Ecological Approaches to Cognition
Essays in Honor of Ulric Neisser

EMORY SYMPOSIA IN COGNITION

Ulric Neisser

(Back row, L to R) Ira Hyman, Philippe Rochat, John Pani, Elizabeth Spelke, Michael Tomasello, Arnold Stoper, Robyn Fivush.
(Front row, L to R) David Jopling, Eugene Winograd, William Hirst, Ulric Neisser, Carolyn Mervis, Robert McCauley, Frank Keil.

Ecological Approaches to Cognition
Essays in Honor of Ulric Neisser

Edited by

Eugene Winograd
Emory University

Robyn Fivush
Emory University

William Hirst
New School for Social Research

LEA LAWRENCE ERLBAUM ASSOCIATES, PUBLISHERS
1999 Mahwah, New Jersey   London

Earlier volumes in the Emory Symposia in Cognition series
were published by Cambridge University Press.

Lawrence Erlbaum Associates, Inc., Publishers
10 Industrial Avenue
Mahwah, NJ 07430

Cover design by Kathryn Houghtaling Lacey

Library of Congress Cataloging-in-Publication Data

Ecological approaches to cognition : essays in honor of
Ulric Neisser / edited by Eugene Winograd, Robyn Fivush,
William Hirst.
   p. cm.
Chiefly papers originally presented at a conference at
Emory University in November 1996.
Includes bibliographical references and indexes.
ISBN 0-8058-2729-3 (cloth: alk. paper).
   1. Cognition—Congresses.   I. Neisser, Ulric.
II. Winograd, Eugene.   III. Fivush, Robyn.
IV. Hirst, William.
   BF311.E27   1999
   153—dc21   98-7417
                                        CIP

Books published by Lawrence Erlbaum Associates are printed
on acid-free paper, and their bindings are chosen for strength
and durability.

Printed in the United States of America
10 9 8 7 6 5 4 3 2 1

Contents

Preface

In November 1996 a conference was held at Emory University to celebrate Ulric (Dick) Neisser's career in psychology. It was a celebration as well as a reunion of Dick's students, colleagues, and many friends. Besides the talks, the weekend included parties and dinners appropriate to the occasion. This volume reflects the talks that were presented during the conference as well as contributions by Eleanor J. Gibson, Karen Adolph, Marian Eppler, and Yohtaro Takano, who were unable to attend the conference. What it may not reflect adequately is the outpouring of affection and respect we saw for an honored and distinguished scholar and teacher. In line with Dick's wishes, all of the contributors were at one time either his graduate students or colleagues at Brandeis, Cornell, or Emory, the three institutions at which he has taught.

Dick Neisser is a rare figure in modern psychology in many ways and especially for the breadth of his scholarship. His theoretical and empirical contributions to our understanding of visual search, attention, visual imagery, memory, and the self are all well known. It is no surprise, then, that this book reflects the breadth and richness, to use one of Dick's favorite words, of the field that he did so much to shape.

We will only briefly outline Dick's biography here. Born in Kiel, Germany in 1928, Dick came to the United States when he was 4 years old. His father, a professor of economics, was part of the early wave of German emigre scholars who foresaw the consequences of the rise of Fascism. Dick grew up in the Philadelphia and New York suburbs while his father taught at the University of Pennsylvania and the New School for Social Research. As an undergraduate at Harvard, Dick was a student of George Miller and carried out his senior research thesis in Miller's laboratory. After graduating *summa cum laude* in 1950, Dick showed his independence of mind by going to Swarthmore to study Gestalt Psychology with Wolfgang Köhler and Hans Wallach. It was clear that behaviorism, so dominant at the time, had no appeal for him. After completing the MA at Swarthmore, Dick went to study at MIT's new psychology department but found its focus on information theory too narrow and did not stay long. Instead, he returned to Harvard, where he completed his dissertation research with S. S. Stevens. By 1957, he had his first teaching job, at Brandeis. There, he was impressed by Abraham Maslow's emphasis on psychology as a force for good. While at Brandeis, Dick carried out his important studies on visual search, the work for which he was best known prior to the publication of *Cognitive Psychology* in 1967.

Few books in psychology have had the impact or staying power of *Cognitive Psychology*. It not only named a new field that quickly came to dominate the discipline, it showed how what had been seen as unrelated research areas such as perception, language, memory, imagery, and thinking could be integrated into a coherent framework. Like Moliere's character who was gratified to learn that he had been speaking prose all his life, a generation of psychologists were pleased to find that they had been doing cognitive psychology. The book was magisterial, lucid, and timely. Its unifying concept was information. In an interview published in Bernard Baars' 1986 book, *The Cognitive Revolution*, Dick said:

> I was convinced that *information* was a central concept, and that you could follow it inward through the organism. There were Gestalt processes at the beginning that were needed to partition the input, and constructive memory processes at the end with a sort of humanistic flavor. I decided to put it all together into a book. (p. 279)

In 1968, Dick and his wife Arden moved to Cornell. There, influenced by J. J. Gibson, Dick modified the strongly constructivist view adopted in *Cognitive Psychology* to take into account the Gibsonian credo that "The information is in the light." In *Cognition and Reality* (1976), he argued for an ecologically based approach to cognition, emphasizing the world outside the laboratory. He criticized mainstream cognitive psychology for lacking ecological validity and, generally, for its excessively narrow preoccupation with internal processes. Contemporary theories of perception, he argued, glorified the perceiver and ignored the richness of the environment. Dick argued that perception, like evolution, involved adaptation to the environment. Commenting later on this marked change in his own views, in spite of the enormous success of his earlier book, Dick said:

> I've always been in the position of liking what other people don't like, so I was a little surprised when cognitive psychology caught on so well. Of course, I had fantasies of success, but I generally think of myself as a marginal, critical theorist. I was caught by surprise, because I'm usually on the outs. And you'll see that I very quickly reestablished my position on the outs. I can't handle the mainstream very well. (Baars, 1986, p. 280)

Although it may be true that Dick does not appear to be able to handle the mainstream very well, to many it appears that the mainstream is in the habit of chasing after him.

Since the publication of *Cognition and Reality*, Dick has consistently applied an ecological approach to cognition. Some examples from memory research are his analysis of John Dean's testimony, involving detailed analysis of the Watergate tapes, his work on the memory of Baker Street Irregulars for Sherlock Holmes stories, and his many publications on the problem of flashbulb memories. In this research, Dick showed that memory for real world events can be studied with the same rigor as laboratory research. When he came to Emory in 1983, it was as an ecologically oriented cognitive psychologist. He founded the Emory Cognition Project and, under its auspices, organized a series of conferences on different topics in cognitive psychology, including categorization and its development, memory and its development, language development, and different aspects of the self. Each conference, at least in part, was concerned with the issues that an ecological approach to cognition presents. Eight of these conferences resulted in books. In addition to cognitive psychologists, contributors included anthropologists, literary scholars, psychiatrists, linguists, and philosophers. A generation of Emory graduate students benefitted from the exciting talks and discussions that characterized these conferences. Special attention should be paid to the pervasiveness of developmental issues in these conferences. It is Dick's strong belief that cognition and its development are inextricably bound up together. This was reflected in the conferences and, more directly, in the guiding role he played in building a single graduate program in cognition and development at Emory.

In recent years, Dick has been interested in intelligence—how it is measured and how social class and racial differences in IQ should be interpreted. This research is a direct result of Dick's deep concern with what psychology can do to make the world a better place. For years, Dick has taught an undergraduate course on intelligence. He was invited to head the American Psychological Association task force that was established to examine recent controversial issues in the study of intelligence. The report of this task force was published in *American Psychologist* in 1996. Subsequently, Dick organized a conference on the Flynn effect, the substantial gain in raw scores on IQ tests spanning decades (Neisser, 1998).

The present volume is organized into three sections: Perception and Its Development, Cognition and Its Development, and Philosophy and Education. The chapters reflect the reach of Dick's influence. There are deep themes running throughout Dick's work, and none more important than that cognition occurs in the world. Cognition is a consequence of the context in which it occurs, a consequence that Dick in so many profound ways has expounded on. That Dick would sound this note with such clarity and purpose is not surprising if one knows Dick because he has always been engaged in the world around him. The intense and careful effort his colleagues and former students clearly put into their chapters in this volume speaks forcefully of his dedication and engagement to his profession and the people in it. But, like all of us, his interactions extend beyond the work place. He dedicated *Cognitive Psychology* to his wife Arden, a constant in Dick's world. As anyone knows who has talked to her or watched Dick interact with her, she has been integral to Dick's work. Dick's dedication reads "for Arden," but it could probably also have read "with Arden."

But the importance of context in thinking is by its nature a two-way affair. Not only has Dick's thinking about psychology benefited from the institutions he has worked at, the students and colleagues he has interacted with, and the people he has shared his most personal and intimate thoughts with, it has also influenced in turn each institution, each student, colleague, and intimate. One of the most extraordinary things about Dick is that not only has he been intellectually sensitive to his surroundings, but that, wherever he has been, he has also created a unique, vibrant world that he has shared, with immense generosity, with others. Every institution he has been part of, every student and colleague he has interacted with, has benefited from his personal and incisive views on psychology. Teachers not only impart information; they encourage ways of approaching a topic, ways of seeing the world, ways of judging quality. Dick's incredibly warm and encompassing embrace of psychology has taught all of us not to see the field through the narrow confines of our specialty. He has encouraged all of us to adopt a critical view, a view from the outside, as it were, informed by the intimate knowledge of an insider. This encouragement, this demand to put research and ideas into as substantial and sizable context as possible, is what makes Dick a truly exceptional figure in psychology. He has given the field a context, a perspective, that will guide our thinking for many years to come. We offer him not only the chapters in this volume but our gratitude.

—*Eugene Winograd*
—*Robyn Fivush*
—*William Hirst*

ACKNOWLEDGMENTS

We gratefully acknowledge Emory University for its continued support of the Emory Cognition Project and for its support of the conference and publication of these proceedings.

REFERENCES

Baars, B. J. (1986). *The cognitive revolution in psychology*. New York: Guilford Press.
Neisser, U. (1967). *Cognitive psychology*. New York: Appleton-Century-Crofts.
Neisser, U. (1976). *Cognition and reality*. San Francisco: W. H. Freeman.

Neisser, U., Boodoo, G., Bouchard, T. J., Boykin, A. W., Brady, N., Ceci, S. J., Halpern, D. F., Loehlin, J. C., Perloff, R., Sternberg, R. J., & Urbina, S. (1996). Intelligence: Knowns and unknowns (APA Task Force report). *American Psychologist, 51*, 77–101.
Neisser, U. (Ed.). (1998). The rising curve: Long-term gains in IQ and related measures. Washington, DC: American Psychological Association.

PERCEPTION AND
ITS DEVELOPMENT

Chapter 1

Direct Perception and Representation in Infancy

Philippe Rochat
Emory University

How to reconcile the rich, immediate experience of perception and action with the schematizing, reconstructing process of higher cognition? This fundamental question is at the core of Dick Neisser's research and theoretical enterprise. As a tribute, I would like to discuss this issue in light of my own recent research in infancy.

If Neisser is at the origin of the cognitive revolution, he is also among the few cognitive psychologists who take perception seriously. As we know, Gibson's influence on Neisser is enormous. It is under Gibson's influence that Neisser became the strong advocate of a more ecologically minded study of higher cognition. Since the theoretical and revisionist stance he took some 20 years ago when he published *Cognition and Reality* (1976), Neisser has spent a great deal of effort attempting to reconcile what is too often viewed as irreconcilable: Gibson's revolutionary insights on perception, with the new wave of research in cognitive science documenting higher thought processes.

A major challenge to Neisser's enterprise is whether Gibsonian views on perception as direct and deprived of reconstruction are reconcilable with the essentially schematic and reconstructive (decomposable) processes of higher cognition that are commonly accounted for by cognitive psychologists. In other words, the question is whether perceptual and representational processes, because of their specific nature, are mutually exclusive or, on the contrary, need to be considered jointly as two inseparable aspects of how the mind works. This question does raise the issue of how well founded Neisser's main theoretical attempt is.

Based on my own recent infancy research, I would like to validate Neisser's attempt to combine Gibson's views with current accounts of higher thought and representational processes. I argue that the attempt to reconcile the direct process underlying perception with the indirect reconstruction involved in higher cognition is necessary based on the fact that the mind works and develops at both levels from infancy. Infants from at least 3 months of age and possibly earlier appear to function at both a direct (perceptual) and indirect (representational) level. These two levels of functioning are neither irreconcilable nor are they reducible to one another. Rather, they are part of the mind's basic architecture as they define distinct processes that develop in parallel, coexist, and interact from the outset of development.

PERCEIVING AND PONDERING THE ENVIRONMENT

The basic misunderstanding between hard-core Gibsonians and mainstream cognitive psychologists rests on the fact that each of them attempts to assimilate two fundamentally distinct and parallel processes as one. Gibsonians spend most of their research efforts trying to demonstrate that perception is veridical and direct. Information-processing people, on the other hand, generate models of the mind that entail the indirect process of a reconstruction. In fact, I would like to suggest that hard-core Gibsonians and mainstream cognitive psychologists are not only talking a different language and reasoning from radically different premises, they are actually accounting for different mental processes that they erroneously construed as being mutually exclusive. Gibsonians are essentially interested in the tight coupling between perception and action that allows animals to move and do things adaptively in the environment. Cognitive psychologists, on the other hand, are interested in modeling the reconstructive process of the mind as it engages in memorizing, thinking, or solving problems.

It is hard not to object to the fact that Gibsonians tend to ignore fundamental aspects that are so much a part of mental life, including memory, imagination, and the conspicuous propensity we have to model and speculate about the environment and our place in it. Alternatively, cognitive psychologists that deal with perception in the confine of their computerized laboratories are obviously minimizing the wealth of information provided by the environment that Gibson insisted on and from which he elaborated his ecological optic (1966, 1979). Ensconced in their assumption of the mind as information storage and schematizing machine, cognitive psychologists commonly overlook the rich fit between the perceiver/actor and its environmental niche.

Gibson's ecological approach to perception points to the fact that in order to make sense of the world, one does not have to engage systematically in a process of reconstruction from peripheral, meaningless bits of sensations to insightful inferences and schemas. Following Gibson, what animals perceive (humans included) is a meaningful environment, rich in information that they learn to pick up via perceptual systems that have evolved to detect them. The light bouncing back to a perceiver's eyes is structured and does not forcibly require higher mental processes to get organized and convey meanings. Gibson convincingly pointed to the fact that light forms a structured array, full of rich, meaningful invariants that are readily available to be picked up. This radical conception is fundamentally in reaction to the traditional, laboratory-based view of perception as a process of meaning attribution of the raw material provided by the sensorium.

What is truly revolutionary in Gibson's approach is that perception is for the first time considered independently from any interpretative (inferential), speculative, or higher order thought processes. Gibson's central contribution is his demonstration that perception does not (always) have to entail representation or some kind of mental reconstruction. In the light, there is information that specifies the perceiver's situation in the environment and what this environment affords him or her for action: whether there are eminent dangers, obstacles, or shelters.

Birds fly at great velocity in dense vegetation and land like lightning on a particular branch of a tree that supports their weight and affords stability. It is doubtful that birds engage in a process of reconstruction and possess a map of each tree and branch they choose to land on. The squirrel I just saw jumping from a high branch to another in my back yard did not noticeably ponder whether the next branch might or might not hold its weight. In regards to such behavior, humans are no exception. They also demonstrate tight perception–action coupling that does not require any pondering and noticeable process of reconstruction. When chased by a grizzly bear, we do perceive without much cogitation and potentially deadly reconstruction that a particular tree affords climbing, therefore safety. Nevertheless, what might be specific to humans is their ability to ponder what did happen, why did it happen, and what will eventually happen next, in addition to respond adaptively to immediate environmental situations, detecting affordances like birds, squirrels, or any other animals do.

Aside from direct perception in the context of adaptation, survival, fitness of a perceiver/actor to its environment, and the appropriate detection of environmental affordances, there is, at least in humans, representation and mental reconstruction (pondering) capabilities. Such process is by definition indirect as it entails the schematizing of events that have happened or will eventually happen in the environment. It is apparent that perceiving à la Gibson and pondering the environment often take place in parallel and are inseparable. For example, I am currently absorbed in trying to convey intelligible (if not intelligent) ideas while my fingers are racing on the keyboard of my computer. I am both cogitating and perceiving/acting adaptively in the ecological niche of my study. There is undoubtedly a double, irreducible process taking place here. At one level, me writing at my computer can be accounted for using Gibson's ecological approach to perception and action. This is the necessary process by which I detect the computer affordances in terms of the workspace it provides and what I perceive. It is also the process by which I track and control the letters that appear on the screen in conjunction with my fingers' movements. If this aspect of the overall writing process I am engaged in is necessary and complex in itself, it is obviously not sufficient to account for what is presently on my mind. There, the Gibsonian account becomes theoretically mute. What guides my perception and the control of my fingers on the keyboard is the meaning I would like eventually to convey to future readers. What I am thinking about right now is not how my fingers feel while hitting the keys or how the letters appear and pile up on the screen. I perceive all those things, but that is not what I am thinking about. What is on my mind is eminently representational and reconstructive in nature: laying down meaningful ideas that represent, in my own mind and because I am a psychologist interested in these questions, what is happening when we perceive and do things in the world.

Most of our activities in the environment entail both tight perception–action coupling and larger goals that are represented. A baseball example should convince anyone who shares Neisser's passion for the sport. It is not unusual to witness a runner moving swiftly toward first and second base while checking if the ball he just hit will make it above the fence to transform the hit into a homer. On one hand, he is controlling his gait accurately to step on each base while pondering and predicting whether the ball will make it beyond the fence. In addition to the tight perception–action coupling manifest in the player's behavior, there is also the representation of the game's rule that gives meaning to both his action and his pondering. At one level, the player is perceiving and running to control his gait. At another, he is involved in assessing the situation and predicting its outcome by looking at the ball's trajectory. In the meantime, all the rules of the game are in his mind.

Perceiving and pondering the environment are real processes that take place on different time scales. Actions that are tightly coupled with perception are based on information that is picked up online (literally in flight for the bird landing on a branch or the gannet plunging toward its prey as described by Lee & Reddish, 1981). In contrast, pondering and the processing of information in representation are, by definition, detachable from the online monitoring of action. Pondering entails such things as planning, predicting outcomes, comparing outcomes with anticipated goals, and reflecting back on past events. In a sense, pondering and the processing of information in representation transcend the immediacy of ongoing perception–action couplings. Ultimately, they monitor actions (past, present, and future) in relation to larger, meaningful goals: safety for the man chased by the bear, intelligibility for the writer in his attempt to convey ideas.

In short, it appears that rather than contradictory, perceiving–acting in the environment and pondering–representing the environment are dual but complementary processes. There is indeed no reason to consider ourselves as either perceivers and actors in an information-rich environment or as theorists and schema crunchers, imaging, rationalizing, anticipating, and learning from past experiences. In actuality, we are both. Neisser's theoretical challenge, as I understand and value it, is to capture how these two processes relate to one another.

Next, I would like to suggest that such dual mode of functioning is an early fact of life and that even neonates engage in more than simply tightly coupled perception and action patterns of behavior. They already have rudimentary (functional) goals that organize their action beyond the immediacy of perception and mere sensorimotor responding. The remaining chapter is organized as follows:

I first try to show that much of the newborn's wakeful activity is oriented toward oral goals (i.e., ingesting food, contacting objects that afford sucking, bringing hands in contact with the mouth). These observations suggest that from birth, infants express rudiments of anticipatory behavior, hence early signs of pondering regarding future outcomes. Neonates are not confined to the online monitoring of perception and action but appear to express future-oriented behavior guided by unambiguous functional goals. However, the functional goals guiding newborns' behavior are yet limited and appear to expand drastically by the second month of life.

In the following section and based on some recent observations, I illustrate that by 6 to 8 weeks, a marked developmental change occurs with the emergence of new anticipatory behavior in relation to novel functional goals. Infants start to respond to people with mutual gaze and smiling, react to the sudden disruption of affective dialogue with the mother and, in general, display a renewed interest toward objects that furnish their environment. I try to show that they start to engage in new, systematic monitoring of the self, objects, and others. At this phase of development, infants drastically enlarge the range of functional goals that guide their perception–action systems as well as their pondering of the environment. Functional goals become increasingly objectified and external to the body (i.e., the oral zone).

Finally, in a last section I try to demonstrate that by 3 to 4 months and in parallel to marked perceptual and action development (e.g., the emergence of systematic reaching and progress in postural control), infants start to manifest unambiguous representational abilities. I present evidence that at this age, aside from directly perceiving affordances, infants start to ponder their environment in relation to future outcomes that are actively imagined and represented.

THE ORAL GOALS OF THE NEONATE

The mouth of the newborn is a primordial organizing force of early development. At birth and during the first 6 weeks of life, the wakeful activity of the infant seems to revolve mainly around the mouth. The propensity for oral contact is what appears to be an important, robust aspect of behavioral development during the first weeks of life. We have suggested elsewhere (Rochat, 1993; Rochat & Senders, 1991) that the behavioral propensity for oral contact constrains much learning in early infancy and defines important avenues of behavioral changes. This propensity for oral contact is deep-seated in the behavioral organization of the newborn and is probably part of the biological endowment of the child (i.e., not originating from postnatal experiences). For example, it is not unusual to witness bruised wrists and hands in newborns at delivery caused by intense sucking engagement in the womb. Ultrasonic recordings document such hand-to-mouth and sucking activity in the fetus during the last trimester of pregnancy (de Vries, Visser, & Prechtl, 1982).

Not that long ago, newborn behavior was considered as essentially confused (disoriented) and chaotic (disorganized). Pioneer infancy researchers, such as Spitz (1965) (but see also Mahler, Pine, & Bergman, 1975; Piaget, 1952; among many others and in the footsteps of the newborn blooming buzzing confusion suggested by James, 1890), presented newborn behavior as "random, unstructured, and . . . inconsistent" (Spitz, 1965, p. 54). Current research leads to a radically different view. It appears on the contrary that newborn behavior is, in some respects, remarkably organized and oriented toward meaningful aspects of the environment, in particular food.

We recently collected data on sucking by very low birth weight, premature infants that illustrate how well prepared and organized infants come to the world (Rochat, Goubet, & Shah, 1997). These observations also point to the predetermination of oral goals (i.e., feeding) that organize much of early behavioral development. In Rochat et al. (1997), we recorded sucking behavior by tube-fed premature infants at 36 weeks of gestational age. Sucking was recorded via the positive pressure variations infants applied on a rubber nipple introduced in their mouth 5 minutes before, during, and after nasogastric gavage feeding. What we found is that infant sucking increases significantly during gavage, indicating that mere stomach cues or temperature changes in the tube during feeding engage infant sucking, a complex activity that appears to be part of a larger action system, namely the feeding system.

This observation with very low birth weight (VLB) premature infants demonstrates how remarkably well organized infants come to the world, predetermined to tap into environmental resources such as the nipple as a source of nutrition. Interestingly, VLB premature infants are not yet physiologically mature enough to be fed orally due to the fact that the coordination between breathing and swallowing depends on soft palate growth normally occurring during the last weeks of pregnancy. This explains in part the necessity to feed premature infants enterally (via nasogastric tubing), delaying oral feeding. However, the enhanced sucking engagement we recorded indicates that infants are already prepared to respond in particular ways in relation to specific contexts (i.e., feeding). Again, what is remarkable is that young infants demonstrate that they do not behave in a vacuum but rather act adaptively in relation to predetermined environmental resources (i.e., the nipple). These resources represent functional goals that orient behavior at birth and are the primordial source of anticipation, possibly of representation.

Neonates spend up to 20% of their waking hours with their hand(s) contacting the oral region (Korner & Kraemer, 1972). Contrary to Piaget's (1952) assumption that hand–mouth contacts by neonates are merely accidental, with genuine hand–mouth coordination emerging only by the second month, recent research shows that these contacts at birth are rather systematic and anticipatory in nature. Butterworth and Hopkins (1988), performing a microanalysis of upper limbs and mouth movements in instances where neonates bring one of their hands to the oral region, demonstrated that this behavior did not appear to be driven by reflex mechanisms such as the Babkin and the rooting reflex. These authors reported instances where infants bring their hand directly to the mouth without prior contact to the perioral region. A fine grain analysis of hand trajectory reveals flexibility and variability, rather than spatio-temporal rigidity and fixedness as would be expected if this behavior was merely driven by a reflex mechanism. Interestingly, Butterworth and Hopkins described episodes in which newborns open their mouth in anticipation of contact. This behavior is illustrated in Fig. 1.1A displaying a picture I took of my daughter Cléo, 10 minutes after her birth, in which she engaged in hand-to-mouth transport. This snapshot reveals the unambiguous opening of the mouth in apparent anticipation of manual contact. It portrays precisely the observations and analyses reported by Butterworth and Hopkins.

In subsequent studies, we confirmed Butterworth and Hopkins' (1988) report, demonstrating further that hand–mouth coordination by neonates

A

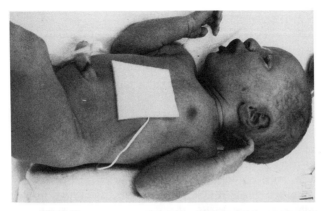

B

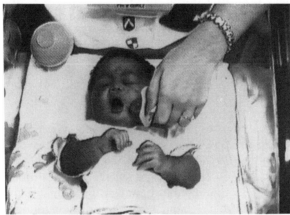

C

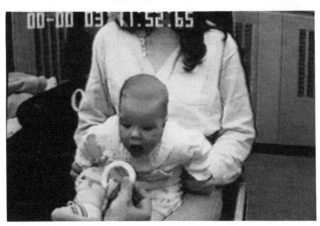

FIG. 1.1. Oral goals and engagement by young infants: Hand–mouth coordination in a neonate with mouth opening in anticipation of manual contact (1A); rooting response by a newborn infant with mouth open and tongue protrusion as the head orients toward the tactile stimulation (1B); oral capture of an object by a 4-month-old infant with both hands constrained, preventing her to reach (1C).

is controlled by sucrose delivery (Rochat, Blass, & Hoffmeyer, 1988). We found that following the delivery of a drop of water with 12% sucrose on the baby's tongue, and in addition to an engagement in mouthing and tonguing activities, infants systematically brought one hand to the mouth and maintained contact for long periods of time. Hand–mouth transports and contacts increase by 50% following sucrose delivery compared to pretest and posttest baselines (Rochat et al., 1988). In another study in which we attempted to capture further the underlying mechanism of hand–mouth coordination by neonates, we observed that following sucrose stimulation and the establishment of hand–mouth contact, upper limb movements tend to stop and overall calming takes place (Blass, Fillion, Rochat, Hoffmeyer, & Metzger, 1989). The coordinated action appears to be brought to completion once hand–mouth contact occurs. This fact is interpreted by Blass et al. as indicating that hand–mouth coordination in the neonate might serve the function of providing the infant with something to suck on, once the sucking (feeding) system is engaged. This interpretation is supported by a study in which immediately following sucrose delivery, the infant was presented with a rubber pacifier inserted in her mouth. Pacifier insertion is shown to suppress hand–mouth coordination typically following sucrose delivery. The pacifier appears to facilitate and bring to balance the newborn's sucking/feeding system (Blass et al., 1989). Once the pacifier is introduced into the newborn mouth, a dramatic inhibition of upper limb movements toward and around the mouth is observed, confirming the idea that hand–mouth coordination, at birth, is an integral part of the feeding/sucking system.

Once engaged, the feeding system appears to orient the newborn toward objects that afford sucking. This orientation probably underlies the neonate's mouth opening in anticipation of a manual contact illustrated in Fig. 1.1A.

Another example of oral anticipation is the robust rooting response of the neonate that is commonly assessed by pediatricians in their neurobehavioral testing of neonates immediately after delivery. As shown in Fig. 1.1B, the rooting response is not merely characterized by a head turn in the direction of the perioral stimulation. It also entails a mouth opening and sucking engagement with tongue protrusion in what appears to be the expression of an oral goal (Koupernik & Dailly, 1968). Typically, newborn rooting behavior, as for hand–mouth coordination, is brought to completion when a suckable object comes into oral contact and the infant is able to suck on it. As suggested by Prechtl (1957), head turning and rooting by newborns are a preliminary to food intake and are actions that subserve the homeostasis of the body's energy content. Again, this would suggest that the rooting displayed by newborns is not merely reducible to a tight (innate) coupling between perception (stimulus) and action (response), but rather is fundamentally goal-oriented and ultimately driven by the anticipation of an oral goal.

If oral goals (i.e., contacts with a suckable object) organize much of newborns' wakeful behavior, similar goals continue to determine the emergence of important behavior emerging by the second, and even the fourth month of life. I have documented that when 2-month-olds start to engage in systematic manual–haptic exploration of objects, they tend first to bring them to the mouth (Rochat, 1989). Up to approximately 4 months, the mouth remains the main locus of spontaneous object exploration (Rochat & Senders, 1991). Interestingly, when 4-month-old infants start to reach systematically for objects they see, they do so primarily to bring them in contact with the mouth. This is illustrated by Fig. 1.1C displaying a 4-month-old infant that is just starting to reach and to whom an object is presented for reaching with the mother holding both of her hands down to the side. Prevented to use her hands in order to reach and eventually transport the object to the mouth, the infant manifests the new strategy of leaning forward to directly capture the object orally. Obviously, the infant adaptively discovered new means to achieve the same goal. As Bruner (1969) did before us, we suggested elsewhere that the oral capture of the object is an important factor driving the emergence of systematic reaching behavior by the fourth month (Rochat & Senders, 1991).

The observations outlined indicate that immediately after birth, infants are not merely sophisticated responding machines endowed with the sensory power to discriminate the stimuli they are bombarded with. In contrast, they suggest that neonate behavior corresponds to sensorimotor movements that are organized in action systems that are driven by specific functional goals, in particular feeding and oral contacts. A major feature of early development is that from oral goals that appear to guide infants' behavior and anticipation during the first 4 to 6 weeks of life, new functional goals emerge that expand infants' perception, action, and attention to their environment. By 6 weeks, infants form novel expectations and appear to become newly attuned to external things and events beyond their own bodily sphere.

THE OBJECTIFIED WORLD OF THE 2-MONTH-OLD

There is a key developmental transition by the second month of life. Parents commonly report increasingly gratifying social exchanges with their infant who starts to smile and respond in reciprocal ways. I would like to illustrate that at this phase of development, infants drastically enlarge the range of functional goals that guide their perception–action systems, not only in relation to their caretakers, but also in relation to the self and to objects. In general, the functional goals guiding the infant's perception, action, and anticipation emerge as increasingly objectified and external to the body. Infants appear to wake up to an objectified environment.

Infants, for example, start to use their hands not only to touch themselves and bring them to the mouth, but also to transport grasped objects for oral exploration (Rochat, 1989, 1993). By 2 months, the oral zone remains a focal point of infant behavior. However, it appears that the mouth becomes increasingly oriented toward an exploratory function, in addition to nutrition. Beside sucking, infants start to manifest more biting, tonguing, and lip movements while experiencing an intraoral object that is eccentric in comparison to the biological shape of the nipple in terms of shape and texture (Rochat, 1983). In our culture, solid food is commonly introduced starting the second month, this practice contributing to a change in the functional status of the mouth as an exploratory system in the context of feeding. It is via oral exploration (i.e., chewing, biting, and tonguing) that infants learn to process and select food that is either ingestable or not ingestable. In addition to the transit and extraction of liquid food via sucking, the introduction of solid food transforms the mouth into a checking and processing point from which food is either swallowed or rejected.

Relative to the whole body surface and aside from the finger tips and the inside of the hands, the mouth concentrates the highest density of tactile–haptic receptors. By the second month, infants tap increasingly and in new ways into the haptic power of the mouth. In addition to chewing and swallowing in the context of feeding, they start to use their mouth to explore nonedible physical objects. At birth, when infants are presented with a small object for grasping and once they have a good hold of the object, they will not tend to bring it to the mouth for oral contact and exploration (Rochat, 1993). As we have seen in the preceding section, this is not due to a lack of hand–mouth coordination. Rather, it is due to limited attention and interest for grasped objects that are not yet integrated in larger intermodal exploratory activities. Note however that immediately after birth, infants do engage in differential oral and manual responding when presented with objects varying in texture and elasticity (Rochat, 1983, 1987). This oral and manual exploration is still rudimentary and tightly linked to feeding, becoming more playful and gratuitous by the second month.

By 6 weeks, infants appear increasingly interested by objects for the sake of their novelty and the discovery of their affordances aside from feeding purpose. It is indeed during the second month that infants are commonly described by caretakers as opening up to the world, becoming more playful and interested, hence more interesting for those who spend time with them.

Aside from the anticipatory activity of the newborn discussed in the preceding section, neonatal imitation (Meltzoff & Moore, 1977), and few studies reporting categorical perception at birth (Bornstein, Kessen, &

Weiskopf, 1976; Slater & Morison, 1991), evidence suggesting that infants 1 month and younger can recognize objects and recall past events are sparse. Potentially representational activities by neonates are still limited to activities that are focused on the own body, and in particular to activities that are centered around the mouth (i.e., mouth opening, tongue protrusion). For 1- to 2-month-olds, evidence of object recall and recognition starts to abound. For example, infants are reported to look longer at an object matching the shape and relative elasticity of a pacifier they explored in a preceding oral familiarization (Gibson & Walker, 1984; Meltzoff & Borton, 1979). Interestingly, in a recent study Meltzoff and Moore (1994) reported that 6-week-old infants not only develop a new repertoire of oral imitation (e.g., tongue protrusion to the side in addition to midline), they also display remarkable attempts to explore and improve the matching between the modeled action and its imitation. This observation is not reported in newborns and points to a qualitative change in the imitative ability of the infant that appears to become more differentiated and objectified.

If by the second month infants show a marked increase in their propensity to engage with objects outside of their own bodily sphere, they do not lose track of themselves and their own body effectivities in the world. They start to show particular attention to the effect of their own action beyond the context of oral goals (i.e., feeding or oral contacts). For example, Lewis, Sullivan, & Brooks-Gunn (1985) attached to one wrist of 2-month-olds a cord connected to a music box that triggered interesting sounds and sights when pulled. Compared to a baseline period where the cord was not attached to the box, infants learned within 3 minutes to instrument the appropriate arm action to trigger the music box. The frequency of arm pulls are reported to increase significantly and infants displayed enhanced positive affects via significant increases in smiling. Interestingly, during a second (extinction) baseline, infants are reported to continue to pull at even a higher rate in an apparent attempt to obtain the reinforcing consequence. They displayed a marked reduction in smiling and a significant increase in an anger expression during this extinction phase. These observations suggest that infants at this age start systematically to explore themselves as agent of action and transformation in the environment. With this exploration, they learn new ways to impact on objects and develop expectations about what should happen next in particular environmental situations and following particular self-generated actions. In other words, they seem to be engaged in pondering the environment as well as perceiving and acting in it. I would suggest that there is more than direct perception as they act with a plan or some kind of a representation of future outcomes. It is doubtful that the accompanying emotional expressions of anger reported by Lewis et al. (1985) are automatic responses, but rather are revealing of the infant's anticipation of a planned action that is violated by the surreptitious experimental manipulation of disconnecting the manipulandum. A similar example with infants of the same age will be discussed later in relation to the still face phenomenon.

In collaboration with Striano, we are currently collecting data that appear to confirm the observations of Lewis et al. (1985), but in a different experimental context. In an experiment that we just started, we are analyzing how 2-month-old infants monitor different types of auditory feedback that are contingent to each pressure they apply orally on a rubber pacifier introduced in their mouth for sucking. Infants sit between two speakers. After a 90-second baseline where they have the opportunity to suck and explore a soft rubber pacifier introduced in their mouth with no contingent sounds, they are tested successively in two 90-second experimental conditions with different auditory feedback following each suck.

In one (Analog + Contingent) condition, each time the infant applies a minimum amount of pressure on the pacifier, he or she simultaneously hears a trill of discrete computer generated sounds that are ascending and descending in pitch frequency. This ascending-descending pattern of sounds matches exactly and online the actual pressure variation applied orally by the infant on the pacifier. In other words, in this condition infants are provided with an auditory equivalent of the effort they generate orally on the nipple. There is a perfect spatiotemporal overlap of the positive pressure variation recorded on the nipple and the sound frequency change infants hear via the speakers.

In another (Contingent Only) condition, each time infants apply a minimum amount of pressure on the pacifier, they hear a 2-second trill of discrete sounds with randomly distributed pitch frequency. This pattern of sounds is contingent with the infant's sucking but does not match the actual pressure variation applied orally by the infant on the pacifier. In other words, in this latter condition infants are provided with a temporally equivalent but spatially incongruent (nonanalog) auditory feedback of the effort they generate orally on the nipple.

Following tests in these two conditions, infants are tested in a second baseline with the pacifier introduced in their mouth for sucking but with no auditory feedback. Infants' oral activity is recorded via an air pressure transducer connected to the pacifier. The transducer itself is connected to a computer that records online sucking and other positive pressures applied by the infant on the pacifier. Based on the recording of positive pressures applied by the infant on the pacifier in the different conditions, we are analyzing sucking frequency and amplitude over testing time.

The aim of this research is to document further the monitoring by young infants of the consequences of their own action and the exploration of their own body effectivities. In general, we intend to capture when infants start to discriminate among different traces of their own actions.

The basic idea guiding the research is that by 2 months, infants develop a novel sensitivity to their own effectivities, starting to explore and possibly to recognize themselves in the auditory consequences of their own action. The systematic exploration of such consequences is viewed as the potential mechanism underlying an early objectification of the self (Rochat, 1995).

I present next a sample of preliminary results obtained in the Rochat and Striano project. Figure 1.2 illustrates the oral response of a 2-month-old infant across the two baselines with no auditory feedback and the two experimental conditions with contingent sounds that are either analog (Contingent + Analog condition) or spatially incongruent (Contingent Only condition). The figure displays successive positive pressure variations applied by this particular infant on the pacifier in the successive conditions, each repeated twice in an alternate order.

As shown in Fig. 1.2, the infant displays remarkably fast learning of the auditory consequences of the oral pressures she applies on the pacifier. In comparison to the second baseline, the infant demonstrates a lower rate of sucking on the nipple during the first baseline. Very quickly this infant learns to use her mouth as an instrument to generate sounds aside from sucking and oral–haptic exploration of the pacifier as discussed in the preceding section. Aside from evidence of instrumental learning, the results obtained with this infant reveal two other interesting facts. In relation to the two auditory feedback conditions, she responded at a markedly higher rate in the Contingent + Analog condition where the sound matched her oral effort on the pacifier. The spatial congruence between what the baby does on the pacifier and the auditory equivalent produced by her action seems to determine her enhanced sucking engagement. Watson (1984) proposed that young infants' instrumental learning is enhanced when the consequence of the learned action is not perfectly contingent. Based on the results of the baby presented in Fig. 1.2, it seems that the learning is not only dependent on the timing of the consequence as, in both experimental conditions, there is perfect contingency (i.e., every time the infant sucks or applies pressure on the pacifier it produces a simultaneous auditory feedback). The only time the infant might have acted on the pacifier without a simultaneous auditory consequence is in the Contingent Only condition and during the 2-second burst of random sounds triggered by a preceding pressure. However, Watson's assertion should have predicted a reversed outcome compared to what this infant actually demonstrates. What appears to be an important determinant of the infant's oral–auditory exploration is not only the temporal link between the two, but the spatial congruence that matches the infant's haptic effort on the nipple and the simultaneous auditory perception of this effort. This is what makes the Contingent + Congruent experimental condition more engaging for this 2-month-old.

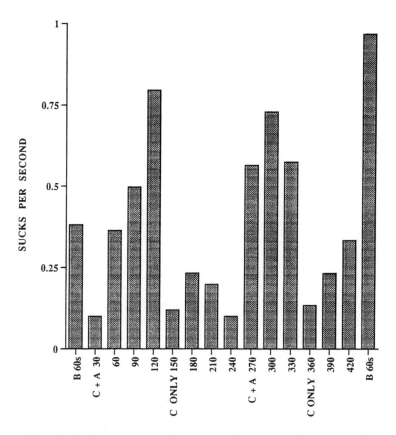

FIG. 1.2. Positive pressure applied on a pacifier (mean sucks per second) as a function of time (sec) and successive experimental conditions: no auditory feedback (beginning and end baselines (B)), contingent and analog auditory feedback (C + A), and contingent only auditory feedback (C only).

Finally, another remarkable fact is what can be observed in the second baseline at the end of the graph presented in Fig. 1.2. Similar to what is reported by Lewis et al. (1985), the infant engages in renewed oral activity during this extinction phase. Again, this would suggest that after only 6 minutes of learning opportunity, the infant already developed expectation as to what should happen when sucking on the nipple. Although we did not videotape the infant's facial expression, both the mother and the experimenter who witnessed the testing session reported that the baby became perturbed and more agitated, displaying an overall facial expression change during the extinction phase of the second baseline. It is doubtful that this reaction was due to fatigue, the infant engaging in more oral activity at during this last phase of the experiment. We intend to document precisely these reactions in subsequent testing by videotaping infants' facial expressions as Lewis et al. have done.

In summary, we interpret these preliminary observations as evidence that the infant displays in her oral activity more than mere instrumental learning. She engages in a differential perception–action coupling while exploring the contingent auditory consequence that is either congruent or incongruent with what she is doing on the pacifier. In addition, this particular infant demonstrates some probing of the situation and anticipation of an outcome (i.e., results of the second baseline). Again, these observations reveal that very early in development and in the context of expanding new goals, infants learn both: to act adaptively in coupling with perception and to anticipate outcomes.

As mentioned previously, by the second month infants open up not only to the world of objects but to the world of people. They start to reciprocate and share attention in bouts of turn taking, displaying what Trevarthen (1993) described as primary intersubjectivity. The study of 2-month-olds interacting with their mother is revealing of both their developing perceptual skills and representational abilities. A phenomenon that has been widely documented by 5- to 6-month-old infants (Muir & Hains, 1993; Toda & Fogel, 1993; Tronick, Als, Adamson, Wise, & Brazelton, 1978) is the still face, where the mother is asked in the middle of a playful interaction with her infant to adopt a neutral, frozen (static) expression while staring at her child. As already described, infants are systematically reported to show distress, including dramatic gaze aversion and smile reduction. It is not yet clear what exactly determines this robust response of the infant and more research is needed, particularly with infants in their second month as they start to develop interactive skills.

A lean interpretation of the still-face phenomenon is that it is essentially determined by the sudden removal of crucial perceptual cues by the mother that disable the infant in monitoring ongoing social exchanges. The mother becomes suddenly still, silent, and is commonly asked to refrain from touching her infant (but see Muir & Hains, 1993, demonstrating the stress reduction factor of touch in a still-face situation). Dynamic visual, auditory, and tactile cues are indeed suddenly and conspicuously absent in the still-face situation. Interestingly, and based on our own recent observations at the Emory Infant Lab, mothers have a very difficult time adopting a steady still face while interacting with their infant. They report an uncontrollable urge to interact and intervene when their child starts to show distress, notwithstanding the difficulty of maintaining a serious facial composure in front of their contact-craving infant.

Another way to look at and try to account for this phenomenon is to postulate that beyond the sudden absence of crucial perceptual cues, infants react to the situation because they do not expect their mother to behave in such a way. Obviously, this interpretation does not dismiss the importance of the sudden removal by the mother of perceptual informa- tion that might directly specify social exchanges and reciprocity with her infant. It does, however, assume that infants do anticipate certain behavior in their mother or any other caretakers, probing their reactions as a func- tion of what they do and the social context they are in (e.g., whether they are entertained, fed, put to sleep, or changed).

I would like to share another set of preliminary observations that seem to go in the direction of this latter interpretation. These observations come from two different ongoing research projects with 2-month-old infants, started recently in collaboration with Blatt and Querido at the Emory Infant Lab. In one study, we place the infant in front of a female experi- menter for approximately 3 minutes of free play interaction in which the experimenter tries to engage the infant with high-pitch voices and fun faces to make him or her smile, without engaging in any touching. Between bouts of lively interaction, the experimenter adopts a still face for up to 30 seconds or until the infant starts to show marked distress and first signs of fussing. During each still-face episode, the experimenter displays one of three different facial expressions that are commonly described as per- ceptually discriminated by infants of this age and even younger (e.g., Field, Woodson, Greenberg, & Cohen, 1982): a) an emotionless facial display corresponding to the neutral face used in existing still face studies; b) a happy face with frozen ("say cheese") smiling expression; and c) a sad face with inverted U mouth, puckering lips and broken eyebrows.

First observations of infants in this situation indicate that they react differentially to the still-face situation depending on the experimenter's facial expression. In the neutral, regular still-face display, all infants react according to what is documented in existing literature: marked gaze aver- sion and smile reduction. In contrast, it appears that infants show persist- ence in gazing at the experimenter when she adopts either a happy or sad still face, with maybe more gaze at the happy expression. Again, these observations are preliminary and more analyses are required to confirm these first results. However, such results are promising, in support of the idea that infants are probing the experimenter during still-face episodes. This probing depends on the static emotional cues that are available. Happy or sad faces appear to be meaningful for the infant in the social context they are in and therefore are potentially less disruptive. In contrast, the neutral emotionless expression is meaningless for the infants to the extent that it does not fit any of their expectations about people and how they usually react while interacting with them. This interpretation is rea- sonable considering that it is not the mere sudden immobility of the experimenter that triggers the reported stress in infants, but what they read in the facial expression of the person they are interacting with. This reading goes beyond direct perception, probably tapping also into a rudimentary representation of what an adult person is, or at least should be in relation to them (highly expressive, whether happy or sad, but never neutral or emotionless in intimate, playful interactions).

In a second ongoing project, infants are placed in front of the experimenter who engaged in a repetitive, ritualized peek-a-boo routine following a 30-second period of free-play interaction. This routine includes three distinct phases: a greeting phase ("Hi baby, look at me") with the experimenter leaning forward, closer to the infant; a hiding phase with the experimenter bringing both hands in front of her face and saying "Peek-a-boo!" and a release phase with the experimenter removing her hands from her face and moving away from the infant while saying softly "Aaaaaah!" This routine has fixed sequences in a crescendo–decrescendo overall pattern or script. This pattern of tension and release is often described as a feature young infants are particularly sensitive to in their interaction with others (Stern, 1985).

After a 30-second period of free play and interaction, the experimenter engages in a series of seven successive peek-a-boo routines over a period of approximately 1 minute before resuming free play. This sequence is repeated twice in two different conditions. In one condition, the peek-a-boo script is organized in the order of the three sequences just described (Normal condition). In another condition, the three sequences of the peek-a-boo are randomly organized and distributed over the seven repetitions of the script (Scramble condition). The experimenter wears an inconspicuous earphone, listening to a tape of successive random sequences of the peek-a-boo routine she follows, adopting the same tone of voice as in the Normal condition. In the Normal condition, the experimenter is attuned to the infant's attention and relative engagement with her, prior to starting each peek-a-boo routine. In contrast, in the Scramble condition, the experimenter follows the prerecorded order and hence is not attuned to the infant's ongoing attention. Furthermore, the scrambled order breaks the regularities of the crescendo–decrescendo pattern, removing the opportunity for the infant to develop expectancies based on some representation of the script.

We just started this research but preliminary observations are again promising. Two-month-olds appear to react differently in the scramble compared to the normal condition. The infants seem to smile less and to be generally less engaged. If these observations are confirmed by future analyses, this would again suggest that by 2 months, when infants start to reciprocate and respond socially, they do not merely express the direct perception of people's social (playful) affordances. They also start to read meaningful social events, elaborating specific expectations about people's behavior in a social (playful, interactive) context. They rapidly pick up complex regularities in the interactive flow with caretakers, developing expectations in routines that are offered by adults to entertain the infant. Interestingly, these routines (e.g., peek-a-boo, paddy cakes) are structured to be easily picked up and represented by the infant: not too long, punctuated by tension and release, with a mix of sharp sounds and interesting visual events that are particularly engaging for the infant. These routines are widely used and compulsively rehearsed by adults. The generalized use by adults of such infant appropriate routines scaffolds young infants' ability to anticipate and represent social events, beyond the direct perception of social affordances.

ACTION DEVELOPMENT AND REPRESENTATION BY 3- TO 4-MONTH-OLD INFANTS

By 3 to 4 months, infants manifest an increasing sense of their own agency in relation to objects, as well as unambiguous representational abilities. Recent infancy literature provides abundant evidence that by 4 months, infants predict outcomes of their own action on objects as well as the outcome of perceived events occurring independently of their own agency.

At the level of perception and action, this age is marked by the emergence of object manipulation. Infants start to contact and grasp objects they see (von Hofsten & Lindhagen, 1979) and develop fine manipulatory activities in conjunction with vision, including scratching, banging, and fingering of grasped objects (Rochat, 1989). In this novel propensity to bring objects in contact with the hands and to engage in protracted manual, oral, auditory and visual inspection, infants discover novel affordances and new effectivities of their own body. They learn what objects afford for manual action, aside from sucking, chewing, biting, and tonguing with the mouth. This is obviously an important development that enlarges the infant's possibilities for action and opportunities to learn objects' affordances. It is also a source of learning about the ecological self (Neisser, 1991): a sense of self as a situated agent in the environment.

When infants start to reach and do things manually with objects, it provides them with enhanced opportunities to plan actions and to learn about the outcome of their own actions. We have seen in the preceding section that from birth and clearly by 2 months, infants already demonstrate some anticipation of the consequences of their own actions. However, 3- to 4-month-old infants develop new perceptuo-motor activities (i.e., reaching) that provide rich opportunities for the parallel development of novel anticipation and probing: particular contact, particular manipulation, and specific effect on objects with new visual, haptic, and auditory consequences (e.g., the anticipation of a particular sound and shiny movements of a metal rattle that the infant might grasp and shake in front of her eyes).

As proposed by Piaget (1952) many years ago, eye–hand coordination, and in particular the emergence of systematic reaching behavior, corresponds to more than an important landmark of perceptual and motor development. It also corresponds to the emergence of planning and clearly intentional action. When infants start to reach, they do not only express eye–hand coordination and the detection of an object's reachability, they also manifest intention to do particular things with them such as banging them, pushing them, or bringing them to the mouth (Rochat & Senders, 1991). Again, aside from direct perception and action, planning, anticipation, and representation underlies early reaching behavior (see for example the research of Clifton, Rochat, Litovsky, & Perris, 1991, demonstrating anticipation and representation in 6-month-old infants reaching for various-sized objects in the dark).

I would like to briefly present more observations on 3- to 4-month-old infants we recently collected at the Emory Infant Lab (Rochat & Morgan, in press). These observations demonstrate that by 3 months, infants develop a sophisticated sense of their own body as agent in the environment. They also show that infants are actively engaged in detecting and exploring objects' affordances, as well as in the process of recognizing and planning actions on objects.

As part of a larger research program on self-perception and exploration in infancy (Rochat & Morgan, 1995a, 1995b), we presented 3- to 4-month-old infants with an online view of their own legs projected onto a large video monitor. In one condition, they saw only their legs dressed with black and white striped socks. The infants were seated in a reclined position in front of the TV and could not see their legs directly. In different experimental conditions, infants saw either their legs (No Object condition), or their legs plus an object on the screen (Object condition). In the No Object condition, a tie microphone was placed under the infant's feet so each time she moved her legs, she heard a rustling/scratching sound coming from an amplified speaker located centrally on top of the TV (see Rochat & Morgan, 1995a for details). In the Object condition, the microphone was placed inside the object, producing the rustling/scratching sound only when touched or kicked by the infant. The object consisted of a white disk with black polka dots centrally supported by a metal spring. The microphone was placed inside the spring and only the polka dot disk (6 cm in diameter) was visible from above on the screen. In order to contact and kick the object, the infant had to perform a full lateral extension of the ipsilateral leg.

In the No Object or Object conditions, infants were presented successively for 2 minutes with two different views of their own legs: an Ego view or a Reversed Ego view. Each view was provided by different cameras placed above and slightly behind the infant. The Ego view corresponded to the view infants would have looking down directly at their own legs. The Reversed Ego view reversed the legs from left to right and was obtained by a special camera with a reversed tube. In the latter situation, when infants moved their right leg to the right, they felt it (proprioceptively) moving to the right but saw it on the left side of the TV screen moving to the left. In other words, the Reversed Ego view provided a conflict between seen and felt movement directionality of the legs.

In analyzing both looking time at the display and overall kicking activity while looking at the display, we obtained the following results. In the No Object conditions, infants spend significantly more time looking at the display and kicking with their legs when they are presented with a Reversed Ego view compared to an Ego view. Interestingly, the reverse was true in the Object Condition: Infants tended to look significantly longer at the display and kicked more while presented with the Ego view compared to the Reversed Ego view. Overall, what these results mean is that infants attended to the display differently in the presence or absence of the object. In the absence of the object, infants are more engaged both proprioceptively and visually in the context of a conflictual presentation of their own legs on the screen (Reversed Ego view). This latter view that alters the familiar visual–proprioceptive calibration of the legs appeared to be more interesting to the infant and associated with enhanced exploration compared to the congruent and familiar Ego view. In contrast, infants appear to look more and kick more at the familiar Ego view when orienting their leg activity toward an object in space. When there is an address in space where they aim their leg activity, they prefer to look at the view that corresponds to the familiar visual–proprioceptive calibration of their legs and that will help them to guide them successfully toward the object to obtain the sound. When merely contemplating their own legs on the screen with no object, infants prefer to explore the incongruent view of their legs that provides a novel conflict between visual and proprioceptive information.

These observations indicate that infants' attention did depend on the context they were in and the action they planned. They show detection of what the particular experimental condition (Object or No Object) affords for action and detected the effectivities of their own leg movements in relation to the goal of producing an interesting sound. In addition, infants demonstrated that they are resourceful in relation to what they plan to do and the context of the task they are engaged in. Again, they focused more on what is perceptually familiar (Ego view) in the context of a spatially oriented action that is required by the task. In contrast, they focused more on what is perceptually unfamiliar and novel when the task required only contemplation of the legs.

In parallel to perceiving, acting, and detecting the affordances provided by the experimental situation, these results also suggest that infants recognize different goals attached to the task: spatially oriented action in one condition and self-exploration in the other. In addition to perception, action, and the detection of affordances, infants also express an engagement in relation to two radically different goals: kicking the object or exploring novel visual–proprioceptive feedback of the legs. Infants appear to function interchangeably in relation to these two goals that correspond to doing (perceiving–acting, i.e., kicking) and probing (recognizing and representing, i.e., exploring novel, unfamiliar calibration of the legs in relation to familiar one).

The research example just provided pertains to observations of infant perceptions of their own action and their own effectivities on objects. I would like to provide further evidence of representation by 4-month-old infants who are not engaged in self-produced movements and in the perception/anticipation of their consequences, but rather who are placed in a situation where they observe and predict the outcome of events that occur independently of their own action. These kinds of situations remove the infants further from a doing mode and force them to adopt a more contemplative view on objects and events around them, probing them on the basis of representation rather than direct perception and concrete actions.

I will not rehash here the pioneer work of Spelke, Baillargeon and their collaborators showing that around 4 months, infants start to display specific anticipation regarding the outcome of partly occluded events (e.g., Baillargeon, 1995; Spelke, Breinlinger, Macomber, & Jacobson, 1992). The cleaver studies that these researchers have accumulated over the past 15 years demonstrate that early on, infants develop precise expectations regarding the behavior of objects that surround them. These expectations are interpreted as the expression of a core physical knowledge, or aboriginal collection of formal (represented) principles such as spatial continuity, objects' boundedness, and the principle of no action at a distance underlying physical causality (e.g., Spelke et al., 1992; but also Leslie, 1984).

I present some recent data in support of the view that as infants develop marked ability to do things with objects (e.g., reaching and manipulating), they also start to demonstrate unambiguous abilities to probe events beyond direct perception and the detection of affordances. These data demonstrate that by 4 months, infants are clearly capable of representing things they cannot perceive directly and can only infer from previous perception. In particular, the research provides evidence that by this age, infants can track mentally and hence represent invisible spatial transformations.

In a series of studies performed in collaboration with Hespos (Hespos & Rochat, 1997; Rochat & Hespos, 1996) we placed groups of 4- and 6-month-olds in front of a puppet stage on which a colorful Y-shaped object disappeared behind an occluder. As shown in Fig. 1.3, the object either fell vertically from the top of the stage behind the occluder (Translation

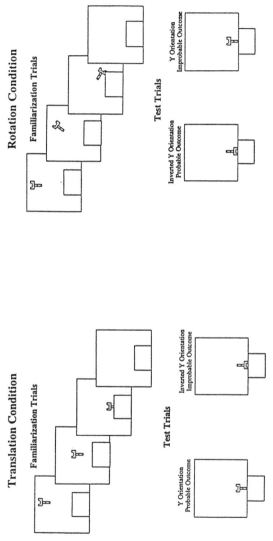

FIG. 1.3. Illustration of the familiarization trials in which the object disappeared either by falling (Translation Condition) or rotating (Rotation Condition) behind the occluder, reappearing during Test Trials either in a probable or improbable orientation outcome (Hespos & Rochat, 1997; Rochat & Hespos, 1996).

condition) or rotated behind the occluder disappearing at 4 o'clock (Rotation condition). Following six familiarization trials in each condition, the infant's visual attention was measured in two pairs of test trials in which following the object's disappearance, the occluder was lowered, revealing the object resting at the center of the stage in either a probable orientation outcome or improbable orientation outcome. The probable orientation outcome corresponded to how the object should have looked following its partly occluded trajectory. In contrast, the improbable orientation outcome corresponded to a 180° inversion of the object. In the improbable test trials, an Experimenter surreptitiously inverted the object from behind the stage prior to lowering the occluder. The rationale of such a procedure (i.e., violation of expectation paradigm) is that if infants formed accurate expectations regarding how the object should look behind the occluder, they should show enhanced visual attention to the outcome of the transformation that violated their expectation compared the one that is congruent with it. In other words, infants should look longer at the improbable compared to the probable test outcome. The rationale of this procedure has been validated by multiple infancy research in many different laboratories.

In three different experiments, each time with different infants, and with slight variations on the display that controlled for any potential residual perceptual cues specifying the movement of the object behind the occluder, we found that from 4 months of age, infants looked systematically longer at the improbable compared to the probable test outcome. These results are remarkably robust and point to sophisticated representational abilities by young infants.

If we admit that these results are the expression of specific expectations that call for more than direct perception, on what bases are these expectations formed and what do they tell us about the infant's ability to probe the environment? Based on our research, we conclude that at least by 4 months, infants are capable of generating dynamic mental imagery. This dynamic imagery or representation capability prolongs the information given by perception and allows infants to predict both visible and invisible spatial transformations. Infants demonstrate an implicit understanding that objects continue to exist when out of sight and behave in a spatially continuous way when moving behind an occluder. In our research, the infant saw the object disappear behind the occluder and managed to map onto invisible (represented) displacements the final orientation outcome of the object once it reappeared. As the object was still visible, they detected the object's characteristics, its starting orientation, motion, trajectory, and progressive occlusion. Once behind the occluder and in order to anticipate the final orientation outcome of the transformation, infants resorted to their imagination, in particular to some representational ability that enabled them to track mentally the object's spatial transformations as it moved behind the occluder. It is based on this mental tracking that infants discriminated between the probable and improbable orientation outcome.

Note that infants did take into consideration the motion and trajectory of the object and their longer looking at the improbable outcome was not merely based on the static matching of the starting and ending orientation of the object. A control group of infants familiarized with the object resting in the starting orientation looked equally at the object in either the probable or improbable orientation at the bottom of the stage in subsequent test trials. Furthermore, in the experimental situation, the novel (improbable) orientation outcome did match the starting orientation in the translation condition only. In the rotation condition, the improbable (novel) orientation was actually the same compared to the starting orientation (see Fig. 1.3). In other words, the Translation and Rotation conditions that each infant passed successively controlled for the eventuality of a mere static matching process (Rochat & Hespos, 1996).

Considering that infants did not merely memorize and compare the static orientation of the object at the top and bottom of the stage, and because no perceptual cues were available to track the object as it moved behind the occluder, the anticipation of its final orientation could only be based on mental tracking. Again, infants showed unambiguous representational abilities, and in the rotation condition demonstrated some rudiments of mental rotation that extended the information given by perception.

CONCLUSION: PERCEPTION, ACTION, AND REPRESENTATION DEVELOP IN CONCERT FROM BIRTH

What I tried to achieve in this chapter is to discuss and provide some evidence that from birth, infants demonstrate goal orientation and anticipation that implies some rudiments of representation in addition to finely tuned perception–action coupling and the direct perception of what objects afford for action. I argued that doing and probing in the environment are dual but complementary processes that are expressed from the outset of development. As suggested by Gibson (1979), the former might essentially be based on direct perception and the detection of veridical information specifying the environment. The latter implies schematizing, memory, and imagination, and is a fundamentally reconstructive process that cognitive psychologists have traditionally attempted to account for. The challenge is to reconcile these two processes, not to consider them as mutually exclusive and theoretically incompatible as Gibsonian or information processing people too often argue. Neisser's major effort of the past 20 years has been to face this challenge, and the observation of young infants validated this effort.

The relation between direct perception and representation, how they differ, interact, and eventually contribute to the acquisition of knowledge is not only an adult cognition problem. It is also a fundamental issue of cognition in infancy.

From birth, infants are both sophisticated perceiver–actors and future-oriented probers of their environment. They suck effectively and are quick to detect the suckability of objects they contact orally (e.g., Rochat, 1983, 1987). On the other hand, they act in relation to goals, anticipating oral contacts that bring to completion coordinated actions (e.g., Blass et al., 1989; Butterworth & Hopkins, 1988; Rochat et al., 1988). If there is direct perception in the neonates, it does not account for the control of all behavior at birth. Newborns already show signs of prospection and antici-pation, their behavior organized toward goals that apparently bypass the immediacy of direct perception and its tight coupling to action.

By the second month, the codevelopment of perception, action, and representation becomes increasingly evident as infants start to manifest interests beyond their own bodily sphere and in particular toward objects and people. When they engage in socially elicited smiling, for example, they do not appear to do so merely in a direct (immediate) fashion but rather in reference to a meaningful reading of the person's emotional expression and what should happen next in their social exchanges. Similar expectations are expressed by 2-month-olds in the context of learning novel perceptual consequences of their own actions on physical objects.

If the research examples I used to describe the behavior of infants 2 months and younger might still leave some room for an interpretation in terms of direct perception and affordance detection, the examples of be-havior by 3- to 4-month-olds are unambiguously linked to the infants' ability to prolong perception via the power of their imagination.

In conclusion, direct perception and representation are facts of the mental life of babies, as they are part of our adult life. The apparent co-existence and codevelopment of these two processes from birth under-scores the importance of understanding how they relate and complement each other. This understanding is at the core of Neisser's project and the observation of young infants demonstrates how essential this project is.

ACKNOWLEDGMENTS

The author expresses his appreciation to Sue Hespos and Tricia Striano for their help and comments. The research presented in this chapter was supported by grant No. SBR-9507773 from the National Science Foundation.

REFERENCES

Baillargeon, R. (1995). Physical reasoning in infancy. In M. S. Gazzaniga (Ed.), *The cognitive neurosciences* (pp. 181–204). Cambridge, MA: MIT Press.

Blass, E. M., Fillion, T. J., Rochat, P., Hoffmeyer, L. B., & Metzger, M. A. (1989). Sensorimotor and motivational determinants of hand-mouth coordination in 1–3 day old human infants. *Developmental Psychology, 25,* 963–975.

Bornstein, M. H., Kessen, W., & Weiskopf, S. (1976). Color vision and hue categorization in young infants. *Journal of Experimental Psychology: Human Perception and Performance, 2,* 115–129.

Bruner, J. (1969). Eye, hand, and mind. In D. Elkind & J. H. Flavell (Eds.), *Studies in cognitive development, essays in honor of Jean Piaget* (pp. 223–236). New York: Oxford University Press.

Butterworth, G., & Hopkins, B. (1988). Hand-mouth coordination in the new-born baby. *British Journal of Developmental Psychology, 6,* 303–314.

Clifton, R. K., Rochat, P., Litovsky, R., & Perris, E. E. (1991). Representation guides infant reaching in the dark. *Journal of Experimental Psychology: Human Perception and Performance, 17*(2), 323–329.

de Vries, J. I. P., Visser, G. H. A., & Prechtl, H. F. R. (1982). The emergence of fetal behaviour: I. Qualitative aspects. *Early Human Development, 7,* 301–322.

Field, T. M., Woodson, R., Greenberg, R., & Cohen, D. (1982). Discrimination and imitation of facial expressions by neonates. *Science, 221,* 1208–1210.

Gibson, E. J., & Walker, A. S. (1984). Development of knowledge of visual-tactual affordances of substance. *Child Development, 55,* 453–461.

Gibson, J. J. (1966). *The senses considered as perceptual systems.* Boston: Houghton Mifflin.

Gibson, J. J. (1979). *The ecological approach to visual perception.* Boston: Houghton Mifflin.

Hespos, S. J., & Rochat, P. (1997). Dynamic representation in infancy. *Cognition, 64,* 153–188.

Korner, A. F., & Kraemer, H. C. (1972). Individual differences in spontaneous oral behavior in neonates. In J. F. Bosma (Ed.), *Third symposium on oral sensation and perception* (pp. 335–346). Bethesda, MD: U.S. Department of Health, Education and Welfare Publications.

Koupernik, C., & Dailly, R. (1968). *Développement neuro-psychique du nourrisson: Sémiologie normale et pathologique* [Neuro-psychological development in infancy: Normal and pathological semiotic]. Paris: Presses Universitaires de France.

Lee, D. N., & Reddish, P. E. (1981). Plummeting gannets: A paradigm for ecological optics. *Nature, 293,* 293–294.

Leslie, A. (1984). Spatiotemporal continuity and the perception of causality in infants. *Perception, 13,* 287–305.

Lewis, M., Sullivan, M. W., & Brooks-Gunn, J. (1985). Emotional behavior during the learning of a contingency in early infancy. *British Journal of Developmental Psychology, 3,* 307–316.

Mahler, M. S., Pine, F., & Bergman, A. (1975). *The psychological birth of the human infant: Symbiosis and individuation.* New York: Basic Books.

Meltzoff, A. N., & Borton, R. W. (1979). Intermodal matching in human neonates. *Nature, 282,* 403–404.

Meltzoff, A. N., & Moore, M. K. (1977). Imitation of facial and manual gestures by human neonates. *Science, 198,* 75–78.

Meltzoff, A. N., & Moore, M. K. (1994). Imitation, memory, and the representation of persons. *Infant Behavior and Development, 17,* 83–99.

Muir, D. W., & Hains, S. M. (1993). Infant sensitivity to perturbations in adult facial, vocal, tactile, and contingent stimulation during face-to-face interactions. In B. de Boysson-Bardies (Ed.), *Developmental neurocognition: Speech and face processing in the first year of life* (pp. 171–183). Amsterdam: Elsevier.

Neisser, U. (1976). *Cognition and reality.* New York: Freeman.

Neisser, U. (1991). Two perceptually given aspects of the self and their development. *Developmental Review, 11,* 197–209.

Piaget, J. (1952). *The origins of intelligence in children.* New York: International Universities Press.

Prechtl, H. F. R. (1957). The directed head turning response and allied movements of the human baby. *Behaviour, 13,* 212–242.

Rochat, P. (1983). Oral touch in young infants: Response to variations of nipple characteristics in the first months of life. *International Journal of Behavioral Development, 6,* 123–133.

Rochat, P. (1987). Mouthing and grasping in neonates: Evidence for the early detection of what hard or soft substance afford for action. *Infant Behavior and Development, 10,* 435–449.

Rochat, P. (1989). Object manipulation and exploration in 2- to 5-month old infants. *Developmental Psychology, 25,* 871–884.

Rochat, P. (1993). Hand-mouth coordination in the newborn: Morphology, determinants, and early development of a basic act. In Savelsbergh (Ed.), *The development of coordination in infancy* (pp. 265–288). Amsterdam: Elsevier.

Rochat, P. (1995). Early objectification of the self. In P. Rochat (Ed.), *The self in infancy* (pp. 53–71). Amsterdam: North-Holland.

Rochat, P., Blass, E. M., & Hoffmeyer, L. B. (1988). Oropharyngeal control of hand-mouth coordination in newborn infants. *Developmental Psychology, 24,* 459–463.

Rochat, P., Goubet, N., & Shah, B. (1997). Enhanced sucking engagement by preterm infants during intermittent gavage feedings. *Journal of Developmental and Behavioral Pediatrics, 18*(1), 1–5.

Rochat, P., & Hespos, S. J. (1996). Tracking and anticipation of invisible spatial transformations by 4- to 8-month-old infants. *Cognitive Development, 11,* 3–17.

Rochat, P., & Morgan, R. (1995a). Spatial determinants in the perception of self-produced leg movements by 3–5 month old infants. *Developmental Psychology, 31,* 626–636.

Rochat, P., & Morgan, R. (1995b). The function and determinants of early self-exploration in infancy. In P. Rochat (Ed.), *The self in infancy* (pp. 395–415). Amsterdam: North-Holland.

Rochat, P., & Morgan, R. (in press). Two functional orientations of self-exploration in infancy. *British Journal of Developmental Psychology.*

Rochat, P., & Senders, S. J. (1991). Active touch in infancy: Action systems in development. In M. J. Weiss & P. R. Zelazo (Eds.), *Infant attention: Biological constraints and the influence of experience* (pp. 412–442). Norwood, NJ: Ablex.

Slater, A., & Morison, V. (1991). Visual attention and memory at birth. In M. J. Weiss & P. R. Zelazo (Eds.), *Infant attention: Biological constraints and the influence of experience* (pp. 256–277). Norwood, NJ: Ablex.

Spelke, E. S., Breinlinger, K., Macomber, J., & Jacobson, K. (1992). Origins of knowledge. *Psychological Review, 99,* 605–632.

Spitz, R. A. (1965). *The first year of life: A psychoanalytic study of normal and deviant development of object relations.* New York: Basic Books.

Stern, D. (1985). *The interpersonal world of the infant.* New York: Basic Books.

Toda, S., & Fogel, A. (1993). Infant response to the still-face situation at 3 and 6 months. *Developmental Psychology, 29,* 532–538.

Trevarthen, C. (1993). The function of emotions in early infant communication and development. In J. Nadel & L. Camaioni (Eds.), *New perspectives in early communicative development* (pp. 48–81). New York: Routledge.

Tronick, E. Z., Als, H., Adamson, L., Wise, S., & Brazelton, T. B. (1978). The infant's response to entrapment between contradictory messages in face-to-face interaction. *Journal of the American Academy of Child Psychiatry, 17,* 1–13.

von Hofsten, C., & Lindhagen, K. (1979). Observations on the development of reaching for moving objects. *Journal of Experimental Child Psychology, 28,* 158–173.

Watson, J. S. (1984). Bases of causal inference in infancy: Time, space, and sensory relations. In L. P. Lipsitt (Ed.), *Advances in infancy research* (Vol. 6, pp. 152–165). Norwood, NJ: Ablex.

Chapter 2

Obstacles to Understanding:
An Ecological Approach
to Infant Problem Solving

Karen E. Adolph
New York University

Marion A. Eppler
East Carolina University

THE PROBLEM OF MOBILITY

This chapter focuses on a very basic and practical kind of problem solving—safely navigating the ground ahead. The problem of mobility is manifold. From their first crawling or walking steps, infants must find their way amidst myriad threats to balance control. The ground is covered with a variety of surfaces—slippery linoleum, deformable playpen mattresses, sloping driveways, and household stairs. Paths are cluttered with furniture, toys, and other obstacles. Interesting places to visit lurk around the corner or behind a door. All the while, infants' own bodies and skills are continually changing. Infants' top-heavy proportions gradually slim down, and the ratio of muscle mass to fat increases. Infants' proficiency at locomotion changes from week to week as babies master belly crawling, progress to hands and knees, cruise sideways along furniture, and finally walk upright.

Solving the problem of mobility in a real world environment is a continual decision process. Figuring out where to go and how to get there requires coordination of skills across a number of psychological domains and time scales: coping with the sheer biomechanics of moving the limbs in a gravitational field, contending with different ground surfaces and their effects on balance control, gathering perceptual information about the ground ahead and about infants' own propensities, searching out alternative means to traverse a surface or reach a location, and so on.

31

Moreover, human mobility is not a solitary enterprise. Problem solving is normally a joint endeavor. Typically, infants' first steps are into the waiting arms of an encouraging caregiver. Parents give a warning shout and rush to the rescue when babies decide to climb out of their cribs or tackle the household stairs. Parents physically structure infants' environment by gating stairs and removing dangerous obstacles. They decide whether babies are held, restrained in a high chair or playpen, or allowed to roam around on the floor. Reciprocally, infants can request help when they get stuck under the kitchen table or thwarted by a closed door. Infants can glance at caregivers' faces for clues about what to do in potentially risky or ambiguous situations (e.g., Sorce, Emde, Campos, & Klinnert, 1985).

OBSTACLES TO UNDERSTANDING

Traditionally, research on infant locomotion has focused on normative descriptions of the ages and stages of motor milestones. Pioneering investigators in the 1930s and 1940s provided the first qualitative descriptions of changes in infants' gait. Each stage-like transition marked a small developmental milestone toward erect locomotion. Gesell and Ames (1940), for example, identified 22 ministages in the development of crawling, from worm-like forward movements with the belly on the floor to more erect crawling on hands and knees or hands and feet. McGraw (1945) and Shirley (1931) described seven stages in the development of walking, beginning with newborn reflexive stepping movements to intentional walking toward the end of infants' first year.

Historically, the early pioneers may have done their jobs too well. The prevailing focus on normative stage-like changes in gait led psychologists to consider locomotor development as a series of isolated biomechanical events. Typically, child development textbooks and infant assessment scales represent locomotor development with a catalog of infant reflexes and a series of line drawings in a milestone chart. Divorced from its context in a complex environment of surfaces, places, and people, infant locomotion appears separate from skills in perceptual, cognitive, and social domains.

Moreover, for the past 50 years, researchers explained infants' progress through the requisite locomotor stages as the result of neuromuscular maturation. Progress from one stage of prone progression to the next resulted from fluctuations in muscle strength, endogenous changes in body dimensions, and maturation of the neural substrate (Gesell & Ames, 1940). Similarly, infants' eventual triumph over gravity in upright positions reflected growth changes and increasing myelination of the corticospinal tract (McGraw, 1945). In fact, clinicians typically assess infants' brain development by observing changes from more obligatory, reflexive movements to more flexible, intentional control of limb movements.

NEW ROUTES TO UNDERSTANDING

Our aim in this chapter is to provide an illustration of how infant locomotion can be rescued from the isolated pages of a textbook milestone chart and resituated in the rich world of everyday mobility. We focus on identifying and understanding connections across different domains of infant development—physical maturation, changes in exploratory activity, advances in attention and perceptual differentiation, emerging cognitive abilities, and the social context of infant locomotion. In particular, emphasis on the adaptive nature of locomotion provides new means for understanding processes of change, both on a developmental time scale as infants progress from crawling to walking, and in real time as babies make decisions from step to step.

The ideas in this chapter were inspired by two complementary tenets of Neisser's work: an emphasis on ecologically valid, functionally relevant tasks, and a call to coordinate findings across traditionally disparate domains. Neisser (1982) argued that an obstacle to progress in perception and memory research has been a focus on isolated laboratory phenomena and domain-specific models. The accumulated facts typically bear little resemblance to everyday activities in real-world contexts. How might researchers overcome these limitations? The first challenge is to discover the important questions. This requires examination of behavior in tasks that capture the fundamental aspects of natural, everyday activities. The second challenge is to discover a broader unifying framework. The solution may lie in the connections between different domains of development (Neisser, 1994).

We have adopted these two tenets of Neisser's work by focusing on the development of adaptive locomotion and by attempting to integrate several traditionally disparate domains of infant problem solving. Our debt to Neisser is also a practical one. Our empirical work for this chapter began at Emory University under Neisser's tutelage. In fact, our first experiments were conducted in Neisser's office. We pushed his desk and file cabinets into the far corners of the room, padded the walls and floor with rubber gymnasium mats, and placed in the center of the office an obstacle course for toddlers, complete with four differently textured slopes and stairs. Fortunately, Neisser was in England when we first constructed the padded playroom, and after his return, we moved our infant gymnasium to less auspicious lab space on the third floor of the Emory Baptist Church, but that is another story.

AN ECOLOGICAL STUDY OF MOBILITY

We illustrate the promise and feasibility of a functional, integrated approach to mobility with a large, longitudinal study of infants' locomotion over slopes (Adolph, 1997). The basic plan was to create a laboratory analogue of everyday problem solving. We used a single locomotor task to observe concurrent changes in traditionally disparate research domains—biomechanical, perceptual, cognitive, and social—and a detailed longitudinal design to track changes over multiple time scales—from step to step, trial to trial, and week to week. As we describe next, results revealed a very different picture of developmental change from the traditional stage-like transitions between motor milestones and very different sorts of underlying mechanisms from the traditional emphasis on neuromuscular maturation.

Slopes. The slope task contained several essential ingredients. First, slopes are novel, allowing first-hand observation of how infants make adaptive decisions about the ground ahead. Babies have little exposure to slanted ground surfaces in everyday situations. Parents limit infants' experience with ascent and descent by gating household stairs and closely monitoring infants when they clamber down furniture and laps.

Second, steepness is a relative variable, providing a way to observe adaptive responding over developmental changes in infants' bodies and skills. The slant of a hill is safe or risky depending on a set of objective, biomechanical constraints—infants' current level of crawling or walking proficiency and whether the goal is to go up or down. Thus, the same relatively steep, risky hill for a weak and tipsy crawler can be a relatively shallow, safe hill for a strong and sturdy crawler. Likewise, the same safe hill for a proficient crawler can be relatively risky when the baby faces it from a new, more precarious, upright walking position.

In addition, relative risk depends on the direction of traversal. Biomechanically, infants' bodies are better suited for crawling or walking uphill. Infants support their weight on a fully extended limb, requiring less muscle strength, and the moving limb contacts the hill midway through the swing cycle. Gravity naturally constrains forward momentum and infants' hands are in a good position to stop a fall. In contrast, biomechanical constraints are more stringent for crawling or walking downhill. Infants support body weight on a bent arm or leg, requiring more muscle strength, and the moving limb travels a longer distance before contacting the hill. Infants must brake forward momentum to resist gravity and their hands are in an awkward position to catch themselves if they begin to fall.

Third, infants' exploratory activity provides an avenue for understanding the basis of online decision making. There are multiple sources of information to specify whether hills are safe or risky for maintaining balance. For example, infants can obtain information about postural stability from optic flow as they perch on the starting platform or generate motion parallax as they peer over the edge. Touching the slope provides information about surface friction and slant from torques generated at wrists or ankles and shearing forces between the surface and infants' hands or feet. Moreover, babies can test consequences for balance control by hanging arms or legs over the brink, or exploring other means of traversal. The most direct route is to plunge over and observe the consequences.

Fourth, multiple locomotor methods are possible on slopes, so that we can observe how new strategies enter infants' repertoires and how babies select among them. On uphill slopes, infants can walk, clamber on all fours, or simply avoid going. On downhill slopes, babies can walk; crawl; slide down sitting, spread-eagled headfirst, backward feet first; or stay put on the starting platform. Backing is especially interesting because it involves an initial detour away from the goal as babies get into position and it involves relinquishing visual guidance because babies' heads are pointed in the wrong direction.

Finally, the slope task simulated important elements of an everyday social context. The infants' goal was to reach their parents, who waited at the top or bottom of the slopes offering their babies enticing toys and cheerios. An experimenter stood nearby to rush to the rescue if infants began to fall. Regardless of outcome, trials ended with infants reunited with their parents amidst more praise and affection. Normally, parents would not put their babies on the brink of potentially risky slopes, and parents would provide explicit verbal coaching (e.g., "be careful," "slide down"). In this task, however, parents maintained a positive demeanor on all trials and a constant stream of verbal praise and encouragement (e.g., "come on over here," "you can do it"), and they never cautioned their babies or told them what method of locomotion to use. Nonetheless, the experimental arrangement allowed us to observe whether infants chose to figure out what to do on their own, sometimes appealed to adults for help, or required direct physical assistance from vigilant caregivers.

Longitudinal Design. The study was designed to control for duration of infants' everyday locomotor experience, spanning the traditional locomotor milestones from the onset of independent mobility. Fifteen experimental babies were observed every 3 weeks, from the infants' first week of crawling until several weeks after they began walking. Fourteen additional control infants were tested at three matched session times to control for experience on slopes in the laboratory (infants' first and tenth weeks of crawling, and infants' first week of walking). Thus, infants' age and everyday locomotor experience were similar across experimental and control groups; only practice on laboratory slopes differed. Overall, there was a total of 221 test sessions and 7,325 trials on slopes.

Procedures. We tested infants' ability to cope with slopes on a large adjustable walkway. Starting and landing platforms were flat, but the middle section of the walkway sloped up or down in 2° increments from 0° to 36°. The walkway was cushioned with soft carpet and safety nets were strung along each side. Wooden posts at the corners of the starting and landing platforms provided infants with manual support for keeping balance. Infants began each 60s trial at one end of the walkway. Crawlers started each trial in a prone position, facing the hill from their typical crawling vantage point, and walkers started each trial in an upright position, facing the hill from their typical walking vantage point. Parents stood at the far end and encouraged their infants to come up or down, while an experimenter followed alongside infants to ensure their safety (Fig. 2.1). Trials ended after infants started onto the hill or after 60s, whichever occurred first.

At each test session, the experimenter used a psychophysical staircase method to identify the boundary between safe and risky slopes (Adolph, 1995, 1997). Slope boundaries were the steepest hills babies could crawl or walk up or down. The slope boundaries provided a measure of the objective biomechanical constraints on locomotion, as well as a way to compare responses across infants and across sessions relative to each baby's current level of crawling or walking proficiency.

The experimenter coded each trial online as success (crawled or walked safely), failure (tried typical method but fell), or refusal (slid down, climbed

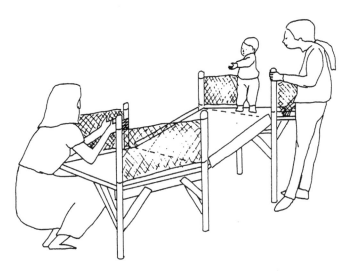

FIG. 2.1. Adjustable walkway used to test infants' actions on uphill and downhill slopes. *Note.* From "Perception of affordances of slopes in crawling vs. walking infants," by K. E. Adolph, M. A. Eppler, & E. J. Gibson, 1993, *Child Development, 64,* p. 1161. Copyright 1993 by the University of Chicago Press. Reprinted with permission.

up, or avoided going). For the purpose of estimating slope boundaries, failures and refusals were treated as equivalent, unsuccessful outcomes. In general, the experimenter presented steeper slopes after successful trials, and she presented shallower slopes after failures or refusals. The process continued until the experimenter narrowed in on a slope boundary according to a 67% criterion (steepest hill with at least 67% successful trials, and at least 67% unsuccessful trials at the next 2° increment and all steeper hills). Easy baseline slopes (0° to 6°) were interspersed with more challenging ones to maintain babies' interest. All trials were videotaped for later analysis.

After testing on slopes, the experimenter obtained additional measures of biomechanical factors—infants' body dimensions and their crawling or walking proficiency on flat ground. Measures of infants' weight and height provided a crude index of size. Leg length and head circumference provided more detailed indices of body proportions, and Ponderal Index related infants' height and weight in an overall chubbiness index.

Coders scored infants' crawling proficiency on flat ground from videotapes of babies crawling back and forth over the flat walkway. More skillful crawlers have higher velocities and fewer crawling cycles (faster, larger movements). Coders calculated standard measures of walking proficiency from the footprints infants left as they walked over a strip of butcher paper with inked tabs on the soles of their shoes. Better walkers take larger steps and have smaller lateral distances (less splaying) between their feet.

Biomechanical Changes. There was a wide range in ages and styles when infants acquired independent mobility. Fifteen infants began as belly crawlers, making forward progress with their bellies dragging along the ground or hopping along in a sort of arm prop-belly flop pattern. Thirteen infants first crawled with a more erect hands-and-knees or hands-and-feet gait. All of the belly-crawling babies eventually crawled on hands and knees prior to walking. Onset ages for belly crawling ranged from 5.26 to 9.60 months and onset ages for hands-knees crawling ranged from 4.77 to 11.77. One control infant never crawled, but proceeded straight to walking. Overall, there was a wide range in ages when infants began walking independently (9.27 to 14.89 months). Infants' variable onset ages resulted in varying durations of total crawling experience (from 0.39 to 8.58 months) and a wide range in ages at each test session.

Infants' bodies and skills changed from week to week. Across sessions, all infants became bigger. However, babies' legs grew faster than their heads and torsos, so that the overall effect was more mature, less top-heavy body proportions. Similarly, height increased faster than weight so that Ponderal Index decreased, meaning that infants' bodies became more slender and cylindrical.

Infants' locomotor proficiency increased over weeks of crawling, and again over weeks of walking. On flat ground, infants' crawling velocity increased and number of crawling cycles decreased, meaning faster movements and larger crawling steps. Although babies showed improvements over both belly crawling and hands–knees crawling periods, in general, hands–knees crawling was more functionally efficient for moving on flat ground. Likewise, infants' footprints showed increase in step length and decrease in step width, indicating better postural control during periods of single limb support (e.g., Bril & Brenière, 1992, 1993).

Moreover, changing biomechanical constraints were reflected in infants' changing ability to locomote over hills. Slope boundaries depended on whether infants were going up or down and on the duration of infants' experience crawling on their bellies, hands and knees, and walking (Fig. 2.2).

Over weeks of crawling, slope boundaries increased. In general, going uphill was easier than going down. Belly crawlers were at an advantage for downhill slopes because they could slither down headfirst, oblivious to balance requirements. Uphill slopes were more difficult for belly crawlers because they could not support body weight on extended arms. In contrast,

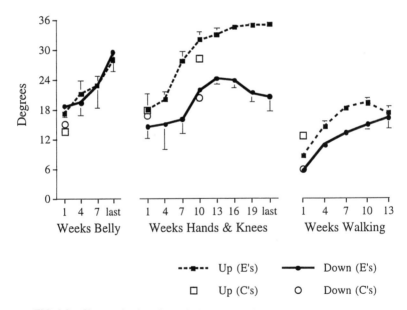

FIG. 2.2. Changes in slope boundaries over weeks of locomotor experience for the three modes of locomotion (E = experimental group; C = control group). *Note.* From "Learning in the development of infant locomotion," by K. E. Adolph, 1997, *Monographs of the Society for Research in Child Development.* Copyright 1997 by the University of Chicago Press. Reprinted with permission.

hands–knees crawlers had more trouble going downhill, where keeping balance is crucial, but hands–knees crawling facilitated improvement in uphill boundaries, where infants could take advantage of their leg strength.

Over the transition from crawling to walking, infants' slope boundaries sharply decreased. The decrement was dramatic and uniform. In their first week of walking, infants displayed a narrow range of slope boundaries limited to very shallow hills. Over weeks of walking, slope boundaries steadily increased. As in crawling, going uphill was easier than going down.

Results showed expected correlations between the various biomechanical measures. Infants' body dimensions were related to their ages at crawling and walking onset. Bigger, fatter babies tended to achieve each locomotor milestone later than smaller, slimmer infants. Infants' height, weight, leg length, and head circumference were positively correlated with age at crawling onset; height and leg length were positively correlated with age at walking onset. In addition, slimmer, longer babies were more proficient at crawling and walking on flat ground and on slopes. Better performance on flat ground predicted steeper boundaries on slopes, suggesting that the staircase estimates were reliable. Moreover, there were no differences in body dimensions, locomotor proficiency, or slope boundaries between experimental and control infants, suggesting that changes in infants' physical ability on slopes resulted from changes in their bodies and everyday locomotor skills, not from practice on slopes in the lab.

Perceptual Judgments. The critical perceptual question was whether infants could adapt responses to their current physical abilities on slopes. Changing slope boundaries meant that relative risk depended on each infant's current level of locomotor skill. If infants distinguished safe from risky hills, they should use their typical crawling or walking position on safe hills and select an alternative, less precarious position for risky ones.

A go ratio provided an index of the accuracy of infants' perceptual judgments. The go ratio was defined as the percentage of trials on which babies attempted their typical method of locomotion on hills steeper and shallower than their slope boundaries:

$$(\text{successes} + \text{failures}) \ / \ (\text{successes} + \text{failures} + \text{refusals}).$$

Success is rare on hills steeper than infants' slope boundaries, by definition; therefore, go ratios on risky hills primarily reflect the ratio of failures to refusals. Likewise, failures are, by definition, rare on hills shallower than infants' slope boundaries, so that go ratios on safe hills primarily reflect the ratio of successes to refusals.

At the slope boundary, the go ratio is $\geq .67$, by definition. However, the ratio varies freely from 0 to 1 on slopes shallower and steeper than the boundary. Perfect perceptual judgments would imply two patterns: (a) a high go ratio on safe hills shallower than the slope boundary, where probability of success is high; and (b) a low go ratio on risky hills steeper than the slope boundary, where probability of falling is relatively high. Infants might err on the side of caution with a low ratio on perfectly safe slopes, or they might err on the side of boldness with a high ratio on risky hills. In addition, adaptive responses should show lower go ratios on risky downhill slopes compared with up. Falling while going downhill was relatively aversive, and the experimenter had to rescue infants to prevent injury. In constrast, failures while going uphill were relatively inconsequential because babies could catch themselves if they began to fall.

Infants' perceptual judgments reflected the different task constraints of going up versus down. On uphill trials, infants often attempted hills where they were likely to fall, despite falling on previous trials and in previous sessions. Crawlers usually struggled at the base of impossibly steep uphill slopes for the entire duration of the trial, sometimes getting partway up, then sliding back down. After lengthy frustrated attempts, they tried equally hard moments later at the next impossibly steep slope. Walkers usually adopted a similar strategy, getting a running headstart on two feet and flinging themselves at impossibly steep inclines. Sometimes persistance paid off and infants eventually reached the summit, and infants were able to catch themselves on trials where they fell. As a result, week after week, both for crawling and for walking, infants' average go ratios were close to 1.0 on safe and risky hills alike (top panel of Fig. 2.3). In fact, there were only three uphill protocols in the entire data set where infants' go ratios on risky slopes decreased below .50.

In contrast, perceptual judgments on downhill trials showed a very different pattern. Go ratios showed two learning curves, one over weeks of crawling and one over weeks of walking (bottom panel of Fig. 2.3). In their first weeks of crawling, infants plunged over the brink of impossibly risky downhill slopes, requiring rescue by the experimenter to prevent babies from tumbling headlong; on average, risky go ratios were high at .68. Over weeks of crawling, infants became increasingly discriminating, attempting only safe hills and refusing to crawl down risky ones. For babies who began crawling on their bellies, go ratios continued to improve over the transition from belly to hands and knees. By their last weeks of crawling, perceptual judgments became nearly perfect; average go ratios on risky hills were .11.

Surprisingly, there was no transfer from crawling to walking. When the same discerning crawlers faced downhill slopes the next week from their new, upright walking position, again they went right over the precipice. In the first weeks of walking, average go ratios were just as high as in infants' first weeks of crawling, near .65. Then, infants learned all over

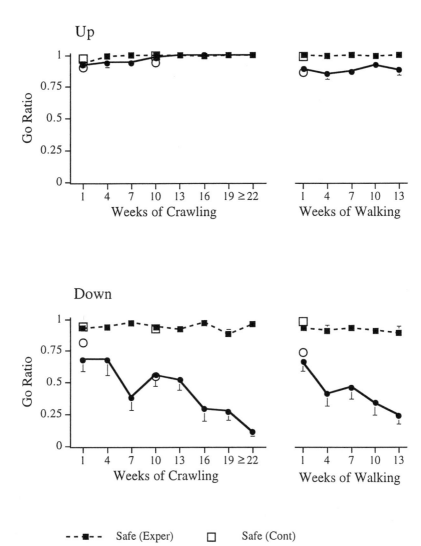

FIG. 2.3. Infants' perceptual judgments over weeks of locomotor experience for uphill (top panel) and downhill (bottom panel) slopes. Go ratio = (successes + failures) / (successes + failures + refusals). Trials are grouped into safe (shallower) versus risky (steeper) hills relative to infants' slope boundaries. *Note.* From "Learning in the development of infant locomotion," by K. E. Adolph, 1997, *Monographs of the Society for Research in Child Development.* Copyright 1997 by the University of Chicago Press. Reprinted with permission.

again to distinguish safe from risky hills as walkers. Over weeks of walking, go ratios on risky downhill slopes gradually geared in to infants' slope boundaries, decreasing to .24 by week 13 of walking. Decrease in go ratios was no faster the second time around.

In fact, we were so surprised to see formerly cautious crawlers responding indiscriminately to risky slopes as walkers that we added an additional experimental manipulation. At the end of each downhill walking protocol, the experimenter tested infants' judgments in both postures over six consecutive trials on the steepest 36° slope (two trials in their new upright posture, two in their old familiar crawling position, then two from a walking position again). Over half the children showed failure to transfer from trial to trial. They went straight over the brink in an upright position, then slid down safely when facing hills from their old crawling vantage point, then again went over the edge in a walking position. Occasionally, when the experimenter started babies in a prone, crawling position, infants stood themselves up and walked over the edge, as though preferring to be hapless walkers rather than discerning crawlers. Examination of consecutive trials at other increments of slope showed similar results. After falling at one increment, babies were most likely to attempt the same precarious position on the same hill, moments later on the very next trial. There was no evidence of within-session learning to prompt adaptive responses.

Apparently, infants learned to gauge their abilities on slopes from crawling and walking over flat ground during everyday experiences at home. There were no differences between experimental infants exposed to dozens of trials each month on slopes in the laboratory and control infants who only came to the laboratory three times. Moreover, duration of everyday locomotor experience (number of days since onset of crawling or walking) was a stronger predictor of infants' go ratios than infants' test age or any other variable. Learning, however, required vast exposure to everyday crawling and walking. On average, infants' go ratios on risky hills did not decrease below .30 until the sixteenth week of crawling and the thirteenth week of walking.

Exploratory Activity. Because crawling and walking boundaries changed from week to week, infants' increasingly adaptive go ratios on downhill risky slopes could not have resulted from simple associative pairing between a particular behavior and a particular degree of slant. Rather, infants' go ratio curves suggest that infants' decisions were based on information obtained online at the start of each trial.

To examine the informational basis for infants' decisions, coders scored infants' exploratory activity on the starting platform. Latency to begin traversal provided an index of the duration of infants' visual exploration. In addition, coders noted whether infants maintained orientation of head and eyes toward the landing platform. Frequency of touching slopes with hands or feet provided a measure of infants' haptic exploration. Coders included only active touch accompanied by visual exploration, where infants rubbed or patted the slope or rocked over their hands or feet at the brink, all the while maintaining orientation of head and eyes in the direction of traversal. Each measure of exploratory activity was calculated independent from slope boundaries and go ratios. Exploration reflected infants' behavior before they started onto slopes, whereas slope boundaries and go ratios were determined by infants' behavior after they crossed the brink. In principle, refusals did not require prolonged exploration (e.g., infants could immediately choose an alternative method and slide down hills), and successes and failures did not prohibit prior exploration (e.g., infants could hesitate and touch hills, then plunge heedlessly over the brink nonetheless).

Overall, infants were extremely selective in distributing their exploratory behaviors. Long looks and frequent touches were rare. On most trials throughout the duration of the experiment, infants started onto slopes after only a brief glance. Median latencies were a tenth of a second and the median number of touches per slope was 0.

As in previous experiments (Adolph, 1995; Adolph, Eppler, & Gibson, 1993), exploration on uphill slopes was most rare and most indiscriminate. In most cases (over 80% of uphill trials), babies began dashing onto hills as soon as the experimenter released them at the start of the trial (top panel, Fig. 2.4). This means that infants' judgments were based only on a momentary glance as the experimenter lowered babies toward the starting platform. As shown in the figure, long looks and touches prior to ascent were limited primarily to the first 4 weeks of crawling. However, in these sessions, babies hesitated and touched safe and risky hills indiscriminately and exploratory looking and touching were rarely followed by refusals. In subsequent weeks of crawling and walking, infants flung themselves forward onto hills nearly as soon as the experimenter placed them on the starting platform.

In contrast to uphill trials, infants explored more before going down hills (over 40% of downhill trials) and over sessions, infants' exploratory behaviors became more discerning (bottom panel, Fig. 2.4). Infants' latency and touching showed a gradual gearing in toward risky hills steeper than their slope boundaries. As in previous studies (Adolph et al., 1993; Eppler, Adolph, & Weiner, 1996), infants explored more when they were new crawlers than when they were new walkers. In their first weeks of crawling, infants' latency and touching were relatively high and distributed over both safe and risky downhill slopes. Over weeks of crawling, there was a steady decrease in latency and touching on safe and risky hills, no change from low levels of exploration over the transition from crawling

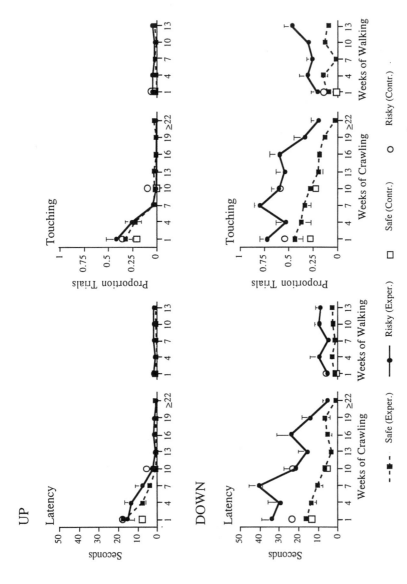

FIG. 2.4. Exploratory behavior (latency to begin traversal and active touching) over weeks of locomotor experience for uphill (top panel) and downhill (bottom panel) slopes. *Note.* From "Learning in the development of infant locomotion," by K. E. Adolph, 1997, *Monographs of the Society for Research in Child Development.* Copyright 1997 by the University of Chicago Press. Reprinted with permission.

to walking, and gradual increase in exploration on risky hills over weeks of walking.

Moreover, as infants' exploratory activity on downhill slopes became more selective, it also became more efficient. Across sessions, infants' exploratory activity and go ratios changed in tandem. Over weeks of crawling, latency and touching on risky hills paralleled infants' go ratios. All three measures showed increasing specificity as values geared in toward risky hills. This means that crawlers actually explored less as their responses became more adaptive. Over weeks of walking, latency and touching on risky hills mirrored infants' go ratios. Exploration on risky hills increased as go ratios decreased.

Usually, infants hesitated for several seconds prior to their first touch, suggesting that visual information prompted the touch; average latency before infants' first touch was 6.08s. The most popular touches were rocking or stepping movements with hands or feet as infants rotated over their wrists or ankles. Rocking movements were most nerve-wracking to observe because infants perched right at the brink of the hills and their bodies sometimes rotated more than 90° over their supporting limbs. In addition, infants occasionally obtained haptic information by patting, rubbing, or poking the hill with a hand or foot, keeping the knees or a foot on the starting platform while the moving limb probed the slope ahead.

Cognitive Strategies. After infants had decided that hills were risky for their typical crawling or walking method, they were left with the problem of figuring out an alternative way to go. On refusal trials, infants could discover a viable means of travel during the course of the trial, or retrieve a suitable climbing or sliding position from the existing options in their repertoires.

The least imaginative solution was avoidance. Infants always had the option to simply stay put on the starting platform until the end of the trial. However, avoidance was frustrating and it was infants' least preferred alternative. On impossibly steep upward hills, infants had few choices: attempt to clamber up on all fours or avoid going. Overall, infants avoided ascent on less than 2% of uphill trials. Instead, crawlers attempted a futile crawling position and walkers attempted to go upright or switched to crawling. In fact, remaining stuck on the starting platform was so frustrating that infants occasionally detoured off the end of the starting platform and crawled or walked around the apparatus to their parents at the far side.

On risky downhill trials where more options were available, infants replaced avoidance responses with various sliding positions. In infants' first weeks of crawling, they avoided descent on 100% of refusal trials. By their last week of crawling, avoidance decreased to 1% of refusal trials and avoidance remained under 9% of all refusal trials over weeks of walking.

However, avoidance was never replaced by a single preferred sliding position. Instead, each baby used a flexible variety of sliding positions on refusal trials in and across sessions: sliding in headfirst prone, sitting, and backing positions over weeks of crawling, and all of the sliding methods over weeks of walking. Across sessions, nearly every infant used each of the sliding positions at least once. More striking, within sessions, most infants used more than two sliding positions in their last weeks of crawling and over all weeks of walking. Variety in locomotor methods was linked with the adaptiveness of infants' responses. Infants using more methods tended to have lower go ratios.

On some downhill trials, infants shifted smoothly to an alternative position and immediately slid down, as though retrieving a known solution from their repertoire of locomotor methods. However, many downhill trials revealed a more exploratory selection process. Similar to the means/ends exploration observed in object tasks (e.g., Piaget, 1952; Willatts, 1989), infants sometimes explored various means of traversal by testing various sliding positions while still on the starting platform. Babies sometimes sat down and hung their legs over the brink, or pivoted into a backing position and looked over their shoulders down the hill, and so on. Coders measured this sort of means/ends exploration of different locomotor methods by counting the number of discrete shifts in position before infants started onto slopes. Refusals required zero shifts to avoid traversal, and only one shift for an alternative climbing or sliding position. Multiple shifts would suggest that children explored various means of reaching the landing platform by testing what different positions felt like before committing themselves to going.

Means/ends testing was especially important for selecting among headfirst, sitting, and backing descent methods. Sliding headfirst was easiest but ended most often in a mishap at the bottom of the hill. Sliding in sitting or backing positions were more difficult cognitively, but were safest. Although every baby could sit independently from the first weeks of testing, infants had to view the sitting position as a means of locomotion rather than a stationary posture. Backing was even more complex. From their first weeks of testing, every baby had the requisite components for using the backing position (shift to a prone position, pivot in circles on their bellies, push backward). However, the backing position required infants to execute an initial detour away from the landing platform, then scoot backward with their faces turned away from the goal. In fact, sliding headfirst prone was infants' first sliding position, and sitting and backing positions appeared last in infants' slope repertoires.

Multiple shifts in position increased over weeks of crawling and walking (Fig. 2.5). Average number of shifts exceeded 1.0 after infants' sixteenth week of crawling and after their thirteenth week of walking, suggesting

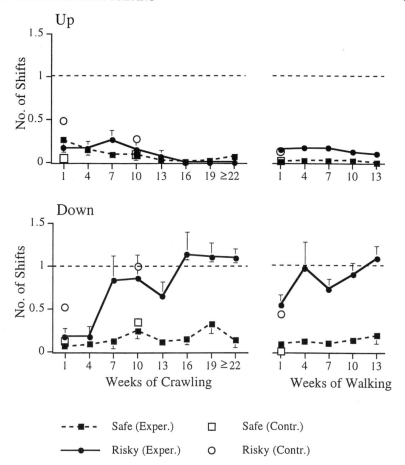

FIG. 2.5. Means/ends exploration (number of discrete shifts in posture prior to embarking) over weeks of locomotor experience for uphill (top panel) and downhill (bottom panel) slopes. *Note.* From "Learning in the development of infant locomotion," by K. E. Adolph, 1997, *Monographs of the Society for Research in Child Development.* Copyright 1997 by the University of Chicago Press. Reprinted with permission.

that babies actively explored various ways to go down. In most cases, multiple shifts resulted in selection of an alternative sliding position (75% trials) rather than avoidance. Moreover, most shifts in position followed long latencies and touches, and nearly every shift trial (99%) resulted in refusals, suggesting that infants shifted position after deciding that hills were risky for their typical method of locomotion.

Walking infants showed an additional type of means/ends behavior by use of the posts at the corners of the starting platform. Similar to adults' use of a railing to navigate a tricky patch of ground, walking infants sometimes used the posts at the brink of the hill for manual support while shifting position or touching the slope with their feet (10% of shift trials and 22% of touch trials). Apparently, threats to balance control led infants to view the posts as a simple tool or means enroute to the goal.

Social Context.   The slope task simulated important elements of an everyday social context. During each trial, an experimenter followed alongside infants to provide assistance if necessary. The babies' goal was to reach their parents, who offered a steady stream of positive encouragement and directed infants' attention to attractive toys and cheerios waiting at the end of every hill.

The go ratio curves for uphill and downhill protocols showed that infants did not learn to rely on the experimenter for rescue. Although the experimenter stood nearby on uphill trials, all infants safely caught themselves if they began to fall. On downhill trials, the experimenter did rescue infants on every occasion where they began to fall, and these near falls appeared to be relatively aversive. However, over the sessions infants became more cautious rather than more reckless, suggesting that infants learned to rely on their own judgments about safe versus risky hills.

More interesting were infants' social expressions directed to their parents and the experimenter. Despite adults' constant positive demeanor and verbal encouragement on every trial, infants could choose to appeal to their parents or the experimenter for help. Coders scored infants' social expressions on the starting platform by the frequency of infants' vocalizations (babbling, whining, and crying) and infants' gestures (pointing at the slope, head shakes "no," arm gestures to the parents such as "gives" and "pick-me-ups," and clinging to the experimenter's body or arm).

Overall, infants emitted social expressions on 16% of trials. Frequency of social expressions was comparable to infants' rate of exploratory touching (16% of trials), but on most trials infants started onto hills without a peep. (Note: Social expressions tended to occur on touch trials, but sometimes infants touched without emitting social expressions and sometimes they emitted social expressions without touching.) Preliminary analyses indicate that vocalizations and gestures became increasingly geared to task constraints (Stergiou, Adolph, Alibali, Avolio, & Cenedella, 1997). Similar to infants' patterns of exploratory looking and touching, crawlers displayed more social expressions than walkers, and social expressions were initially most indisciminate. Infants emitted most social expressions in their first weeks of crawling, and did so on both uphill and downhill, safe and risky slopes. Over weeks of crawling, social expressions gradually became limited to risky downhill slopes. Levels of social expressions remained relatively low over the transition from crawling to walking and, over weeks of walking, social expressions increased slightly on risky downhill slopes. Surprisingly, experienced crawlers gestured equally often as walkers, despite crawlers' reliance on hands and arms for locomotion. In other words, crawlers shifted to sitting or kneeling positions to use their arms for social expressions rather than balance control.

Differential social expressions in experienced crawlers and walkers provide additional evidence that infants eventually discriminated safe from risky hills. These results suggest that infants may contribute to the maintenance of their safety by emitting differential amounts of social expressions in potentially risky situations. Furthermore, regardless of infants' intentions when they vocalized or gestured in early weeks of crawling and walking, adults interpreted their behaviors as expressions with social intent. In everyday situations, even indiscriminate social expressions may function to alert parents when infants are on the move.

Moreover, the slope task was nested in a larger social context—infants' changing exposure to ascent and descent tasks at home. Parents filled out a daily diary noting infants' home experience going up and down stairs and clambering down from furniture. Frequency of exposure to ascent and descent was constrained by the layout of infants' homes and by parents' decisions to allow their babies access to various ascent and descent situations. For example, parents of beginning crawlers babyproofed their homes by gating household stairs and parents permitted babies to go up stairs before they allowed infants to come down. Coders scored frequency of experience with ascent and descent as the number of entries in parents' diaries between each crawling or walking session divided by the total number of days between sessions.

Infants' home experience with ascent and descent increased over weeks of crawling and over weeks of walking. At best, infants were exposed to home stairs and furniture on half of the days between test sessions, and long-time crawlers had more home ascent/descent experience than infants who crawled for only a short time. In addition, infants tended to have more experiences going up stairs than going down as crawlers and more experiences descending furniture than descending stairs as walkers. Infants with stair experience always went up in a crawling position and most went down in a backing position (2 babies bumped down in a sitting position). All infants with experience descending furniture went down backward feet first.

In infants' last week of crawling, duration of crawling experience, amount of home ascent/descent experience, and age varied freely. In that target session, home experience going up and down stairs and furniture was correlated with infants' test age, body dimensions, and crawling proficiency on flat ground. Apparently, parents provided their babies with access to potentially risky ascent and descent situations at home when babies were older, were more maturely proportioned, and displayed more everyday locomotor skill. Moreover, although duration of crawling experience was a stronger predictor of infants' judgments on risky hills, home experience on stairs and furniture was also positively correlated with infants' go ratios on risky downhill slopes. Infants with more home ascent/descent experience tended to have more adaptive, lower go ratios.

UNDERSTANDING CHANGE IN INFANT LOCOMOTION

Coping with slopes required flexible problem solving. Infants' growing bodies and changing locomotor skills resulted in weekly changes in their physical abilities to go up and down slopes. Adaptive mobility meant that infants matched their locomotor responses to these changing biomechanical constraints. The only way for infants to make online decisions about safe versus risky hills was to obtain information from their own exploratory movements. Despite infants' occasional appeals for help, parents and experimenters left infants to figure it out for themselves. Moreover, in the case of risky hills, infants also had to decide which alternative method of locomotion to use.

Learning From Everyday Locomotor Experience. What spurred adaptive responses on slopes? Traditionally, researchers accounted for locomotor development with single cause, maturational mechanisms linked with infants' ages or stages of postural control. However, our focus on adaptive locomotion suggests a more complex explanation. If age were the sole impetus for change, we would expect one smooth go ratio curve on risky hills over weeks of crawling and walking. If adaptive responding resulted from the stage-like transition from crawling to walking, perhaps driven by the shift from a more stable quadruped posture to a less stable upright one, we would expect high go ratios on risky hills over weeks of crawling and an abrupt decrease in go ratios after walking onset. Instead, change resulted from learning via everyday locomotor experience. Infants showed two go ratio curves on risky downhill slopes, one over weeks of crawling and one over weeks of walking, and infants showed increasing sensitivity to the different biomechanical constraints of going uphill versus going down. Duration of crawling or walking experience over flat ground at home was the strongest predictor of infants' perceptual judgments and exploratory behavior on slopes. However, as described later in this chapter, physical growth, locomotor proficiency, and infants' age may also play a role.

What Infants Learn. What might infants learn from everyday crawling and walking experience? A likely answer is that infants learn to predict whether they are going to lose their balance. Detecting threats to balance control requires information about the limit of permissible postural sway. Infants will fall over if their body moves outside their base of support without sufficient muscle strength to pull themselves back into position. When the ground is too steep (or too slippery or too compliant), infants must reduce postural sway by stiffening their bodies or, in extreme cases, switch to a different method of locomotion. Exploratory looking and touching movements yield information about whether the ground surface is safe or precarious for keeping balance in infants' current crawling or walking posture. Exploratory means/ends shifts in position yield information about balance control in alternative climbing and sliding positions when infants decide that their typical method of locomotion is impossible.

Results suggest that infants may learn to detect information for permissible sway posture by posture rather than task by task, such that information obtained from exploratory looking and touching movements generalizes to new ground surfaces and to changes in infants' body dimensions, but is specific to well-practiced postures and vantage points. Everyday practice keeping balance in a crawling posture, for example, may help infants to gauge how fast and far their bodies can rotate as they sway back and forth over their wrists, and how much muscle force infants can muster to counter rotational forces. Such learning would transfer to a novel crawling task. However, in an unfamiliar upright posture, all bets are off. Walkers' bodies sway around the hips or ankles rather than the wrists, compensatory sways are generated primarily in leg or back muscles rather than the upper body, and infants' base of support is reduced to the space between their feet.

Accordingly, infants in this study showed both impressive generalization from home crawling or walking experience to crawling or walking over slopes and a striking lack of transfer between crawling and walking postures. Despite weekly changes in infants' crawling styles and crawling proficiency, crawlers' go ratios decreased and their exploratory behaviors became more discerning. Likewise, despite weekly changes in infants' walking ability, go ratios decreased and exploratory behaviors became more efficient. However, over the transition from crawling to walking, perceptual judgments and functional outcome of exploratory movements were impaired.

Online Problem Solving. In the end, adaptive locomotion requires infants to make online decisions. The end product of development is the ability to monitor action adaptively, online, from one step to the next. The data suggest that what infants learn from everyday home experience is a repertoire of increasingly effective exploratory movements for obtaining information about balance control as infants face each new surface a few steps ahead.

Most often, infants started onto slopes after only a brief glance at the hill. Nearly every uphill trial and more than half of the downhill trials had latencies of less than 1s. This means that infants decided on a locomotor method as they were lowered toward the starting platform, sometimes their typical crawling or walking method and sometimes an alternative position. The functional outcome of quick glances improved dramatically over weeks of experience; failures decreased, and successes and refusals increased. Information gleaned from a quick look may include the distance of the surface from infants' eyes or the angle of slope relative to the plane of gaze.

If a brief glance hinted at something amiss, infants paused for a longer look. Infants typically maintained orientation toward the landing platform during the time that they hesitated. Across sessions, long looks were followed by infants' typical method and alternative locomotor methods in approximately equal proportions, and the functional outcome of long looks improved with weeks of experience. Prolonged looking involves movements of infants' eyes, heads, and bodies as they generate compensatory postural sway on the starting platform and peer over the edge. These movements produce visual and mechanical information for balance control (e.g., Lee, 1994; Mark, Baillet, Craver, Douglas, & Fox, 1990) and visual information about the properties of the ground ahead.

When concerted looking suggested risky ground, infants obtained additional information from touching. Most touches followed long looks, suggesting that visual information prompted the touches. Infants probed the slope with hands and feet—usually stepping and rocking movements at the brink of the hill—all the while looking at their limbs and the ground. Over weeks of crawling or walking, touches became increasingly efficient. They were shorter in duration and more likely to be followed by successes or refusals rather than failures. Coordinated looking and touching yields information about the slant and friction of the hill by generating rotational forces at wrists or ankles, shearing forces between the limb and the surface, and additional visual information from optic flow patterns and motion parallax.

When exploratory looking or touching suggested danger from falling, children explored alternative locomotor methods. Shifts in position were followed by refusals, indicating that infants had already decided that slopes were risky. On most trials, infants discovered an appropriate alternative and used it. Over weeks of crawling, infants replaced avoidance responses on downhill slopes with alternative sliding positions and they continued to use their sliding positions over weeks of walking. Apparently, means/ends exploration yields information for keeping balance in less practiced locomotor postures, such as the various sliding positions for going down hills.

Characterizing Change. Infants showed a protracted period of learning enroute to adaptive, online decisions on slopes. Most researchers have characterized infant learning as an additive, enrichment process of construction via transformation of schema or simple associative pairing (e.g., Piaget, 1952; Rovee-Collier, Greco-Vigorito, & Hayne, 1993). A construction process means that children build the requisite knowledge from the ground up by sequencing or reorganizing smaller, component movements in their repertoires. For example, in the slopes task, a construction process would be evidenced by a gradual increase in exploratory behaviors as infants compile the full array of movements required for online decision making.

The slopes data, however, point to an alternative characterization of learning as a subtractive, sculpting process of gradual differentiation and selection (Gibson, 1969, 1988, 1991; Gibson & Gibson, 1955). A differentiation/selection process implies two things. First, the essential information for adaptive decision making must be available from the beginning of independent mobility. That is, physiological sensitivity and ability to execute appropriate exploratory movements are prerequisite for a differentiation/selection process to operate. Second, a differentiation process would predict that within sessions, infants' responses should be graded, with infants' most accurate judgments on hills most remote from their slope boundaries and infants' least accurate judgments on hills most similar to their slope boundaries. Across sessions, a differentiation/selection process should show increasing specificity as exploratory movements and locomotor responses become more honed and efficient. Given the raw materials to start, the developmental task is to obtain the necessary information, understand its relevance for locomotion, and select an appropriate locomotor response.

Consistent with a differentiation/selection process, the evidence indicates that information for balance control is available at the start of mobility. Even neonates show physiological sensitivity to visual information for surface slant. Infants looked differentially at displays of surfaces slanting to different degrees (Slater & Morison, 1985). Moreover, infants have the requisite skills for obtaining visual and haptic information for slant via self-initiated exploratory movements. In cross-sectional studies, newly crawling infants exhibited differential visual and haptic exploration on steep hills compared with shallow ones in both locomotor and nonlocomotor tasks (Adolph et al., 1993; Eppler et al., 1996). Likewise, in the current study, babies executed the full range of exploratory looking and touching movements in their first weeks of crawling. However, the data suggest that sensitivity and differential exploration is not enough for adaptive responding. Infants must learn the relevance of information obtained from exploratory looking and touching. In the current study and in previous experiments (Adolph et al., 1993), new crawlers explored steep and shallow hills differentially, but plunged over the brink of impossibly steep hills nonetheless without testing a single alternative sliding position.

In accordance with the differentiation/selection account, infants' perceptual judgments were graded in sessions and showed increasing attunement across sessions. In each session of crawling and walking, infants' judgments were always most accurate on the riskiest hills most remote from infants' slope boundaries, and most indiscriminate on slopes slightly steeper than slope boundaries. The most dramatic learning across sessions was on hills slightly steeper than infants' slope boundaries. Likewise, infants' exploratory movements showed a pattern consistent with a differentiation process. Exploratory looking and touching were scaled to infants' slope boundaries, showed increasing specificity across sessions until exploration was limited to risky hills, and showed improvement in functional outcome of trials following each type of exploratory movement. Infants in cross-sectional samples also showed graded perceptual judgments and exploratory behaviors (e.g., Adolph, 1995). Apparently, infants must learn to glean the relevant information for accurate judgments.

Mediating Effects of Biomechanical Factors. A central problem for a differentiation/selection characterization of learning is an account of how so much information becomes available so early. What factors might prompt infants to generate appropriate exploratory movements to enable them to distinguish safe from risky terrain? Presumably, if infants' early exploration in their first weeks of crawling resulted from deliberate forethought, beginning crawlers also should have shown adaptive responses on perilously risky hills. Likewise, if new crawlers' high levels of social expressions reflected functional knowledge of the consequences of risky slopes, infants should have avoided traversal.

Results of the current study suggest that useful exploratory movements, social expressions, and locomotor methods may originate in a serendipitous confluence of biomechanical factors. Infants' changing body dimensions, variable movements, and the physical constraints of the ground surface can load the deck for spontaneous emergence of new motor patterns. Like cases of exaptation in evolutionary development, infants may discover functionally useful movements in the course of attempting to do something else. Discovery in this case does not require deliberate forethought, only that infants must recognize a good thing once they have got it.

In fact, mediating effects of biomechanical factors may explain infants' relatively indiscriminate, high levels of exploration and social expressions in their first weeks of crawling and infants' low levels of exploration and social expressions in their first weeks of walking. In their first weeks of crawling, most infants were weak, top-heavy, and poorly proficient. Infants' heavy heads kept their eyes pointed toward the ground and their weak arms kept body weight distributed back toward the legs from step to step. Even on flat ground, infants hobbled along, pausing, patting the floor, and rocking back and forth over their wrists between bursts of crawling steps (e.g., Goldfield, 1993). Initially, beginning crawlers may have executed the same looking and touching movements on the brink of slopes as they did on flat ground due to the biomechanical constraints of their new quadruped posture. Infants could look at the floor, sway to and fro, and generate torques around their wrists without understanding the relevance of these movements for guiding locomotion. Thus, exploratory movements may have entered infants' repertoires serendipitously, and later, after weeks of crawling, infants used the same exploratory movements intentionally to obtain information about the ground ahead.

Likewise, gathering sufficient energy to move forward meant that new crawlers were in a relatively high state of arousal. Infants' first vocalizations in the slope task may have emerged spontaneously as a result of overall physiological arousal. Later, infants' more specific use of vocalizations, arm gestures, and clinging behaviors reflected intentional appeals for help. Furthermore, in this case, function may precede intention. Regardless of their intent, infants' vocalizations function to alert caregivers when infants are in transit, and adults in the slope task responded to all whining and babbling vocalizations as intentional social expressions.

Biomechanical constraints may also explain the low levels of exploration in infants' first weeks of walking. New walkers have especially poor balance control during periods of single leg support (e.g., Bril & Brenière, 1992, 1993). Infants' body weight shifts forward with each step, so that infants must quickly place their moving leg before they fall over. Unlike crawling, there is no serendipitous, safe pause in forward momentum at the brink of a risky surface. This means that walkers must have decided ahead of time to stop and touch slopes; once their leading leg was planted over the brink, it was already too late. In contrast to crawling where the head naturally points downward and infants have to work against gravity to lift their heads, in upright locomotion, the natural position for head and eyes is straight ahead. Rotating the head downward shifts infants' center of mass forward and threatens balance control. Instead of pausing, looking, and touching serendipitously, new walkers could only have stopped to look or touch hills based on their initial glance as they were lowered toward the starting platform. In fact, even experienced walkers may have had difficulty keeping upright balance while executing exploratory peering movements and touching movements with their feet. Many experienced walkers held the corner posts at the brink of slopes while peering downward or touching hills with their feet, as though requiring additional support to keep balance. In contrast, only one crawler on only one trial held a post for support.

A similar serendipitious biomechanical scenerio also may explain the origins of new locomotor movements. Like exploratory movements and social expressions, new locomotor methods may emerge spontaneously in the context of doing something else. For example, changing biomechanical constraints may have facilitated spontaneous discovery of new descent methods by placing infants in opportune, new situations. Most infants appeared to discover the backing position on slopes by accident, in the course of trying to crawl down steep hills (Wechsler, 1995; Wechsler & Adolph, 1995). As infants' bodies became more maturely proportioned and as their crawling proficiency improved, infants spent more trials on steep slopes. Accomplished crawlers started down on hands and knees with their arms stiffly extended in front, legs tightly flexed under their buttocks, and weight pushed back toward their rumps. Gravity pulled infants' legs around until babies found themselves sliding down sideways or backward feet first. Infants sometimes said, "uh oh" or "oh no" and several infants crawled back up to the starting platform and looked down the hill in puzzlement. After experiencing one or more serendipitous backing trials, infants began executing the backing position on purpose before leaving the starting platform.

It is important to note in these examples that infants' behaviors were not random thrashing or trial and error learning. But, in their first incarnation, neither were behaviors necessarily deliberately focused toward their functional relevance. Instead, infants' repertoires of exploratory movements, social expressions, and locomotor methods may emerge in the context of a goal directed task, with inherent variability in the system. The origins of such basic tools for solving the problem of mobility may be overdetermined by the vissitudes of development. Once in infants' repertoires, recognizing the functional relevance of these movements is hard won over weeks of crawling and walking.

CONCLUSION

The problem of mobility was of central concern for developmental psychologists in the first half of this century. Traditional research programs focused on neuromuscular changes in the biomechanics of locomotion. Divorced from everyday function for the past 50 years, infant locomotion was relegated to descriptions of age norms and postural stages outside the central issues of psychological development. Only recently have researchers begun to overcome the conceptual obstacles of monolithic change mechanisms and oversimplified laboratory tasks.

Our aim in this chapter was to illustrate a new research agenda for understanding how infants solve the problem of moving. As Neisser (1982) argued, the real challenge is to design ecologically valid, functionally relevant tasks that lead investigators to discover the important questions. Further, an integrated approach that examines behavior across traditionally disparate domains may point toward more general theories of learning and development.

POSTSCRIPT

In his book, *Memory Observed*, Neisser (1982) shared an old adage, "Education is what is left over when you have forgotten what you have learned" (p. 5). We wish to reassure our teacher that we have not forgotten all the important lessons. For example, Neisser emphasized clear communication skills in his students. One way that he operationalized good writing was the eight-letter rule. Drafts of our writing returned from his desk with all lengthy, awkward, technical terms circled. One memorable episode was when we asked Neisser to help fund the mailing of our first feedback letter to parents. He agreed to pay, but there was a stipulation: We first had to pay him 5 cents for every word over eight letters long. The newsletter was quickly rephrased so that parents could actually understand the findings.

We end with a personal note to Dick. A quick check of this manuscript indicates that we have violated the eight-letter rule to the tune of 56 dollars and 5 cents. Should we pay you now or is there time for one more revision?

ACKNOWLEDGMENTS

This work was supported by Individual National Research Service Award grant #MH10226-02 from NICHHD, Sigma Xi Grant-in-Aid-of-Research award, and a faculty development grant from Carnegie Mellon University. Additional support was provided by NICHHD grant #HD22830 to Esther Thelen and by funding from the Emory Cognition Project. Portions of this research were presented at the April, 1993 and March, 1995 meetings of the Society for Research in Child Development in New Orleans and Indianapolis.

REFERENCES

Adolph, K. E. (1995). A psychophysical assessment of toddlers' ability to cope with slopes. *Journal of Experimental Psychology: Human Perception and Performance, 21,* 734–750.

Adolph, K. E. (1997). Learning in the development of infant locomotion. *Monographs of the Society for Research in Child Development, 62*(3, Serial No. 251).

Adolph, K. E., Eppler, M. A., & Gibson, E. J. (1993). Development of perception of affordances. In C. Rovee-Collier & L. P. Lipsitt (Eds.), *Advances in infancy research, 8,* 51–98. Norwood, NJ: Ablex.

Bril, B., & Brenière, Y. (1992). Postural requirements and progression velocity in young walkers. *Journal of Motor Behavior, 24,* 105–116.

Bril, B., & Brenière, Y. (1993). Posture and independent locomotion in early childhood: Learning to walk or learning dynamic postural control? In G. J. P. Savelsbergh (Ed.), *The development of coordination in infancy* (pp. 337–358). Amsterdam: North-Holland.

Eppler, M. A., Adolph, K. E., & Weiner, T. (1996). The developmental relationship between exploration and action on sloping surfaces. *Infant Behavior and Development, 19,* 259–264.

Gesell, A., & Ames, L. B. (1940). The ontogenetic organization of prone behavior in human infancy. *The Journal of Genetic Psychology, 56,* 247–263.

Gibson, E. J. (1969). *Principles of perceptual learning and development.* New York: Appleton-Century-Crofts.

Gibson, E. J. (1988). Exploratory behavior in the development of perceiving, acting and the acquiring of knowledge. *Annual Review of Psychology, 39,* 1–41.

Gibson, E. J. (1991). Prospects for a new approach to perceptual learning. In E. J. Gibson (Ed.), *An odyssey in learning and perception* (pp. 607–616). Cambridge, MA: MIT Press.

Gibson, J. J., & Gibson, E. J. (1955). Perceptual learning: Differentiation or enrichment? *Psychological Review, 62,* 32–41.

Goldfield, E. C. (1993). Dynamic systems in development: Action systems. In L. B. Smith & E. Thelen (Eds.), *A dynamic systems approach to development: Applications* (pp. 51–70). Cambridge, MA: MIT Press.

Lee, D. N. (1994). Body-environment coupling. In U. Neisser (Ed.), *The perceived self: Ecological and interpersonal sources of self-knowledge* (pp. 43–67). Cambridge, England: Cambridge University Press.

Mark, L. S., Baillet, J. A., Craver, K. D., Douglas, S. D., & Fox, T. (1990). What an actor must do in order to perceive the affordance for sitting. *Ecological Psychology, 2*(4), 325–366.

McGraw, M. B. (1945). *The neuromuscular maturation of the human infant.* New York: Columbia University Press.

Neisser, U. (Ed.). (1982). *Memory observed: Remembering in natural context.* New York: Freeman.

Neisser, U. (1994). Multiple systems: A new approach to cognitive theory. *European Journal of Cognitive Psychology, 6,* 225–241.

Piaget, J. (1952). *The origins of intelligence in children.* New York: International Universities Press.

Rovee-Collier, C., Greco-Vigorito, C., & Hayne, H. (1993). The time-window hypothesis: Implications for categorization and memory modification. *Infant Behavior and Development, 16,* 149–176.

Shirley, M. M. (1931). *The first two years: A study of 25 babies: Volume I. Postural and locomotor development.* Minneapolis: University of Minnesota Press.

Slater, A., & Morison, V. (1985). Shape constancy and slant perception at birth. *Perception, 14,* 337–344.

Sorce, J., Emde, R., Campos, J., & Klinnert, M. (1985). Maternal emotional-signaling: Its effect on the visual cliff behavior of 1-year-olds. *Developmental Psychology, 21,* 195–200.

Stergiou, C. S., Adolph, K. E., Alibali, M. W., Avolio, A. M., & Cenedella, C. (1997). Social expressions in infant locomotion: Vocalizations and gestures on slopes. In M. A. Schmuckler & J. M. Kennedy (Eds.), *Studies in perception and action IV* (pp. 215–218). Mahwah, NJ: Lawrence Erlbaum Associates.

Wechsler, M. A. (1995). *Strategy acquisition and strategy choice in infants descending slopes.* Unpublished senior honors thesis, Middlebury College, Middlebury, VT.

Wechsler, M. A., & Adolph, K. E. (1995, April). *Learning new ways of moving: Variability in infants' discovery and selection of motor strategies.* Poster presented to the Society for Research in Child Development, Indianapolis, IN.

Willatts, P. (1989). Development of problem-solving in infancy. In A. Slater & G. Bremner (Eds.), *Infant development* (pp. 143–182). Hillsdale, NJ: Lawrence Erlbaum Associates.

Chapter 3

Descriptions of Orientation and Structure in Perception and Physical Reasoning

John R. Pani
University of Louisville

In every species that has cognition, individual organisms take account of the orientations of things (see Fraenkel & Gunn, 1940). Ants leave their nests and search great distances for food or for other ant colonies. How does an ant find its way back? It appears that ants see stripes in the sky, due to their sensitivity to the polarization of sunlight. As an ant forages, its average heading is encoded as an angle relative to the stripes in the sky (e.g., Schone, 1984). To return home, the ant reverses direction.

Human use of information about the world is extended over space and time and has flexibility beyond that of other species. When a human behaves, it may be to determine the age of a fossil, to move a single atom a few microns, or to launch mechanical sensors into the atmosphere of another planet. But despite our differences from ants, understanding orientation is as important to us as it is to them. Along with most other vertebrates, for example, we have a vestibular sensory system dedicated to perception of the local vertical. Much of our cortical organization involves orientation-sensitive neurons or populations of neurons (see Kandel, Schwartz, & Jessel, 1995). Our perceptual intuitions readily inform us that a hill is steep, that a picture frame is tilted, or that a stack of books is leaning too far over. Everyday language encodes these terms: steep, tilted, and leaning, and many more besides. Metaphors based on orientation are common in language (e.g., Lakoff & Johnson, 1980). We are inclined to things, make oblique references, try to get the best angle, to be an upright person, and to avoid the slippery slope of a tempting argument. As humans

59

have developed rigorous descriptions of space in mathematics, science, and engineering, concepts of orientation have remained central.

I suggest in this chapter that an understanding of orientation is essential for humans in high level perception, imagination, and physical reasoning.[1] In one obvious sense this is an appropriate topic for a chapter that honors Dick Neisser. People's understanding of orientation has long been of interest to those who take an ecological view of perception. It is perhaps even more fitting that the work I discuss owes as much to the Gestalt views of Max Wertheimer, and to modern views of perceptual organization, as it does to J. J. Gibson and the ecological tradition. In my years as Dick's friend and colleague, and as a member of his Perception Group, I have found that he welcomes ideas of all kinds, so long as they represent a serious effort to understand people and their ways.

My claims about orientation are based on the results of four research projects in which normal adults reasoned about fundamental physical properties of the world. One project concerned people's ability to recognize and describe simple rotations, or to predict their outcomes (Pani, 1993; Pani & Dupree, 1994; Pani, William, & Shippey, 1995). A second project concerned prediction of the outcomes of elementary projective transformations, such as the casting of shadows or the drawing of pictures (Pani, Jeffres, Shippey, & Schwartz, 1996). A third project concerned an elementary spatial relation, the fact that two planes always intersect at one line. Participants in experiments demonstrated the edges that would be formed by the intersections of surfaces (Pani, William, & Shippey, 1998). And a fourth project concerned the understanding of elementary 3-D shapes. Participants studied, remembered for a brief time, and then physically represented a set of basic solids (Pani, 1994; Pani, Zhou, & Friend, 1997).

In developing an overall view of this work, I suggest that the perception of orientation is a type of description. The mental models of physical events that sometimes underly reasoning also comprise a type of description of the events, which I call their base organizations. Success in reasoning depends on finding a fit between perceptual description of a situation and the description that is needed for reasoning. Such a fit involves either transitive relations from one description to another or a reinforcement among descriptions with like properties. Examination of these descriptions, and of the fit between them, characteristically reveals three nested sets of properties of the world that are especially useful for people. The most specific set is the spatial properties of alignment, including parallel, perpendicular, coincident, vertical, and horizontal. These are a subset of the properties that comprise the symmetries (in the modern sense of invariance

---

[1]A sensible description of spatial relations requires a description of location and distance as well. In the present chapter, however, I concentrate on the topic of orientation.

across transformation). And the symmetries in turn are a subset of the singularities. Fundamental singular properties include maximum, minimum, same, and orthogonal. Sensitivity to these three sets of properties leads to descriptions that are efficient, distinctive, nonarbitrary, and pragmatically useful.

ORIENTATION

Description

To clarify what I mean by the term description, I return briefly to the insects. Bees navigate by the sun, as ants do, but bees add something even more wonderful. Bees return to the hive and communicate the heading to food to their hivemates. Although bees can navigate by the polarization of light, as ants do, this is not the system that provides the information communicated at the hive. Rather, bees encode the vertical in which the sun lies, and they encode the angle of their heading relative to this vertical, as illustrated in Fig. 3.1. I call this the ground angle, because it is the angle within a horizontal plane between the heading of the bee and the vertical in which the sun is located. To communicate the ground angle, bees return to the hive and perform the famous waggle dance (Gould & Gould, 1988; von Frisch, 1967). Standing on a vertical wall of the hive, a bee takes the

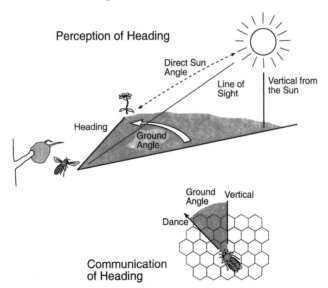

FIG. 3.1. The honey bee encodes the heading to flowers in terms of the ground angle.

vertical direction to symbolize the direction of the sun. The bee shows the ground angle by dancing at this angle relative to the vertical.

There is an obvious alternative angle that the bees could encode. Instead of projecting the sun in the vertical, and encoding the ground angle, bees might have evolved to encode the direct angle between their heading and the sun (see Fig. 3.1). This is the angle that would be suggested by many discussions of visual information in human perception, and bees could use and communicate this angle without loss of information or efficiency of communication.

Perception is at the minimum a partial mapping between the structure of the immediate world and the structure of potential behaviors. Perception of orientation is a mapping from certain relations among things in the world, those relations that can be expressed in angles. For a given orientation, the relations often can be organized in more than one way. Bees might have evolved to use the direct angle between a heading and the sun, but instead they use the ground angle (no doubt for a very good reason). Saying that perception is a type of description makes explicit that the mapping between the environment and behavior concerns certain relations in the environment and not their alternatives. And if bees have settled on particular descriptions of orientation, it is a fair question to ask, what descriptions do people use?

Human Description of Orientation

Cardinal Directions. For anything to have an orientation—for it to be steep, to lean, to be upright, or horizontal—there must be some structure in the object for which orientation will be determined. The simplest structure that fills this role is the line, or axis. Thus, the shape of a telephone pole is approximated by a line. The orientation of an object is given by the angle, or angles, between the structure of the object and a reference system, such as the vertical of the environment. Thus, when the axis of a telephone poll is parallel to the vertical, we say the pole is upright. A wadded piece of paper, approximating a homogeneous sphere, can only be arbitrarily fit with a line, and so it has an arbitrary orientation. It cannot be upside down, lean, or face to the right. (It is considered to have a top by the understanding that top is typically the highest point on an object.)

A number of objects with the simplest orientable structure, a single line (or axis), are shown in Fig. 3.2. They include water pipes, rolling pins, wheels, and plain donuts. For the linear objects (e.g., pipes), the line is the major axis of the object and tells how it points. For the disc-like objects (e.g., wheels), the line is a surface normal and tells how the surface faces. Also shown in the figure are objects characterized by single polar axes. This class of structures includes objects with tops, or fronts, such as mush-

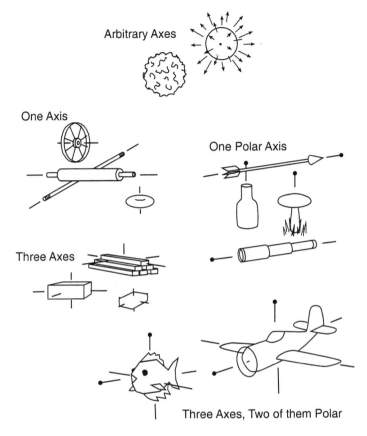

FIG. 3.2. Cardinal directions comprise the orientable structure of objects.

rooms, frisbees, arrows, telescopes, drinking glasses, bottles, trees, and nails.

An axis can be placed through an object anywhere that it has a cardinal direction, a direction that nonarbitarily points or faces in some direction. For example, a variety of three-axis objects also are included in Fig. 3.2, and range from such things as a brick, lumber, mattress, and bar of soap, that have nonpolar axes, to vertebrates (e.g., fish, reptiles, and mammals), television sets, books, vehicles, and buildings; these have three axes and unique ends for two or three of them (i.e., top, front, and side).

Reference Systems. The orientation of an object is given by the angle, or angles, of a structure in the object to a reference system. Suppose there is a solar panel, and its orientation will be described in terms of the way it faces. A system commonly used for such a purpose would include a surface normal on the panel and two orthogonal angles in a polar reference system (so-called spherical coordinates). In terms of these two angles, the solar panel may face upward and South, as shown in Fig. 3.3.

When speaking about our perceptions of surfaces, these orthogonal angles often are called the slant of a surface and the direction of the slant (e.g., Gibson, 1950; Sedgwick, 1986; Stevens, 1983). Determination of these angles requires a polar axis and an equatorial plane that is orthogonal to the axis. The slant of the solar panel (upward) is the angle of a surface normal between the polar axis and the equatorial plane. Direction-of-slant is the direction within the equatorial plane that the surface normal points (South). This direction can be determined by projecting the normal to the equatorial plane (much as bees project the sun) and taking the angle of the projection relative to a reference point in the plane. For large scale geography, this reference point often is North. The sides of the great pyramid at Giza, for example, face North, South, East, and West (due to the relations of the sun to these directions). But reference points for direction-of-slant vary widely. On a baseball field, we might describe a high fly ball as heading down the right field line, or passing between first and second bases.

There is a variety of reference systems that can be used to describe orientation, and the use of a polar reference system is due as much to cognitive structures as it is to the intrinsic nature of things in space. Two advantages of the polar system are immediately obvious from the fact that slant and direction-of-slant are orthogonal dimensions. Decomposing a universe of possibilities into a set of values on dimensions reduces the

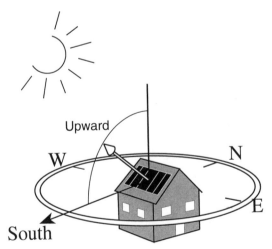

FIG. 3.3. Slant and direction-of-slant in a polar reference system. Adapted from "Orientation in physical reasoning: On the imagination of surfaces to intersect at edges" by J. R. Pani, C. T. William, & G. T. Shippey, 1998, *Journal of Experimental Psychology: Human Perception and Performance.* Copyright 1998, American Psychological Association. Adapted with permission.

number of values that must be taken into account in order to describe the universe. As an example, consider positions in space. With a given spatial resolution, a planar area may have 100 separate locations. If the locations are described in terms of distances along the length and width of the area (i.e., in 2-D coordinates), the entire set of locations can be described with 10 values on each dimension, giving a total of just 20 values and a savings of 80%. Orthogonal dimensions have the further advantage of permitting just one dimension to vary in particular circumstances so that the set of values required to describe the universe can be further reduced (consider Proffitt & Gilden, 1989).

There are many important types of polar axes for humans. Certainly there is the line of sight. Optical texture and perspective gradients useful in vision are related most directly to the line of sight (e.g., Braunstein, 1976). Indeed, most of the orientation-sensitive cells that have been identified in the brain concern orientation defined relative to this reference system (so, indeed, we might have expected bees to use the direct sun angle; see Kandel et al., 1995). Here, however, I am concerned with the understanding of relations among things in 3-D space, and I discuss object axes, transformation axes (e.g., an axis of rotation), and the environmental vertical as basic examples of polar reference systems. It is only with respect to the vertical, for example, that the great pyramid is symmetric (e.g., with all four sides having a single slant to a major axis).

Object Interaction. A major axis or surface normal that expresses a cardinal direction in an object is typically an intrinsic part of that object: It can be determined in the absence of context. Beyond this, the axes of objects are closely related to how objects behave and interact with other things. Arrows fly in alignment with their cardinal direction. Bricks are put into walls in alignment with their cardinal directions. The typical airplane is built so that its control surfaces tip the aircraft about the three orthogonal axes of roll, pitch, and yaw that are aligned with the cardinal directions of the aircraft. This control system is little different from the fins that control the movements and orientations of most fish.

Configurations and interactions among objects can produce geometric structures that are not wholly intrinsic to the individual objects in them, as illustrated in Fig. 3.4. Fences and barriers, which might be formed of linear objects such as ropes, wires, or boards, face perpendicular to their cardinal directions but also parallel with the surface from which they might be approached. The edge of a knife or an axe faces in the direction that it will cut, and this depends on the orientation of the object that includes the edge (see Fig. 3.4).

There are situations in which the geometry of object interaction can substitute for the intrinsic cardinal directions of an object as a description

FIG. 3.4. Illustrations of the geometry of object interaction.

of its orientable structure (especially when positions in space are added to specifications of orientation). Consider such a description of the orientations of flat surfaces.

Orientation Lines.   Once a polar reference system has been chosen, it is not necessary to describe the orientation of a surface using a surface normal. Orientation can be measured for lines on the surface itself, as illustrated in Fig. 3.5. Consider that if a ball is rolled down a flat hill, it follows a particular line. This is the line of least action. It minimizes the angle of the surface relative to the vertical (the polar axis in this case) while maximizing the angle of the surface relative to the equatorial plane (the horizontal; see Fig. 3.5). If balls are started at different positions along the top of the hill, there is produced a family of parallel lines, and any one of these lines may be used to measure the slant of the hill. Hence I call them slant lines.

If steps are carved in the hill, they will be horizontal. The lines formed by the steps will have the maximum angle to the polar axis and the minimum to the equatorial plane. Further, they will face in the direction that the hill faces. Thus, such a family of parallel direction lines gives the

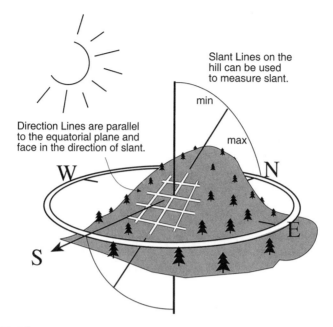

FIG. 3.5. In a polar reference system, orientation lines can give the structure of a plane.

direction-of-slant of the hill. Note that slant lines and direction lines are orthogonal to each other. Overall, they form a set of orientation lines: lines on a surface that exemplify, and can be used to determine, the slant and direction-of-slant of a surface.

Orientation lines express the relationship between a surface and a reference system. Mathematically, they are fairly basic: They give the gradient of the function that defines the surface, and the level set for that function, for the given reference system. Orientation lines on a hillside express orientation in terms of a relation to gravity. In a quite different context, the structure of the head of the hatchet in Fig. 3.4 could be expressed in terms of orientation lines relative to its direction of travel. Here the slant lines would give the direction of the cut, and the direction lines would be given by the edge of the blade. This description of the structure of a plane in terms of how it slices will be useful later in the discussion of projective transformations.

Of course, orientation lines are typically not physically present on a surface. Then again, surface normals are rarely physically present either. Both orientation lines and surface normals are, as it were, soft features of an object that express the possibilities of its interactions (and thus are related to object recognition). When these interactions depend on the presence of a reference axis, such as the vertical, there is a highly cooperative system that joins reference system, object, and description of orientation.

Singular Orientations. For any polar reference system, there are singular orientations of lines and planes, and these are canonical for people. In the singular orientations, the structure of the object has the same orientation as elements of the reference system, as illustrated in Fig. 3.6. The relation parallel is of obvious importance in this context, for this is the relation between two objects in which they have the same orientation. In addition, because a polar reference system has perpendicular elements (the orthogonally related axis and equatorial plane), perpendicular orientations also are important relations between objects and reference systems: An object that is perpendicular to one element of the reference system is parallel to another (perpendicular orientations have a number of other important properties, to be discussed later this chapter).

There is one orientation for planar surfaces in which they are parallel to the equatorial plane and perpendicular to the polar axis. For this one orientation, slant is zero and direction-of-slant does not exist. In the local

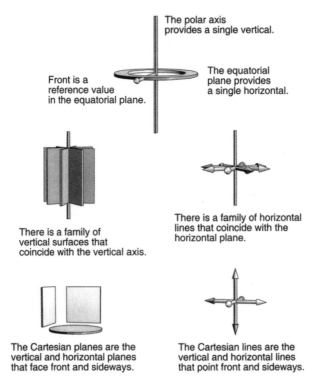

FIG. 3.6. The singular orientations in a polar reference system.

terrestrial environment, these are the horizontal surfaces, exemplified by floors and tabletops. There is also a set of orientations in which surfaces coincide with the polar axis and are perpendicular to the equatorial plane. In the local terrestrial environment, these are the vertical surfaces, exemplified by walls and doors.

The three Cartesian planes are singular surface orientations within a polar reference system (see Fig. 3.6). One of the Cartesian planes is the horizontal. The other two are contained within the set of vertical surfaces. The frontal plane has a direction-of-slant of zero. The sagittal plane, being orthogonal to the frontal, also has a singular orientation (sideways).

Lines also may have singular orientations with respect to a polar reference system. There is one orientation that is parallel to the polar axis and perpendicular to the equatorial plane. For this one orientation, direction of slant does not exist. In the local terrestrial environment, such lines are vertical, or upright. There is a set of orientations in which axes are contained within the equatorial plane and are perpendicular to the polar axis. In the local terrestrial environment, these are the horizontal lines, exemplified by the edges of window sills, steps, and tabletops. The Cartesian axes are singular orientations. One is the polar axis of the reference system. The other two point front and sideways. Overall, the Cartesian lines and planes are embedded within a polar reference system as a set of canonical orientations (once a reference value for direction-of-slant has been selected).

EXPERIMENTS ON PERCEPTION AND PHYSICAL REASONING

These various concepts that concern orientation will now be used to discuss experiments on perception and physical reasoning. The experiments varied widely in detail, and yet there was a basic methodological approach that was used to generate each of them. The tasks concerned easily identifiable objects, properties, or transformations. Displays were seen clearly in 3-D and were viewed with unlimited time (with rare exceptions). Questions for participants concerned properties that are considered both fundamental and elementary in the rigorous description of space. The participants' responses were spatial demonstrations rather than applications of verbal, numerical, or symbolic codes.

Rotation

From an analytical perspective, rotation is one of two fundamental forms of rigid body motion, with translation being the other (see Gibson, 1957; Shepard, 1984). Nature has produced many systems that rotate, from the motion of wrists and elbows to the twirling of maple seeds in the wind. When people build, rotational systems abound. Wheels, gears, propellers, hinges, knobs, cranks, and the needles in dials all are based on the understanding of what can be done with rotation.

The vertical and horizontal of the environment were used earlier as an example of a polar reference system. There are other important instances of polar systems, and when there is more than one of them that matters, they may cooperate or compete with each other. For example, perceiving or reasoning about rotational motion depends on using the axis and planes of rotation as a polar reference system. But whether this occurs depends on the context in which this potential system is viewed (Pani, 1993; Pani & Dupree, 1994; Pani, William, & Shippey, 1995).

Most of us have spatial intuitions about what constitutes a rotation. To put these into words, every point on a rotating object moves in a circular motion, as shown at the upper left in Fig. 3.7. All of these circular motions are in planes parallel to each other, move with a single angular velocity, and are centered along a single line that is perpendicular to the planes of motion. This line through the centers of the parallel circles is the axis of the rotation. I refer to such a description of a phenomenon, a description that encompasses a widely applicable set of spatial intuitions, as a base

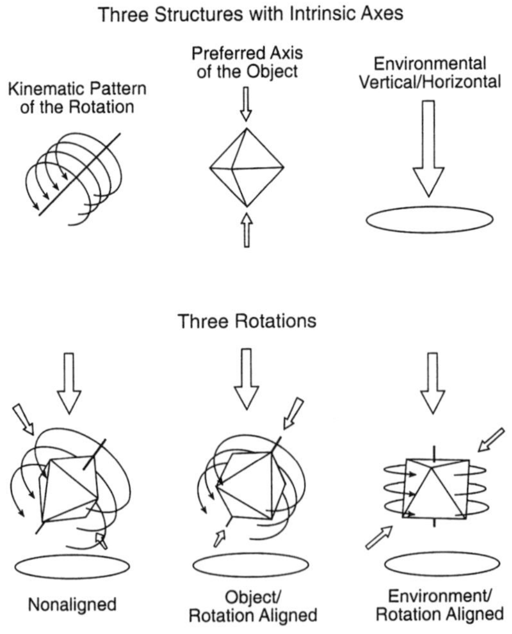

FIG. 3.7.   The motion, the object, and the environment in the formation of a rotation.

organization. The base organization of rotation presents a highly regular kinematic structure, a sort of circular common fate, and one might suppose that a rotation would be recognized as such whenever it occurred.

We can begin to explore the understanding of rotation by noting that objects are not generally seen as clouds of points. Suppose there is an object attached to an axis of rotation, such as a shaft that will turn. And suppose that the object has an obvious structure that will give it an orientation to any reference axis that might be chosen. This object, then, has an orientation to the shaft, the axis of rotation. Physically, if the circular motions of a rotation are to occur, the object must have an invariant slant to the shaft (e.g., be welded to it). This relation must be organized psychologically as well, if the motion is to be seen as a simple rotation. In particular, if the object is seen to have invariant slant to the axis and planes of rotation, the rotational motion may be seen as a continuous change of the direction-of-slant of the object about the axis.

Even though an object continuously undergoes a simple rotation, the motion may not be organized in this way and the rotation may not be seen. This occurs in at least one well-defined situation (Pani et al., 1995; see also Shiffrar & Shepard, 1991), illustrated at the lower left of Fig. 3.7. An object rotates, without a visible shaft; the object has a definite major axis, and hence a definite orientation, but the object axis is not aligned with the axis of rotation; in addition, the axis of rotation is not aligned with the Cartesian reference system of the environment. It is a completely nonaligned (or double oblique) arrangement of the axes for the object, the rotation, and the environment. The result is that the object is not perceived to move in a simple rotation. Instead, it is perceived to have orientation defined in terms of its major axis relative to the vertical. The object is seen to change orientation continuously, but the motion appears to be unfamiliar and rather incoherent. This is not an illusion. Relative to the vertical, the object is indeed not rotating. In other words, perception of the rotation about its axis would be an accurate perception, and perception of the nonrotation about the vertical would be an accurate perception. In the event, the axis of rotation is a weak reference axis, the vertical is a strong reference axis, and the resulting description of space shows the object in a variety of orientations to the vertical. The rotation is simply not seen.

We demonstrated this phenomenon with a task in which participants viewed rotating objects and demonstrated the orientations of the axis and planes of rotation (Pani et al., 1995). The displays were perspective views of opaque solids (as well as a square) viewed stereoptically on a computer screen. Participants were given unlimited time to view each motion and then demonstrated the axis and planes of rotation by placing a stick, with a disc perpendicular to it, in the appropriate orientation into a stand. The options for indicating orientations were in 35° to 45° intervals, so that extreme accuracy was not required. The display remained visible throughout each trial, so that the ability to remember rotations was not an important consideration. The logic behind the method was that if a rotation is seen, it should be relatively easy to indicate the axis and planes of the motion.

The objects used in one of the experiments were the square and the three simpler Platonic solids (the regular polyhedra; see later this chapter). These objects do have preferred axes for people. In the experiment, the objects could be at many orientations to the axis of rotation, and the axis of rotation could be at many orientations in the environment. For the nonaligned rotations, participants had great difficulty determining the axis and planes of rotation. For the object shown in Fig. 3.7, for example, participants required, on the average, 30 seconds to indicate the axis and planes, and then their responses were correct only 46% of the time.

In contrast, perception of a rotation occurs readily in at least two cases with the same general type of display. In one case, the rotation axis remains nonaligned with the Cartesian reference system of the local environment. However, the preferred axis of the object is parallel to the axis of rotation (illustrated at the lower center of Fig. 3.7). Now this axis of the object is fixed in space, and the rotational motion moves around it. The rotation is perceived easily. Participants in the experiment required 13 seconds to indicate the axis and planes of rotation and were correct 82% of the time.

In a second case in which the rotation is seen easily, the object axis and the rotation axis are not aligned with each other. However, the rotation axis is aligned with a Cartesian axis of the environment (illustrated at the lower right of Fig. 3.7). Participants required 8 seconds to indicate the axis and planes of rotation and were correct 95% of the time. In this instance, the axis of rotation is reinforced by a salient axis of the environment. The person can see that the object has an invariant slant to the axis and planes of rotation because the object has the same slant to a Cartesian axis of the environment. (When the motion is aligned with both the environment and the object, the rotation also is seen easily.)

These experiments demonstrate for a fundamental rigid body motion that the understanding of physical phenomena depends very much on understanding how their components are oriented with respect to each other. Further, there is no single measurement system for orientation based on permanent reference axes arranged in a set hierarchy. We must think of a cooperative, sometimes competitive, set of relational structures within a given spatial layout. In this case, there is the motion, with its kinematically defined axis and planes of rotational motion; there is the environment, with its principal axes and planes; and there is the object, with its major axis. Each potential reference system has a strength. Each has a set of parameters that may increase or decrease its strength (e.g., Pani et al., 1995). Finally, there is cooperation such that alignment brings reinforcement and unification among structures. The outcome determines the description of the motion.

Projective Transformation

Projective transformation is one of the fundamental spatial transformations. It is not a rigid body motion (as rotation is), and yet it is common and important. Projection forms the image at the back of the eye, provides the capability for pictures, whether on paper, canvas, or electronic screens (e.g., Kubovy, 1986), and produces shadows. In the manipulation of objects, an intuitive grasp of projection permits us to see that a book can just fit in a space on a shelf, or that a letter will fit through a slot in a mailbox.

A number of experiments on determining the outcomes of projective transformations were completed (Pani et al., 1996). Using a simple three-edged object, shown in Fig. 3.8, we asked people to draw the pictures that would be correct from a particular standpoint or to draw the shadow that would be cast by a light at a given location. In other experiments, the three simpler Platonic solids were shown with rods through them and discs mounted behind them. (These solids are the cube, three-sided pyramid, and regular octahedron; see later this chapter.) Participants were asked to demonstrate the shape of the shadow that would be cast if the rod were in the direction of a light beam shining on the object. Answers were given by matching to a sample of silhouettes.

With just a bit of reminding, adults understand readily what produces projection. As with rotation, there is a base organization of this physical phenomenon, and the question for reasoning concerns whether this organization can be applied successfully to particular situations. The base organization of projective transformation includes an object, a direction of projection (e.g., the direction of a light beam), an image surface, and the image (e.g., a shadow) that is projected onto the surface, as shown in Fig. 3.8. The image depends on the boundary between those rays in the direction of projection that intersect the object and those that do not. This boundary forms a surface, which may be called the projective contour, and the image is just the cross-section of the projective contour at the image surface. In our experiments the objects, and many other parameters of the task, were kept very simple. The major challenge in reasoning about projective transformation was to determine the shape of the projective contour. With objects formed of straight edges and flat surfaces, such as we have studied, the projective contour always was formed of lines and planes, and it was these lines and planes of projection that had to be determined.

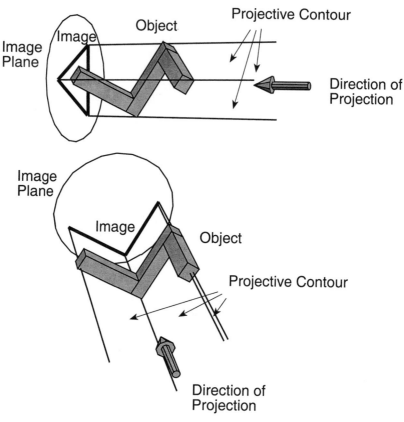

FIG. 3.8. Two illustrations of the base organization of projective transformation. Adapted from "Imagining projective transformations: Aligned orientations in spatial organization" by J. R. Pani, J. A. Jeffres, G. T. Shippey, & K. J. Schwartz, 1996, *Cognitive Psychology, 31*, p. 151. Copyright 1996, Academic Press. Adapted with permission.

The objects in the experiments varied in their orientations to the direction of projection, and the result was that participants were quite good at specifying the outcomes of certain projections but quite poor at specifying the outcomes of others. The projection illustrated at the bottom of Fig. 3.8 led to relatively fast and accurate performance, whereas the projection illustrated at the top led to slow and inaccurate performance. Indeed, these two examples demonstrate the clearest pattern in the results of the experiments: Participants were quite good at determining projective transformations when a cardinal direction of the object was aligned with the projection; when the object was completely nonaligned to the projection, the task was extremely difficult.

One way to describe these results is to say that people can indicate what an object would look like from its cardinal directions, but not from arbitrary directions. Thus, we have shown a trend observed in young children's drawings to continue into adulthood (e.g., Cox, 1992). There are good reasons to move beyond this characterization, however. One reason is that it oversimplifies the data (Pani et al., 1996). A second reason is that we have only an intuitive grasp of what the cardinal directions of the objects in these experiments are, and the problem of explanation is only pushed back a step. The following model is an attempt to provide a more specific and a more broadly applicable explanation by treating the task as an effort to recover the base organization of projective transformation. This model may help to understand how cardinal directions are chosen for objects in the first place.

The account begins with a suggestion that because the individual's primary challenge in this task is to determine the shape of the projective contour (see Fig. 3.8), the direction of projection is adopted as a polar reference axis and the person attempts to determine the positions and orientations of the lines and planes of the contour relative to this axis. It is as though the projective contour was a cookie cutter that sliced through space; the direction of slicing is given, and now the individual edges and surfaces of the cookie cutter must be found. In fact, their slants are already determined, for they always are parallel to the direction of projection (i.e., the lines and planes of projection are vertical in that reference system). The remaining problem, then, is to determine the directions-of-slant of any planes of projection. For those projections that are easiest, the edges of the object that determine the projection are parallel either with lines in the projective contour or with the direction lines of projective planes (see the bottom of Fig. 3.8). It is as if one needed to know the path a blade would cut and was given the direction of travel and the orientation of the edge of the blade at a single point in time (as for the hatchet in Fig. 3.4). This is an instance of a transitive relation from features of the object to the components of orientation required by the task.

For those projections that are so difficult, on the other hand, the edges of the object that generate the projection are oblique to the axis of projection (see the top of Fig. 3.8). There is not a fit between the structure of the object and the orientations of the projective lines and planes. Indeed, there can be interference in determining the projection from looking too closely at the orientation of the object in the environment. The cardinal directions of the object imply the wrong directions in space (an instance of competition between two orientations).

The efficiency of determining the outcome of a projective transformation depends on more than the orientations of the edges of the object to the axis of projection. The global organization of the object is an additional factor that influences the process (along with the orientation of the projection in the environment). I leave a demonstration of this for later, when shape is discussed more fully.

Finding Edges for Surfaces

In a third experimental project, we attempted to demonstrate the importance of the organization of 3-D orientations in a setting that was extremely basic and simple. The fact that two planes intersect in a line is a lawful relation that is demonstrated in each instance that two surfaces join at an edge. We tested people's abilities to view a pair of separated surfaces and then to determine the orientation of the implied line of intersection (Pani et al., 1998). That is, participants in these experiments were asked to demonstrate the orientation of the edge that would be formed if two discs, located quite close together, could shift over or expand so that they interpenetrated. The pairs of surfaces that were displayed either were wooden discs (in one experiment) or accurate computer renderings of discs viewed stereoptically (in other experiments). Participants studied the displays for as long as they wished and then demonstrated the line of intersection to the nearest value in 15° intervals. When the displays were wooden discs, participants demonstrated the line of intersection with a thin dowel that could be held in position by a stand. When computer displays were used, participants demonstrated the orientation of the line of intersection by manipulating the orientation of a computer-rendered double-headed arrow with computer keys, as illustrated in Fig. 3.9. Again, these were realistic displays viewed stereoptically and gave a compelling impression of orientation in 3-D space.

Introspective accounts of a mind's eye that visualizes basic geometric properties of the world suggest that a person should perform this task by imagining two planes to occupy the same space. The individual may then "look" at the edge that is formed and note its orientation. There is, however, a great range of difficulty in this task, depending on the orientations of the surfaces that are shown in each instance. For some pairs of surfaces, mean response time is less than 10 seconds and mean error is less than 10°. For other pairs of surfaces, mean response time is greater than 40 seconds, and mean error is greater than 40°. Even so elementary a task as finding the line of intersection of two clearly indicated planes depends on the nature of the perceptual description of the objects and the fit between this description and what is needed to complete the reasoning.

Three variables in the orientations of the surfaces account for the large range of performance. The first is called degree of fit, and is based on the following analysis: In each trial, completing the task depends on perception of the surfaces, and this begins with perception of slant and direction

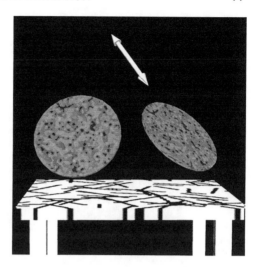

FIG. 3.9. Experimental display for determining lines of intersection. Adapted from "Orientation in physical reasoning: Determining the edge that would be formed by two surfaces" by J. R. Pani, C. T. William, & G. T. Shippey, 1998, *Journal of Experimental Psychology: Human Perception and Performance*, *24*, 283–300. Copyright 1998, American Psychological Association. Adapted with permission.

relative to the vertical. The goal of the reasoning, set by the experimenter, involves determining the line of intersection, a particular line that depends on the two surfaces. The task is an instance of problem solving, then, not so different from the task of a carpenter who must decide how two slopes of a roof will come together and form an edge.

A general strategy for solving the problem is to search for the one line that is common to both surfaces. That common line is, of course, the intersection of the planes. To complete this procedure, we have suggested, the person ultimately attends to one of the surfaces and encodes its slant and direction, relative to the vertical, in terms of orientation lines (as in Fig. 3.5). The person then shifts attention to the other surface and considers whether any of the encoded orientation lines coincide with that second surface. If there is a coincidence, the line of intersection has been found: A line from one surface coincides with the other surface, as illustrated in Fig. 3.10. We call this a fit between descriptions because the person borrows a line from perception and tests to see whether it extends transitively into what is needed for reasoning (i.e., a line of intersection). When there is such a fit between descriptions, the task is relatively easy. But this fit does not always exist (see Fig. 3.10). Hence, the procedure is a heuristic one.

A second variable that accounts for performance is whether or not the line of intersection would have a singular orientation relative to the environment (especially the vertical). People more easily find a line of intersection that would have a singular orientation. This depends once again on a transitive relation. Lines that are contained in the structure of the reference system are extended to a line that is looked for in reasoning.

The third variable concerns the angle that would be formed between the surfaces after their intersection. The angle between two surfaces is

For these pairs, at least one surface has orientation lines (in white)
that match the hypothetical line of intersection of the surfaces (shown
with the arrows). This fit makes finding the line of intersection easier.

For these pairs of surfaces, none of the orientation lines (in white) match
the hypothetical line of intersection of the surfaces (shown with the arrows).

FIG. 3.10. The degree of fit between two surfaces when searching for a
line of intersection.

called the dihedral angle. The line of intersection is the apex of the angle,
and the angle itself is measured in a plane orthogonal to the line of
intersection, as illustrated in Fig. 3.11. (Thus, organization of the dihedral
angle is a special case of a polar reference system, with the dihedral angle
measured in the equatorial plane.) It is easier to imagine two surfaces
joined in a dihedral angle, with the line of intersection at the apex of the

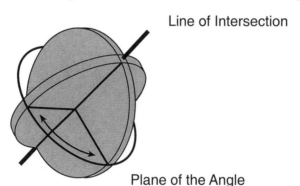

FIG. 3.11. The dihedral angle. Adapted from "Orientation in physical
reasoning: Determining the edge that would be formed by two surfaces" by
J. R. Pani, C. T. William, & G. T. Shippey, 1998, *Journal of Experimental
Psychology: Human Perception and Performance, 24,* 283–300. Copyright 1998,
American Psychological Association. Adapted with permission.

angle, if the surfaces would be perpendicular to each other (i.e., when the dihedral angle is 90°).

The Dihedral Angle. Determining a line of intersection is rather easy with the mathematics of surfaces commonly used by engineers. Generally, these methods are consistent with the geometry of the dihedral angle: They involve finding two surface normals (between which the dihedral angle may be determined) and generating the line of intersection as the line that is perpendicular to the two normals. Indeed, the dihedral angle may be considered a base organization for describing the line of intersection between two surfaces. Methods of search for a line of intersection that proceed from the geometry of the dihedral angle depend on intrinsic properties of the surfaces and have the virtues of a basic mathematical tool (i.e., valid in any context).

In contrast, the importance of the degree of fit and of the orientation of the line of intersection in these experiments shows the importance of context for people in physical reasoning. It demonstrates that descriptions of orientation useful in normal perception of surfaces are extended into reasoning about the surfaces. A transitive movement of one description into another, even though it may be heuristic, is critical to the success of reasoning even for very simple spatial relations.

Nonetheless, the angle between the surfaces did influence performance, and this seems due to an appreciation of the organization of the dihedral angle. People are opportunistic in taking advantage of a variety of sources of information, and many instances of organization may facilitate physical reasoning within a single task.

Shape

The last experimental project to be discussed here is rather different from the others, because it concerns shape alone. Shape has an organization and it is possible to talk about the description of object shape in much the same terms as we talk about the description of object orientation. In fact, it is useful to think of object axes as polar reference axes, and then elementary shape involves the slant and direction-of-slant of the edges and surfaces of an object relative to the object axis (for discussion of object structure, see Biederman, 1987; Hummel & Biederman, 1992; Marr, 1982; Marr & Nishihara, 1978; Rock, 1983). As we pursue this description of shape, certain new topics will be introduced, including those of symmetry, symmetry within orthogonal dimensions, and complexity. Other topics reappear, including the importance of interactions among polar reference axes.

Consider a simple experiment (Pani, Zhou, & Friend, 1997). On a computer screen there was a view of an appropriately shaded solid object, in correct perspective, rotating about the vertical. Such a display gives excellent perception of a virtual object. Participants, who were familiar with the task at hand, studied each display for as long as they wished. The objects that were displayed were the three simpler of the Platonic solids, shown in Fig. 3.12 in two orientations. After terminating a display, the individual fashioned a physical representation of the object, stationary, at the same orientation to the vertical. In particular, the object was imagined at the location of a styrofoam sphere placed in front of the screen where the computer image had been. The individual then put colorful pins into the sphere either where the corners of the shape would be located or where the centers of the surfaces would be, depending on the experimental condition. The only constraints were that the representations should be as accurate as possible and that they preserve the orientations of the objects to the vertical. Generally, participants found the task to be quite straight-forward. For our part, we could examine whether the correct number of features (i.e., corners or surfaces) were preserved in the representations, the accuracy of the representations of the features, and the order in which features were placed into the representation.

The Platonic solids are the five regular polyhedra, on which every corner, edge, and surface is like every other. Greek mathematics gave much attention to these shapes. Plato, coming after most of this study had been completed, considered four of the solids to be the shapes of the atoms of

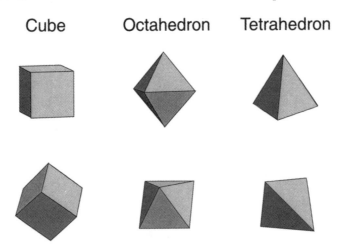

FIG. 3.12. The three simpler Platonic solids shown in two orientations. Adapted from "The generalized cone in human spatial organization" by J. R. Pani, 1994, *Spatial Vision, 8,* p. 495. Copyright 1995, VSP BV. Adapted with permission.

fire, earth, air, and water. Surely, thought Plato, a perfect God would use such perfect shapes for the atoms of the fundamental elements. And Plato was not far wrong. Chemists and crystallographers have established that these Platonic shapes do characterize the shapes of many fundamental atoms and molecules, as well as many microscopic creatures (including, in apparent contradiction of Plato, a large number of viruses).

In a way quite similar to the studies of rotation, we displayed each of the three objects in a variety of canonical orientations. For example, the cube could be shown with opposite surfaces aligned with the vertical, opposite edges aligned with the vertical, or opposite corners aligned with the vertical (see also Hinton, 1979). The outcome of this variation was that for the orientations shown at the top in Fig. 3.12, participants viewed the displays for 17 seconds, slightly less than one revolution. They indicated an incorrect number of features on the objects only 5% of the time. Mean angular error in the placement of the pins around the spheres was 12°. In contrast, for the orientations shown at the bottom of Fig. 3.12, all of these values more or less doubled. Participants looked at the shapes for more than twice as long, an average of 37 seconds. The wrong numbers of pins were used 12% of the time. And when the correct number of pins was used, mean angular error was 20°.

Interaction of Reference Axes. One reason for the sharp contrast in results between the two sets of orientations is that the objects appear to change in shape. This occurs because the salient object axes change with the orientation of the object to the vertical (see also Mach, 1906/1959; Rock, 1983). The change of object axes is the result of a phenomenon that was seen in the perception of rotation: reinforcement and competition among potential reference axes. For example, in one orientation the octahedron is seen to have a pointed top and bottom and to be composed of two pyramids. In another orientation, the same object has a flat top and bottom and is composed of a zigzag arrangement of edges and surfaces. For this object, there is a strong tendency to adopt the axis through the object that happens to be vertical as the major axis of the object (especially when the object rotates about the vertical; Pani et al., 1995). Given the fact that, in different trials, the object actually has different orientations to the vertical, the result is that the object axis changes and the shape of the object is organized in a variety of different ways. Of course, a particular object axis could be made more salient, perhaps by elongating the object along that axis (Pani et al., 1995). Then the shape of the object would not change with a reorientation; only the apparent orientation would. The point here is not that object axes always are mutable. The point is that 3-D shape does depend on an object axis (an object-relative vertical, as it were) and that the selection of this axis depends on a cooperative system into which many variables enter.

Organization of Shape. A second reason for the results of these experiments is that as the shapes of the objects change with orientation, some of them are subjectively very simple for participants and some of them are extremely complex (see also Hinton, 1979). I think that the most important property of the simple shapes, shown at the top of Fig. 3.12, is that they are quite regular instances of the generalized cylinder (GC) about the vertical (for discussion of GCs, see Biederman, 1987; Binford, 1971; Brooks, 1981; Marr, 1982; Pani, 1994; Pani et al., 1997; Zerroug & Nevatia, 1994). GCs are constrained to have cross-sections with a single shape (although not a single size) everywhere along an axis. As illustrated in Fig. 3.13, a GC can be partitioned into a set of regions along the axis and a set of radial positions about the axis. At any given radial position, there will be one direction-of-slant of the features of the object. At any region along the axis, the slants of the surfaces will be relatively uniform, the slants of the edges will be relatively

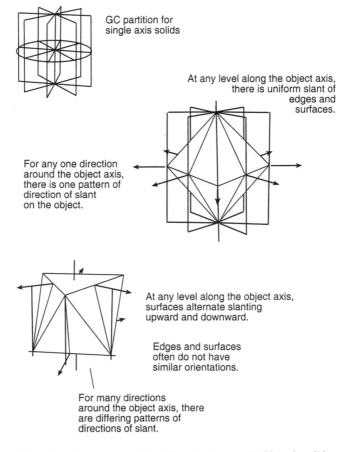

FIG. 3.13. Comparison of the GC and antiprismatic Platonic solids.

uniform, and the slants of the edges and the surfaces will be similar to each other. (The degree of uniformity of the slants of edges and surfaces varies with the shape of the cross-section. For related discussions, see Pani, 1994; Pani et al., 1997; Zerroug & Nevatia, 1994).

This pattern of orientations among the features of a GC Platonic solid comprises a partition of the features into an orthogonal arrangement of slant and direction-of-slant, with the object conforming to a Cartesian product of the values on these dimensions. Such a partition is analogous to the arrangement of a set of locations into a rectangular grid (e.g., like the identical rows and columns of trees planted in an orchard). That is, if the pattern of slants of a GC is known at one position around the axis, then the pattern is known to a good approximation at comparable positions around the axis (e.g., at the centers of the surfaces). And if the direction-of-slant of object features is known at one level along the axis (e.g., the upper half of the object) then it is known at every level along the axis. In all, the object can be described as a relatively simple combination of one set of values of slant and another set of values of direction-of-slant.

In contrast, the shapes at the bottom of Fig. 3.12 are, or have properties of, the antiprisms (Pani, 1994; Pani et al., 1997). In particular, the sides of the shapes are characterized by a 3-D zigzag of edges as well as surfaces that alternately slant upward and downward.[2] In contrast to the GC organization, the pattern of directions-of-slant of features of the object may be different for any given radial position around the object axis. In addition, at any one level along the axis, successive surfaces have very different slants, successive edges change in orientation, and the orientations of edges and surfaces have little in common.[3] This pattern, clearly, does not conform to an orthogonal arrangement of slant and direction-of-slant.

Symmetry. The term symmetry has come to mean invariance across transformation (e.g., Hargittai & Hargittai, 1994; Holden, 1971; Stewart & Golubitsky, 1992; Weyl, 1952). Under this definition, symmetry is the presence of systematic repetition of units of structure throughout an object, where the nature of the repetition is related to the nature of the transformation. Thus, for example, the slats in a picket fence have a translational symmetry (the shape is invariant over translation), mammals have a reflec-

---

[2]The prototypic antiprism, like a regular prism, has a top and bottom with a single regular polygonal shape; the top and bottom differ by a half turn about the object axis, and the sides are formed of equilateral triangles (e.g., Hargittai & Hargittai, 1994; Holden, 1971). The cube, technically, is a trapezohedron about its antiprismatic axis, but I am attempting to reduce the amount of technical language in this chapter.

[3]This type of structure will be most difficult to organize when any global symmetries of the object are not apparent in single views. This occurs in the three simpler Platonic solids, but need not occur for all antiprismatic shapes.

tion symmetry (invariant over reflection), and pinwheels possess a rotational symmetry (invariant over rotation).

In all of the orientations of the Platonic solids, they possess much rotation and reflection symmetry (see later this chapter). For the solids oriented as generalized cylinders to the vertical, this additional regularity makes them especially simple for people. For the antiprismatic shapes, this symmetry helps little. Thus, these classical forms of symmetry may coexist with irregularities of orientation that render the symmetry of marginal value to the human perceiver.

At a higher level of abstraction, however, the distinction between the simple and complex organizations of these objects can be expressed as a difference in symmetry (Pani, 1994; Pani et al., 1997). The simple organizations can be described in terms of two orthogonal dimensions of variation (slant and direction-of-slant), and the variation on each of these dimensions is self-similar across the values of the other dimension (analogous to the orchard). The invariance of direction-of-slant is an abstract form of translational symmetry guaranteed by Binford's definition of the GC as involving a translation of a cross-section with a single shape. This translational symmetry is strongly violated in the antiprismatic shapes. The invariance of slant is a form of rotational symmetry, sometimes approximate, around the GC axis.

Complexity.   Complexity may be considered to be the length of the shortest description that will specify an object (e.g., Attneave, 1954; Gell-Mann, 1994; Leeuwenberg, 1971). In arithmetic, for example, we immediately realize that $9 + 9 + 9 + 9 + 9$ can be converted to 5×9, a shorter description; On the other hand, $9 + 2 \times 5 \div 4 - 7$ is more complex, for most of us, because we are likely to leave it as five numbers and four operations. Symmetry reduces complexity, for it permits descriptions to be hierarchical and efficient. Orthogonal symmetry, such as that seen in the GC Platonic solids, is a special case of the reduction of complexity. Overall, the basic difference between the GC and the antiprismatic organizations of the three simpler Plantonic solids is in the complexity of their descriptions in terms of slant and direction-of-slant relative to object axes.

Shape and Transformation.   The GC and the antiprismatic organization are two types of global organization of shape. It should be pointed out that the global organization of shape interacts with the ability to see or imagine spatial transformations. One demonstration of this was presented in the discussion of rotation, where the relationship between a rotational motion and the preferred axis of an object (e.g., the GC organization) influenced whether the rotation could be seen. The ability to determine projective transformations also depends on the global organization of the object. One way to see this is to leave unchanged the orientation of the object to the direction of a projection (the spatial relation discussed earlier) but to change the orientation of the object to the vertical. The orientation of features of the object to the direction of projection will not change, but the global organization of the object may change as its orientation to the vertical is altered. Such a situation is demonstrated in Fig. 3.14. The shadows that are indicated have identical shapes in the three cases, because the orientation of the object to the projection is unchanged. However, the global organization of the object changes, and it does affect the individual's ability to determine the outcome of such a projection. When the preferred axis of the object is vertical, as at the left, the object appears simple and consistent with the direction of projection. The projection is determined relatively easily. In the situation at the right, the organization of the object is more complex, and is not especially consistent with the direction of projection. Determining the outcome of such a projection is much more difficult (Pani et al., 1996; compare Palmer & Hemenway, 1978; Pani & Dupree, 1994; Rock & Leaman, 1963).

FUNDAMENTAL CONCEPTS AND ISSUES

I have touched briefly on a number of experiments that concerned perception and physical reasoning in normal adults. In every instance, the primary data were contrasts between tasks done well and tasks done poorly. In no instance, however, did perception fail to operate normally. For example, although participants sometimes were unable to see rotations that were present, they nonetheless saw rigid objects changing orientation continuously. And the tasks, for the most part, could be performed well. Participants often were fast and accurate, whether the task concerned identifying the axis and planes of a rotation, determining the outcomes of projective transformations, finding the edge that would be formed from two surfaces, or physical representation of a simple solid. And yet, the tasks

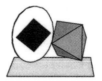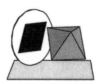

FIG. 3.14. A projective transformation with the object varying in spatial organization. Adapted from "Imagining projective transformations: Aligned orientations in spatial organization" by J. R. Pani, J. A. Jeffres, G. T. Shippey, & K. J. Schwartz, 1996, *Cognitive Psychology, 31*, p. 146. Copyright 1996, Academic Press. Adapted with permission.

sometimes were subjectively difficult, and sometimes large errors were made, for these experiments concern strong constraints on the manner in which people organize things in space. It bears contemplation that an educated adult may claim to be imagining a cube and then indicate an object that has triangular sides (Hinton, 1979; Pani et al., 1997; see also Pani, 1993; Pani & Dupree, 1994).

An explanation of high-level perception and physical reasoning requires an account of the typical descriptions of physical phenomena as well as the manner in which people see or reason with these descriptions in particular situations. In my own efforts after such an account, a certain set of descriptive terms has proven consistently useful. Some of these terms refer to properties of orientation (e.g., cardinal direction, polar reference system, slant, and direction-of-slant). Other terms refer to canonical properties that tend to occur in those tasks that are intuitive and easy for people (e.g., parallel, perpendicular, vertical, and horizontal). A closer look at the set of canonical properties reveals three nested sets of them. The most specific set is the canonical spatial relations, including parallel, perpendicular, vertical, horizontal, coincident, and a variety of others (see later this chapter). These spatial relations are examples of a broader set of canonical properties, the symmetries. The symmetries, in turn, are examples of a quite broad set, the singular properties.

Some Foundations of Useful Structure

Symmetry. A critical component of the present account is that there may be transitivity, or reinforcement, by which the salience of a spatial property is increased through its alignment with something else. The aligned orientations (i.e., parallel and perpendicular) are examples of symmetry, in the general sense of invariance across transformation. Parallel orientations, such as those between the slats in a picket fence, or the columns of a classical building, have translational symmetry. Perpendicular orientations have at least a reflection symmetry. If a flagpole is perpendicular to the ground, for example, the angle between the pole and the ground is the same everywhere (a case of rotation/reflection symmetry). If we consider that the generalized cylinder is also a type of symmetry, as pointed out earlier, then it seems clear that a sensitivity to symmetry is at the heart of much physical reasoning (see also Wagemans, 1996).

The concept of symmetry is not confined to the spatial domain. Rhyme is a type of symmetry. Rhythm, including the rhythm of language, is a type of symmetry. The formal beauty of poetry is just as much an indication of the human sensitivity to symmetry as is the formal beauty of a building in which spatial symmetries have been worked into the design. Blake's (1992/1794) poem not only refers to symmetry, but possesses it as well.

Tyger! Tyger! burning bright
In the forests of the night,
What immortal hand or eye
Could frame thy fearful symmetry?
—William Blake

At least some of the cognitive benefits of a sensitivity to symmetry seem obvious. First of all, where there is symmetry there is repetition and the potential for efficient description. Of course, efficiency is helpful only when a description is sufficiently accurate for its purposes. The many examples of transitivity and reinforcement noted previously were instances in which people found it possible to organize cognition that not only was efficient, but was sufficiently accurate and complete as well.

A second reason for the importance of symmetry is that it is common in the natural world (especially the biological world) and in human arti-facts. Any theory of cognition that suggests that people adapt to their environments should also suggest that people are sensitive to symmetry.

Consider in addition that many of the rather abstract geometric structures that were discussed earlier have high degrees of symmetry, including the base organization of rotational motion (see Fig. 3.7), the relations between cardinal directions and useful interactions (see Fig. 3.4), and polar reference systems (see Fig. 3.3). The base organization of a simple rotation, for example, is one of the most symmetric structures in nature, composed of parallel, perpendicular, and circular relations. And when an object is aligned with a simple rotation, object and motion form a unitary structure. Yet nature can be much more complex than this. The fixed axis rotation is a boundary condition on an infinite set of complex multiaxis motions. And an object need not be aligned with the axis of rotation (as described earlier). The pristine symmetry of the rotations that we find intuitive are a small subset of the motions that nature allows. However, if we consider the things that people construct, we find just such simple motions in alignment with their objects. A rolling pin, for example, is like an axle that produces a simple rotation as well as a translation parallel to the surface on which it rests. Generally, building simple rotational systems with object axes aligned with the axes of rotation has been an extremely effective practice for humans, giving us wheels, pulleys, analog clocks, knobs, and cranks.

Searching for what is useful in life is a sort of filter that leads to an understanding of a small subset of the possible physical relations. These tend to have much symmetry. A thorough analysis may reveal that symmetry is a prerequisite property for many useful physical structures. For example, symmetries arise when things fit together, perform the same function, spread evenly, balance, and so forth. It is a happy coincidence for human cognition that sensitivity to symmetry leads, on the average, not only to efficient descriptions but to pragmatically useful relations among things.

Singularity. There is an important set of properties, the singularities, that includes the symmetries as a subset. Singular properties are qualitatively unique values that arise from comparisons among quantities (see Goldmeier, 1972, 1982; Leyton, 1992; Pani, 1997; Pani et al., 1998; Rock, 1983; Wertheimer, 1950). At a relatively high level of abstraction, the fundamental singular properties appear to be maximum, minimum, same, and orthogonal. At a lower level, familiar singular properties in the domain of spatial relations include straight, aligned, symmetric, circular, vertical, horizontal, midpoint, centered, and gradual (i.e., a smooth gradation). More work needs to be done to determine the process by which singular values become important in cognition. However, two aspects of them seem noteworthy. First, they can be based on ordinal (nonmetric) distinctions, with the notion of same as a null difference. Second, singularities arise from a convergence of ordinal comparisons on to a qualitatively unique value. This value may be specific to a particular set of objects (e.g., biggest), or it may be a natural limit (e.g., straight, circular). In the case of orientation, parallel and perpendicular are single angles, of 0 and 90°, and yet they form qualitative distinctions at the same level as acute and obtuse. Indeed, parallel and perpendicular can be considered to comprise categories of angles with single members.

Singular properties appear to be valuable for several reasons. One of these, surely, is that the unique and qualitative nature of singular properties tends to make them distinctive. Hence, they are relatively easy to see, remember, and imagine. A second advantage of singular values is that they often are the only nonarbitrary ones for particular comparisons. How much profit should a business make? It is best to maximize profit (and minimize cost). How big is a wheel? My younger son, Ethan, recently measured his skate wheels in order to compare them with ones available through a catalog. He soon saw that there are many ways to place a ruler against the face of a wheel. The method that ultimately succeeded was to measure the diameter of the wheel, for it maximizes the value. In a similar way, the angle that is measured between two surfaces, the dihedral angle, typically is measured in a plane perpendicular to the line of intersection of the surfaces (see Fig. 3.11). The angle could be measured in other planes, ones with different orientations to the line of intersection, but the size of the angle changes each time a different plane for the angle is chosen. The perpendicular plane maximizes the angle that is measured. (An additional nonarbitrary plane is the equatorial plane of the global reference system. In this way, the sides of the pyramids at Giza differ by 90°, the differences between their directions of slant.)

Singular properties tend to be distinctive and nonarbitrary. Of course, singularity is valuable only when it leads to descriptions that are useful for present purposes. Hence, it is important that singular properties (e.g., vertical orientations) are common in the world. In addition, people seek out singularity in their efforts to act effectively. They maximize, minimize, and find the point of balance at every level of structure and in every context. With a sensitivity to singularity in general, and symmetry in particular, perception, memory, and reasoning aim toward descriptions that are distinctive, nonarbitrary, efficient, and practical. When the effort succeeds, people are quickly able to see and reason about the relations between things, and cognition seems intuitive.

Learning and Description

A primary question for any investigation of structure in cognition concerns the importance of experience and learning to establishing and refining those structures. Certainly theories of expertise apply to spatial cognition of all varieties. Great athletes, pilots, engineers, geometers, and artists are masters with years of concentrated experience. But what of our everyday understandings of space? What can we say about learning in the areas in which every one of us is a master?

We live in a world with many verticals, parallels, and generalized cylinders. Perhaps, then, the experimental results noted earlier reveal the structure of the environment and our experience in it. There certainly are elements of truth in this suggestion, but it also must be considered that there are many different ways to learn. If the simplest version of empiricism might be taken seriously, that cognitive organization is a reflection of what is common in the world, it is wise to consider rationalist counterarguments to empiricism. I raise these counterarguments in turn.

First, do we truly know the structure of the environment, or do we only think we do? Take the question of why certain simple rotations do not appear to be rotations to us. It could be that they are uncommon. However, there are many motions in the environment that we see as complicated, including falling leaves, tumbling boxes, movements of the hands, and the gyrations of Olympic divers. Such motions may in fact be quite common, and for all I know they might often include simple rotations. It may be that we do not organize these motions in a way that would lead to categorization of them as simple rotations, and then we underestimate their frequency (consider Tversky & Kahneman, 1973). Thus, it may not be that the rotations that people are not good at seeing are in fact rare. They may be common, but not seen as rotations. Overall, the argument from the frequency of events in the world is an empirical argument, and the required evidence has not been generated.

Second, if these empirical studies are ever done, it seems likely that the results will be mixed. There may be a preponderance of verticals in the world. However, I doubt whether the projective transformations that are typically the easiest to imagine will turn out to be the ones that have been seen the most often (e.g., in the casting of shadows). The projective transformation at the bottom of Fig. 3.8 is not more common than the other; it is just geometrically simpler. If this claim is true, then the empiricist argument applied to reasoning about projective transformation must be the weakest one, that there is generalization from what is common in one domain (rotation, possibly) to what actually is uncommon in another.

A third argument concerns the things that people build. When looking at a map of the United States, it generally is quite easy to tell which state borders were inherited from nature, as coastlines, rivers, or mountain ranges, and which borders were more a matter of human concern. When left to nature, borders tend to be irregular, often fractal; when left to people, borders tend to be straight, quite often running North/South and East/West. Have we learned from experience what state borders should look like? If so, it is again a generalization that has gone far from its source. A better argument is that the straight line has a number of practical benefits for the people who need to make and respect borders.

A fourth argument begins with experimental data. Educated adults in the United States have seen the geographic layout of North and South America represented literally thousands of times. And yet in sketching this geography from memory, or in tests of recognition, this geography will be altered by about 2,000 miles (Tversky, 1981; see also Chase, 1986). People take two masses that are diagonally arranged and change them so that they are vertically arranged. Repeated experience over many years clearly has not led to accuracy of representation. Of course, a ready reply is that the particular geographic relations of these continents do not matter to most people. Surely airline pilots who fly between San Francisco and Rio de Janeiro would not make these mistakes. But now the argument for learning depends on knowing what is important and useful to people, and we are no longer discussing a view in which perceptual description reflects what is common. At this point, we may as well turn the argument around. It is not that alignment, symmetry, and singularity are common, and therefore we are sensitive to them. Rather, alignment, symmetry, and singularity are nonarbitrary, reflect the geometry of useful relations among things, are distinctive, and permit efficient perception and cognitive representation. Therefore, we make them common, see them even when they are rare, and presume they are present even when they are not.

The final rationalist argument I raise is one that was important to the Gestalters. Any time that we think about the perception of what is common, there is a chicken-egg problem in deciding whether the perception was conditioned first by repetition or first by the inclination to describe something a certain way, with a subsequent repetition and refinement. Consider an example from the experiments discussed earlier. It might be said that people typically are poor at imagining the tipped cube (shown at the bottom left of Fig. 3.12) because it is a rare orientation for cubes. In contrast, we are adept at imagining the flat cube because it is so common. But consider the view in Fig. 3.15. It shows a view of a block, and its orientation seems common enough. And yet, relative to the egocentric frame of the viewer, the block is a tipped cube. Relative to the room that is implied in the picture, it is a flat cube. Clearly, to say that the flat cube is common is to say that people prefer to describe orientation in an external reference system. Whether, or when, or how people do this is a nontrivial and time-honored empirical question (Attneave & Reid, 1968; Corballis & Roldan, 1975; Franklin & Tversky, 1990; Gibson & Cornsweet, 1952; Hinton & Parsons, 1988; McAfee & Proffitt, 1991; McMullen & Jolicoeur, 1992; Pani & Dupree, 1994; Rock, 1983). The fact is, a claim about what is common in perception depends on claims about the nature of perceptual description.

The solution to chicken–egg problems is not to find which of them came first. Rather, there must be an account of how they evolved together into a system that operates effectively. Certainly an explanation of perception and physical reasoning depends on reference to the objective structure of the world and its affordances for an organism (Gibson, 1979; Shepard, 1984). A second crucial property, on which all can agree, is that the nature of the tasks to be performed, and the goals that have been set, influence the structure of perception and reasoning (see Pani, 1996). But for those cognitive scientists, beginning at least with Mach (1906/1959) and Wertheimer (1950), who think that cognitive organization also is critical, we must take account of the manner in which the descriptions of things are

FIG. 3.15. The tipped cube is not uncommon when an egocentric reference frame is used.

realized (e.g., Biederman, 1987; Cutting, 1981; Hinton, 1979; Johansson, 1975; Palmer, 1977; Proffitt & Gilden, 1989; Rock, 1983; Rosch, 1975). Restle (1979) meant to speak for this view when he said that perceptions are in principle ambiguous. He did not, I think, mean to enter the debate on the degree to which ecological information is rich. To the contrary, I think he presumed the richness of ecological information and believed that nonetheless perception is, in principle, ambiguous. The richness of the world provides options for description. The need to act effectively and efficiently in such a world demands that we adopt one description when others are possible. It is in this context of functionally determined description of an objective and richly structured world that we can explain how a task might be very much easier than one that is ostensibly similar.

Flexibility in Perception

A machine vision system, in an industrial setting, might be given certain permanent reference systems and a set of procedures for measuring particular orientations. For this machine, there would be no question of what descriptions to form. Human perception, in contrast, has evolved to handle uncertainty. This is necessary for a system that will be able to respond intelligently to surprises and that will learn flexibly in changed environments. Competition, transitivity, and reinforcement in the determination of orientation and structure are computational processes that would work well in such a system. The phenomena that have been discussed here, such as changes in the relative salience of rotations, in the ability to determine outcomes of projective transformations, and in the perceived structure of objects, are consistent with the operation of such a perceptual/cognitive system. These phenomena seem part of a cooperative system that learns and responds to objective features of the environment, but that does not presume ahead of time to know just what description is best applied in each new situation.

REFERENCES

Attneave, F. (1954). Some informational aspects of visual perception. *Psychological Review, 61,* 183–193.

Attneave, F., & Reid, K. W. (1968). Voluntary control of frame of reference and slope equivalence under head rotation. *Journal of Experimental Psychology, 78,* 153–159.

Biederman, I. (1987). Recognition by components: A theory of human image understanding. *Psychological Review, 94,* 115–147.

Binford, T. O. (1971, December). *Visual perception by computer.* Paper presented at IEEE Systems Science and Cybernetics Conference, Miami.

Blake, W. (1992). The tiger. In W. Harmon (Ed.), *The Top 500 Poems.* New York: Columbia University Press. (Original poem published 1794)

Braunstein, M. L. (1976). *Depth perception through motion.* New York: Academic Press.

Brooks, R. A. (1981). Symbolic reasoning among 3-D models and 2-D images. *Artificial Intelligence, 17,* 285–348.

Chase, W. G. (1986). Visual information processing. In K. R. Boff, L. Kaufman, & J. P. Thomas (Eds.), *Handbook of perception and human performance, Vol. II: Cognitive processes and performance* (28-1-28-71). New York: Wiley.

Corballis, M. C., & Roldan, C. E. (1975). Detection of symmetry as a function of angular orientation. *Journal of Experimental Psychology: Human Perception and Performance, 1,* 221–230.

Cox, M. (1992). *Children's drawings.* New York: Penguin.

Cutting, J. E. (1981). Coding theory adapted to gait perception. *Journal of Experimental Psychology: Human Perception and Performance, 7,* 71–87.

Fraenkel, G. S., & Gunn, D. L. (1940). *The orientation of animals.* Oxford, England: Clarendon.

Franklin, N., & Tversky, B. (1990). Searching imagined environments. *Journal of Experimental Psychology: General, 119,* 63–76.

Gell-Mann, M. (1994). *The quark and the jaguar: Adventures in the simple and the complex.* New York: Freeman.

Gibson, J. J. (1950). The perception of visual surfaces. *American Journal of Psychology, 63,* 367–384.

Gibson, J. J. (1957). Optical motions and transformations as stimuli for visual perception. *Psychological Review, 63,* 288–295.

Gibson, J. J. (1979). *The ecological approach to visual perception.* Boston: Houghton Mifflin.

Gibson, J. J., & Cornsweet, J. (1952). The perceived slant of visual surfaces—optical and geographical. *Journal of Experimental Psychology, 44,* 11–15.

Goldmeier, E. (1972). Similarity in visually perceived forms. *Psychological Issues, 8*(1), 1–135. (Translation of an article originally published in German in 1936.)

Goldmeier, E. (1982). *The memory trace: Its formation and its fate.* Hillsdale, NJ: Lawrence Erlbaum Associates.

Gould, J. L., & Gould, C. G. (1988). *The honey bee.* New York: Scientific American Library.

Hargittai, I., & Hargittai, M. (1994). *Symmetry: A unifying concept.* Bolinas, CA: Shelter Publications.

Hinton, G. (1979). Some demonstrations of the effects of structural descriptions in mental imagery. *Cognitive Science, 3,* 231–250.

Hinton, G. E., & Parsons, L. M. (1988). Scene-based and viewer-centered representations for comparing shapes. *Cognition, 30,* 1–35.

Holden, A. (1971). *Shapes, space, and symmetry.* New York: Columbia University Press.

Hummel, J. E., & Biederman, I. (1992). Dynamic binding in a neural network for shape recognition. *Psychological Review, 99,* 480–517.

Johansson, G. (1975). Visual motion perception. *Scientific American, 232,* 76–89.

Kandel, E. R., Schwartz, J. H., & Jessel, T. M. (1995). *Essentials of neural science and behavior.* Norwalk, CT: Appleton & Lange.

Kosslyn, S. M. (1994). *Image and brain.* Cambridge, MA: MIT Press.

Kubovy, M. (1986). *The psychology of perspective and Renaissance art.* New York: Cambridge University Press.

Lakoff, G., & Johnson, M. (1980). *Metaphors we live by.* Chicago: University of Chicago Press.

Leeuwenberg, E. L. J. (1971). A perceptual coding language for visual and auditory patterns. *American Journal of Psychology, 84,* 307–349.

Leyton, M. (1992). *Symmetry, causality, mind.* Cambridge, MA: MIT Press.

Mach, E. (1906/1959). *The analysis of sensations,* 5th ed. (C. M. Williams & S. Waterlow, Trans.). New York: Dover. (Original work published 1906)

Marr, D. (1982). *Vision.* San Francisco: Freeman.

Marr, D., & Nishihara, H. K. (1978). Representation and recognition of the spatial organization of three-dimensional shapes. *Proceedings of the Royal Society of London, Biological, 200,* 269–294.

McAfee, E. A., & Proffitt, D. R. (1991). Understanding the surface orientation of liquids. *Cognitive Psychology, 23,* 483–514.

McMullen, P. A., & Jolicoeur, P. (1992). Reference frame and effects of orientation on finding the tops of rotated objects. *Journal of Experimental Psychology: Human Perception and Performance, 18,* 807–820.

Palmer, S. E. (1977). Hierarchical structure in perceptual representation. *Cognitive Psychology, 9,* 441–474.

Palmer, S. E., & Hemenway, K. (1978). Orientation and symmetry: Effects of multiple, rotational, and near symmetries. *Journal of Experimental Psychology: Human Perception and Performance, 4,* 691–702.

Pani, J. R. (1993). Limits on the comprehension of rotational motion: Mental imagery of rotations with oblique components. *Perception, 22,* 785–808.

Pani, J. R. (1994). The generalized cone in human spatial organization. In C. W. Tyler (Ed.), Theoretical issues in symmetry perception [Special Issue]. *Spatial Vision, 8,* 491–502. Reprinted in C. W. Tyler (Ed.). (1996). *Human symmetry perception and its computational analysis* (pp. 383–393). Utrecht: VSP.

Pani, J. R. (1996). Mental imagery as the adaptationist views it. *Consciousness and Cognition, 5,* 288–326.

Pani, J. R. (1997). Descriptions of orientation in physical reasoning. *Current Directions in Psychological Science, 6,* 121–126.

Pani, J. R., & Dupree, D. (1994). Spatial reference systems in the comprehension of rotational motion. *Perception, 23,* 929–946.

Pani, J. R., Jeffres, J. A., Shippey, G., & Schwartz, K. (1996). Imagining projective transformations: Aligned orientations in spatial organization. *Cognitive Psychology, 31,* 125–167.

Pani, J. R., William, C. T., & Shippey, G. (1995). Determinants of the perception of rotational motion: Orientation of the motion to the object and to the environment. *Journal of Experimental Psychology: Human Perception and Performance, 21,* 1441–1456.

Pani, J. R., William, C. T., & Shippey, G. T. (1998). Orientation in physical reasoning: Determining the edge that would be formed by two surfaces. *Journal of Experimental Psychology: Human Perception and Performance, 24,* 283–300.

Pani, J. R., Zhou, H., & Friend, S. M. (1997). Perceiving and imagining Plato's solids: The generalized cylinder in spatial organization of 3D structures. *Visual Cognition, 4,* 225–264.

Proffitt, D. R., & Gilden, D. L. (1989). Understanding natural dynamics. *Journal of Experimental Psychology: Human Perception and Performance, 15,* 385–393.

Restle, F. (1979). Coding theory of the perception of motion configurations. *Psychological Review, 86,* 1–24.

Rock, I. (1983). *The logic of perception.* Cambridge MA: Bradford/MIT Press.

Rock, I., & Leaman, R. (1963). An experimental analysis of visual symmetry. *Acta Psychologica, 21,* 171–183.

Rosch, E. (1975). Cognitive reference points. *Cognitive Psychology, 7,* 532–547.

Schone, H. (1984). *Spatial orientation.* (C. Strausfeld, Trans.). Princeton, NJ: Princeton University Press. (Original work published 1980)

Sedgwick, H. A. (1986). Space perception. In K. R. Boff, L. Kaufman, & J. P. Thomas (Eds.), *Handbook of perception and human performance, Vol. 1: Sensory processes and perception* (21-1-21-57). New York: Wiley.

Shepard, R. N. (1984). Ecological constraints on internal representation: Resonant kinematics of perceiving, imagining, thinking, and dreaming. *Psychological Review, 91,* 417–447.

Shiffrar, M. M., & Shepard, R. N. (1991). Comparison of cube rotations around axes inclined relative to the environment or to the cube. *Journal of Experimental Psychology: Human Perception and Performance, 17,* 44–54.

Stevens, K. A. (1983). Surface tilt (the direction of slant): A neglected psychophysical variable. *Perception & Psychophysics, 33,* 241–250.

Stewart, I., & Golubitsky, M. (1992). *Fearful symmetry: Is God a geometer?* Cambridge, MA: Blackwell.

Tversky, A., & Kahneman, D. (1973). Availability: A heuristic for judging frequency and probability. *Cognitive Psychology, 5,* 207–232.

Tversky, B. (1981). Distortions in memory for maps. *Cognitive Psychology, 13,* 407–433.

Frisch, K. von. (1967). *The dance language and orientation of bees.* Cambridge, MA: Harvard University Press.

Wagemans, J. (1996). Detection of visual symmetries. In C. W. Tyler (Ed.), *Human symmetry perception and its computational analysis* (pp. 25–48). Utrecht: VSP.

Wertheimer, M. (1950). Laws of organization in perceptual forms. In W. D. Ellis (Ed.), *A source book of Gestalt Psychology* (pp. 71–88). New York: Humanities Press. (Abridged translation of a paper originally published 1923)

Weyl, H. (1952). *Symmetry.* Princeton, NJ: Princeton University Press.

Zerroug, M., & Nevatia, R. (1994). *Segmentation and recovery of SHGCs from a real intensity image.* Paper presented at the European Conference on Computer Vision, Stockholm.

Chapter 4

Height and Extent:
Two Kinds of Size Perception

Arnold E. Stoper
California State University

There was a time even before Cornell, and even before *Cognitive Psychology* was written—and I was there. I was Dick's graduate student and assistant at Brandeis University. To prove it, there is a published Neisser and Stoper (1965) paper on the topic of visual search, admittedly not the most widely cited paper in the literature. Even in those prehistoric (and, forgive me, precognitive) days at Brandeis, Dick had a deep-seated mistrust of experiments done with subjects held in head restraints in dark rooms while, in his later words, "the experimenter illuminated their retinae at his own pleasure" (Neisser, 1976, p. 25).

Although he didn't use the term *ecological validity* then, Dick always placed a high value on the similarity of the experimental situation to ordinary life. This attitude was not a common one in experimental psychology in those days, and it left a deep and lasting impression on me.

My particular research interests were always more hard-core perception than Dick's. The perception of motion was always a favorite topic of mine, and my dissertation involved the problem of perceived stability of the world during saccadic and pursuit eye movements (Stoper, 1967, 1973). It was characteristic of Dick to agree to spend much time on my dissertation, all the while encouraging me to follow my own ideas, even though my dissertation topic was not very close at all to his own research interests. Dick left Brandeis at the end of my second year of graduate school, but he continued as my advisor, with the advising done by mail.

Since the Brandeis days, Dick's research interests and mine had diverged even farther. A few years ago, however, he became interested in the topic of a paper of mine concerning the relation of eye height to apparent size, and recently, to my great delight, he did his own investigations of this problem with Wraga (Wraga & Neisser, 1995). I would like to present on this occasion some of my adventures and conclusions in dealing with this area.

For a time after graduate school, despite Dick's warnings, the attractions of head restraints, dark rooms, and illuminating other people's retinae at my own pleasure were more than I could resist. For the 10 years following graduate school, that is how I spent my research time. Dick had left his mark, however, and I never felt quite right about my carrying on this way.

During this time I did make an occasional foray into the real world, and on one such occasion, when visiting a friend in Santa Cruz, California, I happened upon the Mystery Spot. This is a Santa Cruz version of an illusion that can be seen at various amusement parks and tourist attractions around the country. The Mystery Spot centers around an old wooden shack on a fairly steep hill in the midst of a redwood forest. The shack, according to the proprietors, has slid down the hill; its floor, rather than being level, is parallel to the hill and its angles are all askew. The visitor is treated to various wondrous phenomena here, such as water running uphill, balls that fall at a steep angle to the vertical, and, most interesting to me, people growing and shrinking as they move around the Mystery Spot. (See Banta, 1995, for a description of this and many similar locations in the United States.)

The proprietors of the Mystery Spot explained that a meteorite landed there many years ago. Mysterious forces emanating from its remnants produced the strange phenomena. But, as Dick always said, "Beware of explanations of illusions offered by proprietors of tourist attractions" (. . . well, he could have said that). With this in mind, I decided to try to bring some of these phenomena into the laboratory for a closer look.

The Mystery Spot phenomenon of greatest interest to me is the size perception illusion shown in Fig. 4.1.

This particular illusion takes place without benefit of the tumbledown shack, but it does seem to require the steep hill setting shown here. Two people stand facing each other; the surface on which they stand is perfectly level, as demonstrated by a carpenter's level at the site. Let's say you are the person on the left, standing toward the uphill side, looking toward the downhill side. You look at the person on the right, who appears to be taller than you are by several inches. You now change places with that person so that you are standing on the right. Now the other person appears to be several inches shorter than you are. The dotted figures represent the apparent size of each person as seen by the other person. The illusion is very dramatic and convincing. Let me call this the two-person size illusion.

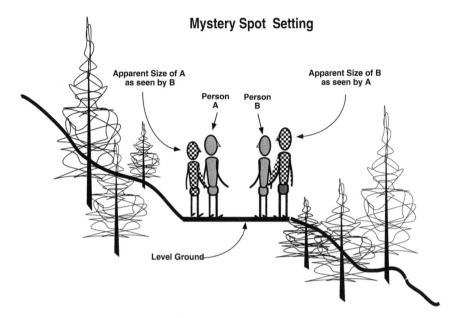

FIG. 4.1. The two-person size illusion at the Mystery Spot. The dotted figures represent each person's apparent size as seen by the other person. They are displaced for clarity; no distance illusion is implied here.

There are other size perception illusions at the Mystery Spot, in particular one that may be better known because it is more easily photographed. In this illusion one person views two other people of equal height with the distorted shack as background. If the shack is higher on the left than on the right, then the person on the left seems shorter than the person on the right. Let me call this the three-person size illusion. This is an illusion very similar to the famous distorted Ames room, and I believe it can be explained along the same lines as that illusion. The classical theory of size perception, dating from the time of Helmholtz, assumes that perceived distance is taken into account along with the retinal image size of the target object. Illusions of size, on this theory, are usually attributed to misperceptions of distance. The Ames room explanation does involve misjudgment of distance; the two observed people are in fact at different distances but appear to be at the same distance. In my opinion the three-person size perception illusion presents no particular challenge to the classical theory of size perception.

The two-person size illusion is considerably more puzzling, however. There is no particular reason to suspect any misperception of distance in the setting shown in Fig. 4.1. What seems to be happening in the situation of Fig. 4.1 is that the slanted background behind the viewed person influences the perception of his or her height.

Most of the other illusory effects at the Mystery Spot can be simply explained in terms of a misperception of the down direction. If a ball falls in some particular direction, but for some reason we perceive down to be some other direction, the ball will seem to fall at a strange angle.

Can we explain a misperception of the downward direction in terms of current perception theory? Another name for the up–down direction is the *gravitational vertical*. The influence of the visual environment on the apparent gravitational vertical or horizontal is a well-known phenomenon; one example of it is Witkin's Rod and Frame paradigm (Witkin & Asch, 1948).

In the Rod and Frame paradigm, a luminous square frame surrounds a luminous rod in an otherwise dark room (see Fig. 4.2). The frame can be tilted to the left or right (i.e., in the roll dimension), or turned off completely so only the rod is visible. An observer, if asked to set the rod so that it is vertical, can do so accurately if the frame is not visible. If the tilted frame is visible, the observer will set the rod somewhere between the true vertical and the direction that is parallel to the sides of the frame. We can describe this as a conflict between two sources of information as to the direction of vertical: (a) the optical information from the frame, and (b) information from the direction of the force of gravity. The optical information is sensed by means of the pattern on the retina; the gravity information is presumably sensed by means of the otoliths in the inner ear, pressure points on the body, and proprioceptive information about the position of the body and the eyes. The visual system evidently resolves the conflict by means of a compromise, and the apparent vertical lies somewhere between the two (but, with this particular stimulus, closer to the gravitational vertical than the optical). Because the true vertical in this case is that defined by the direction of gravity, the tilted frame produces an error in the judgment of vertical.

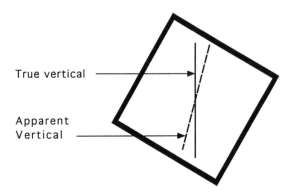

FIG. 4.2. The Rod and Frame paradigm. The apparent orientation of the rod with respect to the gravitational vertical is shifted by the frame.

Given the Rod and Frame paradigm, it is clear how the tilted surrounding of the Mystery Spot could produce a misperception of the gravitational vertical and the direction of down. It is also easy to see how a misperception of the direction of vertical or horizontal could lead to the appearance of a ball falling at an odd direction or water seeming to run uphill. Given the classical explanation of size perception, however, it is not so clear how this misperception of vertical or horizontal would have anything to do with apparent size. To explain the Mystery Spot size illusions we must turn to another approach to apparent size.

Gibson's Direct Perception Theory

Here again, my association with Dick Neisser determined the direction of my thinking. It was through Dick that I became acquainted with J. J. Gibson and his work, and, after Dick went to Cornell, Gibson's way of thinking exerted an even stronger influence on him and also on me. Gibson (1950, 1966) proposed a strategy of size perception that does not assume that perceived distance is taken into account along with the size of the retinal image. Instead, he proposed that there are, in the optical information, certain variables that remain invariant with distance from the observer. These invariants are said to be picked up directly by the observer. Distance can thus be ignored, rather than having to be processed, in the perception of size.

One invariant that Gibson proposed was the number of texture elements covered by an object. Texture elements of the ground surface appear finer as the ground surface recedes from the observer. A distant object will subtend a smaller visual angle, but will cover the same number of texture elements as will a near object of the same size (see Neisser, 1968, for a lucid discussion of Gibson's theory). Another invariant, proposed by Sedgwick (1980), involves the apparent horizon; that is, the line between the earth and sky, visible when an observer looks across a broad expanse of level ground or water. As Sedgwick pointed out, the apparent horizon can be used to determine the visual angle between the apparent horizon and the bottom of the object. The object itself determines another visual angle, the angle between the top and the bottom of the object. If the object is in contact with the ground, these two visual angles will maintain a constant ratio to each other, no matter what the distance to the object. This horizon ratio relation can then serve as an invariant that determines the size of the object.

The role of the apparent horizon may be better understood when it is realized that, although contrary to intuition, the apparent horizon is in fact always at eye level. This is true whether the observer is sitting in a low chair or standing on top of a 50-story building (the curvature of the Earth is negligible at these heights). The line of sight to the apparent horizon is always horizontal, always parallel to the level ground, which means that if it is seen to intersect an object standing on the ground, the linear distance from the base of the object to the intersection point will be one eye-height above the ground (see Fig. 4.3).

If the observer can find a point on the object that is at his or her eye height, this point then determines a kind of yardstick by which the object can be measured. The apparent horizon, in determining the observer's eye level, provides a way to make this calculation no matter what the distance of the object, as long as the observer and the object are standing on the same ground.

Unfortunately for those of you who may wish to rush out and judge sizes by this technique, you will be hard put to find any visible apparent horizons in your neighborhood unless you live on the beach, on a boat, or on the great plains. Fortunately for you, however, you can use a variation of this technique, in theory at least. You do not need to see the actual horizon line to determine the apparent horizon; there is also other information in the optic array you can use. If there are linear perspective cues in the scene, such as relatively straight railroad tracks on level ground receding into the distance, these tracks will converge at a vanishing point. The vanishing point, as any student of perspective knows, lies on the apparent horizon. And, once the apparent horizon is determined, eye height and the size of distant objects can be determined. As Purdy (1958), another of Gibson's graduate students, pointed out, many other aspects of the optical array follow the same geometry as linear perspective. Texture gradient, motion perspective gradient, and binocular disparity gradient can all be used to determine a vanishing point, apparent horizon, eye

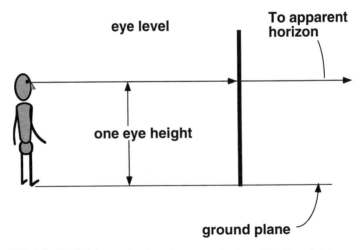

FIG. 4.3.   Eye height, eye level, and apparent horizon. The line of sight to the horizon will intersect any object on the level ground at one eye-height above the ground.

level, and thus the size of any distant object on the same ground plane as the observer. Purdy showed that these perspective cues can determine eye level, even when only a portion of the ground plane is visible.

Setting one's line of sight to level is a very easy and natural task for people to do; you can pick a point at your eye level fairly accurately right now in your present environment. How did you do it? Well, you might have used optical information, as the Gibsonians suggest, but you did not need to. My colleague Cohen and I, among others, have shown that a reasonably accurate determination of eye level can be made entirely on the basis of gravitational and proprioceptive information in completely dark surroundings, without any optical information at all (Stoper & Cohen, 1986). Cohen and Guzy (1995) have shown that this is possible even when the observer is pitched at various orientations.

We have here what seems to be obvious similarity between determination of the vertical in the rod and frame paradigm and the determination of eye level in the paradigm of sloping surroundings. Each paradigm involves both optical and gravitational information. Just as conflicting optical and gravitational information can produce an error in the perceived vertical in the roll dimension, it can produce an error in perceived eye level in the pitch dimension. In fact, a sloping (pitched) environment has been shown to produce an error in judging eye level (cf. MacDougall, 1903; Matin & Fox, 1988; Stoper & Cohen, 1989). If eye level is indeed used to determine size, pitched environment might be expected to produce the kind of misjudgment of size observed at the Mystery Spot. Some anecdotal evidence for such size perception errors in pitched surroundings does appear in the literature (MacDougall, 1903; Matin & Fox, 1988). There is some (although surprisingly little) direct experimental evidence that eye height is used for size judgment (Mark, 1987; Warren & Whang, 1987; Wraga & Neisser, 1995), but these studies did not involve pitched surroundings.

When I visited Matin's lab at Columbia University many years ago he showed me his pitch box, the apparatus he had built to demonstrate the effect of a pitched environment on apparent eye level. Sure enough, as he also showed me, this apparatus produced a dramatic size illusion. The task I undertook was to quantify these size illusions.

METHOD

Apparatus

The method we (Stoper & Bautista, 1992) used involved the pitch box apparatus shown in Fig. 4.4. It is an adaptation of Matin's apparatus.

The pitch box consisted of a wooden box, 244 cm long, 90 cm wide, and 210 cm high. The inside walls of this box were covered with a red

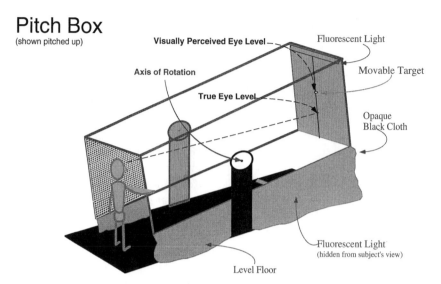

FIG. 4.4. The pitch box apparatus as set up for the eye level task. The opaque black cloth is a skirt extending around the bottom of the pitchbox. In addition, the floor is covered with black cloth.

checkered fabric. The box was suspended with a 66-cm clearance from the floor to allow for rotation. The floor of the pitch box was open, so both the observer and the object stand on the always level floor. Black cloth was draped from the bottom of the walls, and the floor was covered with black material. The floor was visible but difficult to see. The objects to be judged were placed on the level floor at a distance of 163 cm from the subject. A cord, which could move a small target up and down, was attached to the far end of the pitch box for use in the eye level judgment task. The pitch box could be set at three different pitches relative to the horizontal: 15° up (shown in Fig. 4.4), level, and 15° down.

The Matching Method

Our first attempt to quantify the size illusion used the standard method of matching a comparison object to the target. This task is illustrated in Fig. 4.5. The adjustable triangle was mounted on a window shade, and the subject could adjust its height by pulling on a rope. (The triangular shape was used so that the base width increased as the height increased, thus keeping the shape constant with changes in height.)

Subjects were 12 volunteer college students, naive to the purposes of the experiment. In the Height Condition, each subject viewed white target triangles with five different sizes, ranging from 71 cm to 150 cm tall. Each triangle was viewed at three different box pitches and two repetitions for

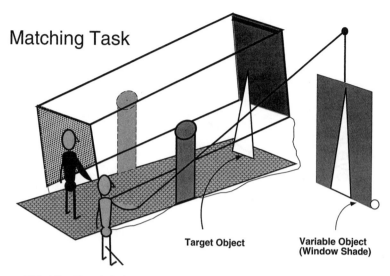

FIG. 4.5. The pitch box apparatus as set up for the matching task. The subject views the target, then comes out of the box to set the variable so that it matches the size of the target.

a total of 30 trials. Full binocular viewing was used, with no head restraint. The instruction was to adjust the variable triangle so that it was the same height as the one viewed in the box.

In the Eye Level Condition, each subject remained inside the box and adjusted the movable target so that it appeared to be at apparent eye level. The subject was instructed that the target was at eye level when the line of sight to the object was parallel to the level ground. This was done for three different box pitches and four repetitions.

The eye level conditions were always run after the height conditions to avoid contamination of the subject's height response by the use of the term *eye level.*

RESULTS

The shift of box pitch from −15° to +15° produced a shift of apparent eye level of 19° (in the same direction as the box pitch), as shown in Fig. 4.6.

This shift is 63% of the 30° of actual shift of pitch, and is in the same general range as the capture of eye level found by Matin and Fox (1988) and other investigators.

The results for the height condition in the matching task are shown in Fig. 4.7. When the pitch box was level, at 0° of pitch, the size of the triangles was judged with reasonable accuracy. When the box was pitched

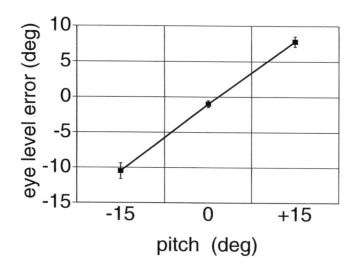

FIG. 4.6. Apparent eye level as a function of box pitch. Average of 12 subjects. Error bars are the standard error of the mean.

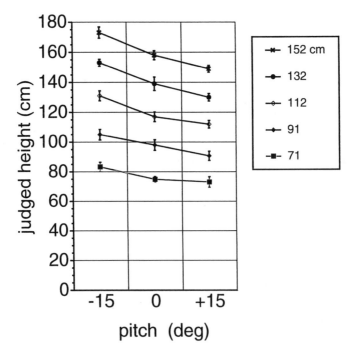

FIG. 4.7. Apparent size of objects as a function of box pitch and actual target size as measured by the matching task. Average of 12 subjects. Error bars are the standard error of the mean.

down, the triangles were always judged to be larger than when the box was pitched up. Although this effect is statistically significant, it is disappointingly small. The shift in eye level produced by the 30° box shift was 19°. At the distance of the target triangles, this corresponds to a shift of 58 cm. The total change of apparent height, however, was, at its best, only 22 cm for the largest triangle and was almost nonexistent, only 7 cm, for the smallest triangle. To us, this small effect did not seem to be consistent with the dramatic reports of the size occurring in the pitch box.

DISCUSSION

At the time I considered the results of the matching task to be a failure. In my own experience, the size illusions in the pitch box seemed in some ways even more dramatic than the those of the Mystery Spot. It is one of the more successful demonstrations at our Psychology Department open house for the general public. Children love to shrink other people, especially their parents. The demonstration produces a volume of amazement vocalizations (oohs and aahs) at least the equal of any other perception demonstration I have witnessed. To me, the small size illusions measured by the matching task simply did not accurately reflect the dramatic nature of these illusions.

The seeming inability to adequately measure what seems to be a powerful illusion is a common occurrence in the field of perception. (The moon illusion, for example, has such a history.) It is an instance of another of Dick's themes, the discrepancy between phenomena in the everyday world and phenomena as measured in the laboratory. In this case, the illusion seemed even more powerful in the laboratory than in the everyday world (if the Mystery Spot can be said to be the everyday world), yet we still could not measure it adequately.

It was only after many more failed attempts that we finally achieved what we consider to be a successful quantification (Stoper, 1990). We did that by using the task described in the next experiment.

The Manual Task

In this experiment we used a Manual Judgment Task, as is shown in Fig. 4.8.

Here conditions were identical insofar as possible to the previous experiment, except the subjects were instructed to indicate the height of each triangle by pointing along the vertical pole shown in the figure. This

Manual Task

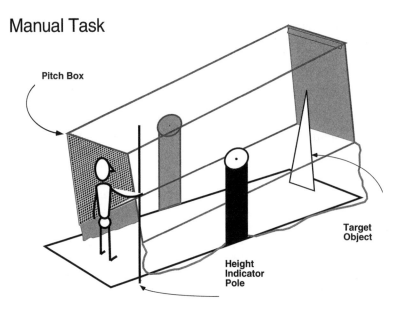

FIG. 4.8. The pitch box apparatus as set up for the manual judgment task. The subject places his finger on the unseen pole so that it seems to be at the same height as the top of the target.

pole could not be seen by the subject. As before, eye level judgments were made after all the height judgments were completed.

RESULTS

The results for the eye level judgments were almost identical to those from the first experiment, despite the fact that 12 different subjects were used.

The functions for all five triangles as measured by the manual judgment method, as shown in Fig. 4.9, are obviously steeper than those for the matching task shown in Fig. 4.7.

In Fig. 4.10, the two tasks are compared directly.

As you can see in Fig. 4.10, the manual task produces approximately double the effect of the matching task. The total effect increases with actual height of the triangle for both tasks. I did not expect this result, but it is consistent with the hypothesis that eye height is used as a yardstick, and that the entire yardstick grows or shrinks with box pitch.

The effect of the 30° shift in box pitch on height judgment can be roughly described as a constant percentage of the triangle height, about 16% for matching and about 30% for the manual task. For the tallest triangle (152 cm), the change in apparent height for the 30° shift was 23

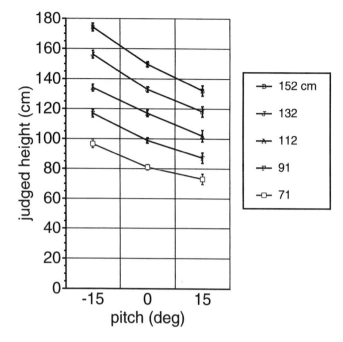

FIG. 4.9. Apparent size of objects as a function of box pitch and actual target size as measured by the manual judgment task. Average of 12 subjects. Error bars are the standard error of the mean.

cm in the matching task and 42 cm in the manual task, or 41% and 75%, respectively, of the 58-cm shift in apparent eye level.

GENERAL DISCUSSION

Why would the manual task be more sensitive to environmental pitch than the matching task? To explain this we must consider a more detailed explanation of how apparent eye level affects perceived size.

Different Types of Eye Level

In the previous discussion and in fact in the way I originally thought about this problem, I was very glib with the term *eye level*. The argument presented is: (a) Eye level is used to judge size, (b) pitched surroundings can affect eye level; therefore (c) pitched surroundings can affect judged size. What this argument glibly slides by, however, is that the term *eye level* is an ambiguous one. The eye level that would result in accurate size perception judgments is a line parallel to the ground plane, even if the ground is

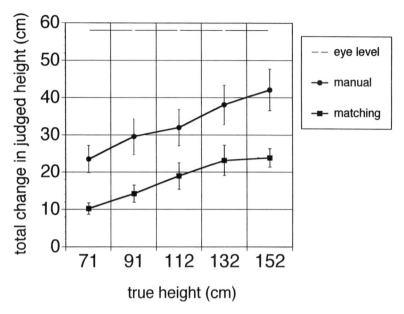

FIG. 4.10. Total change in apparent size produced by the 30° shift of box pitch for the matching task and the manual judgment task. Average of 12 subjects. The error bars are the standard error of the mean. The eye level judgment produced by the same shift of box pitch is represented by a line for comparison purposes.

sloping. The eye level influenced by pitched surroundings is defined in terms of level ground or gravity, rather than the visible ground. We must introduce a more complex terminology in order to avoid logical errors.

In a previous publication, three different types of eye level were described (Stoper & Cohen, 1991). These are shown in Fig. 4.11.

We say a target is at gravitationally relative eye level (GREL) when the line of sight to the target is parallel to the gravitational horizontal. In other words, a plumb bob would always hang perpendicular to GREL. This definition captures the usual meaning of eye level, and the one we intended our subjects to use in making their eye level judgments. We can contrast this with the surface relative eye level (SREL), when the line of sight to the target is parallel to some plane surface. This is the eye level that is implied in Gibson's size perception theory. If we are to pick a point at one eye height above the ground plane, the line of sight must be parallel to that plane; the direction of gravity need not be considered. The third type of eye level shown in the figure, head relative eye level (HREL), need not concern us here.

It is also important to distinguish apparent eye level from the true, physically defined eye level. We say that when the subject attempts to set

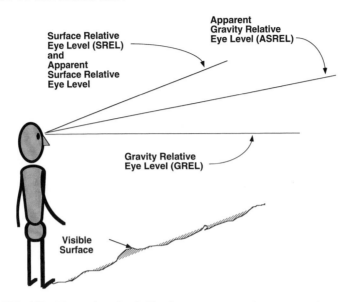

FIG. 4.11. Types of eye level. The figure represents the results of Stoper and Cohen (1991), who showed that apparent GREL is shifted about halfway toward SREL, but apparent SREL is seen veridically, parallel to the surface, and to true SREL.

a target to GREL, his setting defines apparent gravitational eye level (AGREL). Subjects can do this with reasonable accuracy in complete darkness (Stoper & Cohen, 1986), presumably using vestibular (primarily otolithic) and postural information. When the subject attempts to set a target to SREL his setting defines apparent surface relative eye level (AS-REL). Subjects can do this with reasonable accuracy even if the surface is pitched relative to gravity (Stoper & Cohen, 1991), presumably using optical information such as suggested by the Gibsonians, discussed earlier this chapter.

If the observer is standing on level ground, or in a level environment, SREL and GREL coincide. If, however, the ground plane is pitched with respect to gravity, that is, the observer is standing on a hill, there will be an angular difference between SREL and GREL; that angular difference will be equal to the pitch angle, or slope, of the ground plane. This is the condition referred to earlier as conflicting optical and gravitational information; as we said, this conflicting information can produce an error in perceived eye level in the pitch dimension.

To apply this terminology to our present experiment, we must expand the definition of SREL to include any visible structure that suggests a vanishing point, such as our pitch box. The SREL in the case of the pitch box is defined as a line parallel to the longitudinal axis of the box, and intersecting the observer's eye. The true SREL thus changes with the pitch of the box, whereas the true GREL remains level with respect to gravity. I can describe the results of the eye level conditions of the experiments reported here as showing that when the observer attempts to judge GREL the resulting AGREL is shifted in the direction of SREL. In these experiments, as well as many other similar ones, AGREL is shifted approximately 50% of the angular distance between GREL and SREL. Thus, it is always approximately midway between true GREL and true SREL. Stoper and Cohen (1991) also showed that, when the observer attempts to judge true SREL of a pitched environment, the ASREL is shifted in the direction of GREL, but only about 15% of the angular distance between SREL and GREL.

If there are surfaces or structures in the environment that have vanishing points at differing elevations, that is, if they have differing pitch angles with respect to gravity, they will have differing true SRELs associated with them. There is, on the other hand, only one true GREL in a situation. In this particular experimental situation, I must distinguish the SREL of the movable part of the pitch box and the SREL of the floor of the room. An important part of the experimental design is that the movable part of the pitch box has no floor, so the objects to be judged stand on the fixed floor of the room. This floor is covered with black cloth, and is barely visible, but it nevertheless has a true SREL, which is parallel to the true GREL of the observer.

For a long time, although I was convinced that the effect of environmental pitch on apparent size was mediated by eye level, I was bothered by an apparent inconsistency centering around the ability to judge size on a hillside. We have run pilot experiments showing that an observer can look uphill or downhill at an object standing on the hill and judge its size with reasonable accuracy. (I am not aware of any published investigations of this ability.) If any eye level is used to make this judgment, the eye level involved must be the line apparently parallel to the hill, that is, the ASREL of the hill. The observer's only other choice would be the AGREL, which would result in wildly erroneous size judgments on a hillside. The use of ASREL for size judgment would be consistent with the Gibsonian theory of size perception. However, the eye level that is affected by the pitch box is AGREL, not ASREL. Why, then, should the pitch box result in a size illusion?

It was only very recently that a satisfactory (to me) solution of this apparent inconsistency presented itself. This solution involves the concept of an implicit surface and an implicit ASREL associated with it. This implicit ASREL would be assumed coincident with the AGREL unless there is optical information to the contrary; this is just another way of saying that the implicit surface is assumed to be level unless it is seen to be otherwise. Errors in judgment of the AGREL produced by the pitch box could thus produce an error in ASREL, which could thus produce a size illusion.

I can now attempt an explanation of our results using this terminology. I can summarize this discussion with the following assumptions:

Five Assumptions About Eye Level and Pitched Environment

1. Eye level can be used for judging the size of an object assumed to be standing on the same surface (the ground) as the observer, even if this ground is pitched with respect to gravity. The type of eye level used for this purpose is the ASREL of the ground.

2. An implicit ground may exist even though it is not visible, and this ground will have an ASREL associated with it. This means that eye level can be used to judge size even if the ground is not visible.

3. The observer will assume the ground to be level; that is, ASREL will be perceived as coincident with AGREL unless there is optical (or perhaps some other modality) information to the contrary. This assumption, taken together with Assumption 2, implies that, in the case where the ground is not visible, ASREL could be based on AGREL (which, as we have said, can be determined relatively accurately even in complete darkness). This implies that the gravity sensing system can in some circumstances influence the judgment of size. Assumption 3 also implies that, if the ground is not visible, an error in judging GREL will result in an error in judging SREL (in other words an erroneous AGREL will result in an erroneous ASREL).

4. If there is optical information about the direction of SREL, it will be given great weight relative to gravitational information in the determination of ASREL. The experimental evidence of Stoper & Cohen (1991) as to the accuracy of the judgment of SREL, and the resistance of that judgment to influence by gravitational information, has been mentioned previously. Assumption 4 is necessary to explain the observation mentioned in Assumption 1 that an observer standing on a sloping hill will be reasonably accurate in using eye level to judge size. If ASREL were strongly shifted toward GREL on a hillside, observers would strongly overestimate the size of objects situated uphill and strongly underestimate the size of objects situated downhill.

5. If there is optical information about the direction of SREL, it will be weighted about equally with gravitational information in the determination of AGREL. This means that AGREL will be shifted about 50% of the angular distance toward the SREL of the visible environment. The results of the two eye-level conditions presented here, as well as many other experiments, are evidence for this assumption.

Given these assumptions, let us look first at what is presumed to happen in the second experiment reported here, the manual task. In this experiment, the subject attempts to indicate the height of only the top of the object by pointing to a particular place on a nearby pole. (A) AGREL is strongly influenced by the pitch of the box, as our Assumption 5 indicates and as our eye level results show. (B) The floor of the box remains essentially invisible, but by Assumption 2 the subject assumes an implicit floor on which both he or she and the object are standing. (C) The subject assumes the floor to be level, and there being no optical information to the contrary, by Assumption 3 the ASREL of the floor is assumed parallel to, or coincident with, AGREL. (D) The ASREL of the floor is thus also strongly influenced by the pitch of the box. (E) The subject judges the size of the object by means of the ASREL of the floor, and so this size judgment is strongly influenced by the pitch of the box, with errors dependent on that pitch result.

Interestingly, the implicit floor is assumed to be level, and, in fact, it is physically level. Why should this then result in an error in size judgment? The error comes about because the line that is perceived to be parallel to the floor, the ASREL, is not in fact parallel to the actual floor; it is parallel to some nonexistent surface (the implicit surface), which is apparently level. This discrepancy between the ASREL and the true SREL can be said to be the cause of the size judgment errors in the manual task.

Another way of looking at the manual task is to ask what strategy the observer uses in attempting to put his finger at the same height as the top of the object. One reasonable strategy would be to set his finger so that the line between finger and top of the object is parallel to the implicit surface and the ASREL. Because there is a discrepancy between ASREL and true SREL, the observer will put his finger in the wrong place, a place that is a function of the pitch of the box. This error in finger placement will produce the pitch box-dependent size judgment errors.

In our first experiment, a matching task was used. As described earlier, in this task the subject must look at both the top and the bottom of the target, then adjust the variable object so that it appears to be the same size as the target. Now, once again (A) AGREL is strongly influenced by the pitch of the box, as our Assumption 5 indicates and as our eye level results show. (B) In the matching task the subject must look directly at the floor in order to determine the location of the bottom of the target. Even if the actual surface of the floor is invisible, the location of the bottom of the object will give optical information about the orientation of the floor. (C) The floor will not be seen as level. The ASREL of the floor will be strongly influenced by the optical information from the floor, as assumption 4 indicates, but the AGREL will move with the ASREL of the pitch box. Because the perceived pitch of the floor depends on the angle between its ASREL and the AGREL, the perceived pitch of the floor will depend on the pitch of the box. When the box is pitched down, the floor will seem pitched up, and vice versa. (D) If the ASREL of the floor is used to judge size, there will be less or no influence of box pitch on this judgment. The effect of the pitch box will be to cause the entire object to appear higher, or lower, than the observer rather than larger or smaller.

Some anecdotal evidence in support of this explanation is the spontaneous report of many observers when the box is pitched up that the target (or target person) looks as if it is in a pit. The corresponding effect when the box is pitched down is that the target looks higher, or on a pedestal. This latter effect is, for some reason, seldom spontaneously reported.

Given these assumptions, any condition that increases visibility of the floor will decrease the effect of the pitch box. This may be the explanation of the decreased pitch box effect with smaller target objects found in both experiments reported here.

Explanation of the Mystery Spot Size Illusion

We can apply these assumptions to the Mystery Spot two-person size illusion, shown in Fig. 4.1. The person who sees the upward sloping background sees the other person as shorter; the person who sees the downward sloping background sees the other person as taller. One interesting and relevant fact about this illusion is that it only seems to work if the two people are relatively close to each other. The distance used at the Mystery Spot, presumably chosen to optimize the illusion, is under one meter. Why so close? One might reasonably expect that a greater distance would increase the effect because this distance would cause a given angular eye level error to produce a larger error in apparent eye height. We have found, however, in the case of our pitch box that increasing distance beyond a certain point weakens the illusion, and presumably the proprietors of the Mystery Spot also found this to be the case. On the basis of our assumptions, we would expect that any condition that makes the ground more visible would weaken the illusion; this would be the case with increased distance between the two people. Evidently, the people are made to stand close so that they see the ground between them only with difficulty, and this produces a stronger illusion.

On my assumptions, the sloping environment of the Mystery Spot produces an error in judging gravitational eye level (Assumption 5). What would happen if the two people did see the ground between them? They would accurately perceive the surface relative eye level (Assumption 4), but it would be seen as not coinciding with gravitational eye level, so the ground would seem pitched. The other person would simply seem to be uphill or downhill. This would be an erroneous perception, but it would not be a size illusion, just a slope illusion. In other words, because SREL would be judged accurately relative to its surface, it would result in accurate size judgment, but because it is perceived inaccurately with respect to gravity, that perception would result in erroneous slope judgments.

However, if the actual visible ground were ignored, an implicit ground surface would be assumed (Assumption 2). This surface would be assumed as being parallel to the perceived gravitational eye level (AGREL; Assumption 3). The eye level associated with this implicit surface (ASREL) would be assumed coincident with AGREL. Because AGREL is erroneously perceived, ASREL would also be erroneously perceived. This erroneous ASREL would be used to judge size (Assumption 1), resulting in a size illusion. This situation is depicted in Fig. 4.12.

Say you bring a friend to see the wonders of the Mystery Spot (it is well worth the visit, by the way). The friend will, of course, be amazed by the two-person size illusion and, because you have recently read about it, will ask you to explain it. You might say that the illusion depends on the

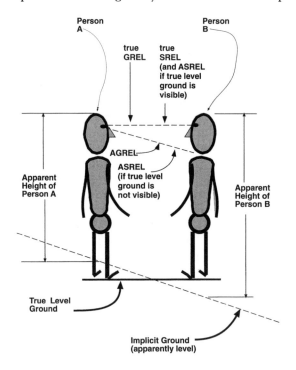

FIG. 4.12. The two-person size illusion explained. The apparent gravitational eye level (AGREL) is shifted from true (see assumption 5) because of the pitched surroundings (shown in Fig. 4.1). The implicit ground is assumed level (see assumption 3). In the case of looking at person B, the implicit ground is assumed lower than the ground really is, hence person B is perceived taller than he or she really is; the opposite is true for person A. If the true level ground were visible, it would override the implicit ground, and would be seen as parallel to the true SREL (see assumption 4). It would still be seen at an angle to the apparent GREL, however, and thus be misperceived as sloping, but would not give rise to a size illusion.

observer not looking directly at the ground, and when this is the case there is an implicit ground, which is assumed to be level. And, you add, the illusion happens because the sloping environment causes a misperception of the slope of the ground between the two people.

But, your friend says, you are contradicting yourself. There is no misperception of the slope of the ground; as you just said, the ground is assumed to be level, and it is in fact physically level. Your friend's statement is certainly true. At this point you might well agree with your friend and decide that what you read must have been confused. Maybe the size change really is due to a meteorite. You might, however, ask your friend to consider the case where person A is looking at the eyes of person B. If they are the same height, that line of sight will be physically level, but it will not be apparently level. The true ground is parallel to that line of sight, but the implicit ground is at some angle relative to it. Therefore, the implicit ground, although it is assumed level with respect to gravity, is assumed to be at some angle relative to the real ground; that is, its slope relative to the real ground is misperceived. This misperception of slope would cause the ground under the viewed person's feet is to be assumed lower or higher than it really is; that person will then seem taller or shorter than he or she really is. Some percentage of friends will still prefer the meteorite explanation, but at least you tried.

Two Size Strategies

Inherent in the earlier assumptions is the implication that an observer may use two distinctly different strategies to judge size. This brings us back to one of Neisser's themes: that perception is an active, constructive process rather than just a passive reception of the stimulus. I think it would be in keeping with Dick's current way of thinking to say there is no such thing as the percept of size of an object; instead there are different strategies for judging size that depend on the reason for wanting to know the size. In the experiments presented here, I seem to have tapped into two different strategies distinguished by the two different tasks set for the subject. I believe they reflect two very different strategies used in the real world. I also believe that these differing strategies are based on differing physiological mechanisms.

The extent strategy is normally assumed in the psychological literature, whether classical or Gibsonian. This strategy requires determination of the location of the topmost point of the object relative to the bottommost point. This strategy would be encouraged by the matching task. In classical size perception theory, the extent strategy is assumed in the taking into account of the size of the retinal image. In Gibsonian horizon ratio theory, the extent strategy is also assumed because one term of the ratio is the angular extent of the object.

Use of the extent strategy, as I have discussed previously, reduces or eliminates the effect of pitched environment on perceived size because it makes salient the actual ground surface on which the object is resting.

The height strategy would involve determination of the location of the topmost point of the object relative to eye level. The bottom of the object need not be considered at all. This strategy would be encouraged in the manual task, where the subject explicitly indicated the level of the topmost point. As far as I know, it is not assumed in any existing theory of size perception. Use of the height strategy, as I have already discussed, is necessary for the occurrence of the effect of the pitched environment on perceived size. The height strategy allows this effect because it allows judgment of size even with the ground remaining essentially invisible.

The Height Strategy

I believe that the height strategy has been unfairly ignored in the size perception literature. In fact, some might argue that the height strategy is not truly a strategy for size judgment, but rather a judgment of location of one point. The height strategy would not distinguish between a tall object standing on the ground and a short object standing on a pedestal. However, many everyday size judgments seem to use the height strategy exclusively. For example, when you judge the height of a person with whom you are in conversation, you rarely bother to look at his or her feet. You seem to judge the person's height by whether, and how much, you must either raise or lower your gaze relative to eye level.

The judgment of whether or not another animal is taller than oneself is biologically an important one for most terrestrial animals, including humans. In other words, we could say it has high ecological validity. This seems to be especially true for males in this society. My 17-year-old (at this writing) son, for example, seems to be exquisitely tuned to the slightest fraction of an inch difference between his height and that of other 17-year-old males in the neighborhood. Many animals increase their apparent height by postural maneuvers (e.g., cats arch their backs) as a threat gesture.

There has been much said (cf. Morris, 1969) about the relation of dominance to height and the custom of putting kings up on thrones or giving them crowns to wear to make them seem more king-like. It is possible that simply raising or lowering the gaze when looking at another leads directly to some emotional reaction. It may be that the dramatic effect of the size illusion at the Mystery Spot and in the pitch box comes directly from the changed apparent direction of gaze induced in these environments.

An elevated gaze to the top of an organism does not necessarily mean that the organism is large. Both increased size and decreased distance would produce an increase in gaze elevation to the top of the other organism. But either large size or close proximity of another organism could be associated with danger and so a high gaze elevation could usefully signal danger without the necessity of analyzing which variable is producing it. Gaze elevation could, in this way, be similar to the time to contact variable, which indicates either high speed toward or close proximity to a surface, either of which requires some avoidance action (cf. Lee, 1976)

In keeping with the possible biological importance of gaze elevation is the simplicity with which it can be accomplished. It is not even necessary to have an optical array providing information as to eye level. The otoliths in the labyrinthine system are sensitive to the orientation of the head with respect to gravity, and this information when used in conjunction with information about the position of the eyes in the head can determine whether the line of sight is level or not. If the line of sight is level, any protrusion above it by a living organism is a basis for fear. The larger the protrusion, the higher the probability of danger.

This brings me to another point of consonance with the outlook of Neisser. The height strategy is not an exclusively visual strategy. It can involve information from the otoliths and can be said to be a multimodal size perception system.

Developmentally, the height strategy seems to come prior to the extent strategy. Young children seem to use it when asked to make a pile of blocks on a low table the same size as a pile on a higher table. Children at Stage 1 (below the age of 6 or so) will make the tops of both piles the same height off the ground, according to Piaget, Inhelder, and Szeminska (1960). They will do this although the extents of the two block piles, the distance between top and the bottom of each pile, may be very different. It is only when they reach Stage 2 that they will take into account both the base and the top of the pile in the comparison.

The height strategy has some serious limitations. It can only be accurate if the judged object is on the same ground surface as the observer. This means it would be of little use to fish or flying birds. Even if the same ground surface condition is fulfilled, the height strategy will be increasingly less reliable as the size to be judged departs from one eye-height. A point exactly one eye-height above the ground will be at eye level no matter what its distance, but if it is some particular angular distance from eye level, its height above ground will depend on its distance from the observer. Thus, an accurate distance judgment would have to be used in conjunction with the elevation of the topmost point of an object in order to accurately determine its height.

The Extent Strategy

The extent strategy also has biological importance. It would be important for those situations where the height strategy fails. It would also be important at close distances, where binocular vision can be used. Such tasks as determination of the graspability of an object would require this strategy.

Real-life determination of size would be a complex interplay between these two strategies, sometimes using one as a standard, sometimes the other. Of course, we are not limited to two; there may be many more strategies, involving complex cycles of interaction, which I would hope would bring joy to Dick Neisser's heart.

ACKNOWLEDGMENT

Some of this research was supported by NASA Cooperative Grant NCC 2-595

REFERENCES

Banta, C. (1995). *Seeing is believing—Haunted shacks, mystery spots, & other delightful phenomena.* Agoura Hills, CA: Funhouse Press.

Cohen, M. M., & Guzy, L. T. (1995). Effects of body orientation and retinal image pitch on the perception of gravity-referenced eye level (GREL). *Aviation, Space, and Environmental Medicine, 66,* 505.

Gibson, J. J. (1950). *The perception of the visual world.* Boston: Houghton Mifflin.

Gibson, J. J. (1966). *The senses considered as perceptual systems.* Boston: Houghton Mifflin.

Lee, D. N. (1976). A theory of visual control of braking based on information about time to collision. *Perception, 5,* 437–459.

MacDougall, R. (1903). The subjective horizon. *Psychological Review Monograph Supplement, 4,* 145–166.

Mark, L. S. (1987). Eye height-scaled information about affordances: A study of sitting and stair climbing. *Journal of Experimental Psychology: Human Perception and Performance, 13,* 361–370.

Matin, L., & Fox, C. R. (1988). Visually perceived eye level and perceived elevation of objects: Linearly additive influences from visual field pitch and gravity. *Vision Research, 29,* 315–324.

Morris, D. (1969). *The human zoo.* New York: McGraw Hill.

Neisser, U. (1968). The processes of vision. *Scientific American, 219,* 204–214.

Neisser, U. (1976). *Cognition and reality.* San Francisco: Freeman.

Neisser, U., & Stoper, A. (1965). Redirecting the search process. *British Journal of Psychology, 56*(4), 259–369.

Piaget, J., Inhelder, B., & Szeminska, A. (1960). *The child's conception of geometry.* New York: Basic Books.

Purdy, W. C. (1958). *The hypothesis of psychophysical correspondence in space perception.* Doctoral Dissertation, Cornell University. [Ann Arbor: University Microfilms, No. 58-5594].

Sedgwick, H. A. (1980). The geometry of spatial layout in pictorial representation. In M. Hagen (Ed.), *The perception of pictures* (pp. 33–88). New York: Academic Press.

Stoper, A. E. (1967). *Vision during pursuit movement: The role of oculomotor information.* Doctoral dissertation, Brandeis University. [Ann Arbor: University Microfilms, No. 67-16,579].

Stoper, A. E. (1973). Apparent motion of stimuli presented stroboscopically during pursuit movement of the eye. *Perception & Psychophysics, 13,* 201–211.

Stoper, A. E. (1990). Pitched environments and apparent height. *Bulletin of the Psychonomic Society, 28,* 517.

Stoper, A. E., & Bautista, A. (1992). Apparent height as a function of pitched environment and task. *Investigative Ophthalmology and Visual Science Supplement, 33,* 962.

Stoper, A. E., & Cohen, M. M. (1986). Judgments of eye level in light and darkness. *Perception and Psychophysics, 40,* 311–316.

Stoper, A. E., & Cohen, M. M. (1989). Effect of structured visual environments on apparent eye level. *Perception and Psychophysics, 46,* 469–475.

Stoper, A. E., & Cohen, M. M. (1991). Optical, gravitational, and kinesthetic determinants of judged eye level. In S. R. Ellis (Ed.), *Pictorial communication in virtual and real environments* (pp. 390–403). Philadelphia: Taylor and Francis.

Warren, W. H., & Whang, S. (1987). Visual guidance of walking throgh apertures: Body-scaled information for affordances. *Journal of Experimental Psychology: Human Perception and Performance, 13,* 371–383.

Witkin, H., & Asch, S. (1948). Studies in space orientation: IV. Further studies of the perception of the upright with displaced visual fields. *Journal of Experimental Psychology, 38,* 762–782.

Wraga, M., & Neisser, U. (1995, November). *Intrinsic and extrinsic size judgments are both affected by perceived height.* Paper presented at the 36th annual meeting of the Psychonomic Society, Los Angeles.

Part II

COGNITION AND ITS DEVELOPMENT

Chapter 5

EPAM to EGO:
A Cognitive Journey

Eleanor J. Gibson
Cornell University

The journey I tell about here was not mine, but I witnessed some of it and occasionally took bit parts by way of argument and exchange of ideas. It would require a full-scale biography (which someone will write eventually) to do justice to this journey. I intend to dwell on three periods along the way. They are not properly stages because the destination was not known but rather periods that mark a time of fruition, leading dynamically to new paths of progress. The first period was quite early in this journey, around the time Ulric Neisser's first book was published in the mid-1960s. The name given the favored style of thinking at the time by the avant-garde psychologists was information processing (although of course Neisser called his book *Cognitive Psychology*). The second period came later when Neisser was a professor at Cornell, intellectual change was in the air, and he moved from a concern with coded information to more naturalistic subject matter. Innovative ideas and methods were rife and there were gifted graduate students trying them out. The third period (still to be completed) brings two, once thought to be opposing, views together, one ecological and the other deeply cognitive; that is, Neisser's reintroduction of the self into psychology, at Emory.

I should point out that I have chosen these three conceptually significant periods in Neisser's career in part because they spurred my own thinking and influenced my research. We have argued together over many issues, but for these periods there are real points of contact and mutual concern. In each case, I intend to comment on Neisser's ideas and work at the time, how they affected myself, and, when possible, where the issue stands now— dead or alive? moving ahead?

ATTENTION AND VISUAL RESEARCH

In the first of the three periods, I dwell on Neisser's work on visual search, both the process he conceived of and a remarkably innovative research procedure that he developed. As it happened, I was influenced by Neisser's ideas and methods even before I knew him. The time was the early 1960s just before his *Cognitive Psychology* (1967) was published. I heard him report on his research at EPA and at the new Psychonomic Society and I was greatly impressed. I was working at the time on the reading process—how children learn to read—and I felt that there was something promising for me there. Psychologists of that generation will remember Neisser's (1964) famous article in *Scientific American* called "Visual Search." He described a technique that he called "vision time without reaction time," putting the spotlight on the cognitive processes of searching for information. Both *search* and *information* were key terms. Conceiving the cognitive process as one of an active, ongoing search, functional and dynamic, was new and very attractive to me. My own concern was (and is) with perceptual search for relevant information about the world as it presently surrounds us. The world could be the scene with people currently performing around us, but the scene has often been restricted for experimental purposes to a set task confined to marks on paper. In either case, the process of finding the information wanted is active, ongoing, and directed. I was interested in how young readers pick up information from a page of print: How do they learn what to look for, where are they focusing? Most important, what is the information?

Information, at that time, was defined by the more modish scientists in bits, either–or choices at a rather atomic level. Psychologists like Miller were eager to apply this definition to psychology (e.g., Miller's article, "What Is Information Measurement?" in 1953 or Garner's 1962 book on "Uncertainty," a term used for measurement of information by computer devotees of Information Theory). Attempts to report psychological data in terms of bits did not prove very helpful, however, in identifying meaningful units for psychological research, even when the matter from which information was to be abstracted was in verbal or numerical form (as it generally was). Neisser did not embrace this definition of information. But in *Cognitive Psychology* (1967) he dealt mainly with information in print, such as alphanumeric or verbal material, or with auditorily presented verbal material. This was coded material, even if not treated as bits, and it fit nicely into programs of research on information processing.

In Neisser's (1964) visual scanning task, a subject searched for a specific target such as a letter, number, or word embedded in a context of more or less similar items. Any feature of the target or context could be manipulated experimentally—meanings, spelling patterns, or phonological features like pronunciation or rhyming. A subject's ability to attend to any of these features and extract them from context could be measured by the time required to locate the target that was placed at varying distances down the list over a long series of trials. In a typical search experiment, a subject scanned a 50-item list that contained a single target, such as a letter, in an unpredictable position. When it was found, the subject pressed a button, permitting search time to be recorded. Over many such trials, the time per item could be calculated. Search time depended on context, such as similarity. One of the results of these experiments was construction of computer models of character and pattern recognition, systems of feature analysis that tested the input. The analysis might be assumed to operate in parallel (as in one called Pandemonium) or sequentially, organized in a decision tree as in the EPAM (Elementary Perceiver and Memorizer) program (Feigenbaum, 1963). The EPAM program was remarkable in that it not only tested for features but presumably learned new ones as well.

Neisser's subjects became very adept with practice at searching for more than one character at a time (Neisser, Novick, & Lazar, 1963), suggesting to some psychologists (including myself) that they were learning to search very economically for the minimal features that differentiated all the targets from their background.

How could these experiments fail to fascinate a psychologist engaged in trying to discover how children learn to extract information from printed characters, the way I then thought of learning to read? I planned similar search experiments to be run developmentally, hoping they would tell me how children gradually developed skill at extracting the information they needed, and perhaps even what that information was. I ran an experiment (Gibson & Yonas, 1966a) in which children in fourth and sixth grades and college sophomores scanned through lists of letters for targets (one or two) in lists of high or low confusability. As we expected, search time decreased with age and was always longer when the target and context were increased in similarity. But fourth graders were quite able to perform the task and found the two-target task no more difficult than searching for one. Evidently strategies for selecting and processing the information required by a search for letters are in place for children who read at a fourth-grade level even with a confusable background and two targets.

What is the information that they can differentiate and use thus effectively? Inspired by Neisser's work and the EPAM model, I thought that the subjects were searching for some optimal letter feature that sufficed for visual differentiation of a target from all the context letters, perhaps a single diagonal, or an x-like feature at the center. In a later experiment we did find an interaction with high visual confusability when third graders were compared with college students. Practice of the task and greater reading competence could account for it. Phonological confusability (similar pronunciation) did not appear to affect competence in a search for a visual target (Gibson & Yonas, 1966b).

These experiments led to further research on both word and letter discrimination and played a role in the theory of perceptual learning that I subsequently proposed (Gibson, 1969). The concept of distinctive features, already appealing to me, was enhanced by Neisser's discussion of feature analysis as a process in visual search. Distinctive features of characters or objects or even places have great utility for visual search tasks (if not for very many others) and I proceeded to examine the notion as a candidate for a theory of perceptual learning. The climax of this research was a gigantic experiment to determine precisely the distinctive features of letters of the alphabet (Gibson, Shapiro, & Yonas, 1968). Same–different judgments given individually by children (7 years of age) and adults yielded reaction times to generate a massive confusion matrix that could be subjected to cluster analysis. Data of both children and adults yielded contrastive features such as straight/curve, diagonally, closed/open, intersection, and so forth. Decision time was longer, the more features shared by a pair of letters. However, *same* decisions for an identical pair were overall shorter than decisions of *different*, so there did not seem to be a feature-by-feature process of comparison in searching for a difference. There was a very direct perception of replication or sameness when such a decision was appropriate.

What kind of theory of perceptual learning suggests itself after such research? A preoccupation with distinctive features of letters was much too narrow to be generally useful, but the notion of perceptual learning as a search for the optional information carrying utility for the task, whatever it be, seemed to me right, and I settled on a selection principle that I called reduction of uncertainty as a principle of perceptual learning (Gibson, 1969). I thought of perception as an active process of seeking information from the world and picking it up directly, rather than a construction of representations or schemata that serve as middlemen in an information-processing chain. As I put it in *The Psychology of Reading*:

> Perceptual learning is learning to extract the relevant information from the manifold available to stimulation, that is, the invariant information that specifies the permanent layout of the environment, the distinctive features of things that populate and furnish the environment, and invariants of events that enable us to predict outcomes and detect causes. (Gibson & Levin, 1985, p. 13)

What is learned surely does include invariants specifying permanent features of the layout and of events, but this research put a heavy emphasis on distinctive features of objects and verbal or written items, bolstered by decision trees for making same–different judgments of letters. All the methods we tried experimentally yielded satisfying contrasts like straight–curve. But there was no hint of research on learning about permanent features of the layout like a traversable surface or lack of it, or the significance of self-perpetrated events like shaking, thumping, or squeezing objects, activities that yield knowledge of properties of real objects in the world.

Perceptual development was characterized, to my mind, by three trends that still play a big role in my theorizing. They are increasing specificity of correspondence between perception and available information, optimization of attention (a manifestation of selectivity), and increasing economy of information pickup (a particularly impressive candidate in learning to read). I thought of reduction of uncertainty as a principle comparable in status to the old notion of reinforcement, providing a basis for a selection process. Discovery of structure or of invariants, for example, reduces uncertainty, provides economy, and is highly reinforcing.

A shortcoming of all the research I have been describing, both Neisser's and my own, was that it was pretty much confined to what James Gibson (1962) referred to as coded information—numbers, letters, and words. To quote Gibson:

> I suggest that the receptors of animals are adapted to register natural information, not coded information. Ordinary stimuli, then, are not signals and the senses do not work by the laws of information transmission that hold for human messages. Men, to be sure, developed a speech code, and later a written code, where the stimuli are arbitrarily related to their objects by convention, but the stimuli for which the senses evolved are related to the objects by laws of ecology, not by convention. (p. 231)

These shortcomings were soon to be redressed in Neisser's work, however. When he became Gibson's colleague at Cornell University, many friendly arguments ensued. Neisser's interest in cognition never flagged, particularly in issues of attention and memory, but in his 1976 book, *Cognition and Reality*, he had changed his views about the kind of information a cognitive psychologist should be concerned with. He shifted his research tasks from signal reception and locating targets like letters and words to tasks such as remembering events of importance in one's life and attending to players in events like games and people in social, communicative situations.

EVERYDAY COGNITION

The opening to *Cognition and Reality* offers a fine introduction to the second period I consider. "Cognition," Neisser said, "is the activity of knowing: the acquisition, organization, and use of knowledge. It is something that organisms do and in particular something that people do" (1976, p. 3). An early chapter was called Ordinary Seeing and it is concerned with perceiving objects, both moving and stationary, picking up the information that the environment offers. I cite two examples of research to illustrate the new direction. Actually, although it was new in the sense of the kind of activities used in the research, the topic of these studies was still attention, the same cognitive function that dominated the earlier research. I choose my examples from a chapter Neisser contributed to a volume prepared on the occasion of my own retirement (Pick, 1979).

An activity involved in a number of these new studies was a ballgame, the players filmed in action so that the ongoing play could be shown to viewers using a procedure referred to by Neisser as selective looking. Earlier experiments on selective listening had given rise to a so-called filter theory (Broadbent, 1958; reviewed in Neisser, 1967). Neisser now thought of perception as pickup of information guided by an anticipatory schema. If everyday perception is an active process of directed search, no filter of unwanted information should be necessary.

A film prepared for selective looking involved two different events superimposed on one another. One event was a ballgame in which three men passed a basketball around, whereas the other was a game involving hand-slapping. The subject had to watch for a single target, either the ball being thrown, or someone being slapped (Neisser & Becklen, 1975). In another film two ballgames were superimposed, the players on one team wearing white shirts, the other black. It turned out to be very easy to follow a game when there were simple distinguishing areas like black or white shirts. But a series of experiments made it clear that perceivers could also follow the designated event on the basis of kinetic information alone. No filtering of a specific feature was necessary; perception was inherently selective.

Is this ability to focus attention, selecting from a complex presentation of events the information that is useful and sought for, an accomplishment of only sophisticated perceivers? Might it even be characteristic of very young perceivers? Neisser and two of his students (Bahrick, Walker, & Neisser, 1981) pursued this question in an experiment with infants of 4 months. They presented the babies, like the adults, with superimposed visual events on film, but used a novel procedure invented by Spelke (1976) to check what the baby was perceiving.

Spelke's method involves simultaneous visual and auditory presentation of an event, a general characteristic of real-life events. We hear what we are seeing and vice versa in a unity that is obvious without our even being aware of it. Spelke presented 4-month-old babies with two filmed events presented side by side so that the baby could be observed looking toward one or the other. One was a film of an adult playing peek-a-boo and the other displayed sounding percussion instruments (a tambourine, drumstick and small drum, etc.). There was a soundtrack for each film, but for any given trial, only one was played. The question was whether the baby's attention tended to be focused on the event currently accompanied by the appropriate sound. The direction of the babies' gaze was recorded. These infants did indeed tend to look selectively at the film specified by the appropriate sound.

In the Bahrick et al. (1981) experiment, two films were actually superimposed while a single soundtrack was played. After several minutes of familiarization, the two films were pulled apart so that a subject's gaze direction could be observed. The exposure now was silent. If the baby had looked preferentially so as to be familiarized with the sound-specified event earlier, attention should now be directed toward the previously silent film, which would be relatively novel. The infant subjects did indeed tend to look at the previously silent, thus novel, film, showing that the ability to attend selectively was present even at 4 months.

How infants perceive natural events was at that time (and now) of great interest to me. I had been engaged in research on infants' visual differentiation of rigid from nonrigid (elastic) substances by means of optical information given over time; that is, the kind of motion displayed when the objects were handled, elastic motion versus rigid rotation (Gibson, Owsley, & Johnston, 1978; Gibson, Owsley, Walker, & Megaw-Nyce, 1979). Whether infants could discriminate and also generalize this contrast properly over different samples of movement was our way of putting the question. Five-month-old infants were habituated to an object undergoing rigid motion in three varying instances. After reaching a criterion of habituation (reduction of looking time), a fourth instance of rigid motion and a nonrigid elastic motion of the same object were presented for dishabituation. Would the babies remain habituated to the fourth rigid motion, hitherto unseen, but look longer (dishabituate) at the nonrigid elastic motion? The infants did, in fact, generalize their habituation to the fourth rigid motion, as distinguished from the nonrigid one. The generalization was maintained even over a change of shape of the object.

We were prompted to ask a new question by the Neisser-inspired experiments described previously. If babies perceived a unitary episode when watching and listening to some event, apparently obtaining corresponding meaningful information specified by both auditory and visual systems, would the same kind of intermodal relation hold for looking and touching? Elasticity and rigidity are properties of substance that are specified simultaneously by optical information obtained by visual regard and by haptic information when the object is manipulated. Do infants recognize the same property specified visually and haptically? These properties of substance carry information for important affordances for infants because they characterize what is chewable or not, what is comfortable to lie on, and what is compact enough to be seized readily. Perceiving affordances of objects and surfaces that have utility for developing action systems is of the utmost importance and very little research existed on the ontogeny of this accomplishment.

We contrived a procedure that provided habituation for the property in one mode, followed by a test for generalization and differentiation in the other mode (Gibson & Walker, 1984). We thought it likely that information obtained for important affordances in the world may be amodal, rather than modality specific, and that differentiation of a particular modality of information for a multiply specified object or event might even develop later than simple detection of what the event or object affords, like hardness or springiness. Several experiments were run in the dark with infants 1 year old who were given an object to handle (either hard or constructed of sponge rubber), and afterward tested with films of similar hard and elastic objects in motion. We compared the time spent looking at one or the other. Knowledge of the substantial property did appear to generalize intermodally. How to put the question earlier?

We decided to allow very young infants (4 weeks old) to mouth a small object that was either hard or spongy. The baby's mother held the object gently in its mouth for 60 seconds. Following this oral familiarization, a simultaneous visual presentation of two identically shaped objects was shown to the baby at an appropriate distance from its eyes, one object undergoing rigid motion, the other elastic. The babies looked significantly longer at the novel substance, suggesting that by 1 month, infants can detect information for substance that is accessible intermodally. They are attending to information for the affordances of objects, not to sensations from separate receptors. In this case, a motion-carried invariant specified the substantial property of rigidity or elasticity.

Neisser's statement that cognition is an activity, something that people do in the acquisition and use of knowledge, led to the strong hypothesis that we attend to things in the world, and that knowledge thus acquired about it is used in later cognitive operations such as problem solving. What is perceived, remembered, and used inductively in thinking is founded on everyday interactions between organisms and the objects and events that surround them. But where is the perceiver in all this? Is it possible that these interactions provide information about the world, and somehow at the same time about the organism doing the perceiving? James Gibson (1979) said, "One perceives the environment and coperceives oneself" (p. 127). Neisser, as always wending his way along a very cognitive route, came to a remarkably similar conclusion.

THE PERCEIVER AND THE SELF

The third period of Neisser's work has to do with the epitome if not the essence of knowing by just about anyone's definition. Know thyself! Is that not supposed to be the ultimate goal of knowledge? Is it not different from knowing that rocks are hard, that something is too far away to reach, or that animals and people move around and communicate? It is certainly different from making models of how static features of coded items are detected. And yet the path leads there. Even in his early days, Neisser worried about who is atop the functioning organism (as information processors do now); who determines where attention is directed? The Freudians and some psychologists (including Koffka) have long had an answer to this: the ego. Neisser had no use for Freud's ego, or for a homunculus, citing the old argument that a little man in the head leads to an infinite regression. But he had said, in his *Cognitive Psychology* (1967):

> If we do *not* postulate some agent who selects and uses stored information, we must think of every thought and every response as just the momentary result of an interacting system, governed essentially by laissez-faire economics. (p. 293)

(Surprisingly enough, that is the way some of us do think of it now.)

There was a way out, he thought then, provided by computer programmers in the form of the executive routine. The regress of control is not infinite: There is a "highest" or executive routine which is not used by anything else (1967, p. 296). "Although there is a real sense in which it 'uses' the rest of the program and the stored information, this creates no philosophical difficulties; It is not using itself" (1967, p. 296). There did remain a philosophical difficulty, however. The executive routine of the program had to be established by the programmer. The computer solution was not really a way out, any more than the standard information processing approach was.

Whether this difficulty was in part responsible for Neisser's later investment of interest and thought in the concept of the self, I am not sure. It may have been. I believe that venture was also prompted by his concern with everyday problems and ways of thinking. The notion of a self plays a role in our thinking from early childhood on. It manifests itself noisily in such well-known phrases as "that's mine" when 3-year-olds compete for a toy; again annoyingly in the young adolescents who are so preoccupied with themselves that their outlook on the world seems to include only what they want to do, where they want to go, and with whom; and exaggeratedly in the paranoid who fancies himself Napoleon or suspects that the rest of the world is after him, stealing from him, or spying on him. But our most persuasive evidence for the importance of a self and for the psychological necessity of a theory to explain its origins is the need to establish one securely in the life of any person.

What is more familiar than the struggle of a grown person to find a domain over which he or she has some control, to carve out a personal niche, a territory that is one's own? This is the theme of biographies and of many novels. For example, First Lady Eleanor Roosevelt was shy and lonely as a child, without control of her life in any way; she was later dominated by her strong-minded mother-in-law and scorned by many women for her lack of beauty and her attempts to compensate for it by working incessantly for social programs, women's rights, and personal equity. She spent her life struggling to find herself, describing it for years in a newspaper column called "My Day."

Is it any wonder that Neisser saw the self as the pinnacle of cognitive structure sorely needing a good psychological theory and a comprehensive description of how it comes about and how it functions? He took on the problem. In the first place, he concluded, the self is not a single thing. He wrote earlier on the "multiplicity of thought" (1976, p. 207). Next he proposed that there was a multiplicity of selves, all combining in the genesis of a human being. This view brought the concept into the realm of psychology and rendered it orderly enough for examination of its ontogeny and its multiple aspects without romanticizing the idea of treating it in the manner of a journalist dwelling on life crises.

Neisser's "Five Kinds of Self-Knowledge" (1988) provided a rational analysis of the concept from the standpoint of a cognitive psychologist. More than that, it encouraged a developmental approach to understanding the concept, beginning with an individual in an ecological setting, a real world. The five kinds of self-knowledge include an ecological self, an interpersonal self, a conceptual self, a temporally extended self, and a private self. So the self ranges from a physical being acting in an earthy environment through a social self, a person with multiple identities and responsibilities, a person with a life history full of remembered experiences, to some kind of inner feeling or awareness that is unique to one alone (making this last self hard to write about). Neisser held a conference on his first two kinds of self (Neisser, 1993), which I was privileged to attend. I am in favor of a self with its feet firmly on the ground, so I was pleased when I was invited to talk about the development of the ecological self.

Thinking about how a self might be defined in terms consistent with an ecological approach to perception was a challenging and interesting problem. If this self is actually perceived, there must be information for it that is available to the perceptual systems, and indeed there is. There is information for one's place in the layout; for the structure and size of one's body; for one's dynamic capabilities; and for one to control both one's own actions and environmental changes that they produce. James Gibson pointed out that perception has many sources of information for the self. One is simply a view of the world, the scene before one's eyes carved out by the shape of one's head, occluding much of the surroundings. As humans, we can turn our heads and bodies to see what was occluded, but this view that you see is very personal.

It turns out that we know quite a lot about the development of such knowledge, and that it begins quite early in infancy. I have been particularly interested in the development of control and the consequent knowledge of agency. Babies discover quite early that they are not robots or chessmen to be moved around (although not in those words), that they effect things themselves, and elicit reactions from others. I wrote an essay about this aspect of the self, the development of agency, called "Are we Automata" (E. J. Gibson, 1995). More important, this excursion into thinking about a very cognitive concept inspired me to do a little philosophizing about the qualities that might uniquely distinguish human behavior, agency being one of them.

I was given further encouragement to reflect on such a nonexperimental, comprehensive topic by an opportunity to address the American Psychological Society on some question that might be of interest to a very large and rather diverse audience, one with no unanimity as to where psychology should be going. Should we all become neurologists? (My answer to this is an emphatic no. The psychology that neurophysiologists take for granted is hopelessly outmoded.) Should we devote ourselves to practical questions, like the best ways to run organizations? Or turn clinician? I called my talk "Has Psychology a Future?"

What should psychology be about? When I was a graduate student, it was about either psychophysics or conditioning in the major graduate schools. As fashions shifted to cognitive psychology, a lot of it was about memory, and now cognitive neuroscience seems to lead the trend. But are there not some broader concepts that will serve better to define what characterizes the subject matter of psychology? That gets to the heart of it and escapes the narrowness of so much of what gets published in our ever more-specialized journals? That we should redirect our attention to and teach our students about?

I threw out some of the traps that psychology has often been caught in—dualism, reductionism, and the nature–nurture dichotomy. I proposed that there are five Hallmarks of Human Behavior (Gibson, 1994) that uniquely distinguish psychology's subject matters so that we should redirect our attention to them and study their development; and that we should study them as they are manifested in behavior (both action and cognition), and leave their neurological underpinnings to the neurologists. The five are:

Agency (the self in control)

Prospectivity (the forward-looking character of behavior)

Flexibility (the transfer of means)

Cognitive creativity (including the multiplication of means of communicating, search for patterns, and moral concerns)

Retrospectivity (the backward-looking character of behavior)

It is obvious that my inclusion of the first of these, agency, is pretty directly attributable to Neisserian influence. What may not be is the last, retrospectivity. I showed him my list when there were only the first four hallmarks. He said, "That's fine, but shouldn't you include retrospectivity too?" On further consideration, I did.

NOW WHERE? A LAST WORD

I should not imply that the impact of Neisser's thoughts on mine has always brought sweet agreement. Often, arguments have resulted. I point out (for fun) the last remarks of his that I might pick a quarrel with. In a recent paper, he offered a new approach to cognitive theory (Neisser, 1994). He suggested that three modules underlie cognition, three basic perceptual systems: (a) direct perception/action; (b) interpersonal perception/reactivity; and (c) recognition/representation.

Now, I not only think the behavior and phenomena he separates into these modules are interactive in a dynamic self-organizing system, I abhor the term module. It was thrust at us by Fodor, who thought the human brain was made up of innately specified, special-purpose modules. He said, "I'm inclined to doubt that there is such a thing as cognitive development in the sense that developmental cognitive psychologists have in mind" (Fodor, 1985, p. 35). Neisser would probably not go along with all of this, but why talk about modules at all?

The notion of distinct special-purpose modules, particularly innately specified ones, goes directly against my hallmark of flexibility. Human behavior is flexible. We can use action systems in flexible ways, even trade one set of acts or strategies for another if needed; we can profit from experiences and apply our wisdom to new and different situations. We do not need to disregard flexibility by dividing behavior into specialized modules. We need to study it, how it comes about, and why sometimes a routine does become specialized and look modular. The worst possible mistake, I think, is to assume modularity and then attribute it to inborn mechanisms in the nervous system. That gets rid of all chance of studying cognitive development. (Makes life easy for Fodor, of course.)

I want psychologists to perform the valuable service of studying their own field as I have defined it and to find out how these wonderful attributes of agency, prospectivity, flexibility, and so on develop and function. There are, I think, principles of behavior and cognition in their own right. It is the psychologist's task to find them and help us understand them. Belittling them by deserting them for reductionist theories, or shutting our eyes to the manifold factors that interact dynamically to organize them so intricately and so wonderfully adaptively is copping out. Ulric Neisser, for one, would never do that, and I am waiting for the next wave of his theorizing.

REFERENCES

Bahrick, L. E., Walker, A. S., & Neisser, U. (1981). Selective looking by infants. *Cognitive Psychology, 13*, 377–390.

Broadbent, D. E. (1958). *Perception and communication.* New York: Pergamon.

Feigenbaum, E. A. (1963). The simulation of verbal learning behavior. In E. A. Feigenbaum & J. Feldman (Eds.), *Computers and thought.* New York: McGraw-Hill.

Fodor, J. A. (1985). Precis of the modularity of mind. *Behavioral and Brain Sciences, 8*, 1–46.

Garner, W. R. (1962). *Uncertainty and structure as psychological concepts.* New York: Wiley.

Gibson, E. J. (1969). *Principles of perceptual learning and development.* New York: Appleton-Century-Crofts.

Gibson, E. J. (1994). Has psychology a future? *Psychological Science, 5*, 69–76.

Gibson, E. J. (1995). Are we automata? In P. Rochat (Ed.), *The self in infant* (pp. 3–15). Amsterdam: Elsevier.

Gibson, E. J., & Levin, H. (1985). *The psychology of reading.* Cambridge, MA: MIT Press.

Gibson, E. J., Owsley, C. J., & Johnston, J. (1978). Perception of invariants by five-month-old infants: Differentiation of two types of motion. *Developmental Psychology, 14*, 407–415.

Gibson, E. J., Owsley, C. J., Walker, A. S., & Megaw-Nyce, J. (1979). Development of the perception of invariants: Substance and shape. *Perception, 8*, 609–619.

Gibson, E. J., Shapiro, F., & Yonas, A. (1991). Confusion matrices for graphic patterns obtained with a latency measure. In E. J. Gibson (Ed.), *An odyssey in learning and perception* (pp. 421–435). Cambridge, MA: MIT Press.

Gibson, E. J., & Walker, A. (1984). Development of knowledge of visual-tactual affordances of substance. *Child Development, 55*, 453–460.

Gibson, E. J., & Yonas, A. S. (1966a). A developmental study of the effects of visual and auditory interference on a visual scanning task. *Psychonomic Science, 5*, 163–164.

Gibson, E. J., & Yonas, A. S. (1966b). A developmental study of visual search behavior. *Perception and Psychophysics, 1*, 161–171.

Gibson, J. J. (1962). The survival value of sensory perception. *Biological Prototypes and Synthetic Systems, 1*, 230–232.

Gibson, J. J. (1979). *The ecological approach to visual perception.* Boston: Houghton Mifflin.

Miller, G. A. (1953). What is information measurement? *American Psychologist, 8*, 3–11.

Neisser, U. (1964). Visual search. *Scientific American, 210*, 94–101.

Neisser, U. (1967). *Cognitive psychology.* New York: Appleton-Century-Crofts.

Neisser, U. (1976). *Cognition and reality.* San Francisco: Freeman.

Neisser, U. (1988). Five kinds of self-knowledge. *Philosophical Psychology, 1*, 35–59.

Neisser, U. (1993). *The perceived self.* New York: Cambridge University Press.

Neisser, U. (1994). Multiple systems: A new approach to cognitive theory. *Emory Cognition Project: Report #27*, Emory University, Atlanta, GA.

Neisser, U., & Becklen, R. (1975). Selective looking: Attending to visually specified events. *Cognitive Psychology, 7*, 490–494.

Neisser, U., Novick, R., & Lazar, R. (1963). Searching for ten targets simultaneously. *Perceptual and Motor Skills, 17*, 955–961.

Pick, A. D. (Ed.). (1979). *Perception and its development*. Hillsdale, NJ: Lawrence Erlbaum Associates.

Spelke, E. S. (1976). Infants' intermodal perception of events. *Cognitive Psychology, 8*, 553–560.

Chapter 6

Unity and Diversity in Knowledge

Elizabeth Spelke
Massachusetts Institue of Technology

At the center of the extraordinary work that Ulric Neisser has so far accomplished is, I believe, a creative tension. On one hand, Neisser is a synthesizer and a unifier, who aims to forge an integrated art and science of cognition. Cognition, as Neisser studies it, cannot be a collection of isolated facts and curiosities; it must be an interconnected system of general principles and common themes. These themes should allow one to see connections between processes as diverse as reaching for objects, identifying faces or words, charting courses through the layout, reminiscing about one's childhood, dreaming, imagining, and arriving at solutions to problems. Neisser's first great step toward this unification—distilled in his book *Cognitive Psychology* (1967)—inaugurated a field. His second step— *Cognition and Reality* (1976), a work at the center of my own intellectual foundations—is an agenda-setting effort to orient the study of human knowledge toward the meaningful problems that perceivers, thinkers, and actors encounter.

On the other hand, the cognitive psychology that Neisser portrayed in those books, and has pursued with ever increasing depth and intensity, focuses on particular cognitive problems and phenomena in all their complexity. Neisser's explorations of different regions of the cognitive landscape—pattern recognition, layout perception, attention, imagery, memory, concepts, the self—are models of how to conduct meticulous, detailed, ecologically oriented studies of rich and complex cognitive phenomena. One cannot hope to understand the mind, Neisser urges, by searching, with simplified laboratory tasks, for the universal building blocks of cognition. Instead, one must study real thinkers, perceivers, and actors facing real problems in their natural context. Neisser's cognitive psychology is a demanding enterprise, for it requires both rigorous attention to the details of particular cognitive phenomena and a consistent search for more general themes and principles that connect these phenomena to broader concerns. Behind his work is the hope that those who study any meaningful aspect of human cognition in depth will shed light on features of human cognition as a whole.

This enterprise faces a problem, however, because the mind seems to have been designed to thwart the efforts of unifiers. Different cognitive achievements appear to result from collections of special-purpose systems, structured in accord with different principles. Although individual cognitive systems must communicate with one another to some degree—a system would be useless if it did not—their interactions appear to be sharply restricted and to fall far short of the ideal of a unitary mind.

Consider, for example, the study of perception. If anything appears to be clear to human consciousness, it is the unity of our perceptual experience: We experience one environment, not diverse collections of surface features, colors, motions, and the like. When one looks more closely, however, this coherence dissolves. As a graduate student in the 1970s, I learned from Neisser about many of the contradictions lurking in our apparently unitary experience of the perceivable world: how perceivers who have stared at a waterfall come to see the surrounding rocks both as moving upward and as maintaining constant positions, or how we see the horizon moon as both closer and farther away than the zenith moon. More recently, cognitive neuropsychologists and other students of perception and action have found further contradictions. For example, Goodale and Milner (1992) describe a brain-injured patient who consistently judges different three-dimensional forms to be indistinguishable in shape and yet shows distinctive and adaptive patterns of reaching for each form. Under certain conditions, moreover, normal subjects judge one disc to be bigger than a second and yet reach for it by opening their hand to a lesser extent (Goodale, 1995). How can the first disc be perceived both as bigger and as smaller than the second disc at one and the same time? Where is the unitary knower who puts these conflicting impressions together?

Contrary to the suggestions of Fodor (1983) and others, the search for the unitary mind seems no more promising when one turns from perception and action to memory and thought. The study of memory has revealed myriad dissociations between what people do and do not remember in different task contexts (e.g., Schacter & Tulving, 1994). For the last two decades, moreover, students of reasoning have focused primarily on the many and varied ways in which human thinkers contradict themselves (e.g.,

Tversky & Kahneman, 1974). If the unity of human thought and knowledge is an illusion, however, is the project of all psychology's unifiers of all persuasions—from Descartes to Locke, Kant to Helmholtz, Kohler to Gibson and Neisser—doomed to fail? Is cognitive psychology just a collection of loosely related facts and phenomena? Should the field of cognitive psychology be replaced entirely by fields like vision and language or even narrower enterprises? Or do studies of different parts of cognition indeed connect in ways that scientists of Neisser's breadth and vision can discover?

Because my own breadth and vision are considerably more limited than Neisser's, I can offer no original, unifying principles for this field. I believe, however, that recent research on cognitive development supports two suggestions that are relevant to the search for such principles. First, studies of young children suggest that the diversity of human cognitive systems has deep roots. Modularity is not an artifact of the growth of habits and skills; rather, domain- and task-specific cognitive systems are present and functional very early in development. Understanding human cognition and its development therefore will require detailed study of all the cognitive systems in the child's repertoire. As Neisser has taught, one cannot devise simplified model tasks and hope to reveal the universal, content-free building blocks of human knowledge.

The second suggestion nevertheless counters the first. Studies of cognitive development suggest that great philosophers and psychologists are not the only creatures with a passion to find unity in the human mind; this passion is shared by the young child. Although children are born with a collection of poorly coordinated, special-purpose perceptual and cognitive systems, they also are born with a propensity to connect these systems and achieve a more comprehensive understanding. Children will not completely succeed at unifying their knowledge: If they did, they would not grow into adults who see the horizon moon as both closer and farther away and the rocks by the waterfall as both stationary and moving. Children's efforts at integration nevertheless give rise to some stunning partial successes, in which distinct systems of knowledge come together to produce new and more effective conceptions. Because of these successes, cognitive psychologists will not achieve a complete understanding of the mind by investigating its modular systems in isolation. We need to appreciate both the unique properties of individual cognitive systems and the common properties across systems that allow children, and adults, to forge connections between them. That is, we all need the kind of vision that Neisser offers.

In the rest of this chapter, I sketch three areas of cognitive development that may reveal emerging connections between children's separate systems of knowledge. First I discuss some developmental changes in infants' representations of objects. Then I turn to one developmental change in children's representations of space. Finally, I speculate about some of the ways in which older children and adolescents may change their understanding of number and geometry over the course of mathematics instruction. In each case, my brief discussion raises many more questions than it answers. My goal is to suggest that Neisser's kind of cognitive psychology—a science combining rigorous, detailed, ecologically oriented studies of particular cognitive processes with a broad and unifying vision—is what is needed to address these questions and approach an understanding of the nature and development of human knowledge.

OBJECTS

My own studies of object perception in infancy began with a question I first considered as a student of Neisser and Eleanor Gibson: Do infants perceive the unity of objects: their internal connectedness, external boundaries, and continuity over space and time? I assumed that the answer to this question would be either "yes" or "no," and that the system by which young children perceive objects would itself have unity and coherence. But research over the last decades casts considerable doubt on this assumption: Infants may have three distinct systems of object representation, each initially uncoordinated with the others.

The first hints of multiple object representations came to me through the dissertation research of Schwartz (1982). Earlier investigations had suggested that young infants perceive the connectedness of a partly occluded, inanimate object by detecting the common motion of its visible surfaces but not by detecting features of those surfaces such as their texture, smoothness, or symmetry (see Kellman, 1993). Schwartz wondered whether infants would use static, configurational properties of an object to perceive the object's unity if the object were more familiar and ecologically significant: a human face. Following Kellman's method, infants were familiarized with a photograph of a center-occluded face and then their looking time to nonoccluded, complete and fragmented faces was compared to that of infants in a baseline group, who viewed the same test displays after a different occlusion display. The study was based on the assumption that infants would look less and less at a display as it became more familiar. If the infants in the experimental condition had perceived a complete face in the occlusion display, therefore, they should show reduced levels of looking at the complete, visible face, relative to infants in the baseline condition.

As in studies with stationary, center-occluded inanimate objects (e.g., Kellman & Spelke, 1983), the 4-month-old infants in the experimental and baseline conditions of Schwartz's study showed the same preferences between the complete and fragmented face displays, suggesting that those who had been presented with the center-occluded face had not perceived a connected object. Although 5-month-old infants did appear to perceive the face's unity, the findings at 4 months puzzled me for two reasons. First, many studies had already shown that much younger infants perceive faces as familiar and meaningful objects (see Johnson & Morton, 1991, for review). Second, the observers in Schwartz's study reported high levels of smiling at the occluded face by all the infants, including the youngest ones (Schwartz, 1982). These reports suggest that the center-occluded face was perceived as a meaningful social object, even by the youngest infants. How could infants recognize the face behind the occluder and yet fail to perceive its connectedness? Was the representational system subserving face recognition failing to communicate with the system that analyzed surface arrangements and motions so as to perceive object unity?

I was inclined to dismiss these questions until Xu and Carey (1994, 1996) showed that the phenomenon is quite general. They focused on infants' perception of the boundaries of two simultaneously visible objects that are adjacent, and infants' perception of the distinctness of two successively visible objects that move into view from behind a common occluder. In some of their studies, the two objects presented to infants were a toy animal and a toy vehicle: objects that infants appear to categorize appropriately by 7 months (Mandler & McDonough, 1993). At 10 months, however, the infants in Xu and Carey's experiments failed to use information for this categorical distinction to perceive a toy duck sitting on a toy car as two distinct objects, or to perceive a toy elephant that appeared from behind an occluder as a different object from a toy truck that previously disappeared behind the occluder. Infants appear to represent the unity, boundaries, and persisting identity of objects by detecting motion and other spatio-temporal information (see Spelke & Van de Walle, 1993; Xu & Carey, 1996), and they appear to represent objects as members of meaningful categories by detecting (little understood) static featural information (see Mandler & McDonough, 1993; Van de Walle & Hoerger, 1996). These two representations, however, do not appear to be coordinated.

Similar conclusions are suggested by studies investigating infants' extrapolations of object motion. In preferential looking experiments, infants who view objects without acting on them appear to extrapolate object motion on paths that are spatio-temporally continuous. If an object moves behind an occluder, for example, infants look consistently longer if events occur that suggest the object has jumped discontinuously from one place to another or has passed through another object in its way (see Baillargeon, 1993). On the assumption that longer looking is a reaction to novel or surprising events, these looking patterns suggest that infants inferred that the object would continue to move on a connected and unobstructed path. In contrast, infants in preferential looking experiments appear quite insensitive to effects of inertia on object motion: If an object moves in a straight line behind an occluder, infants do not look longer at events in which the object reappears along a different line (Spelke, Katz, Purcell, Ehrlich, & Breinlinger, 1994) or after a time interval that is inappropriate to its visible speed of motion (Spelke, Kestenbaum, Simons, & Wein, 1995). Preferential looking experiments therefore suggest that young infants represent the continuity but not the inertia of object motion.

Infants' extrapolations of object motion also have been studied by means of reaching experiments, in which infants' aiming for an object is measured as the object moves into reaching space. Research by Hofsten (1983) provides evidence that infants reach predictively for moving objects, aiming not for the position at which a moving object is currently seen but for a position that it will occupy in the future, when their reach is complete. Predictive reaching, however, is not guided by the knowledge of object motion revealed by preferential looking studies. First, predictive reaching is sensitive to inertia: Presented with an object in linear motion at a constant speed, infants aim and time their reaches so as to intercept the object at a place and time it would reach if it continued moving at constant speed (Hofsten, Vishton, Spelke, Feng, & Rosander, in press; Vishton, Spelke, Hofsten, Feng, & Rosander, 1996). Second, predictive reaching does not appear to be sensitive to the continuity of object motion over occlusion: Infants who have begun to aim for a moving object fail to sustain their reach if the object moves briefly behind an occluder (Hofsten, Feng, Vishton, & Spelke, 1994; Munakata, Jonsson, Spelke, & Hofsten, 1996). The double dissociation between the properties of object motion guiding infants' extrapolations in preferential looking and reaching experiments suggests that separate representations guide infants' extrapolations in these two contexts. Analyses of young infants' failures to search for hidden objects in Piagetian object permanence tasks further support the suggestion that different representations guide object perception versus object-directed action (see Bertenthal, 1996).[1]

In brief, a growing body of research suggests that distinct representations of objects underlie infants' perception of object unity and boundaries, infants' feature-based categorization of objects into meaningful groups, and infants' object-directed reaching and manipulation. If this suggestion is correct, then important developmental changes would seem to occur in early childhood. Between 10 and 12 months, infants begin to use what they know about the features of objects in different categories to inform their perception of object connectedness, boundaries, and persistence over occlusion (Xu & Carey, 1994, 1996). Between 12 and 18 months, infants

---

[1]It remains possible, nevertheless, that a single system of representation captures the spatiotemporal properties of objects and guides both looking and reaching. See Munakata et al. (1996) and Spelke (in press) for discussion.

begin to use what they know about the continuity of object motion to inform their search for objects that have moved from view (Piaget, 1954). The unification of infants' multiple object representations is not complete, for dissociations between the representations guiding reaching, feature-based categorization, and perception of object unity can be found in older children and adults (see, e.g., Kahneman & Treisman, 1984; Krist, Fieberg, & Wilkening, 1993; Piaget, 1976). Nevertheless, the young infant's piecemeal and fragmentary knowledge about objects does become considerably more unified over the course of development. Understanding the processes that create this unity from the diverse representations constructed by infants is a central task for the next generation of developmental studies.

SPACE

In the field of spatial representation, it is well established that humans and other animals form multiple representations of the environmental layout (see Gallistel, 1990; McNaughton, Kneirim, & Wilson, 1994). Spatial representations differ with respect to the coordinate system in which environmental locations are encoded: Representations in various body-centered and environment-centered coordinates guide different actions such as moving the eyes, reaching, or navigating through the layout. Spatial representations also differ with respect to the kinds of information that they incorporate and the kinds of behavior that they support. For example, laboratory rats relocate objects by encoding and recognizing object locations in relation to a configuration of surrounding landmarks (e.g., Suzuki, Augerinos, & Black, 1980). In contrast, rats reestablish their own position when they are disoriented by encoding and recognizing only the large-scale shape of the terrain, independently of the landmarks that guide their search for objects (Cheng, 1986). For rats, separate, modular representations of the environment appear to guide the localization of objects versus the self (see Gallistel, 1990, for discussion).

Recent research by Hermer-Vazquez suggests that these two task-specific, modular systems exist in 1.5- to 2-year-old children (Hermer & Spelke, 1996). Hermer-Vazquez tested children's reorientation and object localization in the same situation Cheng used with rats, in which both the large-scale shape of the environment and its local landmarks in principle could serve to solve either task. For example, the children in an object localization experiment were introduced into a rectangular room with two boxes of distinctive colors, textures, and patterns in adjacent corners. A favorite toy was hidden in one of the boxes, the child's eyes were covered, and the two boxes were moved to the opposite side of the room, such that their lateral positions were reversed (i.e., the box that previously stood on the left side of a short wall now stood on the right side of a short wall). When children were allowed to open their eyes and search for the toy, they searched the box with the appropriate color, texture, and pattern, in the novel location in the rectangular room. In other words, children's search for the object in the movable container was guided by the featural properties of the container and not by the large-scale geometry of the room.

In a parallel reorientation experiment, children were introduced into the same environment, a toy was hidden as in the first experiment, and then the children's eyes were covered and they were disoriented while the boxes were moved. Based on studies of rats, Hermer-Vazquez reasoned that when the toy was first hidden, all the children would encode the object's location in a large-scale geocentric framework. When children were disoriented and encouraged to find the toy, therefore, their first task would be to reorient themselves in that same framework, and their patterns of search for the object would cast light on this reorientation process. Like rats in Cheng's (1986) studies, children searched for the toy in the box that stood in the correct geometric relation to the room, despite the fact that this box differed in shape, color, and texture from the box in which the object was hidden (Hermer & Spelke, 1996)! This search pattern provides evidence that children reoriented themselves in accord with the shape of the environment (the lengths of the walls and the locations of the boxes) and not in accord with the distinctive properties of the container that hid the object. Children's contrasting search patterns in these two studies and others (see Hermer & Spelke, 1996) provide evidence that separate representations of the environment guide children's object localization and reorientation.

If young children form multiple, task-specific spatial representations, however, older children and adults appear to connect these representations. Abilities to construct integrated representations of the environment are revealed in adults' and children's use of spatial language and maps: Older children can follow charts and verbal directions in order both to find objects (as in a treasure hunt) and to orient themselves (as in a piñata game). Evidence for developing abilities to construct unitary representations of the environment also comes from Hermer-Vazquez's tasks. In one series of experiments, adults and children of various ages watched the hiding of a toy in a rectangular room with one blue wall, were disoriented, and then were encouraged to find the toy. Young children searched with equal frequency at the correct corner and at the opposite corner with the same geometrical configuration, ignoring the fact that only the correct corner had the appropriate coloring. In contrast, adults and the oldest children tested—6- to 7-year-olds—confined their search to the single corner with appropriate geometric and nongeometric properties (Hermer & Spelke, 1996). This finding provides evidence that disoriented adults reliably find hidden objects by conjoining information about the shape of the layout with information about nongeometric features of objects and surfaces in the layout. The ability to reorient in accord with unified representations of the environment is not as robust in Hermer-Vazquez's studies as is the ability to reorient in accord with modular, geometric representations: Adults who are disoriented while engaging in an attention-demanding verbal task revert to the young child's pattern of performance, reorienting themselves in accord with the shape but not the color of the environment (Hermer-Vazquez, 1997). Nevertheless, the contrast between the performance of young children and that of adults who are not distracted suggests that cognitive development brings some degree of unity to children's diverse representations of the environment. As in the case of object representation, the developmental processes that produce this integration are not understood.

NUMBER AND GEOMETRY

For my last example of developmental processes that bring unity to initially distinct systems of representation, I turn to higher reaches of human cognition: mathematical knowledge that probably is unique to humans and that typically develops as children attend school.

Research by Gelman and other investigators provides a wealth of evidence that before children begin formal study of mathematics, they have developed a rich set of intuitive conceptions of number and geometry. Young children are able to count and perform simple arithmetic and they have intuitions about the transformations of sets that do and do not change number (Gelman & Gallistel, 1978; Hughes, 1986). Children also have geometrical intuitions about points and lines. Starting at about age 6, one can engage children in conversation about "lines that never turn, that are so thin that they have no thickness, and that go on and on without stopping," and about "points that are so small they have no thickness." Such children will report spontaneously, with near-unanimity, that two straight lines cross at most once, that exactly one line can join any two points, and that exactly one line can pass through a point not on a second line without intersecting that line: a variant of Euclid's fifth ("parallel") postulate (Silberstein & Spelke, 1995).

Nevertheless, there are interesting limits to young children's arithmetical and geometrical understanding. For example, preschool children's notion of number appears to be restricted to the counting numbers and excludes fractions (Gelman, 1991). In addition, 6-year-old children's intuitions about points and lines break down when lines become sufficiently small and points sufficiently dense. Although most children judge that a line segment of visible extent can be cut into two smaller segments and that this process can continue even when the segments are too small to see, they report that successive divisions of the line cannot continue indefinitely: Eventually, cutting the tiniest line segment will result in two indivisible points (Piaget, Inhelder, & Szeminska, 1960; Silberstein & Spelke, 1995).

How do children overcome these limits and arrive at new intuitions about number and geometry, such as the intuitions that there are numbers between any two counting numbers and that any line segment can be divided into smaller segments? In part, these advances appear to depend on children's developing propensity to unify their numerical and geometrical knowledge (Carey & Spelke, 1994). Gelman's (1991) studies of children's developing use of geometrical models, such as the number line, reveal how children come to use intuitions about points and lines to develop intuitions about fractions. For example, many children appear to arrive at the intuition that there are numbers between any two whole numbers by drawing on the intuition that there are points between the demarcated points on a number line. Carey's (1991) studies of children's developing understanding of repeated division of numbers suggests how older children may come to use the early-developing intuition that any whole number can be doubled to arrive at the intuition that any fraction can be halved, and then come to use this new intuition about fractions to extend their intuitions about matter and space. In particular, children may arrive at the understanding that any line segment can be divided in half by drawing on their understanding that any fraction can be so divided. For adults, this unification of number and geometry may never be complete, for we continue to be surprised by its implications (for example, that there are as many numbers between 1 and 2 as there are between 1 and 1000, or that there is no single point next to the point at the end of a line segment). Nevertheless, the student who has come to see a fraction as a point on a line, or the length of a line segment as a fraction, has brought a significant measure of coherence to what were separate systems of knowledge, allowing each system to be extended beyond its initial bounds.

AND COGNITIVE PSYCHOLOGY?

Too briefly and sketchily, I have suggested that human intelligence is caught in a creative tension. On one hand, it is the product of multiple domain-specific, task-specific, modular systems. On the other hand, it is propelled forward by an effort to reconcile the diverse views of the world that different cognitive systems provide. I believe this effort can be seen in the infant who brings together featural and spatio-temporal descriptions of objects, the child who brings together geometric and nongeometric representations of the environment, and the adolescent who brings her emerging understanding of fractions to bear on her recalcitrant intuitions about points and lines. This effort also may be seen in physicists working to build a unitary theory of universe, or in biologists and cognitive scientists seeking mutually consistent theories of brain and mind.

If this creative tension animates human cognition, then perhaps it is not surprising to find it reflected in this generation's most insightful cognitive psychologist. Ulric Neisser's work shows us that cognitive psychology is a difficult enterprise, for we must both do justice to the richness and diversity of human cognitive achievements and relate one achievement to another to find their common ground. His work also shows us how essential both these tasks are, if cognitive psychology is to succeed. Given the diversity of human cognitive capacities, psychologists have no choice but to study each capacity in depth, in its natural context and in all its complexity. Given humans' persistent effort after unity, however, psychologists can never hope to understand any one cognitive capacity fully unless we understand them all. How to forge the right paths between diversity and unity, between the richness of the particular and the power of the general, is a great problem for all cognitive psychologists. Luckily, Neisser has blazed a trail.

REFERENCES

Baillargeon, R. (1993). The object concept revisited: New directions in the investigation of infants' physical knowledge. In C. E. Granrud (Ed.), *Visual perception and cognition in infancy* (pp. 265–316). Hillsdale, NJ: Lawrence Erlbaum Associates.

Bertenthal, B. I. (1996). Origins and early development of perception, action, and representation. *Annual Review of Psychology, 47,* 431–459.

Carey, S. (1991). Knowledge acquisition: Enrichment or conceptual change? In S. Carey & R. Gelman (Eds.), *Epigenesis of mind: Essays on biology and cognition* (pp. 257–291). Hillsdale, NJ: Lawrence Erlbaum Associates.

Carey, S., & Spelke, E. S. (1994). Domain-specific knowledge and conceptual change. In L. A. Hirschfeld & S. A. Gelman (Eds.), *Mapping the mind: Domain specificity in cognition and culture* (pp. 169–200). Cambridge, England: Cambridge University Press.

Cheng, K. (1986). A purely geometric module in the rat's spatial representation. *Cognition, 23,* 149–178.

Fodor, J. A. (1983). *The modularity of mind.* Cambridge, MA: Bradford/MIT Press.

Gallistel, C. R. (1990). *The organization of learning.* Cambridge, MA: Bradford/MIT Press.

Gelman, R. (1991). Epigenetic foundations of knowledge structures: Initial and transcendent constructions. In S. Carey & R. Gelman (Eds.), *The epigenesis of mind: Essays on biology and cognition* (pp. 293–322). Hillsdale, NJ: Lawrence Erlbaum Associates.

Gelman, R., & Gallistel, C. R. (1978). *The child's understanding of number.* Cambridge, MA: Harvard University Press.

Goodale, M. A. (1995). The cortical organization of visual perception and visuomotor control. In S. M. Kosslyn & D. N. Osherson (Eds.), *Visual cognition. An invitation to cognitive science,* Vol. 2. Cambridge, MA: MIT Press.

Goodale, M. A., & Milner, D. A. (1992). Separate visual pathways for perception and action. *Trends in Neuroscience, 15,* 20–25.

Hermer, L., & Spelke, E. S. (1996). Modularity and development: The case of spatial reorientation. *Cognition, 61,* 195–232.

Hermer-Vazquez, L. (1997). *Cognitive flexibility as it emerges over evolution and development: The case of human spatial reorientation.* Unpublished doctoral dissertation, Cornell University.

Hofsten, C. von. (1983). Catching skills in infancy. *Journal of Experimental Psychology: Human Perception and Performance, 9,* 75–85.

Hofsten, C. von, Feng, Q., Vishton, P., & Spelke, E. S. (1994, June). *Predictive reaching and head turning for partly occluded objects.* Poster presented at the International Conference on Infant Studies, Paris.

Hofsten, C. von, Vishton, P., Spelke, E. S., Feng, Q., & Rosander, K. (in press). *Predictive action in infancy: Tracking and reaching for moving objects. Cognition.*

Hughes, M. (1986). *Children and number: Difficulties in learning mathematics.* Oxford, England: Blackwell.

Johnson, M. H., & Morton, J. (1991). *Biology and cognitive development: The case of face recognition.* Oxford, England: Blackwell.

Kahneman, D., & Treisman, A. (1984). Changing views of attention and automaticity. In R. Parasuraman & D. A. Davies (Eds.), *Varieties of attention.* New York: Academic Press.

Kellman, P. J. (1993). Kinematic foundations of infant visual perception. In C. E. Granrud (Ed.), *Visual perception and cognition in infancy* (pp. 121–174). Hillsdale, NJ: Lawrence Erlbaum Associates.

Krist, H., Fieberg, E. L., & Wilkening, F. (1993). Intuitive physics in action and judgment: The development of knowledge about projectile motion. *Journal of Experimental Psychology: Learning, Memory, and Cognition, 19,* 952–966.

Mandler, J. M., & McDonough, L. (1993). Concept formation in infancy. *Cognitive Development, 8,* 291–318.

McNaughton, B. L., Knierim, J. J., & Wilson, M. A. (1994). Vector encoding and the vestibular foundations of spatial cognition: Neurophysiological and computational mechanisms. In M. S. Gazzaniga (Ed.), *The cognitive neurosciences* (pp. 585–596). Cambridge, MA: Bradford/MIT Press.

Munakata, Y., Jonsson, B., Spelke, E. S., & Hofsten, C. von (1996, April). *When it helps to occlude and obscure: 6-month-olds' predictive tracking of moving toys.* Poster presented at the International Conference on Infant Studies, Providence, RI.

Neisser, U. (1967). *Cognitive psychology.* New York: Appleton-Century-Crofts.

Neisser, U. (1976). *Cognition and reality.* San Francisco, CA: W. H. Freeman & Co.

Piaget, J. (1954). *The construction of reality in the child.* New York: Basic Books.

Piaget, J. (1976). *The grasp of consciousness.* Cambridge, MA: Harvard University Press.

Piaget, J., Inhelder, B., & Szeminska, A. (1960). *The child's conception of geometry.* New York: Basic Books.

Schachter, D. L., & Tulving, E. (1994). *Memory systems 1994.* Cambridge, MA: MIT Press.

Schwartz, K. (1982). *Perceptual knowledge of the human face in infancy.* Unpublished doctoral dissertation, University of Pennsylvania, Philadelphia.

Silberstein, C. S., & Spelke, E. S. (1995, April). *Explicit vs. implicit processes in spatial cognition.* Poster presented at the Society for Research in Child Development, Indianapolis, IN.

Spelke, E. S. (in press). Nativism, empiricism, and the origins of knowledge. *Infant Behavior and Development.*

Spelke, E. S., Katz, G., Purcell, S. E., Ehrlich, S. M., & Breinlinger, K. (1994). Early knowledge of object motion: Continuity and inertia. *Cognition, 51,* 131–176.

Spelke, E. S., Kestenbaum, R., Simons, D., & Wein, D. (1995). Spatio-temporal continuity, smoothness of motion, and object identity in infancy. *The British Journal of Developmental Psychology, 13,* 113–142.

Spelke, E. S., & Van de Walle, G. (1993). Perceiving and reasoning about objects: Insights from infants. In N. Eilan, W. Brewer, & R. McCarthy (Eds.), *Spatial representation* (pp. 132–161). New York: Basil Blackwell.

Suzuki, S., Augerinos, G., & Black, A. H. (1980). Stimulus control of spatial behavior on the eight-arm maze in rats. *Learning and Motivation, 11*, 1–18.

Tversky, A., & Kahneman, D. (1974). Judgment under uncertainty: Heuristics and biases. *Science, 185*, 1124–1131.

Van de Walle, G. A., & Hoerger, M. (1996, April). *The perceptual foundations of categorization in infancy.* Poster presented at the International Conference on Infant Studies, Providence, RI.

Vishton, P. M., Spelke, E. S., Hofsten, C. von, Feng, Q., & Rosander, K. (1996, April). *Infant reaching is truly predictive and based on an inertia-like principle at 6 months of age.* Poster presented at the International Conference on Infant Studies, Providence, RI.

Xu, F., & Carey, S. (1994, June). *Infants' ability to individuate and trace identity of objects.* Paper presented at the International Conference on Infant Studies, Paris.

Xu, F., & Carey, S. (1996). Infants' metaphysics: The case of numerical identity. *Cognitive Psychology, 30*, 111–153.

Chapter 7

The Cultural Ecology of Young Children's Interactions With Objects and Artifacts

Michael Tomasello
Emory University

> Man . . . *knows neither how he moves, nor how he remembers; and he has no need to know in order to move or remember, nor does he need to know* before *doing so. But if he . . . forges a tool . . . a design must first act upon him* . . . ; *an* idea *must coordinate what he desires, what he can do, what he knows.*
> —Paul Valéry, *Man and the Sea Shell*

In the 1970s, Ulric Neisser became a Gibsonian ecological psychologist (e.g., Neisser, 1976). This led him inevitably to be concerned with basic processes of perception, but it did not eliminate his longstanding concern with higher mental processes. Indeed, it could be argued that Neisser's major goal in the 1980s was to account for complex cognitive processes within the theoretical framework of Gibsonian direct perception (e.g., Neisser, 1984, 1987). My central thesis in this chapter is that Neisser's goal cannot be reached without an enrichment of ecological theory, specifically an enrichment in which the social and cultural dimensions of human cognition are taken seriously.

My argument centers on a central phenomenon in the ecological approach to perceptual and cognitive ontogeny: young children's interactions with objects and artifacts. Eleanor Gibson (e.g., 1982, 1991), for instance, has been centrally concerned with infants' and young children's exploration of objects and their properties, as have a number of other Gibsonian developmentalists (e.g., Rochat, 1985; Ruff, 1984). Among the Gibsonians, however, there are only a few researchers who have been concerned with the social and cultural dimensions of the process—most prominently Reed (1996), Zukow (1990), and Loveland (1993)—and, in my opinion, they have not fully appreciated the depth with which human cultural life penetrates many of the most mundane instances of object manipulation. In my view, the Gibsonian perspective must be complemented by something like the Vygotskian perspective (e.g., Tomasello, Kruger, & Ratner, 1993; Vygotsky, 1978), which focuses on the structure of cultural environments and how children are adapted for specific types of interaction and learning within these environments. Vygotskian theory is thus ecological but with a much more specific focus on what might be called the cultural ecology of human cognitive development.

My main argument is that human children's encounters with objects, and especially artifacts, are much more deeply social than is generally recognized. These encounters are social not only in the relatively superficial sense that human children come into contact with objects mostly within a social context, they are also social in the much deeper sense that many if not most of the objects with which children interact are artifacts that other persons have designed for specific purposes. In many instances, the purpose of an artifact can only be discerned through adult demonstration or instruction that establishes what "we" do with it, after which the artifact possesses intentional affordances—that is, in addition to the natural affordances for sensory-motor action that have so occupied Gibsonians. I make my argument by looking at four types of objects and artifacts with which most children interact regularly: (a) natural objects (such as rocks), (b) material artifacts (such as tools), (c) symbolic artifacts (such as languages), and (d) material artifacts used as symbols (such as maps).

NATURAL OBJECTS

Human children are very interested in objects and so explore and actively manipulate them with enthusiasm from 3 or 4 months of age (E. Gibson, 1982; Piaget, 1952). They do this much more than nonhuman animal species, including our nearest primate relatives. Thus, McGrew (1977) found that chimpanzees manipulated nonfood objects unattached to any substrate only about 8% of their waking time (most of it for nest building and tool use). The figure for human children is not known precisely, but comparative studies in standardized situations have found that human infants manipulate and explore objects more frequently than apes by several orders of magnitude (e.g., Antinucci, 1989; Vauclair & Bard, 1983).

Vauclair (1984) speculated that the primary reason human children are so interested in objects is the social context in which they encounter them.

Although there are cultural variations in how adults mediate young children's encounters with objects (see Bakeman, Adamson, Konner, & Barr, 1990; Kruger & Tomasello, 1996), in all cultures adults intervene and instruct on occasion. Moreover, from around 10 months of age, children of all cultures regularly engage in social referencing in which they actively check with their caregiver to see if it is safe to approach or touch a novel object in a particular manner. Perhaps most importantly, it has been found that apes raised in human-like cultural environments, in which object manipulation is especially encouraged by human adults, seem to be much more interested in objects than are their wild conspecifics (Call & Tomasello, 1996)—illustrating the effect of the human social environment on object manipulation in a particularly dramatic fashion.

The main point is that in their encounters with natural objects, human children live within a sociocultural context that selectively exposes them to some objects and not others, and provides some form of social guidance in how to interact with objects. Consequently, if we are going to characterize the ecology of human children's encounters with natural objects, the most salient and species-unique aspects of the behavior from an evolutionary point of view are their great interest in manipulating and exploring objects in a good Gibsonian manner and the relatively rich social context within which most of their encounters with objects are embedded—a point that becomes crucial in the case of artifacts.

MATERIAL ARTIFACTS

The objects that nonhuman primates manipulate in the wild are almost exclusively objects unshaped by other hands. On the other hand, human children interact almost exclusively with artifacts prefashioned in some way by adults. Although I know of no quantitative studies of the natural ecology of human children's encounters with objects (and there is clear cultural variability), I can report informally that in one afternoon of observation of one 2-year-old middle-class American child, I saw her actually touch only two natural objects: some pieces of fruit and a leaf that had blown into the window of her Dodge minivan to settle between her titanium car seat and her Power Rangers lunch box. All of the other physical objects she touched were tools, toys, or artifacts of one sort or another, designed for specific types of interactive functions.

As in the case of natural objects, children may explore material artifacts individually and thereby discover some of their important sensory–motor affordances. Again as in the case of natural objects, they may also be selectively exposed to artifacts at the discretion of adults, and they may use adults as social reference points in adopting an emotional attitude toward these artifacts. But in the case of artifacts, social learning of a very specific type comes into play much more than in the case of natural objects—most especially because the intentional affordances of many artifacts are not readily apparent to a naive individual. To understand the conventional use for which many artifacts were designed (i.e., their intentional affordances) it is often necessary to see them being used by other persons.

In this context, there are two types of social learning that must be distinguished. In our work with apes and human infants, my collaborators and I have found it necessary to distinguish between what we call emulation learning and imitative learning more strictly defined (Tomasello, 1990, 1996). Emulation learning is a form of social learning that does not rely on the observation and reproduction of the actual behavior or behavioral strategies of other persons. In emulation learning, an observer watches someone manipulate an object and learns something new about the object as a result, namely some of that object's affordances that he or she did not know existed beforehand. The observer then may use this new information in devising its own behavioral strategy. For example, one primate might crack open a nut that an observing conspecific did not previously know was a food item that could be opened. The observer might then proceed to use this information in devising a way to crack open the nut for itself, using its own existing problem-solving skills.[1] Emulation learning is the major way in which nonhuman primates learn about their environments in social situations, and indeed it also plays a major role in human infants' initial explorations of many artifacts, as illustrated most clearly in the work of von Hofsten and Siddiqui (1993) with 6-month-old infants. I assume that emulation learning could be assimilated to some notion of Gibsonian direct perception of the dynamic affordances of objects displayed in the manipulations of others.

The second type of social learning is imitative learning in which an observer attempts to copy the actual behavioral strategies of others—a type of social learning that may be uniquely human (Tomasello, 1996).[2] This does not mean that the observer blindly mimics the sensory–motor actions

---

[1]Because conspecifics often have similar cognitive processes and motoric abilities, it may often happen in emulation learning that the observer chooses to act in a way that is similar to the behavior of the demonstrator. But this matching of behavior does not necessarily mean that the observer intended to reproduce the behavior of the demonstrator, as in imitative learning.

[2]It is possible that some apes raised and trained by humans may come to imitatively learn some actions on objects (Tomasello, Savage-Rumbaugh, & Kruger, 1993). Whether they are reproducing intentional actions, as opposed to mimicking movements or reproducing results, has yet to be determined, however. More research on enculturated apes' understanding of intentions is needed.

of others—the way that a parrot mimics human speech, for example—but that the observer attempts to reproduce the intentional actions of the other, including the goal toward which they are aimed. Thus, Carpenter (1995) had 1-year-old human infants observe an adult do such things as touch her foot to a box to make its light come on. The infants quite often did the same thing, looking to the light in anticipation and thereby showing that they were indeed reproducing a goal-directed action and not just a sensory–motor movement. The infants behaved in this way even though their natural tendency for interaction with the box would most likely have involved doing something with their hands, not their feet. Tomasello, Kruger, and Ratner (1993) attempted to capture the essential difference between these two major types of social learning by saying that in emulation the observer learns from the demonstrator, whereas in imitation (one form of cultural learning) the observer learns through the demonstrator—imagining herself in the place of the demonstrator and then trying to do what she is doing. We hypothesized that the difference depends on differences of social cognition. Whereas very young infants and nonhuman primates do not perceive the behavior of others as intentional, and so they can only emulate the external results that the behavior produces or perhaps mimic its sensory–motor form, older human children simply perceive Daddy as washing the dishes or trying to open the drawer—not as making specific bodily motions or producing specific changes of state in the environment— and these intentional actions are what children attempt to reproduce. Indeed, in Meltzoff's (1995) study, 18-month-old infants attempted to reproduce the actions that adults were trying unsuccessfully to produce— even though the infant never actually perceived the actions themselves, only various intention cues.

My main point in the current context is this: The affordances that infants and children come to perceive in artifacts via imitative learning may not be of the same type as those they come to perceive in natural objects or artifacts via their own direct explorations and emulation learning. Reed (1996) attempted to argue that they are basically the same, claiming that a mailbox affords the mailing of letters as directly as a solid surface affords walking. But I think there is an important difference. Following Cole (1996), I think it is crucial to distinguish the material aspect of a tool or artifact from its intentional (or ideal) aspect. The intentional aspect of an artifact comes about because humans can in some sense put themselves in the place of (imagine themselves in the role of) other users of the tool or artifact as they observe them using it (leading to imitative learning). On the basis of this observation they perceive what that object is conventionally for for human beings, including themselves, and this perception may be somewhat direct. But this for is a social for; it is the intentions of other persons as embodied in the artifact. This embodiment is simply not a part of natural objects or artifacts considered as physical objects to be grasped, sucked, or otherwise treated as aliments for sensory–motor schemes.[3] It is also possible that after a certain ontogenetic period, children may be able to perceive the intentional affordances of some artifacts without having observed others using them, on the basis of some kind of generalized skill at imagining human users; that is something about which we know next to nothing (although the work of Keil, 1989, and Bloom, 1996, is suggestive). In any case, the important point is that human artifacts come to have for their human users both natural, sensory–motor affordances and, in addition, what we might call intentional affordances.

If the distinction between natural and intentional affordances seems difficult to grasp, let me provide another perspective using a phenomenon of late infancy that makes the point dramatically. Sometimes infants and young children do not use artifacts for the purposes for which they were designed, but instead engage in what has been called symbolic or imaginative play. Thus, a 2-year-old might pick up a pencil and pretend it is a hammer. But as Hobson (1993) pointed out, the child is doing more than simply manipulating the pencil in an unusual way. In early symbolic play the infant also looks to an adult with a playful expression: She knows that this is not the conventional use of this object and that her unconventional use is something that may be considered "funny." One interpretation of this behavior is that symbolic play involves two crucial steps. First, the infant must be able to understand and adopt the intentions of adults as they use objects and artifacts (via imitative learning or perhaps on their own), so that the human intentions in using an artifact are seen as embodied in the artifact; that is, the child first understands how we humans use pencils—their intentional affordances. The second step involves the child "decoupling" intentional affordances from their associated objects and artifacts so that they may be interchanged and used with "inappropriate" objects playfully. Thus, the child comes to use a pencil as one would conventionally use a hammer, smiling at the adult in the process to signal

---

[3]This distinction may underlie the so-called ratchet effect in human cultural evolution (Tomasello, in press-a). That is, as children come to understand an artifact as something that is for a specific human purpose, they may now encounter some new exigency or demand for which the artifact is not well adapted—or discover some new aspect of the artifact's function—and so make a modification in the artifact. Others in the group then perceive this new use, and thus the new intentional affordances of the modified artifact, and adopt it relatively quickly. This results in the ratchet effect in which old uses stay firmly in the group (via imitative learning) until innovations come along and replace them. Over time and generations this process leads to artifacts that embody a kind of cumulative cultural evolution or, said briefly, a "history." Emulation learning cannot lead to cumulative historical change in artifacts because each observing individual on each occasion only perceives the affordances of the artifact for its own already existing behavioral repertoire, not what the object is "for" in the more general social sense that constitutes what I have called intentional affordances.

that this is not stupidity but playfulness. This ability to detach the intentional affordances of objects and artifacts and to interchange them relatively freely in symbolic play is, to my mind, the most convincing evidence we have that the child has indeed learned the intentional affordances embodied in many objects and artifacts in a way that is semi-independent of their material aspects. (It is important to know in this context whether the child has previously seen a pencil used as a hammer in a playful situation by adults—and is just mimicking this use without understanding its symbolic significance—or whether she is doing something truly creative. Research to determine this has not been done, but it is presumably the case that by 2 to 3 years of age, children can create at least some symbolic uses of objects on their own.)

There is very little evidence for symbolic or imaginative play in nonhuman primates, even for apes raised in human cultural environments. There are a few anecdotal observations of enculturated apes manipulating toys that humans consider to be symbolic, such as dolls and the like, but it is not clear that they ever use toys or other artifacts in ways other than the ways they have seen them used (Call & Tomasello, 1996). That is, in many or all cases they may be simply manipulating the dolls the way they have seen humans do it—putting a small spoon to its mouth as humans have done, for example. Although they may have some skills in this regard—we should remain open to the possibility until more systematic research is conducted—if they do not, it would mean that their learning about the conventional affordances of objects is of the same nature as their learning of the more sensory–motor aspects of objects: Pencils simply afford writing and hammering in exactly the same way (because pencils afford both of these actions at a sensory–motor level, as learned individually or via emulation). It is also noteworthy that one of the consistent findings in research with autistic children is their almost total lack of symbolic play. This fits with the current analysis because it is precisely in understanding the intentional dimension of human action that autistic children have their most serious problems (Loveland, 1993).

To summarize: Human children learn the natural, sensory–motor affordances of both natural objects and artifacts through their own explorations, perhaps influenced in some way by the social environment with respect to exposure and social referencing (and perhaps emulation learning). But human artifacts have another dimension that children learn about through cultural learning (i.e., imitative learning) almost exclusively. They do not learn just what they can do with an object, they learn what the object is for—what members of the culture consider the intentional/conventional significance of the artifact—and this constitutes another type of affordance. These intentional affordances become, in a sense, embodied in the artifact in the same way that sensory–motor affordances discovered through direct manipulation become embodied in objects; they are now directly perceived. This process leads over time in a social group to artifacts with a history, as individuals make changes in the intentional affordances of objects and others adopt them. The direct perception of intentional affordances also enables young children early in ontogeny—by a process that is very poorly understood at this point—to detach these intentional affordances from the objects to which they are conventionally attached and to play with them in symbolic or imaginative play.

SYMBOLIC ARTIFACTS

Another line of argument for the importance of the ideal or intentional aspect of artifacts is the existence of artifacts whose materiality is negligible. I am thinking, of course, of languages and some other forms of symbolic communication. My focus in this chapter is on physical objects, and so I do not want to digress too far into the complex subject of language ac-quisition, but language is relevant to the current topic for two reasons. First, by means of its attention-directing function, it is an influence on children's interactions with material objects. That is, if linguistic symbols are viewed as a means by which one person influences the interest and attention of another person, then it is clear that adults often use language to influence children's attention to objects. Moreover, because many lin-guistic symbols are used to indicate whole categories of entities, over time children have their attention drawn to certain features of objects and their taxonomic similarities across objects (e.g., what is common among all things called dog; Mervis, 1987). Particular words often embody different perspectives on objects as well, as when an adult calls the same object on different occasions lion, toy, animal, present from Kimberly, and so on. In all of these ways children's comprehension of various linguistic symbols leads them to pay attention to some aspects of objects and not to others—to learn something of their properties and affordances vicariously, as it were.

In addition, however, linguistic symbols are an interesting kind of artifact in their own right, and one in which the intentional aspect plays an espe-cially important role. A language is a collection of symbolic artifacts used for purposes of communication. These artifacts take the form of words, morphemes, syntactic constructions, and the like—all of which have ma-teriality in the sense that they are constituted by physical sounds, just not the type of materiality that affords sensory–motor manipulations of the kind possible with physical objects. When we ask what a linguistic symbol is for—its intentional affordances—the answer is that people use particular linguistic symbols when they intend for others to attend to particular aspects of things in their shared environments, either physical or conceptual. Linguistic symbols thus have a very salient ideal dimension in terms of the intentions that are embodied in them in a way that is similar to the way that material artifacts have intentions embodied in them. The difference is that these are communicative intentions, and so there is an additional layer of complexity. The intentional affordance of a linguistic symbol is thus the speaker's intentions toward the listener's intentional and attentional states. Knives are for cutting, but words are for directing the attention of other persons—myself included.

Because linguistic symbols are only arbitrarily or conventionally related to their communicative functions, children can acquire them only through some form of imitative learning; one cannot discover on one's own the communicative function of the sound *tree* as used by others. Most prototypically, the process involves a kind of role reversal imitation: The child uses the symbol toward adults as they have used it toward her. The child's use of the symbol thus creates a communicative convention or symbol whose essence is its bidirectionality or intersubjectivity—the quality of being socially shared (Tomasello, in press-b). After the communicative function of a symbol is learned, it may be said that its intentional affordances may be directly perceived in the same way as those of a corkscrew or a mailbox. The existence of symbolic artifacts such as those found in languages thus constitutes additional evidence for the reality of, and indeed the distinctive nature of, intentional affordances.

Children's use of linguistic symbols raises another set of issues with regard to the development of "thinking." These issues are important for current purposes because children will at some point come to interact with and manipulate objects in their thoughts as well as in their hands. They are also issues that the Gibsonians have not accounted for adequately, mainly because their view of sociocultural interactions is not sufficiently rich. The main issue is this: At around 4 or 5 years of age the child begins to use language toward herself, either overtly or covertly (what Vygotsky, 1978, called self-directed or inner speech; see also Wertsch, 1991). This indicates the child's ability to use communicative symbols to direct her own attention—as if she were two separate interlocutors. This internalized attention-directing function is the essence of linguistic symbols as media of cognitive representation: Although they are used exclusively by the self, they embody the way in which past members of the culture have found it useful to focus the attention of others. The use of symbols by individuals in understanding a situation is thus the prototype of Vygotskian internalization and cultural mediation because the symbol that was first used to regulate interpersonal interactions is now being used by an individual to regulate its intrapersonal relation to the world. The use of socially shared symbols to direct one's own attention—and perhaps other symbolic artifacts including narratives and explicit instruction (Bruner, 1990)—is one form of what is meant by the term *thinking*. Indeed, Vygotsky's (1978) studies of thinking were often concerned with preschool and school-age children's internalization of adult instructions to self-regulate their interactions with the environment.

This point of view is relevant in a Gibsonian–Neisserian framework because it conceptualizes cognitive representation not as a "ghost in the machine," duplicating perception in every way, but rather it conceptualizes the more explicit forms of thinking as the internalization of socially created and learned symbols that can be directly perceived in their social uses (see also De Jong, 1990). Moreover, internalization is not itself a ghostly process. In the final analysis it simply boils down to children using symbols toward themselves that others have previously used toward them and that they have previously used toward others; they simply must treat themselves as just another potential recipient of their linguistic communication. This way of looking at human cognitive development naturalizes thinking and cognitive representation by making them a direct result of perceptual and social interactions with the ambient cultural environment and clearly distinguishes them from the disembodied forms of cognitive representation posited by traditional cognitive scientists.

This digression into language and cognitive representation was meant to make three points. First, children's comprehension of language in the context of objects serves to draw their attention to all kinds of properties and affordances of those objects that they might not otherwise have detected for themselves. Second, children's ability to learn language is one more piece of evidence that they perceive and understand the intentions of others as embodied in artifacts. Indeed, the material aspect of linguistic symbols is so evanescent that it could be argued that their intentional aspect is practically the whole of their reality for the child. Third, when children learn to produce language themselves to direct the attention of others to objects—or use some other form of instruction that has been used toward them—they eventually come to treat themselves as recipients of their own communicative or instructional efforts. In using language or instruction to direct their own attention to objects or other phenomena, they are thus engaged in forms of cognitive representation and thinking that are wholly compatible with a Gibsonian–Neisserian ecological analysis in which everything is one or another type of organism–environment interaction. It is just that in the current perspective, the environment and children's ability to interact with it are conceived in a more Vygotskian fashion in which there is an explicitly intentional dimension to the behavior of other persons and their artifacts.

MATERIAL OBJECTS USED AS SYMBOLS

There is one final kind of object that I have not specified, and that is symbolic objects. What I am talking about is not artifacts such as tools that perform functions or even toys like a top or a ball with which one can play—even if one can sometimes play with them symbolically. Nor am I talking about symbolic artifacts such as linguistic symbols or narrative forms that are almost entirely symbolic, with only fleeting materiality. What I am talking about are physical objects created to perform symbolic functions. These range from representational toys such as dolls and toy cars to representational tools such as maps and pictures. It might be a philosophical struggle to distinguish these from other symbolic artifacts such as linguistic symbols in some cases (I am thinking of some forms of art), but for our purposes with young children the key distinction is that these are objects they can physically manipulate. Consequently, their material and symbolic aspects are both potentially perceptible to children and have affordances for them.

Children have great difficulty in understanding these kinds of symbolic objects. Over the past decade, DeLoache (1995) has conducted a series of elegant experiments showing how children in the 2- to 3-year age range have great difficulty with everything from scale models to photographs. For example, in the basic experiment she hides a doll in a real room, shows the children a picture of the hiding process (or a scale model re-enactment of the hiding process), makes sure that at least at some level they understand the correspondence between picture and room (or scale model and room), and then asks them to find the doll in the room. Until 2½ or 3 years old, children are very poor at this task. It is noteworthy that the ability to use a physical object as a symbol is also difficult if not impossible for nonhuman primates. The one enculturated chimpanzee who has been tested did poorly in DeLoache's experimental paradigm (Premack & Premack, 1983) and a number of other chimpanzees and orangutans did poorly in a similar task in which a human attempted to show them the location of hidden food by holding up an object identical to the one under which they could find the food (Tomasello, Call, & Gluckman, 1997). Similarly, it is worthy of note that material artifacts used as symbols are rather late emerging in human history (Klein, 1989), perhaps providing further evidence of their special status.

DeLoache's (1995) explanation for the difficulty that young children have with material objects used as symbols is that these objects create a conflict in the child between their material and symbolic aspects or affordances—what she called the dual representation problem. Young children perceive a doll house as a physical structure to be physically manipulated and explored; to perceive it as a map of something else they have to see it as a symbolic representation as well (see DeLoache, 1995, for a review of evidence supporting this view). One problem with this interpretation, however, is that some other child behaviors would seem to involve dual representation, yet they do not cause children inordinate difficulties. First and most obvious, linguistic symbols are learned and used freely for more than a year prior to the time when children begin to use material objects as symbols skillfully—and linguistic symbols exist as both physical sounds and socially shared symbols. However, as alluded to previously, linguistic symbols have little in the way of tangible materiality to conflict with their symbolic function; they are basically not manipulable physically.

The difficult case is symbolic or imaginative play because in this instance the child is playing with an object that is both manipulable and symbolic. It is widely believed that 18- to 24-month-old children engage in symbolic play with some regularity—although, as mentioned previously, it has yet to be determined the degree to which this play is truly symbolic as opposed to imitative (perhaps the most convincing studies are those of Harris & Kavanaugh, 1993, with 2- to 2½-year-olds). Indeed, in symbolic play the child has a manipulable object with intentional affordances (e.g., a pencil affords grasping and writing) and that can have symbolic significance as well (e.g., the pencil can be a pretend hammer). Why symbolic play emerges developmentally prior to the use of material artifacts as symbols is thus something of a mystery. One possibility is that in symbolic play the child may invoke the two (or three) realities in a sequential manner at her own choosing: The object is first a hammer and then a pencil and then a graspable object. With material artifacts used as symbols, the symbolic aspect is one that has been chosen and designed by the object's maker, not the child, and so it is possible that this design issue puts the two ways of relating to the object in competition simultaneously in a way that the more child-controlled symbolic play does not.

A variation on this theme is that material artifacts used as symbols are symbolic in a different way than play symbols. The idea here is that a map or a doll house is intentionally communicative in the same way as a linguistic symbol. That is, a map is an artifact that someone constructed not to perform a function directly, as a spoon serves its function of obtaining food, but rather to communicate about a particular space to someone else. The intentional affordance is thus of the communicative type in that it embodies the intentions of others toward my intentional states. The child's symbolic or imaginative play does not require her to discern someone else's communicative intention as embodied in the artifact—it just requires her to treat an object alternately as having one of two sets of intentional affordances. Thus, the outcome is that material objects used as symbols inherit the most difficult aspects of both linguistic symbols and pretend play symbols. Like linguistic symbols, they have a more indirect, communicative function; and like play symbols, they have materiality that can potentially come into conflict with their symbolic function.

It is unclear whether any of these speculations represent a fully satisfactory answer to the question of why young children have such a difficult time with material artifacts used as symbols. For current purposes, the important point is that the dual representation hypothesis explicitly recognizes that certain objects have both material and intentional (i.e., intentionally communicative) aspects. And so, once again, we see that the social/intentional dimension of children's experience with objects derives not just from the social interactions within which they are introduced to them, but at some point it also derives from the social dimension that becomes embodied in the objects themselves. And the intentional function of symbolic objects is inherently social and communicative: Someone created this doll house so that I could use it to represent that room next door, or someone created this doll so that I could use it to represent a baby in play. The child can come to use these kinds of symbolic objects, as well as other artifacts, in conventional ways only if she somehow comes to perceive their social/intentional affordances.

Although this is no place to belabor the point, once learned, the communicative function of material objects used as symbols can potentially serve to socially mediate the child's interactions with other objects in ways similar to linguistic symbols. That is, the child may come to use an internalized version of these physical representations for herself—in her own cognitive representations and thinking—in the same way that someone else used them for her. Vygotsky (1978) and others have studied any number of ways that physical objects may be used as cognitive maps, as mnemonic devices, as representations of the sounds of speech, as symbols for mathematical calculations, and so forth and so on, in ways that mediate children's cognitive interactions with their environments even in the physical absence of the mediating devices themselves. Thus, just as linguistic symbols can serve as mediators of cognitive processes, so can other kinds of symbolic artifacts that other persons have created for human use.

To summarize: The significance of children's interactions with material artifacts that have been designed to fulfill symbolic/communicative functions is, once again, that they illustrate the dual nature of artifacts for children. Natural objects have natural affordances for sensory–motor action, but many objects in the child's world have a special kind of social affordance I have termed intentional affordances. These are fairly straightforward in the case of a material artifact: Its intentional affordances are what others use it for (although imaginative play with these may add a layer of complexity). Purely symbolic artifacts such as language require an understanding of a specific type of intentional affordance: the communicative intentions of others. Communicative intentions are others' intentions toward the self's intentional states, and thus they make for another kind of complexity. Material objects used as symbols embody both of these types of complexity—decoupling sensory–motor and intentional affordances and the comprehension of intentionally communicative affordances— and so present children with special cognitive difficulties.

CONCLUSION

Much more than any other species, human beings encounter physical objects in a social framework. Developing humans are selectively exposed to objects by other persons, and they use those other persons as social reference points in deciding how to interact with those objects. In addition, however, there is a much deeper and more pervasive influence of the sociocultural environment on human children's interactions with objects. In the case of both material and symbolic artifacts, children learn about the artifact's conventional affordances via cultural learning (imitative learning) in which they comprehend the intentions of the adult as she uses the artifact. The artifact then comes to embody what we might call intentional affordances, as evidenced most dramatically by the detachment of these affordances from their conventional objects in symbolic play—as well as by the existence of symbolic artifacts such as languages that possess very little materiality at all. The fact that human artifacts accumulate modifications over time, and so come to have a history, provides further evidence that as developing humans learn about artifacts they attend not only to their natural sensory–motor affordances, but also to their social intentional affordances. Material artifacts used as symbols present children with special difficulties (and these kinds of symbols were also late-emerging in human history) because of the special complexities involved in their dual nature as material and intentionally communicative objects. A graphic depiction of the major interactive characteristics of these different types of objects and artifacts is presented in Fig. 7.1.

Most of the Gibsonian analyses of social life extend the concept of affordances to the social world in terms of social affordances: what social beings afford in terms of social behavior (e.g., Loveland, 1993). But for the most part they do not focus on the social matrix in which physical objects and artifacts acquire their conventional significance for children during human ontogeny. The major exception is Reed (1996), who investigated the intentional affordances of cultural artifacts. But Reed treated intentional affordances as basically identical to physical affordances, and I do not believe that they are. Intentional affordances retain their social character, as is most clearly evident in the various phenomena I have

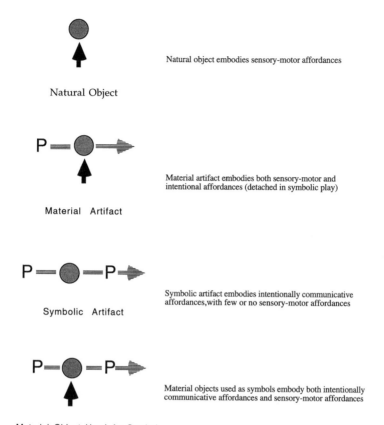

Natural object embodies sensory-motor affordances

Natural Object

Material artifact embodies both sensory-motor and intentional affordances (detached in symbolic play)

Material Artifact

Symbolic artifact embodies intentionally communicative affordances, with few or no sensory-motor affordances

Symbolic Artifact

Material objects used as symbols embody both intentionally communicative affordances and sensory-motor affordances

Material Object Used As Symbol

FIG. 7.1. Schematic depiction of different kinds of interations with objects and artifacts. Black arrow depicts a sensory-motor affordance; P depicts a person; and striped arrow depicts an intentional affordance for a person.

reviewed here, including imitative learning, imaginative or symbolic play, language acquisition, and the use of material objects as symbols. If Gibsonian–Neisserian theory is to incorporate the social dimension of human cognition in meaningful ways, in my view, it will have to incorporate human sociality not just in the sense of social interaction among persons and various types of social influence but also the social dimensions of human beings' interactions with the physical world and, indeed, the inherently social nature of most of the material objects with which they interact.

Let me conclude by pointing out that much of what Neisser has attempted to do theoretically is to extend Gibsonian theory beyond direct perception on the simplest level to the cognitive representation of such things as perceptual categories and, perhaps, some types of affordances: "from direct perception to conceptual structure" in the title of one of his papers (Neisser, 1987). But I believe that a fuller recognition of the social nature of much of our encounters with the physical world would allow for an even richer conceptualization of human cognitive processes, all in a clearly ecological framework. Following Vygotsky (1978), I believe that much light may be shed on human cognition by recognizing the crucial importance of interactions with objects and other aspects of the human environment that are mediated by various forms of social learning: language, instruction, narratives, and other types of symbolic and material artifacts. The hypothesis is that the child internalizes the intentionally communicative dimension of these artifacts and uses them toward herself as others have used them toward her. Just as she represents things for others in language or other symbols, she represents them for herself in those same symbols. In the Vygotskian analysis, the process of using social symbols for oneself constitutes much of what we mean by the term *thinking,* and is a view of cognitive representation that is much more ecologically grounded than the traditional view of pictures or sentences in the head as espoused by the majority of cognitive scientists.

ACKNOWLEDGMENTS

To Dick Neisser for all of his kind and generous theoretical guidance, and other kinds of guidance, over the past 14 years. Thanks to Tricia Striano, Philippe Rochat, and Bill Hirst for helpful comments on an earlier version of the manuscript.

REFERENCES

Antinucci, F. (1989). *Cognitive structure and development in nonhuman primates.* Hillsdale, NJ: Lawrence Erlbaum Associates.

Bakeman, R., Adamson, L., Konner, M., & Barr, R. (1990). !Kung infancy: The social context of object exploration. *Child Development, 61,* 794–809.

Bloom, P. (1996). Intention, history, and artifact concepts. *Cognition, 60,* 1–29.

Bruner, J. (1990). *Acts of meaning.* Cambridge, MA: Harvard University Press.

Carpenter, M. (1995). *Social-cognitive abilities of 9- to 15-month-old infants.* Unpublished doctoral dissertation, Emory University, Atlanta, GA.

Call, J., & Tomasello, M. (1996). The effect of humans on the cognitive development of apes. In A. E. Russon, K. A. Bard, & S. T. Parker (Eds.), *Reaching into thought* (pp. 371–403). Cambridge, England: Cambridge University Press.

Cole, M. (1996). *Cultural psychology: A once and future discipline.* Cambridge, MA: Harvard University Press.

De Jong, L. (1990). Intentionality and the ecological approach. *Journal for the Theory of Social Behavior, 21,* 91–109.

DeLoache, J. (1995). Early symbol understanding and use. In *The psychology of learning and motivation* (Vol. 33). New York: Academic Press.

Gibson, E. (1982). The concept of affordances in development. In W. Collins (Ed.), *The concept of development* (pp. 55–81). Hillsdale, NJ: Lawrence Erlbaum Associates.

Gibson, E. (1991). *Odyssey in learning and perception.* Cambridge, MA: MIT Press.

Harris, P., & Kavanaugh, R. (1993). Young children's understanding of pretense. *Monographs of the Society for Research in Child Development, 58*(1, Serial No. 231).

Hobson, P. (1993). *Autism and the development of mind.* Hillsdale, NJ: Lawrence Erlbaum Associates.

Keil, F. (1989). *Concepts, kinds, and cognitive development.* Cambridge, MA: MIT Press.

Klein, R. (1989). *The human career: Human biological and cultural origins.* Chicago: The University of Chicago Press.

Kruger, A., & Tomasello, M. (1996). Cultural learning and learning culture. In D. Olson (Ed.), *Handbook of education and human development: New models of teaching, learning, and schooling.* Blackwell.

Loveland, K. A. (1993). Autism, affordances, and the self. In U. Neisser (Ed.), *The perceived self* (pp. 237–253). Cambridge, England: Cambridge University Press.

McGrew, W. C. (1977). Socialization and object manipulation of wild chimpanzees. In S. Chevalier-Skolnikoff & F. E. Poirier (Eds.), *Primate bio-social development* (pp. 261–288). New York: Garland Press.

Meltzoff, A. (1995). Understanding the intentions of others: Re-enactment of intended acts by 18-month-old children. *Developmental Psychology, 31,* 838–850.

Mervis, C. (1987). Child basic categories and early lexical development. In U. Neisser (Ed.), *Concepts and conceptual development* (pp. 198–220). Cambridge, England: Cambridge University Press.

Neisser, U. (1976). *Cognition and reality.* San Francisco: Freeman.

Neisser, U. (1984). Toward an ecologically oriented cognitive science. In T. Schlecter & M. Toglia (Eds.), *New directions in cognitive science* (pp. 17–32). Norwood, NJ: Ablex.

Neisser, U. (1987). From direct perception to conceptual structure. In U. Neisser (Ed.), *Concepts and conceptual development* (pp. 11–30). Cambridge, England: Cambridge University Press.

Piaget, J. (1952). *The origins of intelligence in children.* New York: Norton.

Premack, D., & Premack, A. J. (1983). *The mind of an ape.* New York: Norton.

Reed, E. (1996). The intention to use a specific affordance: A conceptual framework for psychology. In K. Fischer & R. Wozniak (Eds.), *Children's thinking: The effect of specific environments* (pp. 221–342). Mahwah, NJ: Lawrence Erlbaum Associates.

Rochat, P. (1985). Object manipulation and exploration in 2- to 5-month-old infants. *Developmental Psychology, 25,* 871–884.

Ruff, H. (1984). Infants' manipulative exploration of objects. *Developmental Psychology, 2,* 9–20.

Tomasello, M. (1990). Cultural transmission in the tool use and comminicatory signalling of chimpanzees? In S. Parker & E. Gibson (Eds.), *Language and intelligence in animals: Developmental perspectives* (pp. 274–311). Cambridge, England: Cambridge University Press.

Tomasello, M. (1996). Do apes ape? In C. Heyes & B. Galef (Eds.), *Social learning in animals: The roots of culture* (pp. 319–346). New York: Academic Press.

Tomasello, M. (in press-a). Social cognition and the evolution of culture. In J. Langer & M. Killen (Eds.), *Piaget, evolution, and development.* Mahwah, NJ: Lawrence Erlbaum Associates.

Tomasello, M. (in press-b). Perceiving intentions and learning words in the second year of life. In M. Bowerman & S. Levinson (Eds.), *Language acquisition and conceptual development.* Cambridge, England: Cambridge University Press.

Tomasello, M., Call, J., & Gluckman, A. (1997). The comprehension of novel communicative signs by apes and human children. *Child Development, 68,* 1067–1081.

Tomasello, M., Kruger, A. C., & Ratner, H. H. (1993). Cultural learning. *Behavioral and Brain Sciences, 16,* 495–552.

Tomasello, M., Savage-Rumbaugh, E. S., & Kruger, A. C. (1993). Imitative learning of actions on objects by children, chimpanzees, and enculturated chimpanzees. *Child Development, 64*, 1688–1705.

Vauclair, J. (1984). Phylogenetic approach to object manipulation in human and ape infants. *Human Development, 27*, 321–328.

Vauclair, J., & Bard, K. (1983). Development of manipulations with objects in ape and human infants. *Journal of Human Evolution, 12*, 631–645.

von Hofsten, K., & Siddiqui, A. (1993). Using the mother's actions as a reference for object exploration in 6- and 12-month-old infants. *British Journal of Developmental Psychology, 11*, 61–74.

Vygotsky, L. (1978). *Mind in society.* Cambridge, MA: Harvard University Press.

Wertsch, J. (1991). *Voices of the mind: A sociocultural approach to mediated action.* Cambridge, MA: Harvard University Press.

Zukow, P. (1990). Socio-perceptual bases for the emergence of language: An alternative to innatist approaches. *Developmental Psychobiology, 23*, 54–71.

Chapter 8

Getting a Grip on Reality

Frank Keil
Kristi Lockhart
Cornell University

In everyday folk psychology, it is common to say that another person understands or fails to understand some aspect of their world. These statements would seem to assume that achieving understanding is an important part of being human and is something that we often find easy to evaluate in others. As teachers, we have to make such judgments quickly and frequently whether our students are 5 or 25. Yet, surprisingly, there has been relatively little work in psychology on what it means to achieve understanding. In this chapter, we focus on one important aspect of that process, how we achieve causal understandings of the world around us, and we argue that Dick Neisser's ideas are enormously helpful in guiding us in this process.

As a way of showing Dick's influence, we talk about how we come to grasp reality, for that metaphor of a hand grasping an object helps illustrate many key insights that Dick has brought to cognition and how those insights have changed its very nature. Dick's influence on cognitive psychology and cognitive science has been extraordinary, more pervasive and at a deeper level than just about anyone else's; and this is especially obvious in such areas as memory, attention, perception, cognitive and perceptual development, and perception in action. The impact of his work on the nature of understanding is also profound.

The grasping metaphor can be illustrated by considering three principles that are embodied in Dick's writings and by then considering the consequences of such principles for an overall view of causal understanding. We can state the principles cryptically as follows:

1. Do not think of the mind as a brain in a vat;
2. Embrace the yin and yang of cognition;
3. Know one's place.

To make some sense of these principles, we now expand on them in the context of causal understanding.

BRAINS IN VATS

Philosophers have long been fond of talking about what sort of mind one would have if one's brain simply sat in a vat of nutrients, with ample blood flow to all its regions, but disconnected from reality (e.g., Putnam, 1975a). To make such accounts more current, we can build in random stimulation of peripheral neurons so as to make sure they do not atrophy from lack of use. These brains in vats cannot perceive in any modality, nor can they act. There are many philosophical issues concerning what such an isolation might do to either a mature or neonatal mind, but the point here is simpler. Despite the gruesome image and the ridiculous aspects of this model, a more covert version has dominated much of the psychology of thinking, including that of concepts and causal understanding. In one of his earlier incarnations, Fodor (1980) called it methodological solipsism and argued that the way to study the mind was syntactically; that is, in terms of the formal computational properties it embodied and not in terms of how those computations linked to reality. Psychology would be best served by looking inward at the isolated mechanics and syntax of mind and not at how the mind worked in a larger context. Most psychologists state their discomfort with methodological solipsism but they have often come close to fully embracing it in actual practice.

Cognitive psychology textbooks of the last few decades are full of information processing flowcharts, where great care is taken to describe the procedures performed by each of several boxes and how they are linked together. We see such models everywhere, in language processing, in attention, in pattern perception, in judgment and decision making, and in the study of concepts and causal understanding. Stimuli in supporting studies are usually made up as a kind of afterthought, arbitrary fuel for the information processing system to show that it could work. It was in fact important to make the stimuli as arbitrary and meaningless as possible as meaningful relations might introduce uncontrollable distortions on the study of the machinery of the mind. There are good reasons, sometimes, for trying to make your stimuli arbitrary and nonsensical, but when it becomes the dominant paradigm, mental solipsism is the result. After all, the brain in the vat could also get random sets of neural stimulations as well.

This bias led to a certain class of questions that endure today: Is a particular kind of information processing largely serial or parallel? Are representations based on sampling over exemplars or on reference to a single summary prototype? Do we think and form representations in largely analogue or propositional ways? Most people think there is a truth to the matter for many of these questions, as do we, but the research suggests that asking such questions in a manner disembodied from real-world context often provides indeterminate results. If we do not use stimuli that reflect important structural properties of the world, we usually do not get very far. One set of arbitrary information suggests one kind of information processing, whereas another arbitrary set but with some different dimensions emphasized may suggest exactly the opposite. Sometimes it seems as if we study psychology the way immunologists might study the immune system if they just looked at how antibodies were formed, not to real-world antigens, but to arbitrary chemical compounds that were varied systematically in some formal space but with no consideration of biologically natural antigens and how they are functionally deployed. Fortunately no immunologists do that; for one thing, the space of possible organic compounds is far too large to allow one to explore how real-world antigens work and how we are adapted to them (see also Piatelli-Palmarini, 1989, for a related discussion of the immune system as a model for models of learning).

There was, however, a different point of view that had a long history in the Gibsonian approach to perception and which Dick Neisser then brought to cognition. The Gibsons (E. Gibson, 1970; J. Gibson, 1961, 1966) and Neisser (1976) demanded that we situate humans in a world with real goals, real tasks, and real consequences for their actions. The information in the world was not arbitrary but critical to an understanding of how we grasped reality; indeed the whole notion of grasping seems incoherent without specifying the structure of what is grasped. Research on the development of cognition and perception was often the first to realize this point. This is why E. J. Gibson's work was so extraordinarily important. Coming from an ecological perspective, she naturally saw why it was critical to think about the infant as an active, exploratory creature learning to navigate a world full of information that afforded different opportunities for that infant. The rest of developmental psychology has increasingly come around to that perspective because children, and especially infants, would not tolerate tasks that asked them to process meaningless information in unrealistic contexts.

From a dramatically different vantage point, the philosophy of science and mind started to converge on similar themes. It is now common to embrace a realism in which there is a true world out there with genuine lawful patterns at levels beyond the merely correlational; there are causal patterns and functional systems and they form distinctive clusters, which is why we have different sciences with different methods, models, and practices (Salmon, 1989). There are not infinite realities out there awaiting yet another social construction; reality is not a completely arbitrary game in which the world can be carved up any old way depending on the whims of the carver. Nature does have joints and we need to pick up on enough of these to get around in the world. That is why science works and why we survive on a daily basis. There may be far more structural patterns than any of us can know, and different people may pick up somewhat different patterns; but such a plurality of ways of construing the world is far different from the logical possibility of infinite ways of carving the world. Reality may have many facets and points of view, but it is not fully arbitrary. To a large extent, the appearance of Dick's *Cognition and Reality* (Neisser, 1976) set the tone for this new point of view. It is interesting how many people resisted the message of that book at first but how much its themes run through the most promising work in psychology today.

To be more specific with the case of concepts and causal understanding, consider how they have been traditionally studied, how Rosch and Mervis (1975) suggested an important change to this strategy, and how the Rosch and Mervis enterprise has been distorted. As we all know, prior to Rosch and Mervis, most psychologists studied concepts in terms of analytic sets of features. The concepts studied had nonsense names, like blik and glibbit, and referred to arbitrary concatenations of feature sets. Given such artificial concepts, research questions were largely forced to focus on general principles of learning. What kinds of functions best described learning curves for concepts with different numbers of positive and negative features? How did other concepts with overlapping features influence learning of related ones? How were logical combinations of features, such as conjuncts and disjuncts, related to learning? You get the idea. Reliable patterns were uncovered, but their import was largely unclear.

Rosch and Mervis (1975) changed this research enteprise by suggesting that there were rich correlational structures in the world that gave rise to patterns of categorization and concepts. Thus, the mind did not simply construct family resemblance concepts; such concepts reflected something about how kinds and properties were distributed in the world. The structure of the mind was certainly also involved because not all possible minds could pick up on natural correlations, but the correlational structure itself was equally central. The emphasis on the structure of the world and how we functionally interact with it was especially strong with the discovery of the basic level of categorization (i.e., categorizing things at the level of chair, not furniture or armchair), where a salient level of categorization occurred as a function of extra dense feature bundles that provided maximum within-category similarity and maximum between-category differences (Rosch, Mervis, Gray, Johnson, & Boyes-Braem, 1976). Dick liked to think of the basic level as the level at which things have the richest afford-ances, a characterization of categorization that is anything but solipsistic.

But, curiously, the study of categorization after these initial discoveries started to become more solipsistic once again. Discussions focused less and less on interactions with the world and the structure in that world and more and more on which kinds of internal probabilistic representations best modeled human performance. Stimuli once again became largely arbitrary as debates revolved around such issues as whether categorization was based on sets of exemplars or summary representations (Smith & Medin, 1985). Later variants asked if probabilistic distributions were better modeled in symbolic terms or subsymbolic connectionist ones. The stimuli started to look more and more like concatenations of arbitrary features with different probability distributions. We had traded in analytic feature sets for more probabilistic ones, but once again seemed to be looking in a very narrow decontextualized way at the machinery of the mind.

This narrowness became especially evident when one considered the tiny number of papers that followed up on the basic-level phenomenon (e.g., Corter & Gluck, 1992; Murphy, 1982; Tversky & Hemenway, 1984). Only a handful of studies explored the basic level further. The basic level could not really be studied at all in a solipsistic manner, and most of the field was not ready to try alternative approaches.

Research on concepts started to shift again, however, as researchers realized that concepts and categorization seemed to often go beyond the probabilistic in ways that involved causal understandings of the world, or intuitive theories. The concepts-in-theories approach evolved in which con-cepts and categorization were seen as intimately linked to understandings of why features were present in categories and why they were interrelated, understandings that were frequently causal (Murphy & Medin, 1985). Much of this perspective came from developmental research where patterns of conceptual change seemed impossible to explain in ways that merely looked at changing weights on feature sets (Keil, 1987). It also came from more attention to naturalistic instances of categorization and concepts, whether it be psychiatric diagnostic categories, metaphor, or how we combined concepts into larger structures. Again, Dick played a major role in this second revolution when he convened a conference at Emory University in 1984 on concepts that recognized this new perspective (Neisser, 1987).

Today the study of concepts has come much closer to an ecological approach. Major categories in the world such as artifacts, natural kinds, and living kinds are now being studied in many different laboratories in ways that assume that members of these categories have different internal structures and different kinds of functional consequences for people. Not surprisingly, people interact quite differently with most artifacts and living things, and one can identify aspects of those things themselves that have important consequences for how people think about them. Plants and animals seem to have much richer, more causally interconnected essences than artifacts (Gelman, Coley, & Gottfried, 1994; Keil, 1989), they may be embedded in taxonomically deeper hierarchies (Atran, 1996), and their surface properties afford different kinds of interactions. Moreover, artifacts themselves break down into other broad categories such as hand tools, vehicles, clothing, and dwellings, each with their own distinctive causal patternings.

People pick up on these importantly different causal patternings and think about such kinds in dramatically different ways. Some argue that the human mind may need special modes of construal to resonate optimally with these different causal patterns (Keil, 1995), just as some perceptual systems seem to be designed for different patterns in more immediately available information (Gibson, 1966). Alternatively, we may just be especially adept all-purpose learners who are able to uncover causal patterns whenever they are relevant to our needs. That is an important issue, but both sides benefit greatly from an ecological approach.

Very recently, we are seeing truly ecological studies of concepts and categories. For example, one series of studies has asked how categorization of biological flora and fauna is influenced by the ecological practices of people who inhabit such environments. Thus, people who practice slash-and-burn kinds of agriculture seem to have predictably different ways of categorizing the biological world from those who practice more conservative agricultural practices (Coley, Medin, Atran, & Lynch, in press). Categorization of both groups is intimately related to the structure of the biological world but there are striking differences as a consequences of the different affordance patterns that arise between these two groups and the living world around them. Categorization here is anything but arbitrary, but there is also not only one way humans can cut up reality.

There are affinities here with what Marr (1982) called the computational level of analysis, which, despite the misnomer, was a level at which the functional aspects of a system are emphasized with links to real-world structure and that was contrasted with the algorithmic and neural levels, which corresponded to specific software and hardware implementations. Some have argued that the distinctions themselves are meaningless and that we should consider cognition and perception as an irreducible complex of all three, but often those who try to erase the distinctions seem to be doing so in the service of working mostly at the algorithmic and neural levels. There is great value to framing and motivating questions at Marr's computational level. Indeed, it often yields great insights without moving to the other levels.

There is also a resonance of ecological psychology with evolutionary psychology, the currently popular calls for psychology to consider behavior in terms of the selective value of cognitive systems to humans as hunter–gatherers in the Pleistocene era (Cosmides & Tooby, 1987). It is too early to know how well that enterprise will turn out, but already it may be not ecological enough in that it does not sufficiently characterize current ecological relations between humans and the world. Instead it engages in much more remote and speculative ecological analysis of humans and prehumans 1 million years ago and how they spent their days as hunter–gatherers. The problem with such analyses is that they often make weakly motivated decisions about what count as relevant behavioral traits and then reason backwards as to how they were selected for. As Gould and Lewontin (1978) pointed out, such a strategy is fraught with problems and often ends up identifying false traits that are indirect consequences of other structures. The ecological approach engages in a more real-time functional analysis.

Imagine, by analogy, focusing on some aspect of a tool, say the patterns in the grain of a wooden handle of a lawn rake. One could then work backwards to ask how people must have designed rakes to have such grain patterns and what made those grain patterns survive over others. But, at least for common department store rakes, no one selects for particular wood grains. The cheapest woods with sufficient strengths are used, and although some particular wood grain, say of basswood, may be more typically found, it is hardly the key to understanding rakes. It might be only a little less silly to ask about how early rakes were used before people had lawns. Maybe some speculative ecological analysis of early tool use would be of some help, but it does not seem too promising. We are not denying the value of thinking about our ancient pasts but we are suggesting that more often, benefits spring from detailed analyses of how we function in current ecological contexts.

THE YIN AND YANG OF COGNITION

In 1963, really in the early dawn of cognitive psychology, Dick published a wonderful piece in the *British Journal of Psychology* called "The Multiplicity of Thought." The article had many extraordinary attributes, of which perhaps the two most dramatic were its prescience and its integration across time and disparate areas of psychology. Dick argued that we cannot understand cognition monolithically; there seem to be intrinsic dualities in thought and these dualities have existed throughout the history of psychology. For example, in Freud's contrast between primary and secondary cognition (Freud, 1965), Dick pointed out how such accounts of thinking seemed incomplete when they failed to recognize this duality. He tried to characterize it in many ways, but his most central way was perhaps also the most clairvoyant: that cognition seemed to have an associative, largely parallel component that often functioned outside awareness and a more serial, rule-like, explicit component that very often was at the heart of current awareness. We can see threads of connectionist versus rule-based contrasts, of explicit versus implicit memories, and many others here.

Most impressive, however, is the extent to which Dick's arguments in 1963 anticipated what is only now being considered as an important theme across much of cognitive science, the hybrid nature of thought. In the last 5 years or so, we see an extraordinary range of converging sources of evidence that something like associative and more rule-like components are both needed. There are signs from computer science, neuroscience, linguistics, and many areas of psychology. Thus, in computer science, models of language processing are increasing, mixing probabilistic–associationist components with parsing rules of grammar. In neuroscience, there are repeated claims of distinct neural processes involved in the associative and rule-based aspects of tasks, whether it be for verb forms or for categorization (Smith, Patalano, Jonides, & Koeppe, 1996). In linguistics we see claims that combine connectionist models of structure with rule-like constraints (Prince & Smolensky, 1997). Finally, in psychology there are many phenomena that are explained in terms of hybrid structures of this sort, whether it be biases in decision making or categorization. In fact, a publication by Sloman (1996) illustrated how this hybrid nature of thought is emerging across psychology and how it owes a primary debt to Dick's 1963 paper.

One controversy is whether these two aspects of thought really require two different mental implementations. Thus, connectionists argue that both aspects can be modeled in a fully connectionist architecture. For example, Clark (1993) discussed how it might be possible to achieve the effect by breaking a network into subnetworks then hierarchically relating them. Similarly, those more fond of symbolic systems argue that associative and rule-like effects can be easily modeled within wholly symbolic systems. At this point, these debates seem indeterminate; moreover, they start to fall into the solipsistic fallacy once again. For our purposes, what matters more is that two functional systems exist of this sort that work in contrasting ways and with different consequences. They may reflect as much something about the nature of kinds of information in the world as they reflect something about the mind in isolation.

With respect to concepts and causal understanding, the arguments for hybrid structure are among the most compelling and come from many sources. Consider, for example, the problem of how one comes to develop understanding in any domain. Any such understanding requires both an identification of the relevant entities in that domain and an explanation of their features clusters and interrelations. Because causation and correlation are not equivalent, we know that typicality relations will not neatly map onto cause and explanation. We might know, for example, that having long hair and hips are both extremely typical of women, but feel that only the hips are causally central to biological females.

It is tempting to think that causal explanatory knowledge might come to fully pervade sophisticated concepts and understanding in an expert domain but such a conclusion is surely wrong. One of the most universal features of human understanding is that it can never be complete. One cannot explain all patterns we observe, even in cases where we know a great deal. Explanation invariably runs out of power as more probing questions are asked. Any parent can tell you how they have been exasperated by a young child's sequence of why and how questions. The exasperation probably has many reasons, but certainly one is that the parent quickly is unable to answer the question. Consider the following sort of interchange between parent and child that might start with the question of why it rains:

C: Why does it rain?
P: Because the clouds get so full of water that it starts to come out of them.
C: How do the clouds get so full of water?
P: Because the sun makes water evaporate into the air and it forms clouds.
C: How does the sun make water evaporate and why does it then form into clouds instead of being everywhere at once?
P: The sun heats up water and. . . .

If the parent is a layperson, she might stop here in exasperation. If the parent is more expert, she might talk about how warmer water evaporates faster and perhaps mutter something about water molecules in air attracting each other. But even the more expert parent soon runs into trouble with further questions about how light causes heat in water or how heat causes evaporation or what sorts of forces pull water molecules together.

Even the best expert in the world will soon come to a point where science does not know the answer beyond general enabling conditions for phase changes of water or attractive forces among molecules. And certainly the vast majority of us will not know at all. It seems likely that most of us, most of the time, have only the most skeletal sets of causal understandings in most domains. But those causal skeletons are certainly not all we know about a domain. We also keep track of the more associative information as well. We may know, for example, a great deal more information about rain and cloud patterns and their correlations with other climatic conditions, but much of this may not go beyond the associative. Thus, we may know that a particular ozone smell often precedes thunderstorms, or that morning breezes in one's home town are generally from the south and afternoon breezes generally from the north; but that knowledge may carry with it very little understanding of even the simplest cause-and-effect relations.

We do not mean to imply that causal information is somehow at odds with or othogonal to associative information. More complex, multilayered networks of association of covariation patterns can often be extremely powerful pointers to mechanisms (Glymour, 1998); but in many other cases, there is too little structure in the associative matrix to specify any causal mechanism or to provide the person with that associative knowledge with an intuitive sense of mechanism.

The more critical point here concerns how the two facets of knowledge do not just coexist but seem to depend on each other. Complete associative knowledge seems doomed to never get off the ground in a learning situation. The number of possible features to attend to in any situation as well as all their possible interrelations will quickly swamp the power of even the most powerful computational system. Something must limit what patterns are likely to be interconnected, and partial models of causal relations in the world are likely to be some of the most powerful and effective limiters. It would seem, therefore, that some degree of causal understanding should be present as early as associative processes are employed. Conversely, causal knowledge needs to be about something, in particular about patterns of covariation.

The origins of such causal understandings are controversial. One could argue that relatively elaborate causal intuitions are intrinsic to humans and form the core of folk psychology, folk physics, and other domains (e.g., Cosmides & Tooby, 1994). Alternatively, one could argue that we are capable of picking up and extracting causal patterns right from the start. The classic Michotte demonstrations of directly perceiving causal relations and the infant studies following up on this phenomenon might be considered part of a model of how causal relations are directly perceived (Leslie & Keeble, 1987; Michotte, 1963). Even more relevant are the many studies conducted by Gibson, showing that young infants can be remarkably sensitive to environmental affordances that are relevant to their current range of abilities (E. J. Gibson, Owsley & Johnston, 1978; E. J. Gibson et al., 1987; E. J. Gibson & Walker, 1984). Perceiving and acting on affordances might not normally be considered causal knowledge, but in fact such abilities may be exactly how the earliest forms of this knowledge emerges. The infant may not be thinking in terms of mental sentences such as, "That surface with undulating motion will cause me great difficulty in crossing it"; but the infant may well be thinking something more like, "I can't move on that, it won't allow me to move across it." Perhaps notions of how objects and environmental configurations enable and/or permit one's own actions are the earliest forms of causal intuitions.

Finally, from a connectionist perspective, initial attention to causal patterns requires that networks be able to learn causal patterns at the same time as they monitor first-order correlations and probabilities. It is not clear how this is to be done without building in some sort of causal primitives into the networks, but that challenge is one of the most exciting and difficult ones in current connectionist research.

Whatever the learning mechanism, it must be understood as being in collaboration with one that simply tabulates frequencies and correlations. Causal schemas, if you will, suggest what feature clusters to attend to and probabilistic patterns suggest how to sharpen those causal schemas. Each kind of knowledge feeds and depends on the other. Ultimately we are going to need a model of cognition that can explain how these two components in essence help to create and nurture the other one.

We can see this interaction in detail when we consider how concepts develop and how they are used and we can see how it helps us understand some apparent contradictions in the literature. For example, in the area of biological thought, there are powerful controversies over whether preschoolers have a distinct way of thinking about the living world, or what some call having an intuitive theory of biology. Some studies show preschoolers as blissfully ignorant of detailed mechanisms concerning such biological processes as inheritance and disease transmission (Carey, 1995; Solomon & Cassimatis, 1995), whereas others suggest that children do treat living kinds as different in terms of their having stronger internal essences and a certain kind of functional architecture (Atran, 1996; Hatano & Inagaki, 1996; Keil, 1995; Wellman & Gelman, 1997).

This apparent conflict can be resolved if one distinguishes between having relatively abstract impressions of causal patterns unique to biological kinds and having concrete knowledge about particular object features and how they causally interact. In many cases, the associative component simply has not tabulated enough concrete details to enable construction of rich concrete mechanisms; yet the ability to see larger-scale causal patterns can remain intact and be part of the first impressions a child has about living kinds. A 4-year-old may know, for example, that both plants and animals tend to have properties that serve the needs of those entities themselves, whereas most artifacts tend to have properties that serve the needs of other entities (Keil, 1995). The 4-year-olds also seem to construe need in a causally neutral way that does not invoke intentions or other mental states. The same child, however, may have no idea of what any of the internal properties of living kinds look like, thus disallowing any concrete mechanisms (Simons & Keil, 1996).

In a related vein, recent work on categorization in children as young as 10 months suggests that they may sometimes generalize over such superordinate categories as vehicles and animals before they generalize at the basic level (Mandler & McDonough, 1993). Mandler (1992) suggested that this ability to pick up on such seemingly abstract categories may be mediated by certain image schemas that often embody causal relations, such as carrying ability, containment, or self-produced movement. It may be the affordances are strongest at the basic level, but in some cases, at least, with little experience, the more high-level causal patterns may "pop out" first. How, why, and under what circumstances is a critical research question.

The question remains as to how the earliest causal intuitions might change in character with development. For example, if the earliest causal understandings are best thought of in terms of affordances, one would suspect different developmental time courses for the understandings of living things as opposed to artifacts. For such things as tools, vehicles, and furniture, affordances, in the classic sense, are on what one bases one's understanding of objects, in particular in terms of how they enable one to perform actions. But for most animals, especially nondomesticated ones, understanding the animal may rest less on the animal's affordances for the child and more on a second-level awareness of how the animal is adapted to its niche; that is, the affordance patterns between an animal and its environment. This may well be why the most robust basic-level effects tend to be for artifact categories. To be sure, tigers afford eating us and some fish afford eating, but for many animals, our interactions with them may be minimal yet our understandings rich. It may be that our causal understandings first emerge with those things that have enabling functions for their own actions and that only later do we see more clearly enabling functions between another organism and its environment.

KNOWING ONE'S PLACE

In the last decade or so, Dick has written an extensive series of pieces on the different senses of self and the roles they play in cognition, perception, and development (Neisser, 1988, 1991, 1993, 1994). You will remember that he distinguished five senses of self: the ecological self, the interpersonal self, the extended self, the private self, and the conceptual self. Versions of these are again extremely central and longstanding themes in psychology and ones that cross all its subareas. It is far beyond the scope of this chapter to review these different senses of self in detail, but we do want to show how some of these senses figure critically in the development of understanding. Sometimes we think of understanding as simply having a set of mental propositions that refer to an external state of the world; yet in real-world understandings, it seems that it is critical to know one's own place in terms of all those understandings, a knowledge that critically depends on senses of self.

With respect to concepts and conceptual understanding, several senses are obviously relevant, most obviously the conceptual self. But Dick's sense of the conceptual self is far more than just having concepts and self-concepts. A full characterization of understanding draws on the other senses of self as well, especially the private self and the extended self. Starting with the conceptual self, Dick emphasized the knowing of oneself as a specific individual in his or her own world of experience. He saw these self concepts as varying widely across cultures because they can involve social roles, cognitive models of our bodies and minds built up out of instruction and observation, and trait attributions.

The conceptual self refers back to each of the other four kinds of self to give it depth and texture. Our sense of our own body, our sense of interpersonal events and our memories of such events, and our sense of our private mental lives all influence the kind of conceptual self we develop. With respect to understanding and explanation, the private self is critical to knowing what is public versus private knowledge, that is what everyone knows, and what you may only know yourself, as well as the difference between idiosyncratic knowledge and general knowledge. The extended self tells one how understanding was gathered. Was it firsthand experience of a phenomenon, or was it secondhand and thus subject to different standards of evidence and criticism? If it was secondhand, who gave or imparted that knowledge? We then might invoke the interpersonal self to know whether we trusted that person who imparted the knoweldge.

One of the most distinctive aspects of human knowledge is the extent to which we rely on each other's expertise. Even in the most traditional communities many thousands of years ago, divisions of cognitive labor occurred. Some people specialized more in tool making, others more in food gathering and storage. These specializations occur in all human communities and this is a common message of any middle-school social studies class. But despite its obvious nature, it is surprising how rarely it enters into the study of knowledge itself. There is, to be sure, an active area of work on situated and distributed cognition (e.g., Hutchins, 1995) and work on the emergent properties of cognition in groups, whether they be a bunch of preschoolers or an airline cockpit flight crew. When people work together, they develop patterns of sharing and distributing information that can lead to enhanced performance. This too seems strikingly obvious and implicit in our cultural practices for centuries. But again, there has been very little attention to the consequences for theories of knowledge and understanding. Here, we want to focus on the individual's role in such groups and what each person must know to achieve understanding in relation to the knowledge represented by a group. The different senses of self are critical to understanding this process. This is a very different sense of cultural cognition from that articulated in the situated cognition movement (e.g., Greeno & Moore,

1993; Lave, 1988; Lave & Wenger, 1991; Norman, 1993), which focuses on how knowledge is in the social world. Here we focus on how one must understand the socially distributed nature of understanding and one's role in that process.

Consider a concrete example in everyday life where one develops a partial understanding of cars. It is the idea of partial understanding and how it works that is most relevant here. Most everyone has causal beliefs about cars that they invoke to help explain their cars' behaviors or that they use to guide their actions on their cars. We buy gas when the gauge nears empty because we believe that the low gas levels cause the gauge needle to move toward empty and because we believe that gas is needed to enable the car to move. We check coolant levels because we believe that coolant is causally necessary to keep the engine from overheating. We explain the squeaking noise of the brakes as being caused by worn-out pads. We explain the car's difficulty in starting in the winter because of a belief that cold weather causes more difficulty in getting the engine going. But every one of these causal beliefs is only a partial understanding, and for many of us, pathetically partial. How, for example, does cold weather inhibit a car's starting ability? Many would shrug, some might use analogies to other things that are sluggish when cold, and perhaps a smaller amount would argue that chemical reactions are slower in lower temperatures but, even there, any further expansions of how such temperatures slow reactions are likely to be missing.

A paradox seems to emerge. Although we seem to invoke and favor causal relations wherever possible and use them to outweigh simple first order patterns of association, those causal understandings are woefully incomplete at an individual level. How can we put such weight on cause when it seems to be resting on ignorance? The answer may lie in how we come to understand our own limits and capacities and how to use external knowledge in others.

It is obvious to any adult how little younger children know relative to older ones, but it is much less clear how well they know their own ignorance. To be sure, children often ask for answers but there is a great deal they do not know they do not know and having to learn that ignorance is difficult. It is a cliché that the greater the scholar, the more he or she understands what is not known. Yet we all come to be content with less than full understanding, with a partial understanding that we assume is good enough to get us around in the world. This partial understanding is a division of cognitive labor with enormous consequences. It was described nicely by Putnam (1975b) in his analysis of natural language terms, where he talked about a division of linguistic labor. Thus, most of us use the word *gold* with almost complete ignorance of the chemistry and physics of gold and most of us would freely admit that appropriate experts could show us to be wrong in our initial hunches of what was gold.

More recently, Kitcher (1993), in his book *The Advancement of Science,* talks about a similar division of cognitive labor. He pointed out the enormous importance of appropriate circles of consensus among experts and how their spheres of activity work toward an overall coherence. At a more detailed level, Kitcher tried to explain the dynamics of the cognitive labor in a formal analysis that blends aspects of Bayesian decision theory, microeconomics, and population biology. This highly technical treatment, however, still focuses on a kind of group process and less on what each indvidual has to know about the terrain of knowledge distributed across that group. But it does seem to presuppose such an understanding as Kitcher repeatedly referred to how scientific progress is critically dependent on developing patterns of trust and reliance on others' understanding. More simply, Hardwig (1985) referred to this as the idea of epistemic dependence. He put the phenomenon nicely when he stated that:

> The conclusion that it is sometimes irrational to think for oneself—that rationality sometimes consists in deferring to epistemic authority and, consequently, in passively and uncritically accepting what we are given to believe—will strike those wedded to epistemic individualism as odd and unacceptable, for it undermines their paradigm of rationality. To others, it may seem too obvious for such belaboring. (p. 343)

To be able to identify appropriate experts, to be able to know the limits of one's own knowledge, and to be able to know when one's knowledge is enough, require important senses of self. And in each domain of knowledge, the links to others may be somewhat different. The depth of our expertise can vary enormously as can the ways in which knowledge is structured and distributed across people. Some kinds of knowledge may be assumed to be a kind of universal competence in which differences in expertise are minor, whereas others lend themselves to vast differences in specialization. We do not think there are special experts who can help us understand how to better climb stairs, but we do think there are such experts for how to swim. There is great controversy on whether any adult is more expert than another in how to make moral judgments, but no one doubts differences in expertise in the ability to make legal judgments. For our purposes, we focus on cases where almost everyone sees vast differences in degrees of understanding. In such cases, consider how children come to see such differences and learn to work with them.

By 3 or so, almost all children have mastered some basics of the theory of mind, knowing that others have belief–desire states that help explain their actions (Wellman, 1990). But this achievement neglects the great deal of social understanding that continues to emerge and how the social sense of self is a complex sense that requires much time to develop. For example, consider how young children seem to be excessively optimistic about all aspects of themselves and how those aspects will change with the future. In one set of studies, younger children were confident that almost any negative trait, mental or physical, would improve with age to a positive direction (Lockhart, 1997). Thus, 5-year-olds tend to assume that, even if one is much less musical than most, or even if one is shorter than most, that if one really wants to be more musical or taller than others, one will end up that way as one grows older. They are surprisingly unrealistic about their own limitations and about the stability of those limitations over time.

The sense of self is intimately involved in such studies because it requires knowing one's limitations and their future consequences. This is also true for knowing about one's own state of knowledge. These results suggest that younger children might also be unrealistically optimistic about their future potential for understanding the world. For example, their peppering adults with countless why questions may reflect their beliefs that adults are omniscient in all areas of knowledge and this view may be related to an unreasonable optimism about their own future state of understanding as an adult. Younger children seem to have a poor grasp of what they do not know and how to reduce ignorance in specific ways, and this weak sense of their own understanding is intimately related to a failure to see how understanding is distributed across others.

More broadly, we all come to develop a sense of the broader social terrain of understanding. We develop strong ideas of where we can be confident in our beliefs and where we should have doubts. We may not always be right in such beliefs, but they are critical to how we function. Moreover, we partition the world up into different kinds of knowledge experts and know who to access in what contexts. This partitioning requires a partial understanding of the phenomena in question and our own position in that understanding. You have to know a little physics to know what a physicist is, even if you are not one. These kinds of knowledge divisions are vivid in academic circles, but everyone in all walks of life knows of some such divisions and uses them. Such divisions, however, may depend critically on our partial understandings and the ways in which they make up skeletal theories of the world. We do not just know that there are experts with different labels, like doctors, chemists, and biologists. We know something about the domains of medicine, chemistry, and biology and how we and experts are connected to knowledge about that domain.

We have some hunches about what sorts of explanations are likely to be relevant and who might be able to give them. Similarly, we suspect that there are many possible areas of knowledge expertise that would strike all of us, including children, as implausible because they do not form a coherent domain with common principles. For example, almost everyone would think it strange for there to be an area of study of tires for red cars or of trees with odd numbers of branches. Those just are not likely to be meaningful groups for a conceptual analysis.

Two decades ago, there was a hot area of research on the development of metacognitive awareness. It often involved showing developing patterns in children coming to know that they do not know an answer to a problem. But that is only a small part of knowing one's place in the society of knowledge. As we get older, we also come to know more clearly what we do not know, perhaps why we do not know it, and how we might find it out. It often seems that we know how to achieve a partial level of understanding that is at a functional level that gives us benefits even as we also know that we will have to defer to experts to unpack almost all the details of our causal beliefs.

It is not possible here to give detailed examples of how this knowledge of the social terrain of understanding develops because there simply has not been enough work done. We do suggest however, that different senses of self, very much in the ways suggested by Dick, will be central. Dick's emphasis on the self in this different sense naturally highlights the importance of knowing how one's own knowledge is located relative to the larger landscape of knowledge in a community.

UNDERSTANDING AS NAVIGATION: "EAST IS BIG BIRD?"

One of Dick's favorite books in cognitive science is Gladwin's (1970) *East Is a Big Bird*, an account of the Pulawat islanders of the South Pacific and how they navigate over hundreds of miles of open ocean to tiny distant islands. They do so without charts, compasses, or any other man-made aids to navigation. As one reads Gladwin's account, one sees the Pulawats as moving through the marine environment almost as one might move through a smaller terrestrial environment. They use the stars, the wave patterns, and flora and fauna to provide a continuous flow of information that helps them orient toward the desired location. At any moment they are, if you will, perceiving their path over the water in real time, rather than, say, holding a compass course for a point indicated on a chart.

Our natural understandings may not be so different in character. We understand how most things work and why they are as they are as a consequence of how we interact with them. We engage in an action to understand, whether it be a physical action or a more mental exploratory one. This is where the navigation and grasping metaphors converge. We need to find ways of negotiating the structure of the world so as to act more effectively on it.

The grasping-reality metaphor and the three principles we have mentioned emphasize several aspects of knowing:

1. The active, exploratory nature of how we achieve understanding. We are not merely passive vessels into which knowledge is poured. This point seems obvious and certainly was central to Dewey's approach to education almost 100 years ago; yet it often seems lacking in the study of concepts and understanding.

2. The importance of characterizing the intrinsic structure of what is grasped. Of course we want to know how the mind interprets reality by knowing more about the mind, but to do so also requires a characterization of reality itself. We need to make much more of an effort describing the causal structures of the world and the different levels of those structures if we are to have an adequate account of how we understand and interpret that structure. A related point here is that the world is not homogeneously structured. It is a rich and diverse array of causal structures that link properties together into stable clusters each with their own character, and we must have minds capable of partially picking up on that heterogeneity.

3. The Gibsonian idea of affordances; that is, how properties of some facet of the world interact causally and functionally with our physical and behavioral structures. The notion of affordances may be the key to uncovering how children develop causal undertandings in the first place. In a recent publication, Premack and Premack (1994) suggested that there is a critical contrast between the natural cause of Michotte (1963) and the arbitrary cause of Hume (1951), with natural cause being developmentally more basic. They saw the earliest form of natural cause being that of a naive psychology with aspects of physical causality coming in later. They went on to suggest that, "explanation, embedded in naive theories about the world, is largely a human specialization" (p. 361). This may be right for explicit explanations, but it may be that, in form of affordances, domain-specific appreciations of physical causal patterns are very early and shared with many species.

4. The relative importance of explanation over prediction. When we grasp an object, or more generally navigate our way through a novel, cluttered environment, we tend to respond to the structure of the world in a continuous interactive cycle (another Neisser idea) rather than making extensive predictions and then reacting to them. Building up understanding is like sharpening a lens that helps us see some aspect of the world more clearly or like developing increasing coordinated ways of grabbing rockholds in mountain climbing, even though each successive hold may be novel and unpredictable. It is less like predictions of the sort we are supposed to put forth in journal articles.

5. Finally, the grasping metaphor reminds us that there are often many ways to grasp the same thing depending on our needs, how it is presented

to us, and depending on what we have experienced before. A realist approach to understanding and science, for that manner, does not say we can grasp all of reality or that all of us will grasp it in the same ways. It does say, however, that we succeed in getting about in the world just because we do much better than chance at picking up on those causal patterns that have special consequences for our own actions.

In sum, we strive to explain and understand all that is around us, but, as we have seen, explanation and understanding cannot be understood in terms of the isolated mechanics of the mind and that even when such mechanics are considered in context, an essential hybrid of causal understanding and associative record keeping seems inescapable. Finally, just as we need to know where we are in physical space to be able to navigate further, we need to know where we are in the community of knowledge to be able to successfully increase our understanding there as well. For the community of knowledge that is cognitive science, we will always see Dick Neisser as one of its most central figures.

ACKNOWLEDGMENTS

Preparation of parts of this chapter and some of the studies described herein were supported by NIH Grant R01-HD23922 to F. Keil. Thanks to Bill Hirst for helpful comments on an earlier draft of this chapter.

REFERENCES

Atran, S. (1996). From folk biology to scientific biology. In D. R. Olson & N. Torrance (Eds.), *Handbook of education and human development: New models of learning, teaching, and schooling* (pp. 206–248). Oxford, England: Blackwell.

Carey, S. (1995). On the origin of causal understanding. In D. Sperber, D. Premack, & A. J. Premack (Eds.), *Causal cognition: A multidisciplinary approach* (pp. 268–303). New York: Oxford University Press.

Clark, A. (1993). *Associative engines: Connectionism, concepts and representational change.* Cambridge, MA: MIT Press.

Coley, J. D., Medin, D. L., Atran, S., & Lynch, E. (in press). Does privilege have its rank? Folkbiological taxonomy and induction in two cultures. *Cognition.*

Corter, J., & Gluck, M. (1992). Explaining basic categories: Feature predictability and information. *Psychological Bulletin, 111,* 291–303.

Cosmides, L., & Tooby, J. (1987). From evolution to behavior: Evolutionary psychology as the missing link. In J. Dupre (Ed.), *The latest on the best* (pp. 277–306). Cambridge, MA: MIT Press.

Cosmides, L., & Tooby, J. (1994). The evolution of domain specificity: The evolution of functional organization. In L. A. Hirschfeld & S. A. Gelman (Eds.), *Mapping the mind:*

Domain specificity in cognition and culture (pp. 85–116). Cambridge, England: Cambridge University Press.

Fodor, J. A. (1980). Methodological solipsism considered as a research strategy in cognitive psychology. *The Behavioral and Brain Sciences, 3,* 63–110.

Freud, S. (1965). *The interpretation of dreams* (J. Strachey, Trans.). New York: Avon.

Gelman, S. A., Coley, J. D., & Gottfried, G. M. (1994). Essentialist beliefs in children: The acquisition of concepts and theories. In L. A. Hirschfeld & S. A. Gelman (Eds.), *Mapping the mind: Domain specificity in cognition and culture* (pp. 341–365). Cambridge, England: Cambridge University Press.

Gibson, E. J. (1970). The development of perception as an adaptive process. *American Scientist, 58,* 98–107.

Gibson, E. J., Owsley, C. J., & Johnston, J. (1978). Perception of invariants by five-month-old infants: Differentiation of two types of motion. *Developmental Psychology 14,* 407–415.

Gibson, E. J., Riccion, G., Schmuckler, M., Stoffregen, T. A., Rosenberg, D., & Taormina, J. (1987). Detection of the traversability of surfaces by crawling and walking infants. *Journal of Experimental Psychology: Human Perception and Performance, 13,* 515–523.

Gibson, E. J., & Walker, A. S. (1984). Development of knowledge of visual and tactual affordances of substance. *Child Development, 55,* 453–460.

Gibson, J. J. (1961). Ecological optics. *Vision Research, 1,* 253–262.

Gibson, J. J. (1966). *The senses considered as perceptual systems.* Boston: Houghton Mifflin.

Gladwin, T. (1970). *East is a big bird.* Cambridge, MA: Harvard University Press.

Glymour, C. (1998). Learning causes: Psychological explanations of causal explanation. *Minds and Machines, 8,* 39–60.

Greeno, J. G., & Moore, J. L. (1993). Situativity and symbols; response to Vera and Simon. *Cognitive Science, 17,* 45–59.

Gould, S. J., & Lewontin, R. C. (1978). The spandrels of San Marco and the Panglossian paradigm. *Proceedings of the Royal Society, London, 205,* 581–598.

Hardwig, J. (1985). Epistemic dependence. *The Journal of Philosophy, 85,* 335–349.

Hatano, G., & Inagaki, K. (1996). Cognitive and cultural factors in the acquisition of intuitive biology. In D. R. Olson & N. Torrance (Eds.), *Handbook of education and human development: New models of learning, teaching, and schooling* (pp. 204–248). Oxford, England: Blackwell.

Hume, D. (1951). *Theory of knowledge. Containing the enquiry concerning understanding, the abstract and selected passages from book I of A treatise on human nature.* New York: Nelson.

Hutchins, E. (1995). *Cognition in the wild.* Cambridge, MA: MIT Press.

Keil, F. C. (1987). Conceptual development and category structure. In U. Neisser (Ed.), *Concepts and conceptual development: Ecological and intellectual factors in categorization* (pp. 175–200). Cambridge, England: Cambridge University Press.

Keil, F. C. (1989). *Concepts, kinds and cognitive development.* Cambridge, MA: MIT Press.

Keil, F. C. (1995). The growth of causal understandings of natural kinds. In D. Sperber, D. Premack, & A. Premack (Eds.), *Causal cognition: A multidisciplinary debate* (pp. 286–302). Oxford, England: Oxford University Press.

Kitcher, P. (1993). *The advancement of science.* Oxford, England: Oxford University Press.

Lave, J. (1988). *Cognition in practice.* New York: Cambridge University Press.

Lave, J., & Wenger, E. (1991). *Situated learning: Legitimate peripheral participation.* Cambridge, England: Cambridge University Press.

Leslie, A., & Keeble, S. (1987). Do six-month olds perceive causality? *Cognition, 25,* 265–288.

Lockhart, K. (1997). *Unlearned optimism: Children's beliefs about the stability of traits.* Paper presented at the meeting of the Society for Research in Child Development.

Mandler, J. M. (1992). How to build a baby: II. Conceptual primitives. *Psychological Review, 99,* 587–604.

Mandler, J. M., & McDonough, L. (1993). Concept formation in infancy. *Cognitive Development,* *8,* 291–318.

Marr, D. (1982). *Vision.* San Francisco: Freeman.

Michotte, A. (1963). *The perception of causality* (T. R. Miles & E. Miles, Trans.). London: Methuen.

Murphy, G. L. (1982). Cue validity and levels of categorization. *Psychological Bulletin, 91,* 174–177.

Murphy, G. L., & Medin, D. (1985). The role of theories in conceptual coherence. *Psychological Review, 92,* 289–316.

Neisser, U. (1963). The multiplicity of thought. *British Journal of Psychology, 54,* 1–14.

Neisser, U. (1976). *Cognition and reality.* San Francisco: Freeman.

Neisser, U. (1987). *Concepts and conceptual development: Ecological and intellectual factors in categorization.* Cambridge, England: Cambridge University Press.

Neisser, U. (1988). Five kinds of self-knowledge. *Philosophical Psychology, 1*(1), 35–59.

Neisser, U. (1991). Two perceptually given aspects of the self and their development. *Developmental Review, 11*(3), 197–209.

Neisser, U. (Ed.). (1993). *The perceived self: Ecological and interpersonal sources of self-knowledge.* New York: Cambridge University Press.

Neisser, U. (1994). Self-narratives: True and false. In U. Neisser & R. Fivush (Eds.), *The remembering self: Construction and accuracy in the self-narrative.* Cambridge, England: Cambridge University Press.

Neisser, U., & Divush, R. (Eds.). (1994). *The remembering self: Construction and accuracy in the self-narrative.* Cambridge, England: Cambridge University Press.

Norman, D. (1993). Cognition in the head and in the world: An introduction to the special issue on situated action. *Cognitive Science, 17,* 1–7.

Piatelli-Palmarini, M. (1989). Evolution, selection, and cognition: From "learning" to parameter setting in biology and in the study of language. *Cognition, 31,* 1–44.

Premack, D., & Premack, A. (1994). Levels of causal understanding in chimpanzees and children. *Cognition, 50,* 347–362.

Prince, A., & Smolensky, P. (1997). Optimality: From neural networks to universal grammar. *Science, 275,* 1604–1610.

Putnam, H. (Ed.). (1975a). *Mind, language and reality* (Vol. 2). Cambridge, England: Cambridge University Press.

Putnam, H. (1975b). The meaning of meaning. In H. Putnam (Ed.), *Mind, language and reality* (Vol. 2, pp. 215–271). London: Cambridge University Press.

Rosch, E., & Mervis, C. B. (1975). Family resemblances: Studies in the internal structure of categories. *Cognitive Psychology, 7,* 573–605.

Rosch, E., Mervis, C. B., Gray, W. D., Johnson, D., & Boyes-Braem, P. (1976). Basic objects in natural categories. *Cognitive Psychology, 8,* 382–439.

Salmon, W. C. (1989). *Four decades of scientific explanation.* Minneapolis: University of Minnesota Press.

Simons, D., & Keil, F. C. (1995). An abstract to concrete shift in cognitive development: The inside story. *Cognition, 56,* 129–163.

Sloman, S. A. (1996). The empirical case for two systems of reasoning. *Psychological Bulletin, 119*(1), 3–22.

Smith, E. E., & Medin, D. L. (1981). *Categories and concepts.* Cambridge, MA: Harvard University Press.

Smith, E. E., Patalano, A. L., Jonides, J., & Koeppe, R. A. (1996, November). *PET evidence for different categorization mechanisms.* Paper presented at the 37th annual meeting of the Psychonomic Society, Chicago.

Solomon, G. E. A., & Cassimatis, N. L. (1995, March). *On young children's understanding of germs as biological causes of illness.* Paper presented at the meeting of the Society for Research in Child Development, Indianapolis, IN.

Tversky, B., & Hemenway, K. (1984). Objects, parts, and categories. *Journal of Experimental Psychology: General, 113*, 169–193.

Wellman, H. (1990). *The child's theory of mind.* Cambridge, MA: Bradford Books/MIT Press.

Wellman, H. M., & Gelman, S. A. (1998). Knowledge acquisition in foundational domains. In D. Kuhn, R. Siegler, & W. Damon (Eds.), *Cognition, perception and language, Vol. 2. of Handbook of Child Psychology (5th ed.)* (pp. 523–574). New York: Wiley.

Chapter 9

The Williams Syndrome Cognitive Profile: Strengths, Weaknesses, and Interrelations Among Auditory Short-Term Memory, Language, and Visuospatial Constructive Cognition

Carolyn B. Mervis
University of Louisville

As an undergraduate at Cornell University, I studied linguistics. But I had time for a little bit of psychology, so I enrolled in Dick Neisser's course, Attention and Memory. This was my first systematic exposure to psychological research methods, and I was fascinated. Neisser often asked for volunteers to participate in graduate student research, and I was always willing. The critical experiment for my career involved a study of iconic memory. My data were unusual enough that the graduate student decided Dr. Neisser would want to talk with me himself. And so I went to Dr. Neisser's office, where we had a long discussion about iconic memory and visual perception, as his dog, Max, lounged contentedly nearby. Although my primary interest remained linguistics, I continued to meet with Dick to discuss research methods.

My intent had been to go to graduate school in linguistics and I was on the verge of accepting an offer from the University of Edinburgh when Dick stepped in. He argued that given my interest in language development, I really should become a psychologist, rather than a linguist. He urged me to enter the graduate psychology program at Cornell. And so I did. Throughout the time I was in graduate school, Dick and I continued our research method discussions, although the two of us were never engaged in research on the same topic at the same time. Dick stressed the importance of combining logical reasoning and creative ideas, the necessity of considering all points of view, and being willing to change one's mind. These emphases have remained with me throughout my career.

Last year, for the first time, Dick and I ended up focusing on the same research area, intelligence, simultaneously. We talked frequently about theoretical issues, research design, and questions of data interpretation. Dick always cut to the core of the matter. For me, these discussions led both to new insights and further questions. My research on the nature of intelligence in Williams syndrome is ongoing. In this chapter, I summarize the current state of this research and consider some of its implications.

Williams syndrome is a rare genetic disorder caused by a submicroscopic hemizygous deletion of chromosome 7q11.23. The incidence of Williams syndrome is estimated at 1 per 20,000 live births. The medical phenotype includes a distinctive set of facial features (see Fig. 9.1), a recognizable pattern of malformations including connective tissue abnormalities and heart disease (especially supravalvar aortic stenosis [SVAS]), and infantile hypercalcemia. Williams syndrome is associated with an unusual personality profile: Individuals with Williams syndrome are overly friendly to strangers, very sensitive to and concerned about other people's feelings, overly anxious to please others, and have a very high level of anticipatory anxiety

FIG. 9.1.   A 26-year-old woman who has Williams syndrome.

for both positive and negative future events. Individuals with Williams syndrome typically have mild to moderate mental retardation or learning disabilities. Williams syndrome involves a unique profile of cognitive strengths and weaknesses; this profile is a major focus of this chapter. (For a more extensive description of the Williams syndrome phenotype, see Mervis, Morris, Bertrand, & Robinson, in press.)

A genetic test for Williams syndrome did not become available until 1993 (Ewart, Morris, Atkinson, et al., 1993). Until that time, diagnosis had to be made based solely on phenotypic characteristics. Many cases of Williams syndrome went undiagnosed; at the same time, many people who did not actually have Williams syndrome were given that diagnosis nevertheless (Preus, 1984). Between the very low incidence of Williams syndrome and the relatively high incidence of missed diagnoses and misdiagnoses, research on Williams syndrome was extremely challenging.

I chose to take on this challenge because of a talk I heard Bates (1990) give at the International Conference on Infant Studies in 1990. In this presentation, Bates described Bellugi's pioneering work on the language and cognitive abilities of individuals with Williams syndrome (e.g., Bellugi, Marks, Bihrle, & Sabo, 1988; Thal, Bates, & Bellugi, 1989). Bellugi had found that the language abilities of individuals with Williams syndrome were much better than would have been expected based on their level of general cognitive development. Furthermore, Bellugi argued, her data demonstrated that individuals with Williams syndrome acquire language in the absence of important cognitive abilities that had been considered prerequisite to language acquisition. More generally, Bellugi claimed that her data showed that language was independent of (dissociated from) other aspects of cognition.

This picture of language development in Williams syndrome contradicted my basic beliefs about how language development proceeds. I decided that I needed to follow the development of young children with Williams syndrome to see for myself how these children acquire language. Early in 1991, Bertrand and I finally located a toddler with Williams syndrome and began to observe her acquisition of language. Eventually, we located several other infants and toddlers with Williams syndrome. Our longitudinal study of these children (Mervis & Bertrand, 1997) convinced us that language development was certainly more advanced than many other aspects of cognition in Williams syndrome, but that the cognitive prerequisites for language acquisition were actually in place at the time children with Williams syndrome began to talk. By then, however, I had become interested more generally in the question of the relations between linguistic and nonlinguistic aspects of cognition in school-aged children and adults with Williams syndrome, and the possible genetic basis for the cognitive profile associated with Williams syndrome. In this chapter, I focus on this aspect of my research.

The remainder of this chapter is divided into three sections. In the first section, I present a proposal for an operational definition of the cognitive profile associated with Williams syndrome. I then provide evidence that this cognitive profile measure systematically differentiates between individuals who have Williams syndrome and individuals who have other syndromes, mental retardation of unknown etiology, or borderline normal intelligence. The pattern of findings suggests that there is a genetic basis for the cognitive profile associated with Williams syndrome. In the second section, I consider the research addressing the genetics of Williams syndrome in which I have been involved. I describe the logic behind the strategy my collaborators and I are following in our genotype/phenotype correlation research, and present evidence for a specific genetic basis for one component of the cognitive profile associated with Williams syndrome. In the third section, I consider the implications of the findings of the first and second sections for questions concerning the possible decoupling of language from other aspects of cognition in Williams syndrome.

WILLIAMS SYNDROME COGNITIVE PROFILE

The results of previous studies of individuals with Williams syndrome suggest a characteristic cognitive profile. Auditory short-term memory is a relative strength both in childhood and adulthood. Short-term memory ability has been studied for individuals from the United States (Bennett, LaVeck, & Sells, 1978; Mervis et al., in press; Wang & Bellugi, 1994), Great Britain (Udwin & Yule, 1991), Canada (Finegan, Smith, Meschino, Vallance, & Sitarenios, 1995), and Italy (Vicari, Brizzolara, Carlesimo, Pezzini, & Volterra, 1996). In all these studies, auditory short-term memory was better than would have been expected for the overall level of cognitive ability.

The language abilities of individuals with Williams syndrome have also been found to be relatively good. The results of most studies indicate that language abilities are approximately at the level expected for overall level of cognitive ability. This result has been obtained for individuals from the United States (Bennett et al., 1978; Mervis et al., in press), England (Udwin & Yule, 1991), Germany (Gosch, Stading, & Pankau, 1994), and Italy (Volterra, Capirci, Pezzini, Sabbadini, & Vicari, 1996). Bellugi and her coworkers (e.g., Bellugi, Birhle, Neville, & Doherty, 1992; Bellugi, Klima, & Wang, 1996; Bellugi et al., 1988; Bellugi, Wang, & Jernigan, 1994) have reported that the language abilities of individuals with Williams syndrome are at a higher level than would be expected for the overall level of cognitive ability.

In contrast, the visuospatial constructive abilities of individuals with Williams syndrome have been found to be extremely poor. Studies have been conducted on individuals with Williams syndrome from the United States (Bellugi et al., 1988, 1992, 1994, 1996; Bertrand, Mervis, & Eisenberg, 1997; Mervis et al., in press), England (Udwin & Yule, 1991), and Italy (Milani, Dall'Oglio, & Vicari, 1995). In all these studies, performance on visuospatial constructive cognitive tasks was found to be well below the level expected for overall level of cognitive ability.

This particular pattern of cognitive strengths and weaknesses—definite strength in auditory short-term memory, relative strength in language, and extreme weakness in visuospatial construction—was a pattern I had not encountered previously for individuals with mental retardation or border-line normal intelligence. To determine if this pattern had previously been reported as characteristic of another syndrome involving mental retardation or borderline normal intelligence (e.g., Down, Fragile X, Noonan, Prader-Willi, autism, fetal alcohol), members of my laboratory conducted a literature review. This review confirmed that the patterns of cognitive strengths and weaknesses associated with these other syndromes differed from the pattern for Williams syndrome.

Thus, the cognitive profile for Williams syndrome suggested by previous research may well be specific for Williams syndrome. However, demonstration of the consistency and uniqueness of the cognitive profile for Williams syndrome has been hampered by the lack of an explicit quantitative specification operationalization of the profile. Across previous studies, a wide range of measures was used. In many cases, no norms for these measures were available, leading researchers to base their conclusions on a comparison of small samples of individuals with Williams syndrome to small samples of either individuals with other forms of mental retardation (matched for mental age [MA]) or individuals who were developing normally (whose mean chronological age [CA] matched the mean MA of the Williams syndrome group). In other cases, norms for specific measures were available but different measures were normed on different samples of normally developing individuals, making comparisons across measures less than ideal.

Operationalization of the Williams Syndrome Cognitive Profile

To address these problems, we have recently proposed and tested a systematic method of assessment of the Williams syndrome cognitive profile (WSCP) across a broad age range (Mervis, Robinson, Bertrand, Klein, & Armstrong, 1996). This operationalization was based on a specific pattern of performance on particular subtests of the Differential Ability Scales (DAS; Elliott, 1990), a standardized measure of intellectual abilities. Use of the DAS rather than other measures of intellectual abilities (e.g., the Wechsler intelligence tests) offers two major advantages. First, the DAS was carefully designed to provide specific information about an individual's cognitive strengths and weaknesses across a wide range of intellectual abilities. Second, the large range of possible standard scores on the DAS provides greatly increased sensitivity to differences in ability across subtests. This is particularly important for differentiating among the subtest ability levels of individuals who are at the extremes of the intelligence distribution. The Upper Preschool and School Age levels of the DAS include six core subtests (measuring language, visuospatial construction, and reasoning) which contribute to the child's GCA score (General Conceptual Ability; similar to an IQ score) and also several diagnostic subtests that are not included in the GCA. One of these diagnostic subtests measures auditory short-term memory. Standard scores (*T*-scores) on each subtest range from 20 to 80, with a standard deviation of 10. (In contrast, scaled scores on the Wechsler IQ tests range from 1 to 19, with a standard deviation of 3.) A *T*-score of 50 indicates performance at the 50th percentile.

Our operationalization of the WSCP addresses both mean level of overall performance on the six core subtests (as indicated by the mean *T*-score), and performance on four specific subtests. One of these subtests measures auditory rote memory (digit recall subtest), two measure verbal abilities (naming/definitions and similarities), and one measures visuospatial constructive ability (pattern construction). For each of these measures, the DAS covers the range of performance expected from very low functioning 3-year-olds to very high functioning 17-year-olds (equivalent to adult levels). In determining if an individual fits the WSCP, both absolute levels of performance and also level of performance on certain subtests relative to performance on other subtests are taken into account. An individual was considered to fit the WSCP if he or she met all the following criteria:

1. Pattern construction *T*-score < mean *T*-score (for core subtests);
2. Pattern construction *T*-score < digit recall *T*-score;
3. Pattern construction *T*-score < 20th percentile;
4. *T*-score for either digit recall, naming/definitions, or similarities > 1st percentile ($T \geq 29$).

The first two criteria reflect the expected weakness in visuospatial constructive abilities relative to both overall level of ability and level of auditory short-term memory ability. The third criterion reflects the expected weakness in visuospatial constructive abilities relative to the norming sample of the DAS. (This criterion was designed to exclude from the WSCP high-ability individuals who happen to have stronger verbal skills than spatial skills.) The fourth criterion reflects the expected strength in either auditory short-term memory or language relative to overall level of ability, even for individuals who are very low functioning.

Sensitivity and Specificity of the WSCP

For a cognitive profile to be useful, it should have high sensitivity and specificity. Sensitivity is defined as the proportion of individuals who are expected to fit the profile who in fact do fit it. In the present study, the sensitivity of the WSCP equals the proportion of individuals with Williams syndrome who met all four of the inclusion criteria for the WSCP. Specificity is defined as the proportion of individuals who are expected not to fit the profile who in fact do not fit it. In the present study, the specificity of the WSCP equals the proportion of individuals who did not have Williams syndrome who did not meet all four of the inclusion criteria for the WSCP.

To determine the sensitivity and specificity of the WSCP, we administered the DAS to 81 individuals with Williams syndrome and to 51 individuals who did not have Williams syndrome (mixed etiology group). The DAS was administered and scored according to the standard procedures. The individuals with Williams syndrome ranged in age from 3 years, 11 months to 46 years (mean = 12 years, 7 months). Approximately two thirds of these individuals had been tested for a possible elastin deletion (the genetic test for Williams syndrome); all had tested positive. The remaining individuals had been diagnosed with Williams syndrome by a clinical geneticist with extensive experience with Williams syndrome (Colleen A. Morris), using the criteria of Lowery et al. (1995; these criteria do not include measures of specific cognitive abilities). The DAS may be used to determine IQs for individuals less than 18 years old. Mean IQ for the 66 individuals with Williams syndrome who were less than 18 years of age was 58.52 (sd = 10.87), with a range from 32 to 84.

Individuals in the mixed etiology group ranged in age from 3 years, 3 months to 34 years (mean = 12 years, 6 months). This group included 25 individuals who had a variety of genetic or other congenital disorders (e.g., Down syndrome, Fragile X syndrome, Noonan syndrome, autism, fetal alcohol syndrome), and 26 individuals who did not have any known congenital disorder but had mental retardation of unknown etiology or borderline normal intelligence. Mean IQ for the 41 individuals who were less than 18 years old was 67.61 (sd = 18.25), with a range from 31 to 111.

We began our analyses by comparing the pattern of overall performance of the Williams syndrome group to that of the mixed etiology group. For each group, we determined the distribution of *T*-scores for the pattern construction, naming/definitions, similarities, and digit recall subtests, as well as for overall level of performance on the six core subtests. This information is presented in the box-and-whiskers plots shown in Fig. 9.2. The 50th percentile corresponds to the internal bar in each box; the bottom of the box corresponds to the 25th percentile and the top of the box to the 75th percentile. The end of the bottom whisker corresponds to the minimum score obtained; the end of the top whisker corresponds

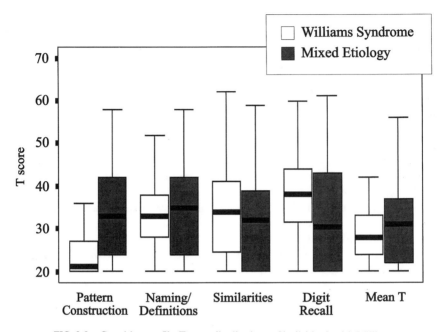

FIG. 9.2. Cognitive profile *T*-score distributions of individuals with Williams syndrome (N = 81) and individuals from the mixed etiology contrast group (N = 51).

to the maximum score obtained, excluding outliers. A visual examination of the data presented in Fig. 9.2 for the individuals with Williams syndrome indicates that the pattern of performance fit well with that found in previous studies. The present sample of individuals with Williams syndrome showed a definite weakness in visuospatial constructive abilities, a relative strength in language abilities, and a definite strength in auditory short-term memory. In contrast, the mean levels of performance of the mixed etiology group were relatively flat across all the abilities measured, and within each ability, performance was much more variable than for the Williams syndrome group. This pattern of performance for the mixed etiology group is partially due to the averaging together of data from individuals who show different patterns of cognitive strengths and weaknesses.

Thus, the overall pattern of findings from the group data portrayed in Fig. 9.2 suggests that, in general, the performance of the individuals with Williams syndrome fit the WSCP, whereas performance of the individuals in the mixed etiology group did not. However, in order to evaluate the fit of individual participants' profiles to the WSCP, the pattern of data from each participant must be considered separately. Accordingly, the four profile inclusion rules described previously were applied to the *T*-scores each individual earned for the various subtests of the DAS and for overall performance on the core subtests. Results indicated that 71 of the 81 individuals with Williams syndrome fit the WSCP, yielding a sensitivity of .88.

The pattern was very different for the mixed etiology group. Of the 51 individuals in that group, 47 did not fit the WSCP, yielding a specificity of .92. The four individuals in the mixed etiology group who fit the WSCP included one high-functioning school-age girl with Down syndrome, two school-age boys with learning difficulties of an unknown etiology, and one adult male, also of unknown etiology.

Included in the mixed etiology group was a particularly interesting subgroup composed of 16 individuals who either had been clinically diagnosed by other geneticists as having Williams syndrome (13 individuals) or for whom the diagnosis had been considered seriously, although never actually made (3 individuals). None of these 16 individuals tested positive for an elastin deletion. These individuals ranged in age from 3 years, 3 months to 30 years, with a mean age of 11 years, 4 months. Mean IQ for the 14 individuals who were less than 18 years old was 69.93 (sd = 21.81), with a range from 31 to 111.

A comparison of this subgroup to the Williams syndrome group is particularly interesting because it offers a contrast between individuals who were clinically considered to have Williams syndrome (or for whom the diagnosis of Williams syndrome had been seriously considered) but who did not meet the genetic criteria for Williams syndrome and individuals who met both the clinical and genetic criteria for Williams syndrome. Of the 16 individuals in the Williams syndrome clinical-only group, 14 did not fit the WSCP. Two individuals were excluded because their *T*-scores for digit recall, naming/definition, and similarities were all at the 1st percentile. The other 14 individuals were excluded because they did not show a specific weakness in visuospatial construction.

In summary, our results indicate that the WSCP, as we operationalized it, is highly typical of individuals who meet both the clinical and the genetic criteria for Williams syndrome. In contrast, the WSCP is seldom found for individuals who do not meet the genetic criterion for Williams syndrome, even if they had been clinically diagnosed with Williams syndrome. This pattern of findings, combined with the fact that Williams syndrome is known to be a contiguous gene deletion disorder, suggests that there is likely to be a genetic basis for the WSCP, in particular, for the extreme weakness in visuospatial construction.

GENETIC BASIS FOR VISUOSPATIAL CONSTRUCTION DEFICITS IN WILLIAMS SYNDROME

As I mentioned in the introduction, Williams syndrome is caused by a hemizygous microdeletion of chromosome 7q11.23. The exact size of the deletion is unknown, but is likely to be between 1 megabase and 2 megabases in length (Morris, personal communication, February 1997). In this range, deletion size varies across individuals (deSilva, 1996; Gilbert-Dussardier et al., 1995). The deletion likely involves at least 10 genes (Osbourne et al., 1996). At the same time, Williams syndrome involves a large number of phenotypic characteristics. Thus, determining the relations between specific genes and specific phenotypic characteristics would be extremely difficult if researchers began by focusing on individuals who had classic Williams syndrome.

An Alternative Strategy for Relating Specific Phenotypic Characteristics of Williams Syndrome to Particular Genes: Studies of SVAS Kindreds

A better strategy for identifying relations between specific phenotypic characteristics and particular genes would be to identify individuals who shared some, but not all, of the phenotypic characteristics of individuals with classic Williams syndrome. If these individuals were found to have smaller deletions (or other types of mutations) in the Williams syndrome region, then fewer genes should be missing (or altered in other ways). The combination of fewer deleted genes and fewer phenotypic characteristics shared with classic Williams syndrome would increase the likelihood of successfully relating specific phenotypic characteristics to particular genes. The fewer the phenotypic characteristics shared with Williams syndrome, the greater the likelihood of success in identifying genotype–phenotype correlations.

This strategy was used initially to identify the region of the genome involved in Williams syndrome. One medical geneticist reasoned that the most central medical characteristic of classic Williams syndrome was SVAS, the heart disease associated with Williams syndrome. Most, but not all, individuals with SVAS also have Williams syndrome. The vascular disease in Williams syndrome is identical to that in kindreds with SVAS (O'Connor et al., 1985; Perou, 1961). Members of SVAS kindreds, however, generally have intelligence in the normal range and do not fit the Williams syndrome personality phenotype. Morris argued that studying individuals who had SVAS but did not have Williams syndrome was the best way to identify the chromosome, and the region of that chromosome, that was involved in Williams syndrome. She began by performing dysmorphology examinations on members of 10 kindreds with SVAS. Across these kindreds, 175 individuals were at risk for SVAS. All of these individuals appeared to have normal intelligence, and none appeared to have the personality phenotype associated with Williams syndrome. Special echocardiographic and Doppler techniques developed by Ensing (a pediatric cardiologist; Ensing et al., 1989) were used to characterize the variability of heart disease in these kindreds. These techniques are particularly valuable because they are sensitive enough to detect cardiac lesions present in individuals who are asymptomatic for SVAS. Based on these data, members of Keating's molecular genetics laboratory demonstrated linkage between the SVAS phenotype and DNA markers on the long arm of chromosome 7 (Ewart, Morris, Ensing et al., 1993). A polymorphism at the elastin locus was completely linked, making elastin a candidate gene for SVAS.

Shortly thereafter, Morris Keating, and Ensing demonstrated that mutations (including deletions) of the elastin gene were indeed responsible for SVAS. A translocation between chromosome 6 and chromosome 7 that disrupted the elastin gene in all members of an additional 4-generation SVAS kindred was identified, showing that mutations of elastin cause SVAS (Curran et al., 1993; Morris, Loker, Ensing, & Stock, 1993). Subsequently, studies of two more SVAS kindreds demonstrated that partial deletions of the elastin gene resulted in SVAS (Ewart, Jin, Atkinson, Morris, & Keating, 1994; Olson et al., 1995).

Given these findings for kindreds with SVAS, Morris and Keating (Ewart, Morris, Ensing et al., 1993) proposed that mutations involving elastin were likely to be involved in Williams syndrome as well. Subsequent submicroscopic deletions of chromosome 7q11.23 (the region in which elastin is located) were identified in individuals with Williams syndrome (Ewart, Morris, Atkinson et al., 1993). Deletions of one elastin allele have since been demonstrated for more than 98% of individuals with Williams syndrome studied (Lowery et al., 1995; Mari et al., 1995; Morris et al., 1994). This finding has led to a simple and accurate genetic test for Williams syndrome: fluorescent in situ hybridization (FISH) using probes for the elastin gene.

Application of This Strategy to Kindreds With Small Deletions in the Williams Syndrome Region

Hemizygous elastin mutations (including deletions) appear to be responsible for the vascular pathology in Williams syndrome. Deletion of one elastin allele likely results in abnormal production of elastin protein, affecting the formation of elastic fibers; the elastic fibers of individuals with SVAS are fragmented and disorganized (Meacham, 1995). Additional physical characteristics of Williams syndrome may also be due to abnormal elastin protein; for a discussion of these characteristics and a possible explanation for how hemizygous elastin mutation results in SVAS, see Mervis et al. (in press).

Abnormalities of elastin protein cannot account for all of the phenotypic features of Williams syndrome. In fact, elastin is only negligibly expressed in human fetal or adult brain cells (Frangiskakis et al., 1996), indicating that elastin is highly unlikely to be involved in either the cognitive or personality characteristics associated with Williams syndrome. To identify genes associated with these characteristics, identification of individuals who had deletions extending beyond the elastin gene but who did not have classic Williams syndrome was critical. The smaller the deletion, the better; fewer genes were likely to be missing, and if the logic underlying this strategy was correct, fewer phenotypic characteristics in common with Williams syndrome were likely to be present. To determine which kindreds were most likely to have deletions that extended beyond the elastin gene, Morris, Keating, Ensing, and I considered the available records for the 13 kindreds involved in the earlier studies.

Members of 11 of these kindreds appeared to have no phenotypic overlap with Williams syndrome beyond characteristics that were likely due to mutations (including deletions) of the elastin gene. Some members of the two remaining kindreds, however, had a history of academic difficulties even though these members had not been identified as mentally retarded. These kindreds seemed the most promising for further study. Molecular genetic studies subsequently identified small deletions in both kindreds (Ewart et al., 1994; Frangiskakis et al., 1996). These deletions were considerably smaller than those found in individuals with Williams syndrome. To determine if members of these kindreds shared any phenotypic behavioral characteristics with individuals who have Williams syndrome, Bertrand, Robinson, Klein, and I assessed the cognitive and personality characteristics of all available members of these two kindreds. Some of the kindred members who had not participated in the original SVAS research agreed to participate in this follow-up study. Morris performed dysmorphology examinations on all available kindred members (including those whom she had assessed previously); Ensing performed echocardiological examinations on these individuals. Additional characterization of the molecular genetics of the two deletions was conducted by members of Keating's laboratory.

Sixteen members of one kindred (K2049), encompassing four generations, were assessed. The pedigree for this kindred is shown in Fig. 9.3. Ten of the 16 were found to have identical deletions of 7q11.23. These deletions, which included the 3' end of the elastin gene, were 83.6 kb in length. (This is much smaller than the classic Williams syndrome deletion of 1 to 2 megabases.) Nine of the 10 individuals with deletions were found to have SVAS (based on either echocardiographic examination or prior surgical records). Five of these 9 individuals also had some facial features characteristic of Williams syndrome; all of these features were consistent with abnormal elastin protein production. None of the 6 individuals without deletions had SVAS.

Eight of the 10 individuals with deletions fit the WSCP. Of the two remaining individuals, one was considered untestable due to a history of

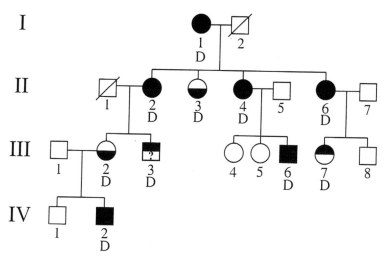

FIG. 9.3. Pedigree for Kindred 2049. Elastin gene deletions are indicated by "D," supravalvar aortic stenosis (SVAS) by a blackened upper portion of the square or circle indicating the individual, and Williams syndrome cognitive profile (WSCP) by a blackened lower portion of the square or circle. "?" indicates that the person could not be tested for the WSCP.

multiple seizures. The other did not fit the WSCP because although her visuospatial constructive ability was impaired relative to her overall cognitive ability, her auditory short-term memory ability was lower than expected for her visuospatial constructive ability. The 8 individuals who did fit the WSCP included 7 of the 9 individuals who had clinical SVAS (including all 5 with facial features consistent with Williams syndrome). The eighth individual who fit the WSCP had a deletion, but did not have SVAS. All 8 individuals had auditory short-term memory and language abilities similar to unaffected kindred members, but had relatively impaired visuospatial constructive abilities. None of the kindred members who did not have deletions fit the WSCP. Fifteen of the 16 members of the kindred had IQs in the normal range. The remaining member, a 4-year-old who had a deletion, demonstrated clinical SVAS and fit the WSCP, had an IQ of 64, indicating mild developmental delay. His performance on all of the subtests that did not assess visuospatial construction was in the normal range, suggesting that his developmental delay could be attributed to problems with visuospatial construction. None of the 16 kindred members fit the Williams syndrome personality profile or had a history of infantile hypercalcemia.

Eight members of the second kindred (K1895), encompassing two generations, were assessed. The pedigree for this kindred is presented in Fig. 9.4. Three of the 8 members were found to have a deletion of approximately 300 kb located at 7q11.23. This deletion included the entire elastin

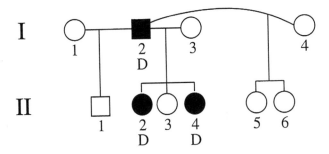

FIG. 9.4. Pedigree for Kindred 1895. Symbols used are the same as in Fig. 9.3.

gene but was considerably smaller than deletions characteristic of individuals with classic Williams syndrome. All three individuals had SVAS, had some facial features consistent with Williams syndrome, and showed an excellent fit to the WSCP. Once again, individuals with deletions had auditory rote memory abilities and language abilities similar to unaffected kindred members, but had impaired visuospatial constructive ability. None of the 5 kindred members who did not have a deletion fit the WSCP. All kindred members had normal intelligence; none fit the Williams syndrome personality profile or had a history of infantile hypercalcemia.

The cognitive abilities of 10 members of four additional kindreds with SVAS included in the 13 kindreds previously studied were also tested to determine if they fit the WSCP. Affected members of one of these kindreds (K1861) had been shown to have a 6;7 translocation that disrupted the elastin gene (Morris et al., 1993). Affected members of the other three kindreds (K1790, K2044, K2260) were found to have point mutations that disrupted one elastin allele. No deletions were found. No member of these kindreds fit the WSCP or the Williams syndrome personality profile or had had hypercalcemia (Frangiskakis et al., 1996). All kindred members had normal intelligence.

Further molecular characterization of the two kindreds that had evidenced deletions of 7q11.23 indicated that the smaller deletion (K2049) was entirely included in the larger deletion (K1985). These deletions are diagrammed in Fig. 9.5. Because the psychological characterization had indicated that members of both kindreds fit the WSCP and had SVAS and some Williams syndrome facial features consistent with elastin protein abnormality but did not share any other phenotypic characteristics with individuals with classical Williams syndrome, the deletion in K2049 was subjected to extensive molecular analysis by members of Keating's laboratory. Except for elastin, no previously characterized gene had been mapped to the Williams syndrome region of chromosome 7q11.23. To determine if the deletion for K2049 included any other genes, the entire 83.6 kb region

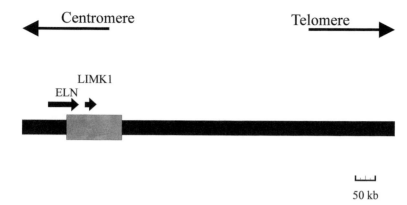

FIG. 9.5. Schematic drawing of the deletions of chromosome 7q11.23 in classic Williams syndrome (black bar) and Kindred 2049 (shaded rectangle).

was sequenced. Only one additional gene was found. This gene, LIM-kinase1, is contiguous with elastin, and was deleted in all affected members of K2049 and K1895. Additional testing confirmed that one copy of LIM-kinase1 was consistently deleted in individuals with Williams syndrome (Frangiskakis et al., 1996; Osbourne et al., 1996; Tassabehji et al., 1996) or in any member of the other four kindreds with SVAS (Frangiskakis et al., 1996). This pattern of findings indicates that hemizygous deletion of LIM-kinase1 co-occurs with the WSCP.

To determine the expression of LIM-kinase1, Northern analyses using mRNA extracted from human fetal and adult tissues was performed. Results of these analyses indicated that LIM-kinase1 levels are higher in the brain than in any other organ for both human fetus and human adult. In conjunction with the WSCP data for the six SVAS kindreds studied, these expression data indicate that LIM-kinase1 hemizygosity contributes to the impaired visuospatial constructive cognitive ability that occurs in Williams syndrome (Frangiskakis et al., 1996).

INTERRELATIONS AMONG LANGUAGE, AUDITORY SHORT-TERM MEMORY, REASONING, AND VISUOSPATIAL CONSTRUCTION

In the preceding sections, I presented evidence that individuals with Williams syndrome show a consistent cognitive profile with relative strengths in auditory short-term memory and language and extreme weakness in visuospatial constructive cognition. I also have shown that there is a genetic basis for this extreme weakness in visuospatial construction. In the present section, I consider the question of how to interpret the consistent finding

of relative strength in language abilities and extreme weakness in visuospatial constructive cognition for individuals with Williams syndrome. Based
on this pattern, Williams syndrome often is argued to provide strong evidence for language modularity—that is, that language abilities are largely
decoupled from other cognitive abilities (e.g., Bellugi et al., 1988, 1992,
1994, 1996; Damasio & Damasio, 1992). The presence of this consistent
cognitive profile, however, does not rule out the possibility that Williams
syndrome might provide strong evidence for the centrality of g (general
intelligence) or central control processes (such as working memory or
analytic ability) to the cognitive abilities of individuals with mental retardation or borderline normal intelligence. To address these possibilities, I
consider the performance of a sample of 50 individuals with Williams
syndrome on measures of intelligence, reasoning, language, visuospatial
construction, and auditory short-term memory. Group performance on
each of the measures is described first. Second, I describe the pattern of
partial correlations among individual performance on these measures.
Third, I consider the amount of variance in the language and visuospatial
construction measures that may be accounted for by individual differences
in auditory rote memory, working memory, and reasoning ability.

Sample, Measures, and Procedure

The sample of 50 individuals with Williams syndrome included all of the
individuals we have tested who were at least 5 years old at the time of
testing, and for whom data were available on the complete set of measures
to be considered in the analyses. The sample included 26 children and
24 adults. The children (12 males, 14 females) ranged in age from 5 years
to 17 years, with a mean age of 10.76 years (sd = 3.66 years). The adults
(14 males, 10 females) ranged in age from 18 years to 47 years, with a
mean age of 30.84 years (sd = 7.80 years).

The Kaufman Brief Intelligence Test (K-BIT; Kaufman & Kaufman,
1990) was used to measure overall level of intelligence. This measure
consists of two subtests: vocabulary (including expressive vocabulary and
definitions) and matrices. This test was used for two reasons. First, the
K-BIT provides age norms for individuals from 4 years to 90 years old.
Thus, the same measure could be used to obtain IQ scores for all of the
individuals included in our sample. Second, administration of the K-BIT
requires considerably less time than administration of a full-scale IQ test.
Note that the K-BIT does not include a measure of visuospatial construction, the area of greatest disability for individuals with Williams syndrome.
Accordingly, for most individuals with Williams syndrome, K-BIT IQs will
be higher than IQs obtained from full-scale measures. The K-BIT IQ distribution, like most other major IQ tests, has a mean of 100 and a standard
deviation of 15. The lowest possible standard score is 40.

The matrices subtest of the K-BIT was used to measure nonverbal reasoning ability. On the early items, the K-BIT matrices include familiar objects and measure understanding of the logical relations among these objects. The later items are composed of abstract geometric forms, similar to those used on Raven's Progressive Matrices (Raven, 1960) and Raven's Advanced Progressive Matrices (Raven, 1965). For each of the K-BIT matrices, individuals are asked to select the picture (from a choice of 5 to 8) that would correctly complete the matrix. Raw scores (number of items correct) are converted to standard scores, taking into account the participant's CA. The K-BIT matrices subtest standard score distribution has a mean of 100, with a standard deviation of 15. The lowest possible standard score is 40.

The K-BIT vocabulary subtest (Kaufman & Kaufman, 1990), Peabody Picture Vocabulary Test–Revised (PPVT-R; Dunn & Dunn, 1981), and the Test for Reception of Grammar (TROG; Bishop, 1989) were used as measures of language ability. On the early items of the K-BIT vocabulary subtest, the participant is asked to name a series of pictures. On the later items, the person is asked to state the word that fits both the verbal and letter clues provided by the researcher. Raw scores are converted to standard scores in the same manner as for the K-BIT matrices subtest. On the PPVT-R, the participant is asked to choose, from a set of four pictures, the one that corresponds to the word said by the researcher. Words tested include object names, action words, descriptors, and abstractions. Raw scores (number of items correct) are converted to standard scores, taking into account the participant's CA. Norms are available from age 2½ years through age 40 years. The norms for the oldest age interval were used for individuals 41 years or older. The PPVT-R standard score distribution has a mean of 100 and a standard deviation of 15. The lowest possible standard score, using the supplementary norms provided by the publisher (American Guidance Service, 1981), is 20.

The TROG (Bishop, 1989) is arranged similarly to the PPVT-R. The researcher says a word or sentence and the participant is asked to select the picture (out of the four available) that corresponds to the researcher's utterance. The TROG is composed of 20 blocks of four items. Each block tests a different grammatical construction, ranging from bare nouns to embedded sentences. Norms are available from age 4 years through adulthood. (See Bishop, 1989, for instructions for assigning standard scores to adults.) The TROG standard score distribution has a mean of 100 and a standard deviation of 15. The lowest possible standard score is "<55."

The pattern construction subtest of the DAS was used to assess visuospatial construction. This measure is the most sensitive test of visuospatial construction available for assessing individuals who have extreme difficulty with visuospatial construction. The participant is shown a colored picture of a block pattern and is asked to construct the pattern using colored cubes. Each cube has one solid yellow side, one solid black side, two sides divided diagonally into yellow and black triangles, and two sides divided vertically into yellow and black rectangles. The initial designs are composed of two cubes; if the participant is able to complete at least three of these patterns, he or she is then asked to complete four-block designs. If the participant is unable to complete at least three of the two-block designs, he or she is asked to perform an easier task. In this task, the individual is shown a colored picture of a block pattern composed only of solid yellow and/or black squares and is asked to copy that pattern using squares that are solid yellow on one side and solid black on the other. The initial designs are composed of two squares; later designs are made up of four or six squares. Points are awarded both for completing a pattern accurately and for speed of completion of correct patterns. Raw scores consist of ability scores, which are converted to standard T-scores based on CA. Norms are available for ages 3 years through 17 years. Following the procedure used for the Wechsler Adult Intelligence Scale–Revised (WAIS-R; Wechsler, 1981), standard scores for the oldest age interval (17 years, 6 months through 17 years, 11 months) were used for individuals 18 years or older. The DAS pattern construction subtest standard score distribution has a mean of 50 and a standard deviation of 10. The lowest possible standard score is 20.

Auditory short-term memory was assessed using digit span tests, with items administered at a rate of one per second. Forward digit span was used to measure auditory rote memory. The participant was asked to repeat a string of digits in the same order as the researcher had said them. Digit strings to be recalled ranged in length from two to nine items. An individual's forward digit span was determined based on the longest string of digits the individual repeated in the correct sequence. The digit strings used were taken from the Test of Auditory Perceptual Skills (TAPS; Gardner, 1985), the WAIS-R (Wechsler, 1981), or the WISC-III (Wechsler, 1991). Standard scores were not computed.

Backward digit span was used to measure auditory working memory. The participant was asked to repeat the string of digits in the reverse order from that produced by the researcher. Digit strings to be recalled in reverse order ranged in length from two to nine items. An individual's backward digit span was determined by the longest string of digits he or she was able to correctly repeat in reverse order. For each individual, the digit strings tested were taken from the same assessment as had been used for measuring forward digit span. Standard scores were not computed.

Most individuals completed the entire assessment battery in 1 day. For a few individuals, the assessment required 2 days of testing. In these cases, test days were spaced as close as possible; intervals ranged from 1 day to 1 month.

Descriptive Analyses of Performance

To graphically present the distribution of standard scores for each of the measures for which these scores were available, histograms were prepared. In Fig. 9.6, the distributions of standard scores for overall K-BIT, K-BIT matrices, and K-BIT vocabulary (productive) are presented. The distribution for PPVT-R (receptive vocabulary) is shown in Fig. 9.7 and the distribution for TROG (receptive grammar) is shown in Fig. 9.8. Finally, the distribution of T-scores for the DAS pattern construction subtest is illustrated in Fig. 9.9. Examination of the histograms for the measures presented in Figs. 9.6, 9.7, and 9.8 suggests a mean level of performance in the range of mild mental retardation or borderline normal ability. For each measure, however, there is also a broad range of ability levels. In contrast, examination of the histogram for DAS pattern construction stand-

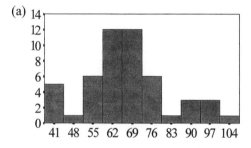

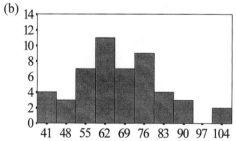

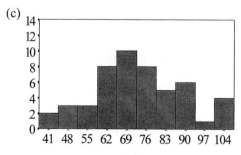

FIG. 9.6. Standard score distributions for (a) overall K-BIT IQ, (b) K-BIT matrices subtest, and (c) K-BIT vocabulary (productive) subtest. (N = 50)

Standard Score

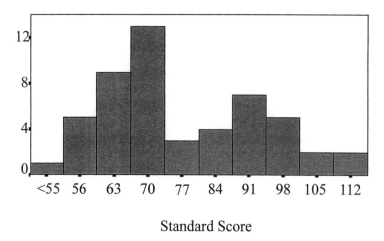

FIG. 9.7. Standard score distribution for PPVT-R (receptive vocabulary). (N = 50)

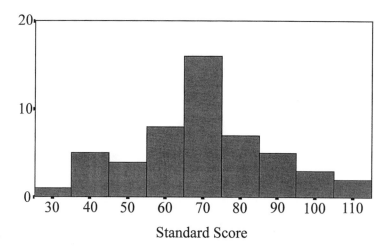

FIG. 9.8. Standard score distribution for TROG (receptive grammar). (N = 50)

ard scores indicates a highly positively skewed distribution, with most participants clustered at the extreme lower end of the ability distribution. The majority of individuals scored at the bottom of the 1st percentile (standard scores of 20 or 21).

Means, standard deviations, and ranges for standard scores for K-BIT IQ, K-BIT Matrices, K-BIT Vocabulary, PPVT-R, TROG, and DAS Pattern Construction are presented in Table 9.1, first for the full sample and then separately for the children and the adults. These numbers confirm the

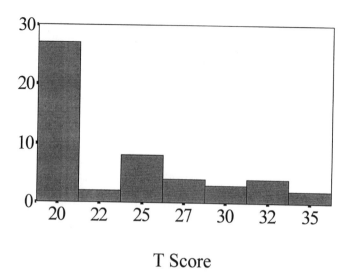

FIG. 9.9. *T*-score distribution for DAS pattern construction subtest. (N = 50)

impressions gained from visual examination of the histograms. Mean level of performance for all measures except DAS pattern construction ranged from 67 (upper end of mild mental retardation) to 76 (lower end of borderline normal). Standard deviations for the K-BIT measures are approximately 15, which is the expected value for the normal population. Standard deviations for the PPVT-R and TROG are slightly higher. Performance ranges from the level of severe mental retardation (generally, the lowest standard score possible on that measure) to somewhat above the expected mean value for the normal population (100). These values suggest that the distribution of ability levels for individuals with Williams syndrome on these measures is approximately the same shape as for the normal population, but with a mean displaced about 2 standard deviations below that for the normal population. In contrast, mean performance on the DAS pattern construction subtest was more than 2½ standard deviations below the normal population mean, and the standard deviation was half that expected for the normal population. The distribution was highly positively skewed, with most individuals clustered at the extreme low end of the ability distribution. The range of performance was extremely restricted; the highest standard score was 1.4 standard deviations below the normal population mean. This pattern of findings is highly consistent with the cognitive profile results presented in the first section.

To confirm that standard scores were significantly lower for DAS pattern construction than for PPVT-R, TROG, or K-BIT matrices, a series of within-participant *t* tests was conducted comparing standard scores for K-BIT

TABLE 9.1
Means, Standard Deviations, and Ranges of Standard Scores on Measures
of Intelligence, Reasoning, Language, and Visuospatial Construction

Measure	Full Sample (N = 50)	Children (N = 26)	Adults (N = 24)
K-BIT IQ	67.04 (15.27) 40–104	68.04 (14.45) 41–96	65.96 (16.35) 40–104
K-BIT Matrices	66.68 (15.10) 40–107	69.54 (13.17) 40–90	63.58 (16.68) 40–107
K-BIT Vocabulary	73.28 (15.94) 40–105	72.23 (16.80) 40–105	74.42 (15.22) 43–101
PPVT-R	69.18 (18.37) 30–110	69.38 (18.83) 35–109	68.88 (18.41) 30–110
TROG	76.20 (16.32) <55–112	73.65 (13.23) 55–99	78.96 (19.03) <55–112
DAS Pattern Construction	23.72 (4.79) 20–36	24.31 (4.56) 20–33	23.08 (5.04) 20–36

Note. Each vertical group of three numbers is composed of mean (first line), standard deviation (second line), and minimum and maximum standard scores (third line). For all the measures except the DAS Pattern Construction, the population mean is 100, with a standard deviation of 15. For the DAS Pattern Construction, the population mean is 50, with a standard deviation of 10. The lowest possible standard score is 40 for the K-BIT measures, 20 for the PPVT-R and the DAS Pattern Construction, and 55 for the TROG.

matrices, K-BIT vocabulary, PPVT-R, and TROG to standard scores for DAS pattern construction.[1] Results indicated that as expected, DAS pattern construction standard scores were significantly lower than standard scores for the other four measures (all $ps < .001$). Within-participant t tests were also used to determine the relation between standard scores on the K-BIT matrices and the three language measures. Results indicated that performance on the K-BIT matrices was significantly worse than performance on K-BIT vocabulary or TROG (both $ps \leq .001$). Although mean performance

---

[1]Standard scores for DAS pattern construction were adjusted so that they were based on a normal population mean of 100 and standard deviation of 15 (the same mean and standard deviation as the other four measures). For comparisons involving DAS pattern construction or TROG, the minimum score was set at 55 (the lowest possible adjusted standard score for these measures). For other analyses, the minimum score was set at 40 (the lowest possible score for K-BIT vocabulary, K-BIT matrices, and PPVT-R without using the extended norms).

TABLE 9.2
Simple Correlations of Raw Scores on Measures of Auditory
Short-Term Memory, Language, Visuospatial
Construction, and Reasoning With Chronological Age

Measure	Full Sample (N = 50)	Children (N = 26)	Adults (N = 24)
Forward Digit Span	.50****	.33	.31
Backward Digit Span	.56****	.40*	.17
K-BIT Vocabulary	.69****	.80****	.26
PPVT-R	.76****	.66****	.34
TROG	.61****	.47**	.56**
DAS Pattern Construction	.47****	.56***	.15
K-BIT Matrices	.37**	.68****	.02

Note. *$p < .05$. **$p = .01$. ***$p < .005$. ****$p \leq .001$.

on K-BIT matrices was lower than mean performance on PPVT-R, the difference was not significant.

The obtained pattern of consistency in standard scores across CA suggests that ability levels increased with increasing CA, at least during childhood, for all of the measures considered. To confirm this impression, simple correlations between standard test raw scores and CA were computed, first for the full sample and then separately for children and adults. These correlations are reported in Table 9.2. The correlations for the full sample indicated a significant increase in ability level for all the standard test measures considered as CA increased. Ability levels increased significantly during childhood for all measures except forward digit span. During adulthood, all correlations were positive.

To determine if standard scores varied as a function of CA, correlations were computed. The highest correlation obtained was +.29 ($p = .04$) for the TROG. Correlations for the remaining measures were extremely low, ranging from −.11 (K-BIT matrices) to +.14 (K-BIT vocabulary), with p levels ranging from .33 (K-BIT vocabulary) to .98 (PPVT-R). This pattern suggests that standard scores are consistent across the age range studied (5 years to 47 years).

Interrelations Among Cognitive Abilities: Partial Correlations

The pattern of cognitive strengths and weaknesses associated with Williams syndrome is relatively unique among groups with mental retardation or borderline normal intelligence. In particular, as demonstrated in the first section of this chapter, individuals with Williams syndrome consistently have extremely poor visuospatial constructive abilities, relatively good auditory short-term memory, and language abilities that are more advanced than would be expected based on level of visuospatial constructive ability. In the present section, I have confirmed the relative strength in language ability for three additional language measures, relative to visuospatial constructive ability. Findings for performance on the K-BIT vocabulary, PPVT-R, and TROG relative to the DAS pattern construction subtest extend the language findings beyond the expressive semantic measures from the DAS to an additional expressive semantic measure and to receptive measures for semantics (vocabulary) and grammar.[2] In addition, I have shown that nonverbal reasoning ability is better than would be expected for level of visuospatial constructive ability but worse than would be expected for level of either expressive vocabulary or receptive grammar ability.

This finding of a consistent pattern of relative strengths and weaknesses across auditory short-term memory, language, nonverbal reasoning, and visuospatial construction does not necessarily mean that these types of cognitive abilities are dissociated from one another in individuals with Williams syndrome. To address this question, examination of the pattern of individual differences on these measures is important. If ability levels on some or all of these measures are not significantly related, then the case for independence of these abilities is enhanced. On the other hand, the finding that ability levels on some or all of these measures are significantly correlated would provide support for the argument that these abilities are not completely independent.

To consider these possibilities, I began by computing the simple correlations among the raw scores for measures of auditory rote memory (forward digit span), auditory working memory (backward digit span), expressive vocabulary (K-BIT vocabulary), receptive vocabulary (PPVT-R), receptive grammar (TROG), visuospatial construction (DAS pattern construction), and nonverbal reasoning (K-BIT matrices). These correlations are reported in Table 9.3. All of these correlations are highly significant ($p < .001$). However, they should not be interpreted as supporting the interdependence of the different cognitive abilities; the significant correlations may be due primarily to differences among participants in CA. To address this possibility, partial correlations among the seven abilities were

---

[2]I have chosen not to test other measures of visuospatial construction for a simple reason: The DAS pattern construction subtest is much more sensitive at the low-ability end than any other standardized test of visuospatial constructive cognition of which I am aware. In particular, the DAS pattern construction subtest is the only measure on which individuals with Williams syndrome may be expected to get at least one item correct. Thus, performance on any other visuospatial constructive measure would almost certainly be worse than on the DAS.

TABLE 9.3

Simple Correlations among Measures of Auditory Short-Term Memory, Language, Visuospatial Construction, and Reasoning (N = 50, df = 48)

	Span F	Span B	K-VOC	PPVT-R	TROG	Pattern
Span F						
Span B	.58****					
K-BIT Voc	.65****	.79****				
PPVT-R	.65****	.81****	.91****			
TROG	.72****	.66****	.83****	.78****		
Pattern	.46****	.61****	.70****	.62****	.62****	
Matrices	.52****	.73****	.77****	.69****	.57****	.64****

Note. ****$p < .001$.

TABLE 9.4

Partial Correlations (Controlling for CA) among Measures of Auditory Short-Term Memory, Language, Visuospatial Construction, and Reasoning (N = 50, df = 47)

	Span F	Span B	K-Voc	PPVT-R	TROG	Pattern
Span F						
Span B	.42***					
K-BIT Voc	.48****	.67****				
PPVT-R	.47****	.71****	.82****			
TROG	.60****	.48****	.72****	.62****		
Pattern	.30*	.48****	.59****	.46****	.47****	
Matrices	.42***	.68****	.77****	.68****	.47****	.57****

Note. *$p = .03$. ***$p < .005$. ****$p < .001$.

computed, controlling for CA. These correlations are presented in Table 9.4. Although all but one of the correlations was reduced once CA was controlled, they still accounted for a significant proportion of the variance between measures. All correlations among backward digit span, K-BIT vocabulary, PPVT-R, TROG, DAS pattern construction, and K-BIT matrices remained significant at the $p < .001$ level. Correlations between K-BIT matrices and the other measures were reduced the least and the correlation between K-BIT matrices and K-BIT vocabulary remained the same even after partialling out CA. Partialling out CA had the most effect on correlations involving forward digit span.

This pattern of partial correlations suggests that the cognitive abilities measured in this study are not independent of each other, even though individuals with Williams syndrome showed a strong and consistent pattern of cognitive strengths and weaknesses. Perhaps the most interesting relations are those involving the three language measures and DAS pattern construction. Previous arguments in favor of the independence of different

TABLE 9.5
Partial Correlations (Controlling for CA and Span B)
among Measures of Forward Digit Span, Language,
Visuospatial Construction, and Reasoning (N = 50, df = 46)

	Span F	K-Voc	PPVT-R	TROG	Pattern
Span F					
K-BIT Voc	.30*				
PPVT-R	.27	.66****			
TROG	.50****	.60****	.45****		
Pattern	.12	.41***	.20	.32*	
Matrices	.21	.57****	.39**	.22	.38**

Note. *$p < .05$. **$p < .01$. ***$p < .005$. ****$p \leq .001$.

cognitive domains have focused on the independence of language abilities from visuospatial constructive abilities in Williams syndrome (e.g., Bellugi et al., 1988, 1992, 1994, 1996). Given that language abilities are not independent of visuospatial constructive abilities in Williams syndrome, it is likely that measures of central processing (or g) mediate between them. If so, correlations between the language measures and the visuospatial construction measure should be greatly weakened when measures of central processing are partialled out. The two best measures of central processing/g for which we have data are backward digit span (a measure of auditory working memory) and K-BIT matricies (a measure of nonverbal reasoning, the ability most strongly related to g).[3] Of these two measures, backward digit span seems the more basic; reasoning ability clearly requires working memory.

Accordingly, I recalculated the correlations between forward digit span, K-BIT vocabulary, PPVT-R, TROG, DAS pattern construction, and K-BIT matrices, controlling for both CA and backward digit span. The resulting correlations are shown in Table 9.5. All of the correlations were reduced substantially below the values found when only CA was controlled. In fact, five of the correlations were no longer significant, even at the $p = .05$ level. Most importantly, the partial correlation between PPVT-R and DAS pattern construction is no longer significant, suggesting that auditory working memory is likely responsible for the significant relation between receptive vocabulary and visuospatial construction. The partial correlations between

---

[3]In principle, it is possible that a measure of spatial working memory would have been more appropriate than a measure of auditory working memory, given that the pattern construction task is clearly a spatial task and matrices may be solved nonverbally. Observation of participants with Williams syndrome in previous studies as they attempted to solve both pattern construction tasks and matrices suggested that these individuals tended to use verbal mediation as an important component of their attempt to solve both tasks. Accordingly, auditory working memory seemed likely to be especially important.

TABLE 9.6
Partial Correlations (Controlling for CA, Span B, and Matrices)
Among Measures of Forward Digit Span, Language,
and Visuospatial Construction (N = 50, df = 45)

	Span F	K-Voc	PPVT-R	TROG
Span F				
K-BIT Voc	.22			
PPVT-R	.21	.58****		
TROG	.48****	.60****	.41***	
Pattern	.05	.25	.06	.26

Note. ***p = .005. ****p < .001.

TROG and DAS pattern construction and between K-BIT vocabulary and pattern construction were reduced substantially, but remained significant at the p = .03 level. The partial correlations between the three language measures, although reduced, remained highly significant.

I then recalculated the correlations between forward digit span, K-BIT vocabulary, PPVT-R, TROG, and DAS pattern construction, controlling for the effects of CA, backward digit span, and K-BIT matrices. These correlations are indicated in Table 9.6. The partial correlations between K-BIT vocabulary and DAS pattern construction and between TROG and DAS pattern construction were no longer significant. This finding suggests that analytic ability may also mediate between language ability and visuospatial constructive ability. Analytic ability is also certainly crucial for correct solution of both simple and complex pattern construction tasks (see Mervis et al., in press). For grammar, it is likely that the role of analytic ability (beyond the role of auditory working memory) is limited to syntactically complex utterances, especially ones that have two possible interpretations (e.g., garden path sentences; see Frazier, 1987). For expressive vocabulary, analytic ability may be useful for determining if the word retrieved from memory is the correct label. The partial correlations among the three language measures remained significant at the p = .005 level. At the same time, the partial correlation between forward digit span and TROG remained significant at the p = .001 level. The partial correlations of the two vocabulary measures with forward digit span were not significant.

To consider the possibility that the still-significant partial correlation between the three language measures (even after controlling for the effects of CA, backward digit span, and K-BIT matrices) might be due to another basic process that was not involved in the relations between language and visuospatial construction, I computed a final set of partial correlations. This time, I controlled for forward digit span in addition to the variables controlled in the previous analyses. Forward digit span is a measure of auditory rote memory, and as such is plausibly important for acquisition of both vocabulary and grammar. This final set of partial correlations is presented in Table 9.7. The partial correlation between K-BIT vocabulary and PPVT-R was hardly reduced at all, remaining significant at the $p <$ .001 level. This finding suggests the possibility that one or more language- or vocabulary-specific variables may play a role in the acquisition of vocabulary. The partial correlation between K-BIT vocabulary and TROG was also hardly affected by controlling for the additional variable of forward digit span. Although the partial correlation between PPVT-R and TROG was substantially reduced after controlling for forward digit span, it remained significant at the $p = .02$ level. These findings suggest that one or more language-specific variables may also play a role in the relation between vocabulary (semantics) and grammar.

Contribution of Central Processes/g to Lexical, Grammatical, and Visuospatial Constructive Abilities

The previous series of analyses indicated that there was a substantial amount of shared variance between lexical, grammatical, and visuospatial constructive abilities. Furthermore, most of the shared variance could be accounted for by measures of central processing/g. I now consider a related question: How much of the variance in lexical ability, grammatical ability, and visuospatial constructive ability may be accounted for by auditory working memory, reasoning ability, and auditory rote memory? To address this question, four separate multiple regression analyses were conducted, one with K-BIT vocabulary raw score as the dependent variable, one with PPVT-R raw score as the dependent variable, one with TROG raw score (number of blocks correct) as the dependent variable, and one with DAS pattern construction raw score (ability score) as the dependent variable. For each analysis, the independent variables were CA, backward digit span, K-BIT matrices raw score, and forward digit span.

Results suggested an important role for central processes for all three abilities, although the magnitude of that role varied across abilities. The

TABLE 9.7
Partial Correlations (Controlling for CA, Span B, Matrices,
and Span F) Among Measures of Language
and Visuospatial Construction (N = 50, df = 45)

	K-Voc	PPVT-R	TROG
K-BIT Voc			
PPVT-R	.56****		
TROG	.57****	.36*	
Pattern	.25	.06	.26

Note. *p = .02. ****p < .001.

contribution of central processes was greatest for lexical ability. The multiple regression analysis for PPVT-R yielded a multiple R of .91 and an adjusted R^2 of .81, indicating that central processes account for most of the variance in lexical ability. The multiple regression analysis for K-BIT vocabulary resulted in almost identical values: a multiple R of .90 and an adjusted R^2 of .80. The multiple regression analysis for TROG yielded a multiple R of .80 and an adjusted R^2 of .61. This analysis suggests an important role for central processes in grammatical ability. At the same time, almost 40% of the variance remains to be accounted for. It is possible that much of this variance may be attributable to processes specific to language. The multiple regression analysis for DAS pattern construction yielded a multiple R of .70 and an adjusted R^2 of .44, indicating that central processes account for slightly less than half of the variance in visuospatial constructive ability. Much of the remaining variance is likely attributable to processes specific to spatial cognition and/or visuomotor integration.

CONCLUSION

Individuals with Williams syndrome show a consistent and unique cognitive profile. Auditory rote memory skills are a definite strength, language abilities (both vocabulary and grammar) are either a strength or at the level expected for overall level of cognitive ability, and visuospatial construction abilities are an extreme weakness. The severe deficit in visuospatial construction appears to be genetically based, due to a hemizygous deletion of LIM-kinase1. It is important to keep in mind, however, that LIM-kinase1 is not the gene for visuospatial construction. Morris, Keating, and I have hypothesized that LIM-kinase1 is part of a genetic cascade necessary for normal visuospatial construction abilities. Hemizygous deletion of LIM-kinase1 disrupts this cascade, leading to impaired visuospatial construction ability in Williams syndrome. Mutations or deletions of other genes in this cascade may lead to visuospatial construction problems in other syndromes.

The language abilities of individuals with Williams syndrome are clearly (and often dramatically) superior to their visuospatial constructive abilities. This finding is frequently interpreted as evidence for the independence (or decoupling) of language from other cognitive abilities (e.g., Bellugi et al., 1988, 1992, 1994, 1996; Damasio & Damasio, 1992; Flavell, Miller, & Miller, 1993). Difference in absolute level of ability does not automatically mean independence, however. Patterns of intercorrelations among language and other cognitive abilities are crucial for addressing the question of independence. In fact, the partial correlation data presented in this chapter indicate strong interrelations among language abilities and other cognitive abilities.

Why might this pattern occur? In the previous section, I suggested that these intercorrelations may be due to g and/or to central processes. Spearman (1904, 1927) showed that intercorrelations among tests are typically positive, forming what he called a positive manifold. g is the component that is common to all of the measures included in the matrix. But the definition of g is unclear. As Neisser et al. (1996) reported, possible interpretations include "a mere statistical regularity (Thomson, 1939), a kind of mental energy (Spearman, 1927), a generalized abstract reasoning ability (Gustafsson, 1984), or an index of neural processing speed (Reed & Jensen, 1992)" (p. 78). The positive manifold may also be described as a set of partially independent factors (Neisser et al., 1996). These factors may correspond to central cognitive processes such as working memory, analytic ability, or rote memory. Intercorrelations among tests vary as a function of IQ; correlations are lowest for extremely bright individuals and highest for individuals with borderline normal intelligence or mental retardation (Detterman & Daniel, 1989; Spearman, 1927). Detterman (1987; Detterman & Daniel, 1989) suggested that these correlations are especially high in individuals with mental retardation because these individuals have deficits in central processes, limiting the efficiency of other cognitive processes. These limitations reduce the variability in level of ability for noncentral processes so that all processes appear to operate at the same low level.

In Williams syndrome, levels of noncentral abilities have not been reduced to the same low level. Language abilities are much better than visuospatial constructive abilities. Nevertheless, correlations among linguistic and nonlinguistic cognitive measures are quite high. The results of the partial correlation analyses indicated that most of the shared variance in measures of language and visuospatial construction could be attributed to working memory and analytic ability, two central processes. This finding suggests that limitations in working memory and analytic ability may underlie the strong correlations among measures of linguistic and visuospatial constructive ability in Williams syndrome.

The finding that the significant partial correlations among measures of language and visuospatial construction are largely accounted for by individual differences in central processes does not provide a measure of the magnitude of the potential contribution of central processes to linguistic and visuospatial constructive processes. To begin to consider the potential importance of central processes to noncentral processes in Williams syndrome, multiple regression analyses for which measures of receptive vocabulary, expressive vocabulary, receptive grammar, and visuospatial construction were the dependent variables were conducted; Independent variables were CA, auditory working memory, analytic ability, and auditory rote memory. These analyses suggested an important role for central processes in all of the noncentral abilities measured. Individual differences in central processes accounted for 80% of the variance in lexical ability, suggesting that central processes are likely to be more important than language-specific processes for vocabulary development. Individual differences in central processing accounted for 61% of the variance in grammatical ability, again suggesting that these processes are important for language ability. Note that central processes appear more central to lexical development than to grammatical development, consistent with suggestions that any language module is likely to be more important for grammar than for vocabulary (e.g., Smith & Tsimpli, 1995). Individual differences in central processing accounted for 46% of the variance in visuospatial constructive ability, again suggesting an important role for central processes. At the same time, these data are consistent with the possibility of a visuospatial module or perhaps a visuospatial construction module.

In summary, the findings from this study provide strong support for the importance of central processes to intelligence in Williams syndrome. At the same time, these findings also suggest the potential importance of modules devoted to specific abilities such as grammar or visuospatial construction.[4] And the findings clearly point to the need for additional research, carefully targeted to measure particular central processes and specific noncentral processes, and to determine how central processes and modules interact. As Neisser et al. (1996) pointed out, debates about intelligence are typically characterized by "strong assertions as well as by strong feelings" (p. 77). Neisser et al. made this comment in response to the debate engendered by *The Bell Curve* (Herrnstein & Murray, 1994). This finding, although to a less dramatic degree, characterizes the controversy regarding the nature of intelligence in Williams syndrome. The solution that Dick proposed—a careful analysis of all the available data, acknowledging both what is known and what is unknown about the topic under consideration—is the same solution he taught me when I was a student. Application of this strategy has greatly strengthened my research on the nature of intelligence in Williams syndrome.

ACKNOWLEDGMENTS

This project was supported by Grant NS35102 from the National Institute of Neurological Disorders and Stroke and by Grant HD29957 from the National Institute of Child Health and Human Development.

---

[4]These findings, although consistent with the potential importance of modules, do not provide unequivocal support for them. For example, the variance not accounted for by the central processes measured in this study may be accounted for in part by central processes that were not measured, such as speed of processing or spatial working memory. Some of the variance may also be accounted for by environmental factors such as parent–child interaction style or amount (or quality) of previous experience with spatial tasks.

I thank the National Williams Syndrome Association, the Williams Syndrome Association Southeast Region, and the Williams Syndrome Association Far West Region for facilitating this work both by helping to identify potential participants and by permitting me to conduct research at national and regional meetings. The individuals with Williams syndrome who have participated in this research and their families have been generous with their time and their commitment to the research; I am very grateful. Byron Robinson, Jacquelyn Bertrand, Bonnie Klein, and Sharon Armstrong collaborated with me on the psychological portion of this research. Deborah Deckner, Sharon Hutchins, Janell Kalina, Echo Meyer, Bronwyn Robinson, Paul Scott, Natasha Turner, and Sara Voelz were involved in data collection, reduction, and/or analysis. Stephanie Nelson assisted with scheduling and field trips. The medical genetics component of this project was conducted by Colleen Morris. The molecular genetics component was conducted by Mark Keating and the members of his laboratory, especially Amanda Ewart, J. Michael Frangiskakis, and Shannon Odelberg. The cardiology component was conducted by Gregory Ensing.

REFERENCES

American Guidance Service. (1981). *Peabody Picture Vocabulary Test–Revised: Supplementary norms tables*. Circle Pines, MN: Author.

Bates, E. (1990, April). *Early language development: How things come together and how they come apart.* Invited paper presented at the International Conference on Infant Studies, Montreal, Canada.

Bellugi, U., Bihrle, A., Neville, H., & Doherty, S. (1992). Language, cognition, and brain organization in a neurodevelopmental disorder. In M. Gunnar & C. Nelson (Eds.), *Developmental behavioral neuroscience: The Minnesota symposium* (pp. 201–232). Hillsdale, NJ: Lawrence Erlbaum Associates.

Bellugi, U., Klima, E. S., & Wang, P. P. (1996). Cognitive and neural development: Clues from genetically based syndromes. In D. Magnusson (Ed.), *The lifespan development of individuals: Behavioral, neurobiological, and psychosocial perspectives* (pp. 223–243). Cambridge, England: Cambridge University Press.

Bellugi, U., Marks, S., Bihrle, A., & Sabo, H. (1988). Dissociation between language and cognitive functions in Williams syndrome. In D. Bishop & K. Mogford (Eds.), *Language development in exceptional circumstances* (pp. 177–189). London: Churchill.

Bellugi, U., Wang, P. P., & Jernigan, T. L. (1994). Williams syndrome: An unusual neuropsychological profile. In S. H. Broman & J. Grafman (Eds.), *Atypical cognitive deficits in developmental disorders: Implications for brain function* (pp. 23–56). Hillsdale, NJ: Lawrence Erlbaum Associates.

Bennett, F. C., LaVeck, B., & Sells, C. J. (1978). The Williams elfin facies syndrome: The psychological profile as an aid in syndrome identification. *Pediatrics, 61,* 303–306.

Bertrand, J., Mervis, C. B., & Eisenberg, J. D. (1997). Drawing by children with Williams syndrome: A developmental perspective. *Developmental Neuropsychology, 13,* 41–67.

Bishop, D. (1989). *Test for the reception of grammar* (2nd ed.). Manchester, England: Chapel Press.

Curran, M. E., Atkinson, D. L., Ewart, A. K., Morris, C. A., Leppert, M. F., & Keating, M. T. (1993). The elastin gene is disrupted by a translocation associated with supravalvular aortic stenosis. *Cell, 73,* 159–163.

Damasio, A. R., & Damasio, H. (1992). Brain and language. *Scientific American, 267*(3), 88–95.

deSilva, N. (1996). *Genotyping Williams syndrome families using polymorphic DNA markers shows variable lengths of the Williams syndrome deletion.* Unpublished honors thesis, Emory University, Atlanta, GA.

Detterman, D. K. (1987). Theoretical notions of mental retardation and intelligence. *American Journal of Mental Deficiency, 92,* 2–11.

Detterman, D. K., & Daniel, M. H. (1989). Correlations of mental tests with each other and with cognitive variables are highest for low IQ groups. *Intelligence, 13,* 349–359.

Dunn, L. E., & Dunn, L. E. (1981). *Peabody Picture Vocabulary Test–Revised.* Circle Pines, MN: American Guidance Service.

Elliott, C. D. (1990). *Differential ability scales.* San Diego, CA: Harcourt, Brace, Jovanovich.

Ensing, G. J., Schmidt, M. A., Hagler, D. J., Michels, V. V., Carter, G. A., & Feldt, R. H. (1989). Spectrum of findings in a family with nonsyndromic autosomal dominant supravalvular aortic stenosis: A Doppler echocardiographic study. *Journal of the American College of Cardiology, 13,* 413–419.

Ewart, A. K., Jin, W., Atkinson, D., Morris, C. A., & Keating, M. T. (1994). Supravalvular aortic stenosis associated with a deletion disrupting the elastin gene. *Journal of Clinical Investigation, 93,* 1071–1077.

Ewart, A. K., Morris, C. A., Atkinson, D., Jin, W., Sternes, K., Spallone, P., Stock, A. D., Leppert, M., & Keating, M. T. (1993). Hemizygosity at the elastin locus in a developmental disorder, Williams syndrome. *Nature Genetics, 5,* 11–16.

Ewart, A. K., Morris, C. A., Ensing, G. J., Loker, J., Moore, C., Leppert, M., & Keating, M. T. (1993). A human vascular disorder, supravalvular aortic stenosis, maps to chromosome 7. *Proceedings of the National Academy of Science USA, 90,* 3226–3230.

Finegan, J.-A., Smith, M. L., Meschino, W. S., Vallance, P. L., & Sitarenios, G. (1995, March). *Verbal memory in children with Williams syndrome.* Poster presented at the meeting of the Society for Research in Child Development, Indianapolis, IN.

Flavell, J. H., Miller, P. H., & Miller, S. A. (1993). *Cognitive development.* Englewood Cliffs, NJ: Prentice-Hall.

Frangiskakis, J. M., Ewart, A. K., Morris, C. A., Mervis, C. B., Bertrand, J., Robinson, B. F., Klein, B. P., Ensing, G. J., Everett, L. A., Green, E. D., Proschel, C., Gutowski, N., Noble, M., Atkinson, D. L., Odelberg, S. J., & Keating, M. T. (1996). LIM-kinase1 hemizygosity implicated in impaired visuospatial constructive cognition. *Cell, 86,* 59–69.

Frazier, L. (1987). Sentence processing: A tutorial review. In M. Coltheart (Ed.), *Attention and performance: Vol. XII* (pp. 559–586). Hillsdale, NJ: Lawrence Erlbaum Associates.

Gardner, M. F. (1985). *Test of auditory perceptual skills.* Burlingame, CA: Psychological and Educational Publications.

Gilbert-Dussardier, B., Bonneau, D., Gigarel, N., Le Merrer, M., Bonnet, D., Philip, N., Serville, F., Verloes, A., Rossi, A., Ayme, S., Weissenbach, J., Mattei, M.-G., Lyonnet, S., & Munnich, A. (1995). A novel microsatellite DNA marker at locus D7S1870 detects hemizygosity in 75% of patients with Williams syndrome. *American Journal of Human Genetics, 56,* 542–544.

Gosch, A., Stading, G., & Pankau, R. (1994). Linguistic abilities in children with Williams-Beuren syndrome. *American Journal of Medical Genetics, 52,* 291–296.

Gustafsson, J.-E. (1984). A unifying model for the structure of intellectual abilities. *Intelligence, 8,* 179–203.

Herrnstein, R. J., & Murray, C. (1994). *The bell curve: Intelligence and class structure in American life.* New York: The Free Press.

Kaufman, A. S., & Kaufman, N. L. (1990). *Kaufman Brief Intelligence Test.* Circle Pines, MN: American Guidance Service.

Lowery, M. C., Morris, C. A., Ewart, A., Brothman, L., Zhu, X. L., Leonard, C. O., Carey, J. C., Keating, M., & Brothman, A. R. (1995). Strong correlation of elastin deletions, detected by FISH, with Williams syndrome: Evaluation of 235 patients. *American Journal of Human Genetics, 57,* 49–53.

Mari, A., Amati, F., Mingarelli, R., Giannotti, A., Sebastio, G., Colloridi, V., Novelli, G., & Dallapiccola, B. (1995). Analysis of the elastin gene in 60 patients with clinical diagnosis of Williams syndrome. *Human Genetics, 96,* 444–448.

Mecham, R. P. (1995). Elastic fiber assembly and organization. *Genetic Counseling, 6,* 157–158.

Mervis, C. B., & Bertrand, J. (1997). Developmental relations between cognition and language: Evidence from Williams syndrome. In L. B. Adamson & M. A. Romski (Eds.), *Research on communication and language acquisition: Discoveries from atypical development* (pp. 75–106). New York: Brookes.

Mervis, C. B., Morris, C. A., Bertrand, J., & Robinson, B. F. (in press). Williams syndrome cognitive profile: Findings from an integrated program of research. In H. Tager-Flusberg (Ed.), *Neurodevelopmental disorders: Contributions to a new framework from the cognitive neurosciences.* Cambridge, MA: MIT Press.

Mervis, C. B., Robinson, B. F., Bertrand, J., Klein, B. P., & Armstrong, S. C. (1996, April). *Williams syndrome cognitive profile.* Poster presented at the meeting of the Cognitive Neuroscience Society, San Francisco, CA.

Milani, L., Dall'Oglio, A. M., & Vicari, S. (1995). Spatial abilities in Italian children with Williams syndrome. *Genetic Counseling, 6,* 179–180.

Morris, C. A., Ewart, A. K., Sternes, K., Spallone, P., Stock, A. D., Leppert, M., & Keating, M. T. (1994). Williams syndrome: Elastin gene deletions. *American Journal of Human Genetics, 55*(Suppl.), A89.

Morris, C. A., Loker, J., Ensing, G., & Stock, A. D. (1993). Supravalvular aortic stenosis cosegregates with a familial 6;7 translocation which disrupts the elastin gene. *American Journal of Medical Genetics, 46,* 737–744.

Neisser, U., Boodoo, G., Bouchard, T., Jr., Boykin, A. W., Brody, N., Ceci, S. J., Halpern, D. F., Loehlin, J. C., Perloff, R., Sternberg, R. J., & Urbina, S. (1996). Intelligence: Knowns and unknowns. *American Psychologist, 51,* 77–101.

O'Connor, W. N., Davis, J. B., Geissler, R., Cottrill, C. M., Noonan, J. A., & Todd, E. P. (1985). Supravalvular aortic stenosis: Clinical and pathologic observations in six patients. *Archives of Pathology and Laboratory Medicine, 109,* 179–185.

Olson, T. M., Michels, V. V., Urban, Z., Csiszar, K., Christiano, A. M., Driscoll, D. J., Feldt, R. H., Boyd, C. D., & Thibodeau, S. N. (1995). A 30 kb deletion within the elastin gene results in familial supravalvular aortic stenosis. *Human Molecular Genetics, 4,* 1677–1679.

Osbourne, L. R., Martindale, D., Scherer, S. W., Shi, X.-M., Huizenga, J., Heng, H. H. Q., Costa, T., Pober, B., Lew, L., Brinkman, J., Rommens, J., Koop, B., & Tsui, L.-C. (1996). Identification of genes from a 500 kb region at 7q11.23 that is commonly deleted in Williams syndrome. *Genomics, 36,* 328–336.

Perou, M. (1961). Congenital supravalvular aortic stenosis. *Archives of Pathology, 71,* 113–126.

Preus, M. (1984). The Williams syndrome: Objective definition and diagnosis. *Clinical Genetics, 25,* 422–428.

Raven, J. C. (1960). *Guide to the standard progressive matrices.* London: Lewis.

Raven, J. C. (1965). *Advanced progressive matrices. Sets I and II.* San Antonio, TX: Psychological Corporation.

Reed, T. E., & Jensen, A. R. (1992). Conduction velocity in a brain nerve pathway of normal adults correlates with intelligence level. *Intelligence, 16,* 259–272.

Smith, N., & Tsimpli, I.-A. (1995). *The mind of a savant: Language learning and modularity.* Oxford, England: Blackwell.

Spearman, C. E. (1904). "General intelligence" objectively defined and measured. *American Journal of Psychology, 15,* 201–293.

Spearman, C. (1927). *The abilities of man.* New York: Macmillan.

Tassabehji, M., Metcalfe, K., Fergusson, W. D., Dore, J. K., Donnai, D., Read, A. P., Proschel, C., & Gutowski, N. J. (1996). LIM-kinase deleted in Williams syndrome. *Nature Genetics, 13,* 272–273.

Thal, D., Bates, E., & Bellugi, U. (1989). Language and cognition in two children with Williams syndrome. *Journal of Speech and Hearing Research, 32,* 489–500.

Thomson, G. H. (1939). *The factorial analysis of human ability.* Boston: Houghton Mifflin.

Udwin, O., & Yule, W. (1991). A cognitive and behavioral phenotype in Williams syndrome. *Journal of Clinical and Experimental Neuropsychology, 13,* 232–244.

Vicari, S., Brizzolara, D., Carlesimo, G. A., Pezzini, G., & Volterra, V. (1996). Memory abilities in children with Williams syndrome. *Cortex, 32,* 503–514.

Volterra, V., Capirci, O., Pezzini, G., Sabbadini, L., & Vicari, S. (1996). Linguistic abilities in Italian children with Williams syndrome. *Cortex, 32,* 663–677.

Wang, P. P., & Bellugi, U. (1994). Evidence from two genetic syndromes for a dissociation between verbal and visual-spatial short-term memory. *Journal of Clinical and Experimental Neuropsychology, 16,* 317–322.

Wechsler, D. (1981). *Wechsler adult intelligence scale–Revised.* New York: Psychological Corporation.

Wechsler, D. (1991). *Wechsler intelligence scale for children–III.* New York: Psychological Corporation.

Chapter 10

Creating False Autobiographical Memories: Why People Believe Their Memory Errors

Ira E. Hyman, Jr.
Western Washington University

The real puzzle about flashbulb memories is quite different: Why do people so often have vivid recollections that are entirely incorrect?
—Neisser (1991, p. 35)

My goal in this chapter is to provide an answer to the puzzle about flashbulb memories that Neisser noticed a few years ago. Before I start down that path, however, I think I should put the chapter-opening quote in context. In 1989, Banaji and Crowder wrote an aggressive critique of naturalistic memory research in which they claimed that such work has found no important discoveries, generalizations, or theoretical understandings. They argued that naturalistic work, by its very nature, is unable to do so. In responding, Neisser (1991) noted a few findings from naturalistic research that he felt should qualify as valuable discoveries—Neisser also argued that these discoveries, based on the nature of the phenomena, would be impossible to document in traditional lab studies. One of the phenomena he discussed was that flashbulb memories, instead of being accurate, detailed, and long-lasting, are often entirely wrong. This led Neisser to ask why people have vivid autobiographical memories that are inaccurate.

In trying to explain how people come to believe their large autobiographical memory errors, I first point out the variety of memory errors that have been observed in both laboratory and naturalistic studies of memory. Not all memory errors are equal. Instead memory errors come in a variety of styles and flavors. In explaining errors, it is helpful to be clear about the type of memory errors under consideration. In this chapter, I offer an explanation of one type of memory error: large autobiographical memory errors of the sort that have been observed in flashbulb memories (McCloskey, Wibble, & Cohen, 1988; Neisser & Harsch, 1992; Southwick, Morgan, Nicolaou, & Charney, 1997) and in false childhood memories (Hyman & Billings, 1998; Hyman, Husband, & Billings, 1995; Hyman & Pentland, 1996; Loftus & Pickrell, 1995; Pezdek, 1995; Pezdek, Finger, & Hodge, 1996). I offer explanations at two different levels of analysis. The first is an expansion of relatively traditional constructivist arguments focusing on the mental activities involved in the creation of autobiographical stories. Although parts of this explanation are useful in addressing other types of memory errors and are drawn from explanations of other errors, I think the nature of these large autobiographical errors warrants its own explanation. The second level is a consideration of why a memory system would be designed this way. I intend to address what memory errors are good for by telling an evolution just-so story.

VARIETIES OF MEMORY ERRORS

Several times in his career, Neisser argued that prior to developing theories, psychology should specify and describe the phenomena to be explained. He argued this in his call for naturalistic memory research (Neisser, 1978). In that publication, Neisser noted that the search for the cause of forgetting is rather strange because forgetting is an incoherent notion. There is no one form of forgetting. Instead there are several different forms of forgetting and, thus, several causes of forgetting. This point formed part of Neisser's argument against global, context-free theories of memory, and this issue seems to be one that critics of naturalistic studies of memory have failed to understand. Neisser used part of that publication to classify the types of memory, and the entire volume *Memory Observed* (Neisser, 1982a), for which the 1978 publication became the opening chapter, can be viewed as a classification of memory phenomena based on the functions of memory (e.g., remembering, testifying, performing, getting things done). Neisser has also written other papers classifying and describing memory phenomena. For example, he classified memory based on the types of things to be remembered (Neisser, 1988a). In addition, he has used the same approach when addressing the self (Neisser, 1988b). I should note that Neisser is not the only memory scholar to call for classifications of memory—for example, there is Tulving's (1983) distinction between episodic and semantic memory, the widely discussed distinction between implicit and explicit memory, and many other forms of memory.

In the study of memory errors, however, there is a tendency to not look for different types of memory errors (although see Roediger, 1996, for a recent exception). In part this may be because traditional studies regarding memory errors have been limited to a few methodologies and materials. There is the work in the tradition of Bartlett (1932) using stories. In this tradition, one looks for the reduction of complex material to the gist and for systematic intrusions into later reports. In addition, there is the research in the eyewitness memory tradition examining the adoption of postevent information into memory of an event. In recent years, however, several new forms of memory errors have been documented (although some of these new errors are actually old ideas dusted off and given new life by creative researchers). Thus I think the time has come to consider a classification scheme for memory errors.

The value in classifying memory errors will be the same as the earlier work that discussed types of memory. As Neisser (1978) noted, the search for a global theory of memory may be a hopeless endeavor if there is no such thing as memory but instead several forms of memory. Thus, we may need several different theories, each focusing on the different forms of memory. No doubt there are some constants, but the valuable work accomplished in the last dozen years looking at dissociations between implicit and explicit memory, for example, shows the value of studying the differences. Similarly, before we search for a global theory of memory errors, such as source monitoring confusion (Johnson, Hashtroudi, & Lindsay, 1993) or fuzzy trace theory (Reyna & Brainerd, 1995), a classification may be in order. In addition, I think we will not make much progress in understanding memory errors if we refer to all errors as false memories or all as instances of gist (Reyna & Brainerd, 1995).

In discussing the forms of memory errors, it seems appropriate to start with the types of errors that Bartlett (1932) noted: gist and intrusions. The gist is the general understanding of what took place. People tend to lose the specifics of an event in favor of a more general understanding of the experience. For example, Bransford and Franks (1971) documented this in clever experiments. I would like to note that this tendency to move to the gist was the cause of a partial failure Neisser and I had in our first research project together. I say partial failure because we did get something valuable on the role of the self in memory, although that was not our original intention (Hyman & Neisser, 1992). We tape-recorded an undergraduate seminar that Neisser taught and several months later asked the students to remember the conversations that took place. We had hoped to find errors in their recollections of the seminar caused by their views of themselves and of Neisser. In many respects, we had hoped to replicate Neisser's (1982b) study of John Dean's memory with Neisser playing the role of Nixon. In that study, Neisser found that Dean's memory was consistent with the sorts of things Nixon said, but that what Dean claimed Nixon said in specific situations was seldom accurate. Unfortunately, we failed in replicating. We could not get the students to be detailed enough in their recalls to ever let their biases show. We gave very precise cues, based on tedious work transcribing the seminar, but the students would say things like: "Neisser said something about that," and "Neisser seemed to not like hypnosis much." The students preferred to report their memories at the gist level and we could not induce them to report specifics. Such statements at the gist level are errors in the sense that they do not match what originally happened but they also preserve the basic idea and in that sense can be seen as correct.

I think there are other forms of memory errors that are related to a movement toward gist, and these errors have been documented in materials other than sentences and stories. For example, there are conjunction errors in which people combine images from two faces into one face (e.g., Reinitz, Verfaellie, & Milberg, 1996), the biasing of memory for location (Huttenlocher, Newcombe, & Sandberg, 1994; Tversky, 1991, 1992), the research on memory for scripts (Nelson, 1986, 1988; Schank & Abelson, 1977), and Neisser's own example, repisodic memory (Neisser, 1982b). In these cases, information from several instances is blended into one more general representation and the general representation is recalled.

The second type of error that concerned Bartlett (1932) was intrusion errors. In contrast to gist memories, intrusions are more clearly errors in that they add information that was not originally present. The additional information may be consistent with or may contradict what was present originally. Intrusion errors seem to occur in memory for stories (Bartlett, 1932), word lists (Roediger & McDermott, 1995), rooms (Brewer & Treyens, 1981), and songs (Hyman & Rubin, 1990; Rubin, 1995). Intrusions are likely related to gist errors. Like gist errors, intrusions are based on a general understanding of a set of experiences. They differ from gist errors by being detailed. In some circumstances, people may choose to describe their recollection at a specific, rather than a general, level. Those specifics will be constructed based on the general understanding. Thus some of the specifics will be accurate, whereas others will be intrusions of erroneous information. When people are remembering a song, for example, they may feel compelled to be detailed and thus intrusions will be apparent (Hyman & Rubin, 1990). In contrast, when remembering the conversations that occurred in a seminar, people may prefer to describe events at a general level. Thus whether gist or intrusions errors occur may depend on the nature of the retrieval context: Do people feel either compelled or comfortable enough to provide specifics as part of their recollections?

Another memory error is what I term an *inference error*. Ross (1989) described several such errors in cases when a person would be trying to remember a previous attitude or mental state. Information concerning previous attitudes may not be available, perhaps because information concerning thoughts and feelings fades rapidly from memory (Brewer, 1988). Thus the person would reconstruct the previous attitude based on the current attitude. For example, currently I do not like President Clinton, I assume that my opinion of him probably has not changed much in the last few years, and thus I am sure that I have never liked him (although for the record I find liking is unrelated to my voting behavior). Generally this inference works and results in claims that are mostly accurate, but sometimes it leads to errors. These errors seem very similar to intrusions, in that a person is filling in something about the past. I think they differ based on the source of the erroneous claim about the past—general knowledge versus current mental states. In addition, the inference errors are not about events. There are other forms of errors that may also be inference errors. Jacoby's false fame paradigm may be an inference error (Jacoby, Kelley, Brown, & Jasechko, 1989; Jacoby, Woloshyn, & Kelley, 1989). In false fame experiments, a person is shown several nonfamous names on day one and asked to make judgments of whether people are famous on day two. They often will claim that a nonfamous name seen previously is famous—incorrectly inferring that familiarity with the name (a current mental state) is due to fame rather than the experience the previous day (see Kelley & Jacoby, 1996, for another similar inference error). Schooler, Bendiksen, and Ambadar's (1997) recent description of the forgot-it-all-along effect may also be an inference error. In a few cases, Schooler et al. found that some people will incorrectly claim to have experienced a time during which a memory for trauma was unavailable, even though independent sources claim the individuals talked about the experience during that time period. These people remember the experience with great emotion and perhaps incorrectly conclude that with so much emotion attached to the memory, they must not have thought or talked about it in years or else they would remember having done so. All of these errors are inferences based on current mental states.

The classic misinformation effect is yet another form of memory error. In misinformation studies, people first experience an event (for example, they watch a video of a car accident), then are given misleading postevent information or misinformation (they are told the car went past a stop sign when it actually was shown passing a yield sign), and finally erroneously claim that they observed the misinformation as part of the event when later tested. Although the explanation of the finding is hotly contested (Belli, 1989; Lindsay, 1990; Loftus, Donders, Hoffman, & Schooler, 1989; McCloskey & Zaragoza, 1985; Zaragoza & Lane, 1994), the occurrence of the misinformation effect is not in doubt.

If one's theory of the misinformation effect is that it is due to the blurring of two experiences into one more general understanding of the event, then one would place these errors as instances of relying on gist.

Many people, however, have suggested that the misinformation effect is an instance of a source monitoring error (e.g., Johnson, Hashtroudi, & Lindsay, 1993). Source monitoring errors occur when a person remembers a piece of information but fails to recollect where the information was learned. In this view, there is no claim of a combined general understanding. For example, people often erroneously attribute verbal statements to the wrong person (Johnson et al., 1993). For the misinformation effect, people did receive the information; they are simply wrong about when and where they received it. Related to source errors are reality monitoring errors. In these a person is confused about whether something occurred or if the occurrence was only imagined: For example, did I call my friend or only think about calling my friend? Johnson and her colleagues have done some nice studies showing that people often confuse actions performed with those imagined. In addition, Goff and Roediger (1996) showed that imagining the action more frequently increases the chances of erroneously claiming that it occurred. I think all of these errors—misinformation effect, source monitoring, and reality monitoring errors—share some features but differ in some features as well; they differ at least in the source of the memory error and the source erroneously claimed for the information. Looking at the common features is useful in formulating general theories but may lead us to miss certain crucial issues.

One of my favorite memory errors, time-slice errors, also may be an instance of a source monitoring failure. Sometimes a person is asked to recall some experience and replies with an event that is clearly inconsistent with what originally took place as recorded at the event or as reported by the person at some other time. Nonetheless, what the person recalls may be an actual experience. As Brewer (1988) suggested, the person may have recalled a true event, but not the event in question—they retrieved the wrong slice of time. With autobiographical memories, this is hard to dismiss as an explanation when a person recalls an event that is apparently wrong. Neisser and Harsch (1992) noted that some of the large errors in remembering flashbulb experiences could be time-slice errors. In my lab, we (Kheriaty, Kleinknecht, & Hyman, in press; Winningham, Hyman, & Dinnel, 1996) have recently found some evidence for time-slice errors—in other words, we have found good reason to believe that both accounts are stories of real events. Of course, time-slice errors may not be due to source confusion but may be due to problems with encoding specificity (Tulving & Thomson, 1973). The cue may be associated with more than one event and thus may serve as a lousy cue. For example, Linton (1982) noted that "last time sending off a paper" was a lousy retrieval cue if you have sent the paper away on a few occasions thinking each time was the last.

So far I've attempted to classify memory errors into just a few categories: (a) gist descriptions, (b) intrusions, (c) inferences, (d) misinformation effect, (e) source and reality monitoring errors, and (f) time-slice errors. I think these categories may fit into two broad groupings based on the process involved in creating the errors; namely schema-based reconstructions and source monitoring failures. Gist errors, intrusions, and inferences all involve reconstructing a recollection based on general knowledge structures. The misinformation effect, source monitoring errors, and time-slice errors are all forms of source monitoring errors. The construction process seems separate from source monitoring errors in which a person retains information but inadvertently attributes it to the wrong event or source. Of course, it may be possible to consider construction errors as source monitoring errors: Is the source of the memory general knowledge structures or a real experience? Doing so, however, misses the process of constructing memories. Further, in many cases a memory is constructed and no source monitoring is performed; people assume the construction is a memory. I think source monitoring is not something we normally bother to do. Nonetheless, I suspect that the construction process sometimes feeds recollections into the source monitoring process. The more successful the construction, the less likely the memory will be recognized as a constructed recollection.

Now, with any classification scheme, especially when you first start, you need an Other category. My Other category holds a few errors that do not seem to fit: boundary extensions in which a person remembers a picture as including more than it did (Intraub, Gottesman, Willey, & Zuk, 1996) and verbal overshadowing in which talking about something nonverbal, such as a picture, seems to reduce access to the original (Schooler & Engstler-Schooler, 1990). I had thought that I could fit these errors into my classification system: boundary extensions as gist-like errors and verbal overshadowing as an instance of the misinformation effect, but one in which the participants create their own misinformation. Unfortunately, both sets of researchers have shown that my simple approaches to explaining the errors do not work. It is for this reason that I suspect that the Other category may grow as researchers study the various errors more closely and find that although they share certain characteristics, they differ in other important features.

My Other category also encompasses the error that I have been particularly interested in lately—complex autobiographical memory errors. These are large errors that are not time-slice errors. Instead, these are instances in which a person creates a false memory. I think some examples of these complex errors are the flashbulb errors observed by Neisser and Harsch (1992) and most of the false childhood memories documented by my group of researchers (Hyman & Billings, 1998; Hyman, Husband, & Billings, 1995; Hyman & Pentland, 1996) and others (Ceci, Huffman, Smith, & Loftus, 1994; Ceci, Loftus, Leichtman, & Bruck, 1994; Loftus & Pickrell, 1995; Pezdek, 1995; Pezdek et al., 1996). They are complex in that they seem to involve many of the other errors: gist errors, intrusions, the mis-information effect, and reality monitoring. Thus I am going to offer an explanation of one form of memory error—false childhood memories. The explanation will work for other related errors, such as being wrong about where you were when you heard the news that the Challenger had exploded. In addition, parts of the explanation are borrowed from research on other errors. I hope it will answer Neisser's (1991) question of how people can come to believe vivid memories that are entirely incorrect.

FALSE CHILDHOOD MEMORIES

In my lab for the last few years, we have been concerned with the creation of false childhood memories (Hyman & Billings, 1998; Hyman, Husband, & Billings, 1995; Hyman & Pentland, 1996). I would be remiss if I did not note that I got started on this research in response to an e-mail exchange with Neisser. As I recall the exchange, we discussed generalizing from laboratory research on memory errors to the possible creation of abuse memories in therapy. Neisser argued that some recovered memories were likely to be false memories. My own memory of the exchange is that I played more ecological than Neisser and suggested the generalization was too large of a step (but I did not save the e-mails and I am not sure I can trust my memory). That is why I started the research: Rather than gener-alize, I wanted to see if people would create false childhood memories.

In our research, we went into an introductory psychology class and asked for permission to send to the students' parents a questionnaire concerning events that occurred when the students were children. We told the students that we were interested in what they could remember from childhood. When we received the returned questionnaires, we invited the students to participate in a series of two or three interviews concerning their memory for the childhood experiences. We asked the students about two to five true events and then threw in a ringer, an event that we were relatively sure had not happened: "When you were five, you went to the wedding of a friend of the family and while running around at the reception with some other kids, you bumped into the table the punch bowl was sitting on and spilled punch on one of the parents of the bride." In the first interview few students claimed to remember the false event. After a few interviews, however, between 15% and 25% of the students not only claimed the event happened but actually provided memories of the expe-rience that included details we never suggested. For example, they de-scribed the parents of the bride, the punch bowl, the reaction of their parents, or the place where the reception took place.

We have found several factors that contribute to the creation of false childhood memories. One of the first things we noted was that how a student responded to the false event in the first interview was related to the eventual creation of a false memory. Some of the students tied the false event to personal knowledge and experience—they talked about whose wedding it could have been, where it would have occurred, and personal and family characteristics related to spilling a punch bowl. Those students who talked about related self-knowledge in the first interview were more likely to create a false memory in later interviews than those who did not discuss related self-knowledge (Hyman et al., 1995). We found that requiring participants to form a mental image and describe that image for any event they failed to recall in the first interview (whether a true or false event), led nearly 40% of the students to create a false memory after three interviews (Hyman & Pentland, 1996). We also found that individual differences in the tendency to have dissociative experiences and in imagery ability are related to the creation of false memories (Hyman & Billings, 1998). Thus we have not only found that college students will create false memories (my original goal based on my exchange with Neisser), but we have also begun to delineate the factors that influence memory creation.

I think these errors share important features with some of the erroneous flashbulb memories observed by Neisser and Harsch (1992). First, these are large errors in autobiographical memories. Second, for at least some participants they are vivid memories. Third, the individuals come to believe their memory errors. In Neisser and Harsch this was evident because the participants did not abandon their false flashbulbs in favor of their original descriptions of where they had been when they were shown their original descriptions—they preferred their current recollections that they must have realized were false. With respect to false childhood memories, the individuals also come to have very believable recollections. Loftus (1993; Loftus & Ketchum, 1994) described one young man who, even after debriefing, continued to feel as if the memory was real. One of Ceci's (Ceci, Huffman, Smith, & Loftus, 1994) preschool-aged participants claimed continued belief in his recollection after debriefing, actually arguing for his recollection by noting that his mother was not there. One woman approached me after I described the work in an upper-level undergraduate class and discussed with me her participation in my studies. She claimed that she still has the memory of spilling the punch bowl. I asked her if she knew the event was false and she agreed the memory was false. Nonetheless, she reported that it still remained a very vivid memory. Thus people do come to have vivid, false memories that seem real—even in the face of debriefing. In the remainder of this chapter I offer two explanations of these errors: one a cognitive explanation that addresses the processes involved in memory creation and the other an evolutionary explanation that focuses on why a memory system would be designed this way.

COGNITIVE PROCESSES INVOLVED
IN FALSE MEMORY CREATION

Three things are necessary for a person to create a false childhood memory. First, the person has to accept the event as plausible. Second, the person has to construct an event image and narrative. Third, the person has to make a source monitoring error: The person has to claim the construction as a personal memory.

Event Acceptance

In order for a person to create a false memory, the suggested event needs to be plausible. That is, the event needs to be something that the person believes could have happened. For example, some subjects in our experiments (Hyman et al., 1995; Hyman & Pentland, 1996) did not create memories of spilling a punch bowl at a wedding because they believed that they had never attended a wedding as a child. They refused to accept the event as a plausible personal experience.

Several factors may influence whether an event is seen as plausible. The source of the suggestion will most likely affect plausibility assessments. In the typical false memory experiment, the suggested event is presented by an experimenter and the information is supposedly based on information from the participant's parents—these are two generally reliable sources of information. Nonetheless, students occasionally did not accept their parents as reliable sources; instead they would suggest that their parent must have them confused with a sibling again.

Not only will the source affect whether an event is viewed as plausible, but also the event itself will matter—whether people view this event as something that happens. For example, most people would not consider that they have been abducted by extraterrestrials as plausible suggestions. Nonetheless others may consider such an event relatively common. Spanos, Cross, Dickson, and DuBreuil (1993) found that belief in alien visitations was the primary variable that differentiated people who claimed memories of UFO experiences from individuals who do not claim such experiences. Of course, the causal direction of that relationship is not entirely clear.

In addition, implications that the experience is not only generally likely but also personally likely will increase willingness to believe an event may have occurred. In this fashion, studies of false feedback (Kelley, Amodio, & Lindsay, 1996) are partially effective because the researchers provide to the participants reasons to believe that an experience happened to them. For example, Kelley et al. told right-handed participants that tests indicated they were born left-handed (the false feedback). The researchers then asked the participants to search for memories consistent with hand-use shaping. Participants were able to generate such memories because the researchers had tied such events to false personal characteristics. The effect might be stronger if tied to actual personal characteristics. This is one reason researchers (e.g., Lindsay & Read, 1994; Loftus, 1993) have expressed concern regarding symptom checklists for repressed memories of child abuse—the lists present abuse as plausible for people who see themselves as having the symptoms.

Groups may also be effective in leading to false memories, in part, through affecting plausibility. If the people in a group are presented as similar to a new person and all of the other members of the group have certain types of memories, then this implies that the experiences are plausible for the new member. Any such feedback—either from a researcher, book, therapist, or group—can provide information that a class of experiences is likely for a particular person.

The basic point is that we can affect people's impression of the likelihood of an event having occurred and that this is the first step in memory creation. For example, with those students who doubted they attended a wedding and thus refused to see spilling a punch bowl as likely, the experimenter could have suggested reasons for this erroneous belief—perhaps the student has repressed memories of weddings, perhaps the parents were embarrassed and thus did not talk about it.

Image and Narrative Construction

A person can believe that an event is likely, or even that the event occurred, but must still construct a memory; an image with a narrative. Since the time of Bartlett (1932), memory construction has been well studied. People do not simply retrieve a memory and replay the experience—memory is not like a videotape. Instead people combine schematic knowledge from various sources with personal experiences and current demands to construct a memory. Memory construction has been demonstrated in material from word lists (Roediger & McDermott, 1995), to songs (Hyman & Rubin, 1990), stories (Bartlett, 1932), and autobiographical memories (Barclay & DeCooke, 1988; Ross, 1989). All memories are constructions.

Several activities make false memory construction more likely. First, tying a false event to self-knowledge will encourage false memory creation (Hyman et al., 1995). Once someone thinks of the false event with some self-knowledge, when the person thinks again about the false event, the person will have actual self-knowledge come to mind as well. The image that the person constructs will thus involve some true information. Encouraging a person to construct and describe an image of a false event also leads to memory construction (Hyman & Pentland, 1996). Probably any activity that encourages people to think about, imagine, and talk about events will lead to the construction of an image and narrative. Thus activities like journaling and dream interpretation may contribute to memory creation.

Source Monitoring Errors

Even if a person believes an event is plausible and constructs an image of the event, he or she still may not think that the event is a memory. All of the participants in Hyman and Pentland's (1996) imagery condition constructed an image and narrative of spilling the punch bowl at a wedding. Many, however, did not claim the image as a memory, instead they noted that this was just an image they had created. In this fashion they had correctly monitored the source of the image. In order to have a false memory, the participants had to make a source monitoring error—they had to claim the image as a personal memory. Many studies have shown that people experience difficulties remembering the source of information they have learned (see Johnson et al., 1993). In addition, source misattributions have been suggested as a primary cause of the misinformation effect—people remember the misleading postevent information and incorrectly claim that the information was part of the original event (e.g., Zaragoza & Lane, 1994). Just because someone claims a suggestion was part of the original (for the misinformation studies) or a personal memory (for the false memory studies) does not mean that a person has forgotten the other (and actual) source of the information. The participant can recall that they heard about spilling the punch bowl from the experimenter and come to believe that they personally recollect it as well. Sources are not mutually exclusive. This point is clear for many autobiographical experiences: I remember the event, I have heard you talk about it, and we have photos of it. In general all three sources will agree on many aspects of the event but each source may also include some unique information. In addition, I may come to claim as part of my recollection one feature that I previously did not recollect and have instead adopted from your version of the event—a source monitoring failure.

The situational demands may affect whether a source monitoring error occurs. For example, if a person shares an image and expresses a lack of confidence that it is a memory, others (an experimenter, members of a group) may tell the person that the image is a memory. In addition, time since a false suggestion may also affect source monitoring errors. Memory for the source of information is thought to fade more rapidly than memory for the content; thus people may remember the false suggestion, forget the source, and attribute the source to their own memory. The number of rehearsals may also increase the chance of a source monitoring error (Zaragoza & Mitchell, 1996). Individual differences may matter for source monitoring errors. Finally, characteristics of the constructed memory may influence the willingness to claim the memory as a personal recollection: Clearer images, more emotion, self-involvement, and plausibility may increase claims of a narrative being a personal memory (Hyman, Gilstrap, Decker, & Wilkinson, in press).

Overview

In writing this section with the order of event acceptance, memory construction, and source monitoring error, I have implied that the processes occur in a linear fashion and are dependent on the preceding step. I actually suspect that the processes are somewhat interactive. For example, constructing a clear image may influence one's assessment of the plausibility of an event having occurred (see Garry, Manning, Loftus, & Sherman, 1996). I think that all three processes are necessary for false memory creation and that they are somewhat independent in the sense that different factors influence each process.

I do not think, however, that all three processes are involved in all memory errors. For example, in most reconstructions of autobiographical experiences, people do not engage in source monitoring even though it may be appropriate: Did that really happen during that meeting or in the previous meeting? Such occasions may more accurately be labeled source monitoring failures rather than errors: One fails to engage the source monitoring process. Other errors probably do not directly involve other processes. When people accept the misinformation as part of the original event, what they have usually done is select it in a forced-choice recognition task. Most likely they did not evaluate the plausibility when they first heard the information (see Greene, Flynn, & Loftus, 1982, for an example of the effects of warning on the misinformation effect). Nor have the misinformed participants constructed a version of the original that included the erroneous information. Instead they have made a source error on a test of the item. If these three processes are involved in some but not all memory errors, then the theoretical framework may help in classifying memory errors. That was why I noted earlier that some errors are schema-based constructions although others are source errors and still others, like false childhood errors and false flashbulbs, are more complex errors.

In closing my cognitive explanation of large autobiographical memory errors, I would like to offer one conjecture about source monitoring errors. Although researchers so far have found distinguishing true from false memories difficult (if not impossible; see Hyman & Pentland, 1996; Leichtman & Ceci, 1995), I wonder if people could be trained to become better at this task. We get little opportunity to learn when we have made an autobiographical memory error or when we have something right. The lack of feedback is due to several causes. First, I think really big errors are relatively rare. People cannot make lots of large memory errors and manage to get around. Instead, small errors seem more likely. Second, the world seldom gives feedback on smaller errors in autobiographical memory. Generally one has to get the gist or tell an amusing story in order for the instance of remembering to be considered successful. Finally, even when someone does get feedback, the feedback is ignored or discounted. Personally, when I find that my recollection is at odds with someone else's, I assume the other person is in error, although usually I am polite enough not to point this out. Unfortunately or fortunately, depending on your view of your memory, there are not many external records of events that can be used to check our recollections. Nonetheless, with some training it may be possible to help someone learn to do this task accurately.

BUT WHAT IS IT FOR?

As another way of explaining these memory errors, I would like to discuss cause at a different level of analysis. I want to discuss why a memory system that seems biased toward errors would be the product of natural selection. Why does memory not work like a tape recorder or a videotape or a computer—why do we not record exact representations of what occurred? This section is more speculative than my cognitive explanation. I also run the risk of only telling an evolution just-so story—a story that makes functional sense of the ability but that is no more likely than any of a dozen other sensible stories. As Pinker (1994) noted for language, evolutionary explanations of cognitive abilities are difficult because we have no direct record of when cognitive abilities developed and the environmental conditions in which they developed. Nonetheless, thinking of current functions and functions during evolutionary history served by cognitive abilities may help in understanding those abilities and in generating new ideas for research.

I think that in many respects, autobiographical memory errors are related to the social function that remembering serves. One of the primary jobs that autobiographical memory serves is social interaction. People talk about the past in order to strengthen social bonds. Groups of people— families, friends, work groups, cultural groups, countries—are defined in some sense by a shared version of history. In the course of talk about the past, people come to agree on a version of their collective memory. In some cases of disagreement, people may immediately adopt the suggestions of others. In others, they may hold both ideas for a while and later forget that the other person is the source of the recollection.

Individuals with the tendency to adopt information from others in social contexts would then be selected—that is, be more likely to survive long enough to pass on their genes. There could be many ways in which the selection could have occurred. These differing selective pressures should lead to interesting predictions about the situations likely to lead to memory changes and the consequences of adopting other people's recollections as one's own. One possibility is selection based on membership in a more cohesive group. When individuals adopt a collective version of history, the group may share stronger social bonds. A shared past may also mean a shared version of the future. Thus, such groups might plan more effectively, be more likely than other groups to obtain resources, and thus be more likely than other groups to grow. But Dawkins (1982) argued that evolution works on individuals, not groups. The focus needs instead to be on what is in it for each member of a group.

A second way in which the social adoption of autobiographical memory information may have been selected is through identification of relatives. Humans and other species care about kinship. Animals sacrifice for kin, share with kin, and warn kin of impending danger. But how does one recognize that some other individual is a relative? Similarity of looks helps, but may not be particularly precise. Basing kinship knowledge on who is around, particularly as one grows up, is better than simply using looks. For a species with some ability to tell and remember stories, telling the family's stories would be excellent evidence of kinship. It would also work well in identifying family members who have traveled or who live a fair distance away. Maybe this is why storytelling is such a pivotal part of many family gatherings. Children should then be adept at adopting a family's stories so that they will be recognized as a member and so they can recognize other family members. This may be one reason why children are generally found to be more suggestible (Ceci & Bruck, 1993). Rather than arguing that children have poorly developed memory abilities, instead I could suggest that memory should be particularly malleable during early ages so that a child can adopt a family's stories. I think I can also make a suggestion for conjunction families (those with adopted children, stepchildren, nonparent adults living in the household). Generally children in these families are more likely to be abused and neglected. Evolutionary biology suggests it is because the children and adults do not share genes—they are not kin. I wonder if sharing memories and developing a shared family history might be related to healthier families. Perhaps having children learn and share family memories can redefine kinship.

Another way in which malleable memories may have been selected is via resource allocation in groups, both families and larger social groups.

Individuals who adopt the stories of powerful others and the majority of others are probably going to receive more resources than those who do not. It probably is not enough to parrot the stories or even to include the other person's views as part of one's own narrative—one has to be sincere. As Wright (1994) argued, the best way to be sincere is to actually believe something, to deceive oneself. I think this means that studies of suggestibility need to pay more attention to the nature of the social relationships between the suggestor and suggestee. Researchers (myself included) have primarily relied on authority figures (see Ceci, Ross, & Toglia, 1987, for an exception with children). Other sorts of individuals should also serve as excellent sources of suggestion: attractive individuals because they usually do well in human social groups, those who display resources, and the dominant members of a group at the least. In addition, social/personality factors may also play a role in how suggestible an individual is. People with lower status in a group may be more suggestible.

A final form of social pressure for malleable memories may come from sexual selection. When attempting to mate with a person, someone may be more likely to adopt that person's world view, version of the past, and goals for the future. I think that who adopts whose memories may depend on the state of a relationship: particularly if the evolutionary biologists are right about when males and females are selective (see Buss, Larsen, Westen, & Semmelroth, 1992; Buunk, Angleitner, Oubaid, & Buss, 1996; Wright, 1994). Early in a relationship, when the male is trying to woo the selective female, the male should be more likely to adopt, and sincerely believe, the female's version of the past and future. Later in a relationship, if the female begins to doubt the male's fidelity, she will be more likely to adopt the male's version of the past. I think we should be able to chart the state of a relationship by looking at the amount of agreement in the couple's independent recollections and at who adopts whose version during cooperative remembering. For example, Langhinrichsen-Rohling and Vivian (1994) documented that in abusive relationships, couples who agree on the level of past violence have fewer problems than those who disagree.

Thus there are several social pressures that may have contributed to the selection of a malleable autobiographical memory system. I hope that reality needs might limit the malleability of autobiographical memory. As perception needs to be generally veridical to enable one to function, so must memory generally be accurate. Thus, individuals with too great an ability to adopt external views would not be selected if their memories become too discrepant with the actual state of the world and their own past. In other words, there is pressure to be malleable as well as to be accurate. This should result in a system that is generally accurate but open to suggestion. On the other hand, people who have very malleable memories might do very well—these may be the people who become politicians because they could so easily adapt to any group! One possibility is that humans may have different strategies they can use based on the situations in which they find themselves. If natural selection has operated on the tendency to have a flexible memory system, then individual differences in memory flexibility should still exist, are worth investigating, and should be tied to many social factors (e.g., attractiveness, social status, popularity).

I am not the only person to suggest memory serves a social function. This is an idea with plenty of roots in psychology (Bruner, 1986, 1987; Edwards & Middleton, 1986a, 1986b; Hyman, 1994; Neisser, 1988c). Nor am I the only person to argue that this should lead to a memory system that is somewhat open to the introduction of errors via conversation (Alper, Buckhout, Chern, Harwood, & Slomovits, 1976; Hollins & Clifford, 1983; Stephenson, Brandstatter, & Wagner, 1983). I want to argue, however, that all the functions that autobiographical memory serves lead to the selection of a memory system open to errors.

One other function of autobiographical memory is self-definition (Baddeley, 1988; Brewer, 1986; Neisser, 1988b). I argued recently that the nature of changes we have observed in the creation of false memories means that the self is a construction created through social interaction (Hyman & Pentland, 1996). But as others have noted, the self is probably one of the forces working to create errors in memory (Greenwald, 1980; Ross, 1989; Spence, 1982). As the self-concept changes, this may lead to changes in memory that keep pace. Greenwald argued that having a consistent self-concept is valuable in the sense that it makes mental life more pleasant and smoothly functioning. Thus a memory system that adapts to changes in the self would have been selected if it led to better functioning.

In spite of everything that I have argued so far, I do not think that the social pressures or self pressure would have been enough to create a memory system open to lots of errors. Autobiographical memory is a late addition, in evolutionary time, to a person's repertoire of memory capabilities. Neisser (1988a) argued that autobiographical memory may have developed out of spatial memory. Tulving (1983) suggested that it grew from semantic memory. It is also possible that autobiographical memory developed from the ability to track social systems and hierarchies. Leaky (1994) noted that the most complex problems primates face are those involving social structure in the group. He thus argued that most human cognitive abilities evolved to aid in those tasks. I am not willing to place bets other than to note that autobiographical memory is bound up with language—I suspect that the two developed together.

No matter what the roots of autobiographical memory, those other memory capabilities must also include a tendency to make errors—to construct a general understanding and to lose the source of information. With just that tendency, the social pressure can then work to select an autobiographical system prone to memory errors. (Just a side note here: Rubin, 1995, argued that such a system will lead to accurate memories that can preserve knowledge over generations if one has multiple constraints defining the specific contents—as is the case in oral traditions.)

Thus I think that a memory system open to errors runs deeper than just the autobiographical memory system. As it turns out, there is good reason for this to be the case because the world around us is constantly changing. Many of the changes take place over such a long period of time that they are not noticeable to humans—I am told that the mountains in my part of the world are rising a few inches a year, but I have yet to notice. Other changes, however, take place in time periods relevant to us. For example, people grow and change. My children have gotten a lot taller in the last few years, I have gained a bit of weight and wear my reading glasses more frequently, my father continues to lose his hair. Places build and change. Old buildings are torn down, new ones are built, trees grow and sometimes are removed as roads widen, airports even sprout entire new terminals when the Olympics come to town. My memory of the people, places, and things I interact with needs to be constantly updated. This enables me to find my way around even though things change, to recognize people even after they get a haircut. It is important to note that we often do not refer to this sort of remembering as an error—the eyewitness to a crime who identifies the culprit even after the person has grown a mustache is thought to be accurate. In most memory studies, however, this person would be scored as having made an error—they selected a face that differed from the original. Perhaps our view of memory errors and accuracies does not mesh with the task the system was selected to perform? Memory evolved to update (see Larsen, 1983, for a similar argument).

Now I want to return to flashbulb memories. With this view of memory it seems odd to suggest the Now Print mechanism that Brown and Kulik (1977) originally proposed. They proposed the flashbulb mechanism when they first observed memories for highly emotional experiences and thought the memories were detailed, long-lasting, and accurate. Memory should not work that way if it has been naturally selected. You should not remember exactly the place, the time of day, and who was with you when the lion jumped out and ate your friend. That situation will never occur again and it will not be useful to constantly be on the lookout for just that situation. Instead, one should have a gist memory for the event that allows one to recognize similar situations (stimulus generalization is the term the behaviorists used) and one should update one's memory of the place where the attack occurred. This is why people with phobias generalize to similar stimuli instead of just showing fear in the situation in which they were previously harmed. Thus one reason why people make errors in flashbulb memories is that in these memories, as in other memories, the event should be updated by new knowledge. With respect to avoiding lions, consider what might happen when two individuals encounter a situation similar to one in which a friend has previously become a lion's lunch. I suspect the person who remembers exactly what happened is more likely to be eaten because that person will not recognize the situation—such individuals do not become ancestors. In contrast, the person who remembers what generally happened will recognize the situation and will be selected to survive and reproduce.

In short, I think that a memory system open to the introduction of errors has been selected by most of the remembering contexts in which humans and other animals have found themselves over the course of time. The exceptions to this rule are two recently created cultural contexts: courtrooms and psychology labs. I think a memory system open to errors has an important beneficial side effect, although this may have been another reason for selection. Memory errors may be related to some forms of creativity. People who combine things in unusual ways or remember events differently are often valued as inventors or artists.

This returns me to the question of why does the human memory system not work as well as a computer's memory or some other technical device, like a tape recorder. I answer that it functions better. I think it functions better if you understand the tasks the human system was selected to perform. I also thinks it performs better if you consider the way the metaphorical comparison objects actually function. My computer may record things exactly, but it also erases completely and writes something new over something old whenever I tell it to do so. It makes no effort to keep track of the source of information—was this part of the original draft of this chapter or did I add it in later? You cannot tell by looking at what shows up on my computer screen at this point. This problem of failing to track source is true for all of our technical comparisons—tape recorders, videotapes, and so forth. Forrest Gump really never met President Kennedy, but you cannot tell that from the movie. At least human memory makes some effort at tracking source. In addition, because computers remember things exactly and do not create general representations of similar events, they do not create knowledge as humans do, nor should we expect them to be creative in the manner that humans are.

CONCLUSIONS

I have tried to talk about why people believe their large autobiographical memory errors. I think it is because they view the event as plausible, they construct a memory that is partially based on true experiences and that is often very vivid, and they erroneously claim the false memory as a personal recollection.

I have also made two other points that seem consistent with much of Neisser's writing on memory. First, before we move toward global theories of memory, we ought to define and describe the phenomena. I have argued that we need to consider the variety of memory errors. I can see the advantages of using a few theoretical ideas to explain all memory errors. Nonetheless, I think there are compelling reasons to focus on explaining the errors independently. Doing so will help us better understand the intricacies of the various forms of memory errors, as is proving to be the case in recent developments concerning the misinformation effect, boundary extension, and verbal overshadowing. Further, there is value in variety. If the field develops multiple theories, then the final understanding at a more global level will be a selection among several competing theories.

The second Neisserian point I have tried to make is that we should consider the tasks the memory systems perform. Human memory was not designed to remember a list of unrelated words. Studying memory in this sort of context may seem a safe means of isolating factors in a controlled environment and, if the findings will generalize, this will be useful (Banaji & Crowder, 1989). However, the functioning of human memory varies with context (Ceci & Bronfenbrenner, 1985; Hyman, 1994). In addition, it is not clear that all memory phenomena can be studied in the lab. Thus we need to study human memory, and memory errors, in the contexts in which they occur.

REFERENCES

Alper, A., Buckhout, R., Chern, S., Harwood, R., & Slomovits, M. (1976). Eyewitness identification: Accuracy of individual vs. composite recollection of a crime. *Bulletin of the Psychonomic Society, 8*, 147–149.

Baddeley, A. (1988). But what the hell is it for? In M. M. Gruneberg, P. E. Morris, & R. N. Sykes (Eds.), *Practical aspects of memory: Vol. 1. Current research and issues* (pp. 3–18). New York: Wiley.

Banaji, M. R., & Crowder, R. G. (1989). The bankruptcy of everyday memory. *American Psychologist, 44*, 1185–1193.

Barclay, C. R., & DeCooke, P. A. (1988). Ordinary everyday memories: Some of the things of which selves are made. In U. Neisser & E. Winograd (Eds.), *Remembering reconsidered: Ecological and traditional approaches to the study of memory* (pp. 91–125). Cambridge, England: Cambridge University Press.

Bartlett, F. C. (1932). *Remembering: A study in experimental and social psychology.* Cambridge, England: Cambridge University Press.

Belli, R. F. (1989). Influences of misleading postevent information: Misinformation interference and acceptance. *Journal of Experimental Psychology: General, 118*, 72–85.

Bransford, J. D., & Franks, J. J. (1971). Abstraction of linguistic ideas. *Cognitive Psychology, 2*, 331–350.

Brewer, W. F. (1986). What is autobiographical memory? In D. C. Rubin (Ed.), *Autobiographical memory* (pp. 25–49). New York: Cambridge University Press.

Brewer, W. F. (1988). Memory for randomly-selected autobiographical events. In U. Neisser & E. Winograd (Eds.), *Remembering reconsidered: Ecological and traditional approaches to the study of memory* (pp. 21–90). New York: Cambridge University Press.

Brewer, W. F., & Treyens, J. C. (1981). The role of schemata in memory for places. *Cognitive Psychology, 13*, 207–230.

Brown, R., & Kulik, J. (1977). Flashbulb memories. *Cognition, 5*, 73–99.

Bruner, J. (1986). *Actual minds, possible worlds.* Cambridge, MA: Harvard University Press.

Bruner, J. (1987). Life as narrative. *Social Research, 54*, 11–32.

Buss, D. M., Larsen, R. J., Westen, D., & Semmelroth, J. (1992). Sex differences in jealousy: Evolution, physiology, and psychology. *Psychological Science, 3*, 251–255.

Buunk, B. P., Angleitner, A., Oubaid, V., & Buss, D. M. (1996). Sex differences in jealousy in evolutionary and cultural perspective: Tests from the Netherlands, Germany, and the United States. *Psychological Science, 7*, 359–363.

Ceci, S. J., & Bronfenbrenner, U. (1985). Don't forget to take the cupcakes out of the oven: Strategic time-monitoring, prospective memory and context. *Child Development, 56*, 175–190.

Ceci, S. J., & Bruck, M. (1993). Suggestibility of the child witness: A historical review and synthesis. *Psychological Bulletin, 113*, 403–439.

Ceci, S. J., Huffman, M. L. C., Smith, E., & Loftus, E. F. (1994). Repeatedly thinking about non-events. *Consciousness and Cognition, 3*, 388–407.

Ceci, S. J., Loftus, E. F., Leichtman, M. D., & Bruck, M. (1994). The possible role of source misattributions in the creation of false beliefs among preschoolers. *International Journal of Clinical and Experimental Hypnosis, 42*, 304–320.

Ceci, S. J., Ross, D. F., & Toglia, M. P. (1987). Suggestibility of children's memory: Psycholegal implications. *Journal of Experimental Psychology: General, 116*, 38–49.

Dawkins, R. (1982). *The extended phenotype: The gene as the unit of selection.* New York: Oxford University Press.

Edwards, D., & Middleton, D. (1986a). Text for memory: Joint recall with a scribe. *Human Learning, 5*, 125–138.

Edwards, D., & Middleton, D. (1986b). Joint remembering: Constructing an account of shared experience through conversational discourse. *Discourse Processes, 9*, 423–459.

Garry, M., Manning, C. G., Loftus, E. F., & Sherman, S. J. (1996). Imagination inflation: Imaging a childhood event inflates confidence that it occurred. *Psychonomic Bulletin & Review, 3*, 208–214.

Goff, L. M., & Roediger, H. L. (1996, November). *Imagination inflation: Multiple imaginings can lead to false recollection of one's actions.* Paper presented at the 37th annual meeting of the Psychonomic Society, Chicago.

Greene, E., Flynn, M. S., & Loftus, E. F. (1982). Inducing resistance to misleading information. *Journal of Verbal Learning and Verbal Behavior, 21*, 207–219.

Greenwald, A. G. (1980). The totalitarian ego: Fabrication and revision of personal history. *American Psychologist, 35*, 603–618.

Hollins, C. R., & Clifford, B. R. (1983). Eyewitness testimony: The effects of discussion on recall accuracy and agreement. *Journal of Applied Social Psychology, 13*, 234–244.

Huttenlocher, J., Newcombe, N., & Sandberg, E. H. (1994). The coding of spatial location in young children. *Cognitive Psychology, 27*, 115–147.

Hyman, I. E., Jr. (1994). Conversational remembering: Story recall with a peer versus for an experimenter. *Applied Cognitive Psychology, 8*, 49–66.

Hyman, I. E., Jr., & Billings, F. J. (1998). Individual differences and the creation of false childhood memories. *Memory, 6*, 1–20.

Hyman, I. E., Jr., Gilstrap, L. L., Decker, K., & Wilkinson, C. (in press). Manipulating remember and know judgments of autobiographical memories. *Applied Cognitive Psychology.*

Hyman, I. E., Jr., Husband, T. H., & Billings, J. F. (1995). False memories of childhood experiences. *Applied Cognitive Psychology, 9,* 181–197.

Hyman, I. E., Jr., & Neisser, U. (1992). The role of the self in recollections of a seminar. *Journal of Narrative and Life History, 2,* 81–103.

Hyman, I. E., Jr., & Pentland, J. (1996). Guided imagery and the creation of false childhood memories. *Journal of Memory and Language, 35,* 101–117.

Hyman, I. E., Jr., & Rubin, D. C. (1990). Memorabeatlia: A naturalistic study of long-term. *Memory & Cognition, 18,* 205–214.

Intraub, H., Gottesman, C. V., Willey, E. V., & Zuk, I. J. (1996). Boundary extension for briefly glimpsed photographs: Do common perceptual processes result in unexpected memory distortion? *Journal of Memory and Language, 35,* 118–134.

Jacoby, L. L., Kelley, C. M., Brown, J., & Jasechko, J. (1989). Becoming famous overnight: Limits on the ability to avoid unconscious influences of the past. *Journal of Personality and Social Psychology, 56,* 326–338.

Jacoby, L. L., Woloshyn, V., & Kelley, C. M. (1989). Becoming famous without being recognized: Unconscious influences of memory produced by dividing attention. *Journal of Experimental Psychology: General, 118,* 115–125.

Johnson, M. K., Hashtroudi, S., & Lindsay, D. S. (1993). Source monitoring. *Psychological Bulletin, 114,* 3–28.

Kelley, C., Amodio, D., & Lindsay, D. S. (1996, July). *The effects of 'diagnosis' and memory work on memories of handedness shaping.* Paper presented at the International Conference on Memory, Padua, Italy.

Kelley, C. M., & Jacoby, L. L. (1996). Adult egocentrism: Subjective experience versus analytic bases for judgment. *Journal of Memory and Language, 35,* 157–175.

Kheriaty, E., Kleinknecht, R. A., & Hyman, I. E., Jr. (in press). Recall and validation of phobia origins as a function of a structured interview versus the Phobia Origins Questionnaire. *Behavior Modification.*

Langhinrichsen-Rohling, J., & Vivian, D. (1994). The correlates of spouses' incongruent reports of marital aggression. *Journal of Family Violence, 9,* 265–283.

Larsen, S. F. (1983). Text processing and knowledge updating in memory for radio news. *Discourse Processes, 6,* 21–38.

Leaky, R. (1994). *The origin of humankind.* New York: Basic Books.

Leichtman, M. D., & Ceci, S. J. (1995). The effects of stereotypes and suggestions on preschoolers' reports. *Developmental Psychology, 31,* 568–578.

Lindsay, D. S. (1990). Misleading suggestions can impair eyewitnesses' ability to remember event details. *Journal of Experimental Psychology: Learning, Memory, and Cognition, 16,* 1077–1083.

Lindsay, D. S., & Read, J. D. (1994). Psychotherapy and memories of childhood sexual abuse: A cognitive perspective. *Applied Cognitive Psychology, 8,* 281–338.

Linton, M. (1982). Transformations of memory in everyday life. In U. Neisser (Ed.), *Memory observed: Remembering in natural contexts* (pp. 77–91). San Francisco: Freeman.

Loftus, E. F. (1993). The reality of repressed memories. *American Psychologist, 48,* 518–537.

Loftus, E. F., Donders, K., Hoffman, H. G., & Schooler, J. W. (1989). Creating new memories that are quickly accessed and confidently held. *Memory & Cognition, 17,* 607–616.

Loftus, E. F., & Ketchum, K. (1994). *The myth of repressed memory: False memories and allegations of sexual abuse.* New York: St. Martin's Press.

Loftus, E. F., & Pickrell, J. E. (1995). The formation of false memories. *Psychiatric Annals, 25,* 720–725.

McCloskey, M., Wibble, C. G., & Cohen, N. J. (1988). Is there a special flashbulb memory mechanism? *Journal of Experimental Psychology: General, 117,* 171–181.

McCloskey, M., & Zaragoza, M. (1985). Misleading postevent information and memory for events: Arguments and evidence against memory impairment hypothesis. *Journal of Experimental Psychology: General, 114*, 3–18.

Neisser, U. (1978). Memory: What are the important questions? In M. M. Gruneberg, P. E. Morris, & R. N. Sykes (Eds.), *Practical aspects of memory* (pp. 3–24). London: Academic Press.

Neisser, U. (Ed.). (1982a). *Memory observed: Remembering in natural contexts.* San Francisco: Freeman.

Neisser, U. (1982b). John Dean's memory: A case study. In U. Neisser (Ed.), *Memory observed: Remembering in natural contexts* (pp. 139–159). San Francisco: Freeman.

Neisser, U. (1988a). Domains of memory. In P. R. Solomon, G. R. Goethals, C. M. Kelley, & B. R. Stephens (Eds.), *Memory: Interdisciplinary approaches* (pp. 67–83). New York: Springer-Verlag.

Neisser, U. (1988b). Five kinds of self-knowledge. *Philosophical Psychology, 1*, 35–59.

Neisser, U. (1988c). Time present and time past. In M. M. Gruneberg, P. E. Morris, & R. N. Sykes (Eds.), *Practical aspects of memory: Vol. 2. Current research and issues* (pp. 545–560). New York: Wiley.

Neisser, U. (1991). A case of misplaced nostalgia. *American Psychologist, 46*, 34–36.

Neisser, U., & Harsch, N. (1992). Phantom flashbulbs: False recollections of hearing the news about *Challenger.* In E. Winograd & U. Neisser (Eds.), *Affect and accuracy in recall: Studies of "flashbulb" memories* (pp. 9–31). Cambridge, England: Cambridge University Press.

Nelson, K. (1986). *Event knowledge: Structure and function in development.* Hillsdale, NJ: Lawrence Erlbaum Associates.

Nelson, K. (1988). The ontogeny of memory for real events. In U. Neisser & E. Winograd (Eds.), *Remembering reconsidered: Ecological and traditional approaches to the study of memory* (pp. 244–276). New York: Cambridge University Press.

Pezdek, K. (1995, July). *Childhood memories: What types of false memories can be suggestively planted?* Paper presented at the meeting of the Society for Applied Research in Memory and Cognition, Vancouver, BC.

Pezdek, K., Finger, K., & Hodge, D. (1996, November). *False memories are more likely to be planted if they are familiar.* Paper presented at the meeting of the Psychonomic Society, Chicago.

Pinker, S. (1994). *The language instinct: How the mind creates language.* New York: HarperCollins.

Reinitz, M. T., Verfaellie, M., & Milberg, W. P. (1996). Memory conjunction errors in normal and amnesic subjects. *Journal of Memory and Language, 35*, 286–299.

Reyna, V. F., & Brainerd, C. J. (1995). Fuzzy-trace theory: An interim synthesis. *Learning and Individual Differences, 7*, 1–75.

Roediger, H. L., III. (1996). Memory illusions. *Journal of Memory and Language, 35*, 76–100.

Roediger, H. L., III, & McDermott, K. B. (1995). Creating false memories: Remembering words not presented in lists. *Journal of Experimental Psychology: Learning, Memory, and Cognition, 21*, 803–814.

Ross, M. (1989). The relation of implicit theories to the construction of personal histories. *Psychological Review, 96*, 341–357.

Rubin, D. C. (1995). *Memory in oral traditions.* New York: Oxford University Press.

Schank, R. C., & Abelson, R. P. (1977). *Scripts, plans, goals, and understanding.* Hillsdale, NJ: Lawrence Erlbaum Associates.

Schooler, J. W., Bendiksen, M., & Ambadar, Z. (1997). Taking the middle line: Can we accommodate both fabricated and recovered memories of sexual abuse? In M. Conway (Ed.), *False and recovered memories* (pp. 251–292). New York: Oxford University Press.

Schooler, J. W., & Engstler-Schooler, T. Y. (1990). Verbal overshadowing of visual memories: Some things are better left unsaid. *Cognitive Psychology, 22*, 36–71.

Southwick, S. M., Morgan, C. A., Nicolaou, A. L., & Charney, D. S. (1997). Consistency of memory for combat-related traumatic events in veterans of Operation Desert Storm. *American Journal of Psychiatry, 154,* 173–177.

Spanos, N. P., Cross, P. A., Dickson, K., & DuBreuil, S. C. (1993). Close encounters: An examination of UFO experiences. *Journal of Abnormal Psychology, 102,* 624–632.

Spence, D. P. (1982). *Narrative truth and historical truth: Meaning and interpretation in psychoanalysis.* New York: Norton.

Stephenson, G. M., Brandstatter, H., & Wagner, W. (1983). An experimental study of social performance and delay on the testimonial validity of story recall. *European Journal of Social Psychology, 13,* 175–191.

Tulving, E. (1983). *Elements of episodic memory.* New York: Oxford University Press.

Tulving, E., & Thomson, D. M. (1973). Encoding specificity and retrieval processes in episodic memory. *Psychological Review, 80,* 352–373.

Tversky, B. (1991). Spatial mental models. *The Psychology of Learning and Motivation, 27,* 109–145.

Tversky, B. (1992). Distortions in cognitive maps. *Geoforum, 23,* 131–138.

Winningham, R. G., Hyman, I. E., Jr., & Dinnel, D. L. (1996, November). *Flashbulb memories? Recollections of O. J. Simpson's acquittal.* Poster presented at the meeting of the Psychonomic Society, Chicago.

Wright, R. (1994). *The moral animal: Evolutionary psychology and everyday life.* New York: Vintage Books.

Zaragoza, M. S., & Lane, S. M. (1994). Source misattributions and the suggestibility of eyewitness memory. *Journal of Experimental Psychology: Learning, Memory, & Cognition, 20,* 934–945.

Zaragoza, M. S., & Mitchell, K. J. (1996). Repeated exposure to suggestion and the creation of false memories. *Psychological Science, 7,* 294–300.

Chapter 11

Revisiting John Dean's Memory

William Hirst
David Gluck
Graduate Faculty
New School for Social Research

In this chapter, we revisit Neisser's classic publication on John Dean's memory (1981). For those unaware of the article, a brief summary is in order. When John Dean, Counsel to President Nixon, testified at the Watergate hearings, he was unaware that the conversations he had with Nixon had been tape recorded. In his formal testimony and during the subsequent interrogation, Dean provided an incredibly detailed account of these conversations, in particular, the conversation of September 15, 1972, in which he reviewed progress in the Watergate affair with Nixon and Haldeman, Nixon's Chief of Staff. This meeting was important to the Watergate hearings because it provided insight into the extent to which Nixon understood that his staff was engaged in illegal activities. The committee spent much effort in trying to determine through careful interrogation whether Dean was telling the truth or falsely recollecting the substance of the meeting. The existence of the tape recordings surfaced only after Dean had finished his testimony, but once the Watergate committee discovered them, they knew that the tapes would provide a perfect means of verifying Dean's testimony. After comparing the testimony with the tapes, the general consensus was that Dean had told the truth.

Neisser saw Dean's testimony about the September 15th meeting and the subsequently discovered tape recordings as an ecologically valid experiment, the kind he had been arguing for since his talk on "Memory: What are the important questions?" (1978). The testimony and tapes raised a host of interesting questions for Neisser. Particularly, Neisser wanted to know in what sense Dean's recollection was an accurate recollection of the September 15th meeting?[1] Dean's testimony was extraordinary. His opening statement alone ran 245 pages. His recollections were so detailed that one investigating Senator referred to Dean as a human tape recorder (Neisser, 1981). Neisser thought that the study of Dean's seemingly tape-recorder-like memory might help psychologists better understand the nature of human memory.

In his groundbreaking book *Cognitive Psychology*, Neisser (1967) reintroduced to the psychological world the work of Frederick Bartlett. Bartlett (1932) showed in a series of brilliant experiments that memory was rarely accurate—verbatim memory was the infrequent exception rather than the rule. People remember the past according to the attitude they have in the present, not by retrieving stored traces of past. Consequently, remembering involves not the reappearance of the stored trace of the past into consciousness, but the reconstruction of this past in the present. For Bartlett, and for Neisser (1981), the notion of a human tape recorder was perfectly ludicrous.

After carefully comparing the testimony and a transcript of the tape recordings, Neisser arrived at a dramatic conclusion, one contrary to the received wisdom of the Watergate committee and the general public. According to Neisser, Dean's memory was far from what one might expect from a human tape recorder. He wrote that "it is clear that Dean's account of the opening of the September 15 conversation is wrong both as to the words used and their gist" (p. 151) and went on to comment that in his recall of the entire conversation Dean "mentions topics that were indeed discussed, but never reproduces the real gist of anything that was said" (p. 152).

There is little doubt that Neisser's conclusion was at variance with that of the Watergate Committee, who after all did not charge Dean with perjury, and that of the general public, who thought Dean had provided crucial insight into the machinations of the White House cover-up. The general consensus was that Dean had done a credible—in some eyes, an incredible—job of recollecting the events unfolding in the White House. As Neisser noted, the highest-placed members of the White House staff that Dean incriminated in his testimony all went to prison, and Nixon resigned.

Neisser was, of course, aware of the divergence between his conclusion and the general view of the veracity of Dean's testimony. In his view, the difference hinged on what is meant by truth, accuracy, and memory. As Neisser noted, these are not "simple notions" (p. 141). As an account of past episodes—the content of episodic memory—Dean's testimony weighs in woefully short. As Neisser noted, Dean did not get the details or even the gist of the episodes right. Neisser's analysis reminded psychologists

---

[1]Neisser examined both the meetings of September 15 and March 21. Our discussion here is confined to the September 15 meeting.

once again of Bartlett's well-taken point, made over 50 years ago, that remembering is reconstructive.

But Neisser's insistence that the testimony is inaccurate does not necessarily mean that the Watergate Committee and the general public were wrong in applauding its accuracy. As Neisser (1981) noted, Dean recollected the semantics—the theme of what occurred—fairly accurately. He did not accurately recall any event in its own right, but did accurately recall information that depends on repeated episodes, rehearsed presentations, or overall impressions. As Neisser put it, [Dean]:

> believes that he is recalling one conversation at a time, that his memory is 'episodic' in Tulving's sense, but he is mistaken. . . . Such memories might be called *repisodic* rather than episodic: what seems to be an episode actually represents a repetition. (p. 158)

In addition to focusing on the repisodic character of Dean's memory, Neisser also emphasized its schema-driven nature. Specifically, Neisser observed that Dean remembered what was self-serving for him to remember—that Nixon congratulated him on a job well done, for instance. Dean remembered what made Dean look good.

Neisser's analysis of John Dean's memory does, then, tell us something about the nature of human memory—that accuracy in our recollection may at times reflect the repisodic rather than episodic character of the memory and moreover that the recollection is schema-driven. The story about John Dean's memory, however, probably does not end with Neisser's analysis. Something as rich as John Dean's memory probably contains more insights than Neisser could legitimately mine in one article. Other rich veins of gold probably exist in the same set of data Neisser examined, especially if one approached the material with a different tact than the one Neisser pursued. That is what we propose to do in this chapter.

In the meeting of September 15, Dean, Nixon, and Haldeman were conversing about the past. Dean was recounting the events surrounding Watergate through conversation with Nixon and Haldeman. We wondered what insights could be gained by treating the September 15 meeting as an instance of conversational remembering. In the last few years, Hirst, Manier, and their colleagues (Hirst & Manier, 1995, 1996; Hirst, Manier, & Apetroaia, 1997; Manier, 1996; Manier, Pinner, & Hirst, 1996) have been interested in conversational aspects of remembering: how remembering is structured by a conversation and how the act of remembering within a conversation shapes subsequent recollections. We wanted to see how their work could help us understand John Dean's memory.

There was another reason for revisiting John Dean's memory. Although Hirst and Manier undertook their work with the tenets of ecological validity in mind, the instances of conversational remembering they solicited had not occurred spontaneously. Hirst, Manier, and their colleagues mainly studied conversational remembering in the context of families. They asked family members to recollect individually an event each member shared with the others, then to recount the event as a group, and finally, in work still underway, to subsequently recall the event individually. In the group re-countings that Hirst, Manier, and their associates solicited, an experimenter probed the family. That is, the recounting was elicited by the experimenter and the family essentially continued recounting the event until everyone agree that there was nothing more to say. However, most spontaneous acts of conversational remembering do not start with a direct memory probe, as in the Hirst–Manier work. Nor do they continue until every participant in the conversation agrees that there is nothing more to say.

The meeting of September 15, then, could provide a more ecologically valid instance of conversational remembering than the recountings collected by Hirst, Manier, and their colleagues. As we note later in this chapter, the mapping between the conversational remembering of the Hirst–Manier fami-lies and the conversational remembering on September 15 is not exact. Nevertheless, we believe that it is close enough to make John Dean's mem-ory a worthwhile extension of the work on family remembering.

THE HIRST AND MANIER FRAMEWORK

The guiding maxim for Hirst and Manier is that remembering is often an act of conversation (Hirst & Manier, 1996; Manier, 1996). People remember their past through conversation with others. A family will gather at Thanksgiving dinner and talk about previous Thanksgiving dinners; one friend will recollect in conversation with a friend the details of his break up with his boyfriend; businesspersons will recall past efforts to do business in meetings with colleagues. Such acts of conversational remembering were occurring in the September 15 meeting of Nixon, Dean, and Haldeman. As even a cursory reading of the transcript of the tape indicates, the recollection of the past emerged out of an energetic conversation among Nixon, Dean, and Haldeman. The average number of idea units between conversational turns is 2.07 idea units.

In asserting that one must study memory by considering what occurs out in the world as well as probing what goes on in the head, Hirst and Manier (1995, 1996) reflected a growing interest in conversational analysis as a means of understanding psychological functioning. Social psychologists have recently shown that several major social psychological findings, such as the base-rate fallacy of Kahneman & Tversky (1973), and the funda-mental attribution error (Ross & Nisbett, 1991), can be partially accounted for by analyzing the conversational demands present in the experimental tests of these finding (Hilton, 1990, 1995). Moreover, Sperber, Cara, and Girotto (1995) argued that the errors observed in the Wason (1968) task, a classic problem in the study of thinking, can be accounted for not by attributing biases to human thinking, but by looking at the conversational demands of the task. Finally, Middleton and Edwards (1990) forcefully called for a discourse approach to psychology, focusing their efforts, as do Hirst and Manier, on memory.

Acts of group remembering could be viewed as involving processes similar to those observed in group problem solving, where the problem is to remember a past event. As in any case of group problem solving, the group usually assigns members specific tasks or roles. This assignment is usually based on a possibly implicit componential analysis of the task. When it comes to remembering, people probably have folk psychological theories of remembering. Protocol analyses indicate that people state that they do at least three things when remembering: retrieve, assess what is retrieved, and provide retrieval cues to further the retrieval (Norman & Bobrow, 1979). When it comes to telling a story about a past episode, we can relabel these activities as narrating, monitoring the narration, and mentoring the narration, as we shall see, labels that admittedly imply more than simply retrieval, assessing, and cueing.

Hirst, Manier, and their colleagues (Hirst & Manier, 1996; Manier, 1996; Manier et al., 1996) were interested in determining whether members of a well-structured group such as a family will distribute these mnemonically relevant roles across the group. Of course, one family member could have each told one part of the episode and then deferred to another family member to recount the next segment. Alternatively, they could have constantly interrupted each other in an attempt to redirect the story according to their own perspectives. Manier, Hirst, and colleagues found that these modes of recounting rarely occurred.

Hirst, Manier, and colleagues classified family members as narrators, monitors, or mentors on the basis of a coding scheme that they developed. Transcripts were divided into idea units, corresponding to a single action or state described by a participant. These idea units were then classified according to the complex coding scheme. Of interest to the present discussion were the three type of utterances:

Narrative Telling (NT) Describes states or events that are linked together (causally, temporalli, or spatially) and that relate to a central topic or theme.
Examples
"We went to all these other places and then we went to Coney Island, and we went to the aquar-

ium. We went to th-um, amusement park and we went to the beach."

Facillitating Remark (FR)   Attempts to spur someone else to further the narrative, provide more details, or "search their memory." Also, may evaluate someone else's narrative with (implicit or explicit) reference to standards of narrative structure.

Examples

"What did we eat there?" "What did you, what else do you remember?" "Keep to the point." "That's irrelevant."

Assessing Statement (AS)   Agrees, disagrees, or in some other way judges the validity of a previous statement that is not an overt request for assistance. Includes a repetition of a phrase just spoken by someone else, as well as responsive utterances like, "oh," "okay," and "sure" (but not responses to overt questions).

Examples

"Yeah, that's right." "No, you're wrong."

Participants were classified as narrators, monitors, mentors, or other on the basis of the frequency of occurrence of these utterance types, using the definitions and formulas listed next. A measure of the strength with which participants held these roles was also devised and is specified next.

NARRATORS   Assume the function of telling the story. Their utterances are meant in some fashion to "further the narrative." Generally speaking, a Narrator's utterances preserve "narrative continuity" (cf. Middleton & Edward's "default continuity"). That is, any given narrative telling is interlinked (either causally, spatially, temporally, or thematically) with narrative tellings that precede or follow it. Characteristically, they might be expected to: utter a large share of the group's metanarrative statements (e.g. "I'm getting off the point"); seek outside confirmation, perhaps by making overt requests for assistance; and endeavor to "contextualize" the narrative.

Narrative tellings must be the preponderant type of structural unit within their contributions to the group conversation. Also, they must utter a greater than chance share of all the narrative tellings uttered by all family members within the conversation. For a family of four, this means that they must utter more than 25% of the narrative tellings uttered by all participants in the conversation.

Strength: $N/2$, where $N =$ (the percentage of the Narrator's narrative tellings out of the total number of structural units he or she contributed) + (the percentage of the Narrator's narrative tellings out of the total uttered in the conversation).

MENTORS   Assume the function of prompting Narrators to further their narratives and provide more details. Encourage Narrators to adhere to standards of narrative form and content, spurring Narrators on by providing criticisms, directions, helpful remarks, substantial queries, and memory probes. Rather than furthering the narrative directly through their own utterances, Mentors guide the narrative telling, often by providing retrieval cues to Narrators in order to elicit further recollections from them.

Facilitating remarks are among the two most frequent structural units within their contributions to the group conversation. Also, they must utter a greater than chance share of all the facilitating remarks uttered by all family members within the conversation.

Strength: $F/2$, where F = (the percentage of the Mentor's facilitating remarks out of the total number of structural units he or she contributed) + (the percentage of the Mentor's facilitating remarks out of the total in the conversation).

MONITORS   Assume the function of explicitly agreeing or disagreeing with the utterances of the Narrator, without taking personal responsibility for constructing the narrative. They attempt to ensure that the narrative, as told by the Narrator, correctly and completely describes the episode, as remembered by the Monitor.

Assessing statements are among the two most frequent structural units within their contributions to the group conversation. Also, they must utter a greater than chance share of all the assessing statements uttered by all family members within the conversation.

Strength: $A/2$, where A = (the percentage of the Monitor's assessing statements out of the total number of structural units he or she contributed) + (percentage of Mentor's assessing statements out of the total in the conversation).

Coding, using the Hirst–Manier scheme (see Manier, 1996, for the latest version) turned out to be quite reliable. More importantly, in most of the acts of conversational recounting Hirst and Manier and others in their laboratory collected (Apetroaia & Manier, in preparation; Hirst & Manier, 1996; Manier, Pinner, & Hirst, 1996), there was a single (or at most two) narrator(s), and in many of the conversations, monitors and mentors could be unmistakably discerned.

The roles family members adopted did not appear to be fixed. They changed from recounting to recounting. Nevertheless, Hirst, Manier, and their colleagues (e.g., Hirst & Manier, 1996) have observed that in many families, there were tendencies toward default roles, roles a family member would adopt *ceteris paribus* (see Hirst & Manier, 1996, for a discussion of this point). In one family, for instance, the daughter narrated more often than anyone else, in particular, when no one family member singly occupied a central role in the story. In the same family, the father always served the role of mentor.

These default roles did not always coincide with what might be called traditional family roles. Parents are not always mentors, for instance. In one family Apetroaia and Manier (1996; see also Hirst, Manier, & Apetroaia, 1997) examined, the children mentored the parents. This distinctive pattern may have reflected the socioeconomic disruption occurring in this family's home country, Romania, where children are often substantially better educated than their parents. Whatever the reason, this family clearly illustrates that conversational roles do not always mirror family roles.

As yet, Hirst, Manier, and their colleagues have not systematically studied why family members adopted the roles that they do. We expect that it is a complex process. Manier (1996) observed that the events described by the narrator were often more significant or important to him or her than to other participants in the conversation. Thus, in one family that he studied, the son served as narrator of a story in which the son was promised a stereo set, but never received it. In another recounting, the mother served as the narrator in a story about preparations to bring her parents to the United States.

Hirst, Manier, and their colleagues were chiefly interested in demonstrating that conversational roles structured what is remembered in the conversation. Consequently, they collected individual recollections before soliciting the group recounting. Such pregroup recountings were usually collected at least a week before the group recounting. Hirst and Manier (1996) compared the pregroup to the group recounting with the idea of seeing whether the role that family members adopted affected what from the pregroup recollections emerged into the group recounting.

Manier (1996) provided the most detailed analysis to date. Among his many findings, he established that for the family he studied, narrators were able to insert into the group recounting more of their unique pregroup recollections than were nonnarrators. This distinctive contribution to the group recounting did not merely reflect the fact narrators talked more than anyone else. Even if one took into account the large output of the narrators, narrators were still more successful in getting their version of the past, as reflected in their pregroup recollection, into the group narrative than was anyone else.

The advantage of the narrator does not mean that monitors and mentors had no effect on the content of the group recollection. Facilitating remarks, for instance, tended to introduce new narrative units, units found in none of the pregroup recollections. Indeed, Manier found that in the family recountings he studied, 22% of the new narrative units were in response to facilitating remarks. It would seem that mentors shape the content of group recountings by introducing new narrative units. They do this not by stating the narrative units themselves, but by eliciting them through facilitating remarks.

Monitors have less of an effect on the content of the group recounting than either narrators or mentors. According to Manier, in the recountings he studied, assessing statements often served as a bridge from the narrative tellings of one participant to the narrative tellings of another. In 50% of the instances Manier examined, the narrative tellings following an assessing statement were offered by the assessor. Thus, monitors, as the chief assessor, had a powerful tool available to them to connect what they wanted to say with what preceded in the group recounting.

What was remembered in the group recounting, then, was not what any single individual family member remembered in their individual pregroup recollections or even the sum of these pregroup recollections. Rather, the pregroup recollections were filtered through and amplified by the conversational roles family members played in the group recounting. As Hirst & Manier (1995, 1996) argued, the acknowledgment of the contribution conversational roles make in shaping acts of remembering is a first step toward a psychology that goes beyond the narrow confines of studying what occurs in the head. Remembering becomes not the reappearance of what is in the head, the retrieval of information stored in an internal mental mechanism, but the reconstruction of the memory through an act of conversing with others. A narrow information processing approach could not account for the contribution of conversational roles because it would never look at the social interactions occurring during the act of remembering.

The influence of conversational roles on memory may reach beyond the confines of the group recounting itself. It also can shape subsequent recollections. As their work suggests, a conversation about the past renders a past episode in a different form than individual participants in the conversation might have offered prior to the conversation. This new rendering could in turn permanently alter the way participants think about the past episode. In this way, the conversational roles that structure conversational remembering could alter all subsequent acts of recollection.

No work in the Hirst–Manier lab to date has considered the contribution the concept of conversational roles could make to understanding the effect of group recounting on subsequent memory, although this work is currently underway in the context of family recounting. We plan to explore it here as well, but in the context of John Dean's memory. We determine the conversational roles adopted by Dean, Nixon, and Haldeman and then examine the effect these roles had on Dean's statement to the Watergate subcommittee. In this way, we can study the way conversational roles shape subsequent recollection. As the literature reviewed earlier suggests, group recounting should affect subsequent recollection. That is, the way Dean, Haldeman, and Nixon talked in the meeting of September 15 and not merely what they said in that meeting, should have consequences for Dean's memory, as evidenced in his statement to the Watergate committee. Neisser illustrated how Dean got it both right and wrong. We want to determine whether this peculiar pattern of remembrance might in part be traced to the conversational roles Nixon, Dean, and Haldeman adopted in the meeting of September 15.

DIFFERENCES BETWEEN THE WORK
ON FAMILY RECOUNTING AND THE DATA
ON JOHN DEAN'S MEMORY

The memories elicited in the research on family recounting and the memories emerging in the September 15 meeting differ in at least one crucial way: the degree to which the recounted memories are shared among participants at the outset of the conversation. Hirst, Manier, and their colleagues (e.g., Manier & Hirst, 1996) have elicited memories about events that all family members participated in: last Christmas, a graduation, a family outing to Coney Island. There was in each instance a single starting point, even though each family member may have experienced the event differently, and also unquestionably recollected the event differently.

The same is not the case for the events recollected in the September 15 meeting. Dean had been tracking the legal maneuverings surrounding the Watergate affair for the White House. He was the chief point man in the White House for Watergate. Consequently, when he entered the Oval Office on September 15, he probably clearly had at his fingertips a vast array of facts about the events that had transpired from the first report of the Watergate break-in to the present troubles in the courts. As a hardworking and conscientious aide, he no doubt had spent many hours keeping abreast of the events as they unfolded, organizing them into a coherent story, and generally mastering the material so that he could talk spontaneously and effectively with others. To use the language of schema theory, Dean entered the Oval Office with a well-established schema about the recent events surrounding Watergate.

The schemata of Nixon and Haldeman probably differed substantially from Dean's. Unlike Dean, their major responsibilities did not focus on Watergate. As of September 15, the White House still felt fairly comfortable about Watergate and seemed certain that it could be contained. They certainly had yet to adopt a siege mentality. As Watergate reached its apex, or depending on your perspective, nadir, Nixon and Haldeman may have spent their entire working day on Watergate. But it is fair to say that as of September 15, 1972, it probably occupied only a small part of their working day.

Nixon and Haldeman, then, were certainly not participating in the events that figured in the discussion of September 15 to the same degree as Dean was. They were not following the various court actions or even the press coverage of Watergate with the same intensity as was Dean. Nor were they aware of the day-to-day progress of relevant Congressional Committees or the G.A.O. (General Accounting Office) audit. Their knowledge of Watergate probably focused on events to which Dean was not privy. They may have known more about the events leading to the break-in than did Dean. They certainly had greater knowledge about the politics of bugging, at least from a personal level, than did Dean.

These differences can clearly be discerned in the September 15 conversation. Dean tended to talk about the events transpiring since the break-in. Thus, he discussed at length the actions of all parties involved on either side of various legal actions and investigations. Haldeman and Nixon discussed more general topics such as widespread use of bugging in the past, the uses of presidential power, the motivations of the other side, and how to get back at one's enemies.

Of course, we can never be certain what Dean, Nixon, and Haldeman knew when they began their September 15 meeting. Pregroup recollections are not available for Nixon, Haldeman, and Dean. Nevertheless, as we hope we have made clear, it is possible to make assumptions about what these preconversational recountings would have looked like if they were available. In particular, we expect that Dean would have had a well-organized, detailed, and readily accessible account of the events transpiring between the break-in and September 15. Inasmuch as the September 15 meeting was convened rather suddenly, Dean probably did not have time to prepare a speech. But he must have had one at least partially prepared for just such a sudden, unannounced occasion. The last thing he wanted to do was to be perceived as out of touch with the data. It is worth noting that the overlearned character of Dean's knowledge makes it quite different from the kind of knowledge underlying the recounting in the Hirst–Manier studies. Their subjects were talking about ordinary events, events that they probably had not thought much about since they occurred. Dean, on the other hand, had been highly focused for several months on the repercussions of the break-in at the Watergate Apartments.

Whereas it is more difficult to specify what a preconversational recollection of Haldeman and Nixon might have looked like, it would undoubtedly be less detailed than Dean's about the events directly related to the repercussion of Watergate and less well-formed and rehearsed. Their schema may have been more about related events, events that may have occurred before the break-in. Their knowledge was probably more like that of the family members in the Hirst–Manier studies—not overlearned and often half-forgotten.

ANALYSIS OF THE WATERGATE TAPES, DEAN'S STATEMENT, AND THE SUBSEQUENT TESTIMONY UNDER INTERROGATION

Transcript

When Neisser set out to check John Dean's memory, he used the available factual record which, at that time, was *The Presidential Transcripts* (Gold, 1974), the book form of the published transcript as it had appeared originally in the *Washington Post* and the *New York Times*. This published version of the transcripts was full of parenthetical notes such as "(inaudible)" or "(expletive deleted)," and ended with "(Note: Further conversation following unrelated to Watergate.).". Our quantitative analysis required that we use an account of the original material that was as close as possible to a verbatim reproduction. Since the time of Neisser's (1981) study, the tapes themselves have become public and are available at the National Archive.

At the start of our attempt to revisit John Dean's memory, Gluck traveled to the National Archive, listened to the original tape, and obtained an unpublished version of the transcript that had been prepared by the Impeachment Inquiry Staff for the House Judiciary Committee at the time of the Watergate Hearings. Significant differences were found between the published transcript, Neisser's point of departure for his study, and Congress' own transcript, our point of departure. In the published transcripts, dysfluencies and overlaps had been removed. Moreover, some statements had been simplified or summarized, resulting in a product that was less a verbatim reproduction than a very highly detailed summary of the conversation. See Table 11.1 for an example illustrating this point. The version of the Impeachment Inquiry Staff also included the expletives that had been deleted, filled in some of the inaudible gaps, corrected several misattributions to the wrong speaker, resolved discrepancies, and filled in material that had been omitted from the published version. Perhaps the most significant change was the addition to the transcript of what followed that had been considered unrelated to Watergate. This included further discussion of an enemies list and of using the I.R.S. against enemies, and plans for staff changes after the election, topics that Dean touched on in his statement and testimony and that were not fully represented in the published transcript.

The final version that we used in the present study went one step beyond that Impeachment Inquiry Staff version. We made several changes to that version after carefully listening to the tape and added some text where

TABLE 11.1
Comparison of Published Transcript and the
Transcript of the Impeachment Inquiry Staff

Published Version	Hirst/Gluck Version
Example #1 (Gold, 1974, p. 59):	
D-Good statistics supporting the finding.	D-And good statistics supporting that. Kleindienst is going to have a—
H-Isn't that ridiculous-	H-Isn't that ridiculous though?
	P-What is?
this silly thing.	H-This silly ass damn thing.
P-Yes (Expletive deleted).	P-Yeah.
	H-That kind of resources against—
	P-Yeah for Christ's sake [unintelligible]
	H-Who the hell cares?
Goldwater put it in context when he said	P-Goldwater put it in context, he said
Example #2 (Gold, 1974, p. 69):	
D-We can blunder down the road anyway.	D-It's a, it's a glimmer down the road anyway, but, uh—
(NOTE: Further conversation following unrelated to Watergate.)	P-It'll look forward to the time that we have the entrance to the Department of Justice and IRS totally under our control . . .
Example #3 (Gold, 1974, p. 59):	
P-The difficulty with using it, of course, is it reflects on Johnson.	P-The difficulty with using it, of course, is that it reflects on Johnson.
	D-Right.
	P-He ordered it.
If it weren't for that, I would use it. Is there any way we could use it without using his name—	If it weren't for that, I'd use it. Is there any way we could use it without reflecting on Johnson?

other transcribers had merely classified the conversation as inaudible. The result of this process was a new transcript that was as close a representation as was possible of what was uttered in the original conversation. As a result of all these differences, the final version was markedly longer than the published version, 1109 idea units versus 486 idea units.

Coding

Prior research on conversational remembering had used conversations created when a group was asked to remember material together. Participants were focused on the task at hand and the conversation was consequently confined to a discussion of past events. The September 15 conversation between Nixon, Dean, and Haldeman also consisted, in great part, of discussion of past events; after all, the task at hand was a review of events related to Watergate. However, unlike the previously studied conversations, future plans and predictions were also included in the naturally occurring conversation, as were remarks (such as greetings, etc.) that could only be classified as relating to the present. To capture this aspect of the conversation on September 15, the following categories were added to the Hirst and Manier coding scheme:

Future (F)   Idea units related to future plans or predictions and therefore, unrelated to memory or group remembering.
Examples:
"I suggest that we're going to have a house cleaning." "I think we are going to fix the son of a bitch." "This is going to be over someday."

Present (P)   Idea units that do not refer to the past or the future, but relate only to the present conversation.
Examples:
"Hi." "How are you? (as a greeting rather than a question)" "I'm getting into this thing."

Other (O)   Units which could not be otherwise coded due to fragmentary content and/or unclear meaning.
Examples:
"and if he (unintelligible)," "Well on the other hand maybe," "our suits are still - ."

The transcript was divided into idea units corresponding to a single action or state described by a participant and coded by two coders. The relevant section of John Dean's statement and the section of his testimony where he was questioned by Senator Baker (which Neisser used in his study) were also divided into idea units and coded by two coders. The coders disagreed less than 10% of the time and discrepancies were successfully resolved.

After the transcripts were coded and the various coding categories tabulated, the statement and testimony were reviewed one idea unit at a time. For each unit, the September 15 conversation was reviewed and any unit that matched in meaning was identified. A one-to-one correspondence as to exact wording or exact meaning was not sought. Rather, if a unit in the statement or testimony matched more than one unit in the original conversation, each match was recorded as contributing to the subsequent unit. If more than one unit in the statement or testimony matched the same unit in the original conversation, the original unit was recorded as contributing to both subsequent units.

RESULTS

Who Occupied What Role

Table 11.2 contains the distribution of the utterance types across the three participants. The figures are stated in terms of the number of idea units. As can be readily seen, the conversation was chiefly between Dean and Nixon, with Haldeman mainly sitting on the sideline. Overall, there were more narrative tellings than anything else, including remarks about the future or the present. The meeting was called to update Nixon about the Watergate affair and the meeting concentrated mainly on recounting what had happened so far in the Watergate affair. As already noted, to the extent that the participants talked about things other than the past, they did so by interweaving talk about the future and present with talk about the past. Consequently, Dean never had a chance to deliver a smooth, continuous narrative about the past. Comments he would make about the past would elicit comments about the future. A typical example of this is as follows:

> Dean: Johnnie has been a, a disappointment . . .
> Nixon: Well he's going to get out. (National Archives, 1996, p. 5)

Table 11.3 contains the proportion of an utterance type that could be attributed to the three participants. That is, it captures who uttered the most of any particular utterance type. The figure in each column adds up to 100%. Table 11.4 contains the proportion of what a participant uttered that belongs to each utterance type. Here the figures in each row adds up to 100%. We have calculated the percentages in Table 11.4 using two methods. For the first method, we examined every utterance in the September 15 meeting. This would include talk about the future and the present as well as talk about the past. In the second method, we only examined talk about the past, excluding talk about the present and future. As can be seen, both methods revealed the same pattern.

TABLE 11.2
Distribution of Utterance Types Across
Participants (in number of idea units)

	Total	NT	FR	AS	Future	Present	Other
Nixon	486	103	55	47	129	20	107
Dean	403	244	6	38	64	2	49
Haldeman	221	76	16	19	58	6	46
Total	1110	423	77	129	251	28	202

TABLE 11.3
Percentage of the Total Units for Each
Utterance Type Contributed by Each Speaker

	Total	NT	FR	AS	Future	Present	Other
Nixon	44	24	71	56	51	71	7
Dean	36	58	8	29	25	7	49
Haldeman	20	18	21	15	23	21	46

TABLE 11.4
Percentage of the Total Units of Each Speaker Belong to Each
Utterance Type (percentage based only on utterance types
involving the recounting of the past in parentheses)

	NT		FR		AS		Future	Present	Other	
Nixon	21	(35)	11	(19)	15	(24)	27	4	22	(22)
Dean	61	(78)	1	(2)	9	(12)	16	0	6	(8)
Haldeman	34	(56)	7	(12)	9	(14)	26	3	9	(18)
Total	38	(57)	7	(10)	12	(17)	23	3	8	(16)

As Tables 11.3 and 11.4 illustrate, according to the Hirst–Manier definitions of narrator, monitor, and mentor, Dean clearly served the role of narrator and Nixon served the roles of monitor and mentor. Haldeman served no definable role. An analysis of the strength of the roles held by the three participants suggests that Haldeman was more of a narrator than anything else. His strength as a narrator was .26. This value is small, however, at least in comparison to Dean's strength of a narrator of .60.

Nixon also made more comments about the future than anyone else. That is, he appeared to be the person in the conversation who would forecast what could happen in the future or outline plans for future action. Examples of both kinds of comments are as follows.

Nixon: It's not going going to be that way anymore and uh . . . (National Archives, 1996, p. 24)

Nixon: Well, the point is they ought to raise hell about this. (National Archives, 1996, p. 30)

Several comments are in order about the roles held by participants in the September 15 meeting. Dean's role of narrator is expected. After all, the meeting was called to update Nixon, and presumably Haldeman, about the events surrounding Watergate. Dean had the job of providing the update. That other participants limited their narrative tellings suggests either they had little to contribute or were genuinely interested in hearing what Dean had to say.

As for Nixon, his tripartite role in the meeting of monitor, mentor, and projector of the future follows almost directly from his position as President. Hirst, Manier, and their colleagues (e.g., Hirst & Manier, 1996) also found instances in which conversational participants held more than one role. Nixon's tripartite role is just another example of such multiplicity. However, there are some problematic aspects of Nixon's role in the meeting, at least problematic for the concepts of conversational roles we have advanced so far in this chapter. In particular, we need to consider carefully what we mean by mentor.

When Hirst and Manier (1996) coined this term in their studies of family recounting, they had in mind recent developmental work focusing on mother–child interactions during acts of remembering (Fivush, 1991). In this work, mothers provided children with retrieval cues and instructions about the narrative direction the child should follow with the aim of helping the child tell a story about a past event, such as his or her day in school. In a real sense, the mothers were mentoring their children, helping them tell the story and more generally teaching them how to recollect the past. The same mentoring function appears to hold in the families studied by Hirst and Manier. For instance, in one family, a father's facilitating remark was not aimed at discovering new information, but in helping his daughter tell a complete story.

Nixon is clearly not mentoring Dean in the sense Hirst and Manier meant when they coined the term. Dean does not have to learn how to tell a narrative about the Watergate testimony. Nor does he need help telling the narrative. He probably could have delivered a nonstop lecture on Watergate if instructed to. He did not have to be taught how to recount the events of the past.

What Dean needed to know from Nixon in the September 15 meeting was what information Nixon wanted and what information should be left out of his recounting. Nixon supplied this guidance in his facilitating remarks. It would be more accurate to say that Nixon facilitated Dean's narration of the Watergate affair rather than mentored it. His facilitating remarks seemed to have a couple aims. They specified what Dean should talk about, as when he said:

Nixon: How did MacGregor handle himself? (National Archives, 1996, p. 5)

They also indicated what Dean should expand on, as in the comment:

Nixon: What the hell do you think is involved? What's your guess? (National Archives, 1996, p. 6)

In coding the transcript, we applied the Hirst–Manier coding scheme, or our expanded version of it, without carefully considering how the context of the meeting of September 15 might differ from the context of experiments on family recounting. We then assigned to Nixon the same role as we found in family members in our family recounting studies on the basis of our coding. This application of the coding scheme and the definitions of narrator, monitor, and mentor was not sufficiently context-sensitive. By their nature, coding schemes abstract away from the complexity of any discourse and urge the investigator to put multivalanced utterances into categorically confining boxes. We only discovered the difference in the role Nixon plays in the September 15 meeting and the role the family members played in their discussions about the past by moving beyond the coding scheme and returning to the text. Each new conversation, each new group or social context does not require a new coding scheme but they do necessitate a critical attitude toward the application of a pre-existing coding scheme, as well as a continued close reading of the text outside the confines of the coding scheme.

In recognition of this point, we henceforth use the term *facilitator* to capture Nixon's role in the September 15 meeting rather the term *mentor*. The exact relation between a facilitator and a mentor deserves further analysis, an analysis that is outside the confines of this chapter. Suffice it to say for the present, mentoring appears to be a specific kind of facilitating, one with goals that reach beyond those of facilitating.

As we have noted, Nixon did more than facilitate Dean's narration. He also monitored Dean when he thought Dean was wrong or when he wanted to agree with Dean. Here we need to make a cautionary remark similar to that made for mentoring. As noted, in the work done in Hirst and Manier's laboratory, subjects began from the same starting point. Before their memory was tested, they all experienced the same event. Under this condition, subjects could presumably legitimately assess the validity of another subject's narrative telling because they had all experienced the same thing. In the situation of the meeting on September 15, there is no reason to assume the participants begin from the same starting point. In some instances, they may share the same knowledge, and when they say, "Yeah," they are indeed confirming that what was said was correct. But in many instances, a "Yeah" may not be an example of monitoring, but merely a social convention to encourage the narrator to continue to talk. We could see both kinds of activities in the September 15 meeting.

> Dean: . . . and I've gone through some of these clippings and it's just phenomenal the uh the amount of coverage this case is getting.
> Nixon: Yeah. (National Archives, 1996, p. 34)

Dean: I stopped doing that about uh two months ago.

Nixon: Yeah

Dean: We just take one at a time and . . . (National Archives, 1996, p. 31)

We have presently found it difficult to distinguish between these two kinds of statements in any systematic fashion, and until we do, we must cautiously interpret any results dealing with assessing statements.

Finally, it should be noted that Nixon spoke about the future more than anyone else. Again, an explanation for this dominance can be found in Nixon's status. The presidency was at stake, and only plans approved, indeed, originating in the presidency may have been deemed appropriate.

That Haldeman served no discernible role in the meeting is not surprising inasmuch as he was only sitting in. Hirst, Manier, and their colleagues also found instances in which family members did not serve any definable role, at least according to the present scheme.

THE EFFECT OF CONVERSATIONAL REMEMBERING, AND THE CONVERSATIONAL ROLES THAT GOVERN IT, ON SUBSEQUENT RECOLLECTION

We are interested in determining whether we can better understand why Dean remembers what he does in his statement by considering the conversational roles Nixon, Dean, and Haldeman adopted in the conversation that transpired among them on September 15. We concentrate here mainly on the narrative tellings in the September 15 meeting. These tellings presumably capture the recollections Nixon, Dean, and Haldeman had of the past events surrounding Watergate. Of course, the September 15 conversation consisted of more than narrative tellings about the past—nonnarrative remarks, such as facilitating statements and assessing statements, as well as statements involving both the present and future were included. Although we comment briefly toward the end of the chapter on nonnarrative statements and present- and future-oriented statements, our main interest is in how the recollections about the past in the meeting of September 15 make it into Dean's subsequent recollections. Specifically, we examine the recollections contained in Dean's statement to the subcommittee, not the subsequent responses to the questioning of the members of subcommittee. This testimony did not differ substantially from the statement and would add a complexity to our analysis that we wanted to avoid at this stage.

About the narrative tellings found in the meeting of September 15, it should be stated at the start that few make it into the statement. There were 422 unique narrative tellings in the September 15 meeting. Only 65, or 15.4%, of them surfaced in Dean's statement to Congress. Can a discussion of conversational roles help us understand which of the 422 narrative tellings made it into Dean's statement?

Narrators and Narrative Tellings

Let us first consider Dean's role as narrator. Dean was more likely to remember what he said in the September 15 meeting than what any other participant said. Whereas Dean offered only 58% of the narrative tellings in the meeting of September 15, 71% of the narrative tellings he recalled in his statement to Congress were his. His reasons for privileging his narrative tellings were probably multifold. Most of them reflect to varying degrees his role as narrator. As noted, what he said may have been rehearsed, indeed, probably overlearned. As narrator, Dean also generated more narrative tellings than anyone else. This generation may have made his narrative tellings more memorable than anyone else's. Work in the verbal learning domain indicates that information generated by an individual may be more memorable for that individual than information generated by someone else (Slamecka & Graf, 1978). This principle may also apply to narrating. Moreover, according to Pinner (see Manier, Pinner, & Hirst, 1996), information that is reconstructed by a participant is more likely to be recollected in subsequent recollections. Finally, Dean wanted to make himself seem more important in the meeting, as Neisser (1981) suggested, and hence may have wanted to give himself, and what he said, a more central role.

Clearly, none of the results we have could be used to support a claim that the narrator's utterances are better remembered than any other utterances. However, this might seem a reasonable hypothesis. Inasmuch as the narrator dominates the recounting, he has an advantage in giving structure and shape to the narration. Consequently, the resulting narration of any participant in the recounting could capture his structure and in particular the narrative tellings of the narrator. In order to test this hypothesis, we would need the subsequent recollections of the nonnarrators in the September 15 meeting. Unfortunately, although both Haldeman and Nixon wrote books, they gave their public accounting after the existence of the tapes was known. They presumably consulted the tapes before making their recollections of the September 15 meeting public.

Facilitators and Facilitating Remarks

The available data does, however, allow us to explore the impact of monitoring and facilitating on John Dean's memory. Consider the role of facilitator. Facilitators utter more facilitating remarks than anyone else. Are the narrative tellings elicited by facilitating remarks more likely to be remembered than those surfacing spontaneously in the meeting?

Narrative tellings elicited by facilitating remarks are likely to be remembered because they either bring to the fore something that may not have been so easily remembered by the participants in the conversation, perhaps because it is not schema-relevant, or because they introduce new narrative units into the recounting that can be assimilated into the existing schemata of the participants. In other words, the mnemonic effectiveness of facilitating remarks will depend in part on the schemata participants have of the solicited material.

As we have already noted, we expect that the schemata Dean had as he entered the Oval Office on September 15 differed markedly from those of Nixon and Haldeman. Specifically, Dean already knew a great deal about the events following the Watergate break-in. Not only did he know a lot, he knew it well and probably had a well-organized schema of this information. Dean came to the meeting prepared to impart to Nixon and Haldeman information about the Watergate affair. The facilitating remarks of Nixon and Haldeman were not intended to teach Dean how to tell his story, but to inform Dean about the story Nixon and Haldeman wanted told. Because Dean was the narrator in the conversation, he undoubtedly had ample opportunity to impart to Haldeman and Nixon the information he found most important. Thus, one might expect that in many of the instances in which Haldeman and Nixon solicited information through facilitating remarks, they were provoking Dean to talk about things he might not have considered of importance. For example:

Nixon: What's the situation on your uh on the on the little red box? (National Archives, 1996, pp. 12–13)

In such instances, Nixon and Haldeman are asking Dean to readjust his conception of the Watergate affair. Simply by asking, they were giving certain information more importance than Dean might have assigned to it. For someone without the well-formed schema that Dean no doubt had, we might expect a readjustment in the conception of the unfolding events. Such a readjustment might have been difficult for Dean. He had been working on Watergate for months and a subtle indication of the importance of an event by his boss may not be enough to make him rip up his preestablished conception of the events and reconfigure it to suit his boss. In other words, Dean may have had difficulty remembering what might be called schema-irrelevant or schema-unimportant information.

Thus, it is possible that facilitating remarks Nixon and Haldeman addressed to Dean may actually have been difficult for Dean to remember.

The elicited narrative tellings did not fit well into Dean's already well-established schema, and hence may be poorly remembered.

The situation is different when Dean solicited memories from Nixon and Haldeman using facilitating remarks. Dean probably solicits information from Nixon and Haldeman because he thinks that from them, he will learn something he does not presently know. Dean's knowledge of Watergate was from careful study of the public events transpiring at that time. Nixon and Haldeman had access to more private activity. They also had a more historical perspective than Dean. Dean clearly was not wrong in hoping that he could discover something new from Nixon and Haldeman.

But Dean solicits information from Nixon and Haldeman not only in the hope of finding out something that he may not already know. He also proffers facilitating remarks because he thinks that the information Nixon and Haldeman may provide will be relevant to the continual construction of his schema of Watergate. It is information he should easily be able to assimilate and consequently, remember.

We find ourselves, then, in a somewhat paradoxical situation: On the one hand, Dean should find it difficult to remember the narrative tellings he provided to Nixon's and Haldeman's facilitating remark. On the other hand, he should find it easy to remember the narrative tellings Nixon and Haldeman provided in response to his facilitating remarks. An analysis of Dean's statement to the Congressional subcommittee investigating Watergate confirms this set of predictions.

We calculated two probabilities: First, we examined the narrative tellings in the conversation that made it into Dean's statement. We calculated the proportion of these in-statement narrative tellings that were elicited by facilitating remarks. We called this proportion the in-statement proportion. Second, we examined the narrative tellings in the conversation that failed to make it into Dean's statement. We then calculated the proportion of these out-of-statement narrative tellings that were elicited by facilitating remarks. We called this the out-of-statement proportion.

Now consider those narrative tellings elicited from Dean by facilitating remarks made by Nixon or Haldeman. For these narrative tellings, we would expect that the out-of-statement proportion should be greater than or equal to the in-statement proportion. The opposite pattern should hold for the narrative tellings elicited from Nixon or Haldeman by facilitating remarks made by Dean: The in-statement proportion should be greater than the out-of-statement proportion.

As Table 11.5 indicates, this configuration of results obtained. That is, the narrative tellings elicited by Haldeman and Nixon from Dean actually were more likely to remain unstated than to appear in Dean's statement. On the other hand, the narrative tellings elicited by Dean from Haldeman and Nixon were more likely to make it into the statement than remain

TABLE 11.5
Proportion of Narrative Statements Elicited by a Participant
Appearing or Failing to Appear in Dean's Statement

	In-Statement	Out-of-Statement
Elicited from Dean	.19	.31
Nixon or Haldeman	.21	.06

unsaid. In other words, narrative tellings following facilitating remarks only make it into subsequent recollections if they can be assimilated into existing schemata. The statements elicited from Dean by Haldeman and Nixon could not be easily assimilated: Dean might not have thought they were important and hence had trouble finding a place of importance for them in his preexisting schema. The statements elicited from Haldeman and Nixon by Dean could be easily assimilated: Dean asked for the information; he probably thought it was relevant, and hence probably had little trouble assimilating this information.

Monitors and Assessing Statements

Let us now turn to the monitoring that occurred in the meeting of September 15. There were 129 assessing statements in the meeting of September 15. Most of them were positive assessing statements—114 positive, 9 negative, and 6 neutral (as in "Oh"). The small number of negative assessing statements is consistent with the findings of Manier (1996) in his work with families. People generally do not appear to question the narrative tellings of other participants in a conversation. In the September 15 meeting, 16% of Haldeman's assessing statements were negative, 11% of Dean's were negative, and only 4% of Nixon's were negative. Nixon, of course, as a monitor, offered substantially more assessing statements than anyone else—72 of 129 assessing statements.

We examined two different sets of narrative tellings: (a) those that were assessed, and (b) those that followed an assessment. According to the work of Manier et al. (1996), an idea unit raised in a group recounting should be better remembered by a participant if he aided in the reconstruction of the idea unit. Manier et al. included assessing statements as a sign of participation. Sixty-six assessing statements followed a narrative telling. The remaining 63 followed statements about the present or future or nonnarrative statements. Only 8% of the 66 assessed narrative tellings made it into the statement, a percentage that is markedly below the 16% of the narrative tellings in general that made it from the conversation to the statement. The same pattern obtained even if we confine our focus to those assessing statements made by Dean. Fifteen of his assessing statements followed narrative tellings, and only 13% of these made it from the conversation to the statement. Thus, in this particular instance, assessing a narrative telling conferred no mnemonic advantage to that telling. This unexpected result is difficult to interpret inasmuch as the assessing statement we examined may, as noted, not even assess, but merely encourage a speaker to continue talking.

Firmer results are possible when we look at the bridging role of assessing statement. Here it does not matter whether the statement truly assesses or merely served as a linguistic tool for furthering the conversation. Manier (1996) found that 50% of the assessing statements in the family he studied served as bridges to the narrative tellings of the assessor. Such bridging did not occur as frequently in the September 15 meeting. Of the 35 assessing statements that were followed by a narrative telling, only 26% of them could be defined as a bridge—that is, the narrative telling was uttered by the same person who offered the assessing statement.

Whereas bridging may not have occurred as frequently in the September 15 meeting, it did confer a mnemonic advantage to the narrative telling that followed it. If the assessing statement is offered as a bridge connecting the previous narrative tellings of one participant with the narrative tellings of the assessor, then one might expect that the tie between these two sets of narrative tellings might be quite tight or integrated. If so, the second set of narrative tellings should be remembered along with the first set. We tested this hypothesis somewhat grossly by examining whether the narrative telling that immediately followed a bridge assessment was more likely to make it from the conversation into the statement than would a narrative telling in general. This rough test of the hypothesis, if anything, understates the possibility of an effect. Nevertheless, we could discern a trend in the expected direction: 20% of the bridged narrative tellings made it into the statement compared to 16% of narrative tellings in general. Moreover, 44% of bridged narrative tellings surfaced in his statement to the Watergate subcommittee compared to 19% of his narrative tellings in general. Thus, assessing statements like facilitating remarks may, under specific circumstances, serve a mnemonic function.

Remarks About the Future

Finally, we turn to statements about the future or the present. These properly have little or nothing to do with remembering. Nevertheless, an examination of the relevant data provides at least two interesting findings. First, in his statement, Dean's recall of the various roles each participant took mirror what occurred in the conversation. Not only did Dean recollect more assessing statements and facilitating remarks as originating from

TABLE 11.6
Percentage of the Total Units for Each Utterance Type Contributed
by Each Speaker according to Dean's Statement
(Percentage of the Total Units for Each Utterance Type Contributed
by Each Speaker in the September 15 meeting, in parentheses)

	NT		FR		AS		Future		Present	
Nixon	12	(24)	100	(71)	50	(56)	70	(51)	100	(71)
Dean	71	(58)	0	(8)	50	(29)	19	(25)	0	(7)
Haldeman	17	(18)	0	(21)	0	(20)	12	(23)	0	(21)

Nixon and more narrative tellings as originating with himself, he also remembered that Nixon provided the majority of the remarks about the future. See Table 11.6 for the relevant data.

The second finding touched on what Dean remembered about what Nixon said. As Table 11.6 illustrates, Dean did not remember the narrative tellings offered by Nixon very well. Although Nixon offered 24% of the narrative tellings in the meeting of September 15, Dean remembered him as offering only 12%. Or to state the point slightly differently, Dean remembered only 8% of the narrative telling of Nixon in the September 15 meeting, whereas he remembered 19% of his own. This difference may not be terribly surprising until one contrasts it with Dean's memory for Nixon's comments about the future. In the September 15 meeting, Nixon made around 50% of the remarks about the future, but Dean attributed 70% of them to Nixon. Indeed, Dean remembered 23% of the remarks Nixon made about the future, but only 13% of his own and 9% of those made by Haldeman. Clearly, Dean's memory for what Nixon said was not uniform. It was bad for Nixon's narrative tellings; good for Nixon's comments about the future.

GENERAL DISCUSSION

What have we learned in revisiting John Dean's memory from a conversational perspective? First, the participants in the meeting of September 15 adopted conversational roles, just like the family members in the studies of Hirst, Manier, and their colleagues (e.g., Hirst & Manier, 1996). Dean was responsible for updating Haldeman and Nixon about Watergate, and hence, not surprisingly, he adopted the role of narrator. Haldeman had no discernible role, or at least only a minor role in the meeting. This relatively passive stance probably reflected the fact that Haldeman was merely sitting in on the meeting. Nixon provided input into the meeting in the main through facilitating remarks and assessing statements, among other nonnarrative utterances. He also made more remarks about the future than anyone else. He did little narrating. Rather he assessed, encouraged Dean and Haldeman to talk, queried Dean and Haldeman, and spoke about the future. Nixon's function here was in part not so much as a mentor and monitor, but as a facilitator and monitor—indicating what he wanted to know and guiding Dean in his narration.

The observable conversational roles that emerged in the September 15 meeting are important for the study of John Dean's memory because they do not merely structure the conversation but also have mnemonic consequences. Elsewhere, Hirst and Manier (1996) have explored the way conversational roles shape the act of remembering in a conversation. Our focus here has been on the effect these conversational roles have on subsequent memory.

Clearly, as narrator, Dean told his story in the September 15 meeting, and it is this story by and large that he remembers in his statement. That he remembers this information is not surprising: After all, he probably recited in the September 15 meeting things that he had overlearned in the many months he had spent mastering the Watergate affair. We would have liked, of course, to determine the extent to which Dean's rendering of the events surrounding Watergate reshaped what Nixon and Haldeman already knew about the affair. Unfortunately, this data is not available.

What is available is the effect assessing statements and facilitating remarks in the conversation had on subsequent memory. In approaching John Dean's memory, it became clear that we could not merely consider the conversational interactions alone—the assessing statements and facilitating remarks by themselves. Nor could we merely consider the schemata Nixon, Haldeman, and Dean possessed when they began their meeting. Both conversational interactions and schemata had to be taken into account.

We demonstrated that conversational interactions mattered. Narrative tellings were not uniformly remembered. Rather, memorability of a narrative telling could be traced to the conversational context in which it emerged. For instance, Dean was more likely to remember narrative tellings that he solicited from Nixon or Haldeman through the device of facilitating remarks than information Nixon or Haldeman offered unsolicited. Dean was also more likely to remember narrative tellings that were connected to other participants' narrative tellings through bridging assessment than through narrative tellings in general. In other words, narrative tellings solicited through facilitating remarks or assessing statements had a mnemonic advantage under some conditions.

We could specify some situations where a mnemonic advantage did not emerge. A person may enter a conversation with such a well-established schema that what anyone says or how he or she interacts with others in the conversation will have little or no impact on the schema. One could possibly add new information to the schema—especially if the new information can be easily assimilated into the schema—but one cannot easily alter the schema.

Such a situation appears to hold for Dean. He probably knew the details about the events following Watergate extremely well. Thus, nothing Nixon or Haldeman could do, either by narrating the events themselves or by trying to solicit a different rendering through facilitating remarks, could alter Dean's perspective on the events. Dean's subsequent memory for narrative tellings solicited through facilitating remarks by Nixon and Haldeman was actually worse than his memory for the narrative telling in general. Moreover, Dean's memory for the narrative tellings offered by Nixon and Haldeman was worse than his memory for narrative tellings in general.

Our set of results cannot be reduced to analysis of the status of the participants; that is, the power relations that exist among the participants. One might expect that power relationships would have an effect on memory, with one more likely to remember something said by a powerful person than a less powerful individual. At least in the complex dynamics clearly at play in the meeting of September 15, this did not appear to be the case.

In particular, although Dean no doubt acknowledged that the President was the most powerful person at the meeting, he also probably had more confidence in his own expertise about the events that transpired since the Watergate break-in than he did in the expertise of the other participants. More important, he knew what he knew very well. On the other hand, Dean realized that Nixon was his boss and what Nixon thought about future actions concerning Watergate, as well as his prognostications about the way the affair would unfold, probably was worthy of attention. From this perspective, it is not surprising that Dean failed to remember well the narrative tellings offered by Nixon, but did remember well his remarks about the future. Power alone cannot explain what Dean remembered about what Nixon said.

We suspect that no single approach to the complex conversation occurring on September 15 can fully accomplish the task of accounting for John Dean's memory. We only want to underline the need to consider conversational and social components. Toward the beginning of this chapter, we argued that remembering must be considered a social process, an act of communicating. As such, we argued, it could not be fully understood merely by referring to internal processing. However, we found that we could not escape from the use of some of the vocabulary associated with internal mnemonic processing. We found it necessary to evoke the idea of schema to explain why Dean was unaffected by the facilitating remarks of Nixon and Haldeman. We explained the effect of bridging assessing statements by referring to the degree to which new information can be assimilated into existing schema. And we treated facilitating remarks as retrieval cues, at least to some extent. Each of these explanations evoked a tried and true principal of memory, verified by careful experiments that treated memory solely as an internal mechanism. If traditional principles of memory are serving as a major explanatory vehicle, than why evoke a social component?

Such a line of argument neglects that facilitating remarks, assessing statements, narrative tellings, and all other conversational ploys occur not in random fashion but by virtue of the social interactions underlying the conversation. To be sure, facilitating remarks may in many cases be viewed as retrieval cues, and as such, may not seem to add much to the theoretical armature available to the student of memory. But some participants in a conversation are more likely to offer facilitating remarks than others, as our discovery of conversational roles in the September 15 meeting, as well as their repeated discovery in the Hirst–Manier work on family recounting, indicates. A subsequent memory of the events discussed in a conversation, then, will not only reflect the isolated effect of facilitating remarks on memory, but the preponderance of facilitating remarks offered by an individual adopting the role of facilitator. Consequently, the facilitator, by virtue of his facilitating remarks, has a unique and personalized effect on the subsequent memories of conversation participants. The same is true for narrative tellings and narrators, assessing statements and monitors, and other conversational moves and the mnemonically relevant conversational roles underlying these moves. Clearly, the effect of conversation on subsequent memory must be understood at least in part in terms of the social interactions that led to adoption of particular conversational roles.

In revisiting John Dean's memory, then, we have seen an aspect of John Dean's memory that Neisser's (1981) initial visit did not touch on. We have discovered that Dean's recollections of the information imparted in the conversation of September 15 was not merely a reflection of what he knew about the Watergate affair before the September 15 meeting, what he heard in the meeting, what his self-interests were, or what was repeated across meetings. Rather, his recollections reflected in part the social interactions occurring in the meeting and in particular, the conversational roles Dean, Nixon, and Haldeman adopted at the meeting. Too often the social component of memory is treated as a side show. Our visit with John Dean suggests that it should really be placed in the main ring.

REFERENCES

Apetroaia, I., & Manier, D. (in preparation). Children mentoring their parents: Effects of authority and expertise on conversational remembering in a Romanian family.

Bartlett, F. C. (1932). *Remembering*. Cambridge, England: Cambridge University Press.

Fivush, R. (1991). The social construction of personal narratives. *Merrill-Palmer Quarterly, 37,* 59–82.

Gold, G. (1974). *The White House transcripts.* New York: Bantam.

Hilton, D. J. (1990). Conversational processes and causal explanation. *Psychological Bulletin, 107,* 65–81.

Hilton, D. J. (1995). The social context of reasoning: Conversational inference and rational judgment. *Psychological Bulletin, 118,* 248–271.

Hirst, W., & Manier, D. (1995). Opening vistas for cognitive psychology. In L. Martin, K. Nelson, & E. Tobach (Eds.), *Sociocultural psychology* (pp. 89–124). New York: Cambridge University Press.

Hirst, W., & Manier, D. (1996). Social influences on remembering. In D. Rubin (Ed.), *Remembering our past* (pp. 271–290). New York: Cambridge University Press.

Hirst, W., Manier, D., & Apetroaia, I. (1997). The social construction of the remembered self: Family recounting. *Annals of the New York Academy of Science.*

Kahneman, D., & Tversky, A. (1973). On the psychology of prediction. *Psychological Review, 80,* 237–251.

Manier, D. (1996). *Family remembering: Autobiographical remembering in the context of family conversations.* Unpublished doctoral dissertation, New School for Social Research, New York, New York.

Manier, D., Pinner, E., & Hirst, W. (1996). Family remembering. In D. Hermann, C. McEvoy, P. Hertel, & M. K. Johnson (Eds.), *Basic and applied memory research.* Mahwah, NJ: Lawrence Erlbaum Associates.

Middleton, D., & Edwards, D. (Eds.). (1990). *Collective remembering.* London: Sage.

National Archives. (1996). *White House Tapes (Watergate Prosecution Force File Segment). Transcript of Conversation, Sept. 15, 1972, 5:27–6:17 PM, Conversation No.: 779-002.* (Available from the National Archives)

Neisser, U. (1967). *Cognitive psychology.* New York: Appleton-Century-Crofts.

Neisser, U. (1978). Memory: What are the important questions. In M. M. Gruneberg, P. E. Morris, & N. Sykes (Eds.), *Practical aspects of memory.* London: Academic Press.

Neisser, U. (1981). John Dean's memory: A case study. *Cognition, 9,* 1–22.

Norman, D. A., & Bobrow, D. (1979). Descriptions: An intermediate stage of retrieval. *Cognitive Psychology, 11,* 107–123.

Ross, L., & Nisbett, R. E. (1991). *The person and the situation.* New York: McGraw-Hill.

Slamecka, N. J., & Graf, P. (1978). The generation effect: Delineation of a phenomenon. *Journal of Experimental Psychology: Human Learning and Memory, 4,* 592–604.

Sperber, D., Cara, F., & Girotto, V. (1995). Relevance theory explains the selection task. *Cognition, 57,* 31–95.

Wason, P. C. (1968). Reasoning about a rule. *Quarterly Journal of Experimental Psychology, 20,* 273–281.

PHILOSOPHY AND EDUCATION

Chapter 12

Bringing Ritual to Mind

Robert N. McCauley
Emory University

By attending to Dick Neisser's principal methodological admonition in an unexpected domain, religious ritual, and his experimental findings in a more familiar domain, flashbulb memory, our understanding of both domains may improve. To consider how nonliterate societies, in which some religious rituals may be repeated only once in a generation, transmit religious systems may snap into focus how research on flashbulb memory may illuminate these topics. Conversely, to consider the persistence and continuity of some nonliterate, traditional religions for hundreds—perhaps even thousands—of years (at least until they faced such destabilizing forces as missionaries, colonialism, world wars, and industrialization) should begin to clarify why a broadly ecological study of such religious systems might prove suggestive for research on flashbulb memory and on memory in general.

Putting that last claim more sharply (and more tendentiously), the transmission of secret, infrequently performed, nonrepeated religious rituals in nonliterate societies[1] seems to pose as formidable a challenge for long-term memory as social life is ever likely to present. Understanding that process,

---

[1]On the ritual form theory that Lawson and I (McCauley & Lawson, 1998b) propose, literacy is not the most critical consideration determining the variables a religious system enlists to aid in its transmission. Nonrepeated religious rituals in literate cultures manipulate exactly the same variables, although usually less dramatically. (See the final paragraphs of the section on religious transmission and memory).

therefore, may offer insight into some variables that contribute to effective long-term recall. Alternatively and, even more tendentiously, the religious systems of some of the most isolated, technologically undeveloped cultures in the world have for millennia exploited many important variables shown to enhance recall in controlled, scientific research.

In the second section of this chapter I briefly examine some issues surrounding the transmission of religious systems from one generation to the next. I survey some general considerations concerning the role of memory in the transmission of cultural materials and consider the impact of literacy on this process. Finally, I sketch a case for the special interest of the transmission of infrequently performed, secret, nonrepeated religious rituals in small, nonliterate cultures for ascertaining how memory dynamics are enlisted in the transmission of religious systems.

The third section reviews some suggestive findings from the last decade or so from the work of Dick Neisser and others concerning outstanding recall for some extraordinary events that occurred outside psychologists' laboratories and independently of any experimentalists' manipulations.

Be warned. This is neither a comprehensive survey by an expert in the field nor a detailed examination of a narrow research program by a qualified experimentalist, but something more like shamelessly opportunistic looting of some particularly suggestive scientific findings in the service of a speculative theory, which Lawson and I advance in *Rethinking Religion* (1990) and subsequent work.[2]

The final section aims to substantiate—by means of a short illustration—the comments I made in the second paragraph.

RELIGIOUS TRANSMISSION AND MEMORY

Evolutionary thinking about the sociocultural realm has enjoyed a renaissance over the past two decades. Theories of cultural evolution, sociobiology, evolutionary psychology, and cognitive anthropology (in at least some of its incarnations) are (different) manifestations of this trend. Although evolutionary accounts of cultural phenomena at the psychological level suffer from some vaguenesses concerning both the ontological commitments and the mechanisms underlying the processes in question, unlike sociobiology, they have postponed worries about biological determinism and eschewed dismissive conceptions of mental life.

Considering the psychological foundations of cultural forms in an evolutionary framework reorients research on a topic like religious ritual. In

---

[2]See Lawson and McCauley (1993), McCauley (in press), and McCauley and Lawson (1993, 1996, 1998a, 1998b).

this framework, the central questions include how cognitive factors contribute to rituals' transmission and persistence. On this view tradition and cultural change are best understood as the propagation and mutation of "cultural representations" that provoke in people who possess them "public behaviours that cause others to hold them too" (Sperber, 1996, p. 100). Broadly, the argument is that the nature of the human cognitive system differentially encourages the generation or the learning or the recollection of some cultural representations as opposed to others and, therefore, that these cognitive considerations constitute selection pressures on cultural representations and, indirectly, on the cultural forms for which they are responsible.

On the face of it, religious rituals seem paradigmatic cases of such public behaviors. Religious rituals are typically both provocative and public in all of the right ways. Explicitly connected with an entire constellation of cultural representations (which collectively make up what Lawson and I, 1990, called a religious system), religious rituals as cultural forms are not only self-perpetuating—sacrifices to the ancestors, for example, do not merely model subsequent performances of that ritual—but they also invoke a host of cultural assumptions about, among other things, the ancestors themselves. Performing the sacrifice increases the probabilities of replicating each of the associated cultural representations in the religious system. Distinguishing between actions and beliefs is perfectly reasonable, but in cultural evolution these two types of cultural representations often prove intimately intertwined.

Two characteristics of many religious rituals—the frequency of their performance and their stability—enhance the probabilities of their subsequent transmission (all other things being equal). Customarily, these characteristics jointly insure that religious rituals remain memorable—a necessary condition for their persistence as cultural forms.

Religious systems exploit frequency to solidify memory for many religious rituals. Participants must perform some religious rituals repeatedly—sometimes even daily (e.g., see Whitehouse, 1995)—so that such rituals become as familiar as any other daily routine.

Psychologists construe the cognitive foundations of such actions in terms of scripts. Arguably, a ritual is the prototype of a scripted action. A script is a cognitive representation for "a predetermined, stereotyped sequence of actions that defines a well-known situation" (Schank & Abelson, 1977, p. 41). The script shapes recollections of such actions. Although participants may be unable to distinguish particular past performances, the attributes that those performances share in common constitute the framework of the thoroughly familiar routine that the script represents. The scripts, rather than recollections of individual episodes, are the resulting knowledge structures.

When participants perform rituals routinely, their actions become habitual and automatic. Their memory for carrying out these action sequences is largely procedural. In nonliterate cultures in particular, where exegetical traditions may be utterly unknown, participants may have a much richer sense of how to proceed than they have for what they are doing (Barth, 1975; Rubin, 1995). Even if participants are largely incapable of formulating this knowledge about how to proceed propositionally, they still know how to do what must be done. Their knowledge is implicit (Reber, 1993; Roediger, 1990).

The relative stability of many religious rituals results, at least in part, from their frequent performance. Frequently encountered instances of the same form leave less room for variation in memory. Each new performance forestalls distortions. That mechanism does not completely explain ritual stability, however, because in part, it presumes it. At least two other considerations also contribute to the stability of religious rituals.

One of these considerations is the peculiar character of their publicity. Religious rituals regularly require activity that is both collective and coordinated. Such coordination presupposes participants' abilities to anticipate one another's actions. Because the success of religious rituals often depends on the cooperation of numerous participants, this imposes important constraints on their performance.

A second consideration concerns the special sort of cultural representations associated with religious rituals. Reducing variation in action is a mark of ritual (Staal, 1979). Typically, religiously required ritual minimizes variation because that is what the relevant culturally postulated superhuman agents (CPS-agents hereafter) usually demand. Many religious representations and those concerning CPS-agents, in particular, possess practical and epistemic authority that is renowned for being substantial, automatic, and unquestioned. If the gods dictate actions of a specific form, participants usually comply.

To summarize, then, both the frequency and the stability of many religious rituals facilitate their retention, which is a necessary condition for their transmission. To the extent that those rituals serve as cues for and implicate a host of further religious representations, their retention is also a prominent catalyst for the propagation of religious systems generally.

As many scholars have observed (e.g., Goody, 1987), however, literacy renders most of these concerns about memory superfluous because literacy enables a religious community to standardize many (although not all!) aspects of rituals in books, manuals, and sacred texts. This largely eliminates any need either for elevated levels of recall or for any other extraordinary devices for reaching a consensus about such matters in a religious community. Various new technological and institutional forms reliably accompany the development of literacy. Formal education and schooling are among the most important. Such cultural arrangements can greatly affect the knowledge a culture possesses and the cognitive styles it fosters (Scribner & Cole, 1981).

Literacy may also change our standards for what counts as satisfactory recall. Hunter (1985) argued that extended verbatim recall of a text of 50 words or more occurs only in literate cultures.[3] This should not be too surprising because humans are notoriously weak at remembering extended passages word for word without the aid of an independent, authoritative text (or other form of inscription) to guide them.

Rubin (1995) in effect cautioned against imposing unrealistic expectations—grounded on transactions in literate cultures—on memory and transmission in oral traditions. He noted that although the singers of epics in existing oral traditions (embedded in larger literate cultures) may claim the ability to sing familiar epics verbatim, even comparisons of multiple performances by the same singer fail to sustain those assertions.

On many fronts these singers' accomplishments are impressive, however. Through extensive exposure, the singers of epics and ballads have developed a tacit mastery of their respective genres' constraints. Rubin showed how multiple constraints on the forms of such materials render them quite regular on many fronts and jointly impose substantial restrictions on the range of viable variation; that is, on the range of versions that the relevant community will recognize as tokens of the same type. Although the various constraints each genre imposes on its materials restrict their modification, by no means do they rule it out altogether.

Our conceptions of the conditions of transmission and of the resulting operative form of recall should not hinge on the model employed in parlor games and even in the laboratory much of the time. This model

> has been ... to pass a piece from one person to the next with no individual seeing more than one version ... In oral traditions, it would be unusual for this pattern to occur. Many versions of the same piece are heard, often from different people. (Rubin, 1995, p. 133)

The interpersonal connections, according to Rubin, are multifarious like those between the nodes in a net rather than like the isolated, sequential links in a chain. Frequently, participants have multiple experiences with (what are regarded as) the same cultural materials. Nor are they typically restricted to a single performance, if they, in turn, transmit this cultural knowledge to others.

Often, multiple versions of some cultural product circulate, all of which fall within the scope of admissible variation. Communities collectively

---

[3]This claim is not uncontroversial. H. Whitehouse (personal communication, Summer 1997) maintained that evidence exists of more substantial verbatim recall of linguistic materials in nonliterate societies than Hunter (1985) allowed for.

uphold these practices, sanctioning opportunities for instruction, consulta-
tion, rehearsal, and performance as well as for tacitly negotiating the range of
acceptable variants. It is at least as much through the practices of the engaged
community as it is through any prodigious mnemonic accomplishments of
individual cultural experts that these materials are retained and transmitted.

Rubin's study concentrates on oral traditions (e.g., ballad singing in
North Carolina) embedded in literate cultures. Rubin held, correctly I
think, that these oral traditions largely enjoy lives of their own, comparatively insulated from the impact of literacy on both the practitioners and
the larger culture.[4] This insulation bears on production. For example,
Rubin (1995) reported that when asked to compose a new ballad about a
train wreck, three of eight North Carolina ballad singers commenced singing their compositions immediately after reading the newspaper account
of the incident. This insulation also bears on the assessment of performances. Although, when tested from 6 to 12 months later, these singers
showed recognition memory well above chance for their own stanzas, not
one could recall even a single stanza from the ballad he had composed.
The point is that such limitations in no way impugn these subjects' status
as expert ballad singers. Thus, cultural systems undergirding such practices
enlist social and cognitive dynamics that operate to some extent independently of the influences of literacy (see footnote 1).

A useful strategy both for glimpsing these forces in isolation and for
learning what other cognitive devices assist in the propagation of religious
systems is to study the transmission of such materials in the absence of
literacy and any other cognitive prostheses involving symbolic codes. This
is to study the transmission of religious systems in settings that more closely
approximate the emergence of such systems in prehistory.[5] How do small

---

[4]This and many other important points of agreement notwithstanding, Rubin's analyses
are of limited usefulness for my purposes here. First, his study focuses on subjects' memories
for linguistic materials. I am concerned with their memories for (ritual) actions. These two
types of cultural materials are often intimately connected, but sometimes they are not. What
interests me most are precisely the nonlinguistic considerations that contribute to enhanced
memory for actions. Second, Rubin (1995) held (again, correctly, I think) that memory in
oral traditions is usefully thought of as a "well practiced skill dependent on extensive
experience" (p. 146). Rubin held, for example, that ballads and counting-out rhymes are
considerably overlearned. As will become clear in the final section of this chapter, extensive
and elaborate rituals are performed only once per generation in some nonliterate cultures
with only limited preparation and rehearsal. In the case of the Baktaman (Barth, 1975),
neither extensive experience nor overlearning are even possible for the initiations.

[5]Rubin is less helpful here. His comments about the connections between literacy and
religion reflect the prevailing biases of most contemporary scholarship on that topic,
inadvertently favoring the few (text-based) world religions over the thousands of religious
systems that have existed in completely nonliterate settings in human history. Rubin (1995)
suggested that it is quite difficult to imagine "religion without writing" (p. 320), yet religion
as a cultural form predates the invention of writing and to this day some religious systems
prevail exclusively in nonliterate cultures. (See Lawson & McCauley, 1993.)

communities of nonliterate hunter–gatherers or practitioners of primitive forms of agriculture without sophisticated technology or permanent settlements remember and transmit religious rituals that are lengthy and elaborate? That question's import is especially striking once we contemplate two further factors.

The first is that in such conditions, life is notoriously nasty, brutish, and short. The first two adjectives may no longer be politically correct, but the third is uncontroversial. The evidence about peoples at the dawn of human history as well as about traditional societies now indicates that average life spans are very short. Barth (1975), for example, noted that the Baktaman of New Guinea (whose ritual practices undergo scrutiny in the final section of this paper) are "essentially limited to two living generations" (p. 25). (In 1968 only 6 of 82 persons below puberty had a living grandparent and 39 had lost one or both parents.) Such societies do not have the benefit of a large cohort of elderly cultural experts. Barth reported that neighbors of the Baktaman, the Augobmin, lost all of the members of their most senior generation in a very short time and, consequently, lost the final three stages of male initiation in their religious system.

Frequency effects cannot explain participants' memories of all religious rituals because some occur quite rarely either in the life of the community or, at least, in the lives of individual participants. The classic rites of passage are the most obvious examples of these sorts of rituals (although they are not the only ones). Most religious systems—at least ideally—initiate, marry, and bury individual participants only once, hence these rites of passage are examples of what Lawson and I (1990) called nonrepeated rituals. (These rituals contrast with repeated rituals such as sacrifices.) Still, in many religious systems, including most in the United States, participants can observe such nonrepeated rituals even when they are not directly involved in them themselves. So frequency influences memory for these rituals, too, when they are publicly accessible. In some religious systems, however, three further circumstances—either separately or in combination—pose additional barriers to proposals that look to frequency primarily for explaining participants' memories for these rituals.

First, in many religious systems these rituals are not publicly accessible. In these systems, most participants only experience these rituals once, vis-à-vis on the one occasion when they go through them themselves. Second, often not only is each participant's experience private, but demands for secrecy discourage after-the-fact disclosures. Many religious systems surround all or parts of these nonrepeated rituals in secrecy, their frequent performance notwithstanding. Third, in some religious systems all of the members of an age cohort undergo a rite of passage at the same time. Depending on the range of ages included, this can make for extremely infrequent performance of these rituals. Barth (1975) estimated that approximately 10 years on average separates successive performances of any of the various degrees of male initiation among the Baktaman. For different reasons, even some repeated rituals are performed quite infrequently. In areas in southwestern India, several years often separate performances of the Vedic Agnicayana ritual (Somayajipad, Nambudiri, & Nambudiri, 1983).

The comparative frequency with which repeated as opposed to nonrepeated rituals are performed raises interesting theoretical issues. The general theory Lawson and I (1990) have defended, which concentrates on participants' cognitive representations of their religious rituals, explains a variety of those rituals' features. Although students of religion have long recognized many of these features, the theory accounts for them in a unified and principled fashion. The theory yields an ordered set of ritual types, categorizing rituals by how and where representations of CPS-agents figure in their formal descriptions. The typology sorts out all of those long-recognized features of religious rituals, including whether rituals are repeated or not. All of the rituals that fall into the odd-numbered types— those types where CPS-agents first appear in structural descriptions of rituals functioning as agents—are nonrepeated rituals. The significant theoretical point (developed at length in McCauley & Lawson, 1998) is that, contrary to appearances, ritual form and not frequency of performance is the decisive variable determining which memory dynamics predominate with any particular ritual (contrary, for example, to the position White-house, 1992, endorsed). Here, however, I must set these theoretical matters aside. The aim in this chapter is simply to explore some mnemonic devices—other than the ones based on frequency or literacy (especially)— employed in the transmission of religious ritual.

FLASHBULB MEMORY AND ENHANCED RECALL FOR ACTIONS

In the previous section I provided reasons why focusing on frequency effects at the level of individual psychology or on the effects of literacy at the level of culture may not suffice to explain the transmission of all religious rituals and, thus, the transmission of religious systems generally. If psychological research on memory is to aid in accounting for the transmission of those nonrepeated religious rituals performed either highly infrequently or secretly or both—in the preliterate past or in contemporary nonliterate cultures, then we must explore different quarters of that literature. The critical criteria for relevant studies will be (a) minimal reliance on frequency effects, (b) no reliance on literacy, and (c) evidence of comparatively impressive long-term recall for actions, especially, but for persons and places as well. (In most theories of ritual, and especially in mine and Lawson's, actions, settings, and persons are pivotal analytical concepts.)

What follows is a highly selective discussion of some promising findings in the recent experimental literature on memory for actions. The discussion explores some recent investigations of flashbulb memory, ending with a summary and short discussion of the extraordinary findings reported in Neisser et al. (1996). What is of interest about these studies are the variables that seem to make for virtually ceiling-level effects—concerning accuracy and confidence in particular—for subjects' recall for actions, settings, and persons.

Typically, flashbulb memories concern our recall for features of the circumstances in which we learned of some startling event rather than our recall of the startling event itself, which we may not have experienced even indirectly (by way of some electronic medium; Colegrove, 1899/1982). These experiences are what Larsen (1988) called reception events. Brown and Kulik (1982), who first proposed the flashbulb metaphor, characterized these memories as ones in which

> almost everyone testifies that his recall of his circumstances is not an inference from a regular routine. It has a primary, "live" quality that is almost perceptual. Indeed, it is very like a photograph that indiscriminately preserves the scene in which each of us found himself . . . (p. 74)

Because flashbulb memories usually concern recollections connected with events that are isolated, unexpected, and arousing, they seem to arise independently of "such well-established determinants of memory as primacy or recency or repetition" (Brown & Kulik, 1982, p. 25). Brown and Kulik speculated that a special neural mechanism may automatically register all available information connected with the context when learning suddenly of a significant novelty that is emotionally arousing.

Brown and Kulik noted that their metaphor variously suggests brevity, surprise, and indiscriminate illumination (of the circumstances at learning). The first two suggestions seem to make sense. All things being equal, brief episodes seem easier to remember than longer ones. Prolonged episodes not only introduce more material; they almost inevitably introduce more complex material as well. Similarly, surprise seems no surprise. In his study of Swedes' memories for how they heard about the assassination of Olof Palme, Christianson (1989) found that his subjects' initial assessments of how surprising they found the news proved a significant variable in predicting their overall recall a year later. On the other hand, however, surprise does not appear to be a necessary condition for flashbulb memories. Winograd and Killinger (1983) found that many subjects had flashbulb memories for reception events concerning such events as the resignation of Richard Nixon or the death of a close relative after a prolonged illness, which were not very surprising—at least by the time they occurred.

As to the third of these suggestions, even Brown and Kulik (1982) emphasized that the illumination is not altogether indiscriminate. Some details surrounding such reception events seem to stand out, whereas others seem less memorable. The former includes such details as our actions (and what was going on generally) just before learning the news, the place where we learned it, and at least some of the persons present. (These seem important items when thinking about memory for rituals.) The less memorable details include that indefinitely large class of apparently peripheral matters such as which shoes we were wearing or what was hanging on the walls or the color of the car in front of us.

In Christianson's (1989) study of memories for learning of the Palme assassination, subjects recalled central details reasonably well after 1 year. Their recall proved much less, however, for a wide range of peripheral information. Christianson held that what his subjects have remembered are the standard components or gist of a narrative account of the reception event. Following Neisser's (1982) earlier proposal that narrative structure "does more than explain the canonical form of flashbulb memories; it accounts for their very existence" (p. 47), Christianson also suggested that the rehearsal and conventions associated with the formulation of stable narratives rather than any special neural mechanisms are primarily responsible for the form of flashbulb memories, for the consistency of subjects' reports over time, and, therefore, for a good deal of their (apparent) accuracy as well.

Christianson's study does not provide overwhelmingly compelling evidence about accuracy, however, because he did not collect his initial data until 6 weeks after Palme was killed. It seems reasonable to suppose that those 6 weeks provided ample time for subjects to have told their stories repeatedly and, in the process, to have consolidated their narratives according to the conventions to which Christianson (1989), Neisser (1982), and others have pointed. (Rubin, 1992, suggested that what I am calling narrative consolidation may occur in as little time as a week.) The accuracy of Christianson's subjects about the gists of their narratives 1 year later may have resulted from nothing more than their simply telling an already familiar story with an utterly conventional form another time rather than accurately recalling their reception event for the Palme assassination. The fact that most of Christianson's subjects told the same general stories approximately 58 weeks after this event as they told 6 weeks after it is interesting, but it does not show that those initial 6-week-old stories were, in fact, accurate accounts of how they learned that Olof Palme had been assassinated.

Comparatively speaking, however, Christianson's study is exemplary on this front. The salient problem with most treatments of flashbulb memory (including Brown & Kulik's, 1982, study) until the last few years has been the failure of researchers to determine the accuracy of their subjects' responses. In light of both their detail and the profound vividness and confidence regularly associated with flashbulb memories, this concern might seem needlessly scrupulous. But various studies of eyewitness memory have indicated that neither subjects' confidence about nor the precision of their recollections reliably predicts their accuracy (Wells & Murray, 1984). The critical questions are, first, whether flashbulb memories are accurate and, second, whether similar dissociations between confidence and accuracy can arise even for flashbulb memories.

More than 15 years ago, Neisser (1982) supplied two anecdotes that suggested that flashbulb memories are not always accurate (although it has turned out that one of those examples, specifically, Neisser's own memory of how he learned about the attack on Pearl Harbor, may not have been as inaccurate as he then thought—see Neisser, 1986). It was the explosion of the space shuttle Challenger that gave Neisser an opportunity to ascertain experimentally whether those two anecdotes were rare exceptions or genuine indicators that our confidence in such memories may often be unfounded.

Within 24 hours of the Challenger accident, Neisser and Harsch (1992) obtained reports from subjects about the circumstances under which they learned of the explosion. They then tested subjects' recall 2½ years later and then again about 6 months after that. (On neither occasion did subjects know in advance that they would be asked to recall this material.) Their findings were intriguing. Most important, many of Neisser and Harsch's confident subjects, who otherwise gave every evidence of possessing an accurate flashbulb memory in this situation, were completely wrong in their recollections about all of the tested items from their initial report. This group included 3 of their 13 maximally confident subjects, who—with respect to the relative accuracy of their responses—said that they were absolutely certain.

The visual vividness of subjects' recollections predicted their accuracy no more reliably than their levels of confidence did. Although some subjects reported highly vivid mental imagery associated with their memories, they too were, sometimes, completely wrong. Neisser and Harsch were so startled by these findings that they decided to interview their subjects, approximately 6 months later (roughly 3 years after the explosion of the Challenger). They wanted to see if, among other things, their first test or the intervening 6 months affected subjects' recollections and to discover what cues, if any, might suffice to aid subjects' recall.

Those second interviews supplied the second of two findings, which, according to Neisser and Harsch (1992), impugn "the simplest form of the emotional strengthening hypothesis" (p. 30). The first finding (from their tests at 2½ years) was the absence of any significant connections between emotion and recall. Although the initial questionnaire did not ask for precise measures of subjects' emotional states, it had elicited detailed statements about subjects' emotions. No coding scheme that Neisser and Harsch devised for subjects' responses yielded any grounds for regarding emotion as a predictor of subjects' accuracy. It is worth noting that Neisser and Harsch explicitly excluded expressions of surprise from these measures of emotion. Although what is surprising often produces strong emotions, it does not always do so. Second and even more telling, in the interviews the original memories (as recorded in their questionnaires) of the subjects who were mistaken "seemed to have disappeared entirely" (1992, p. 30). Neisser and Harsch could find no cues that could elicit the correct memories in their subjects. They even let subjects peruse their original questionnaires! Apparently, a couple of these subjects were so confident about the accuracy of their current recollections that, in order to discredit their responses to the initial questionnaire, they argued that people sometimes misreport events at first!

Besides raising problems for theories of flashbulb memory that look to emotional arousal as a decisive variable, Neisser and Harsch's findings also offer some support for Neisser's earlier conjectures about the central role of narrative. Although many of their subjects seemed utterly incapable of accurately recalling their original accounts of the events in question, the stories subjects told at 2½ years did prove strikingly consistent with the stories they gave in their interviews 6 months later.

Neisser and Harsch's study provides abundant evidence for the fallibility of flashbulb memories.[6] Many of their subjects totally missed the mark yet claimed to be highly confident about the accuracy of vivid memories concerning their reception of what they took to be emotionally stimulating news. Understandably impressed by these findings, Neisser and Harsch concluded that "[f]lashbulb memories . . . may be appreciably less reliable than other cases of vivid and confident recall" (p. 30).

This conclusion is undoubtedly true about some of their subjects' flashbulb memories but not about all of them. Some of Neisser and Harsch's subjects, who were also absolutely certain about the accuracy of their rec-

---

[6]Brewer (1992) argued, however, that the inaccuracies of Neisser and Harsch's subjects may not be as grievous as their analysis suggests. He maintained that they were probably problems of retrieval, not problems of reconstruction. He suspects that many were accurately remembering events from the day when they heard about the Challenger. They were just not remembering the events they described in their initial questionnaires. They were recalling the wrong time slice.

What Neisser and Harsch (1992) called "TV priority" (p. 25) may be evidence for this conjecture. The difference between the large number of subjects who misremembered that they had first heard about the Challenger on television versus the small number who misremembered that they had not was significant.

ollections, had every right to be so confident because they accurately re-called all of the items on which they were tested. Their flashbulb memories were completely accurate.

The explosion of the Challenger might simply not have been the sort of event that all of Neisser and Harsch's subjects found either sufficiently significant or sufficiently surprising. The question remained whether some events can produce accurate flashbulb memories across an entire popula-tion in the way that John Kennedy's assassination is popularly thought to have done. Neisser and his colleagues found evidence that the 1989 Loma Prieta earthquake did for those who experienced it.

Neisser and colleagues (1996) in both Georgia and California studied subjects' memories concerning the Loma Prieta earthquake in 1989. This was a standard study of memory for *reception events* for the subjects in Georgia; however, for the Californians, the study, in part, concerned mem-ory for an event that subjects had *experienced* first-hand as well. Subjects in this experiment filled out questionnaires from as little as twenty-four hours to as much as three weeks after the quake (see note seven below).

The experimenters tested subjects approximately eighteen months later, focussing in particular on three items for which they had data that apply to both direct experiences and reception events, viz., place, others present, and activity just before the target event. The experimenters compared Californians' memories of their experiences during the earthquake both with their memories for how they learned about the collapse of the Oakland Bay Bridge and with Georgians' memories of how they learned about the earthquake. The Georgians' memories proved least accurate. The Califor-nians' memories for their experiences were most accurate, and the Cali-fornians' memories for how they heard about the Bay Bridge were in between. All of the differences were significant.

Those comparisons are interesting, but probably the most important finding in this study concerns the character of the Californians' memories for their first-hand experiences of the earthquake. The accuracy of their responses for the three target items as well as their confidence in that accuracy were at the highest possible levels. None of the Californians made the substantial errors that some subjects made about their reception events in the Challenger study or that some of the Georgians made in this study. Moreover, all of the Californians were quite confident that they had not made such errors. The study seems to demonstrate that some events can produce both startlingly accurate memories for actions, settings, and per-sons and thoroughly confident assessments of their accuracy by those doing the remembering.

Neisser et al. (1996) emphasized one obvious difference between the Californians' ceiling-level-accurate memories in this study and those of subjects in nearly all other experiments on flashbulb memory. The Californians were recalling not a reception event but an event that they themselves had experienced. Not only were these memories more accurate than the Georgians' memories of their reception events, but they were even more accurate than the Californians' (overwhelmingly accurate) memories of their own reception events concerning the news of the Bay Bridge. "Being personally involved in an event is evidently more memorable than just hearing the news of one" (Neisser et al., 1996, p. 346). Directly experiencing an isolated and unexpected event of significance seems to confer substantial mnemonic advantages over just receiving news of one. All else being equal, participants in such events are significantly more likely to remember accurately and to be confident about that accuracy than mere observers are. Still, as Neisser et al. (1996) noted, "most life events and experiences involve 'participation' ... what was so special about participating in the earthquake?" (p. 338).

Their comparative destructiveness, which most people only learn about after the fact, is usually what makes earthquakes momentous. Presumably, it is participation in momentous events, not earthquakes per se, that is special. Neisser et al. (1996) opted for the processes underlying narrative consolidation as the critical variables influencing subjects' enhanced memory here, although they remain uncommitted about which feature of this process is most important. They point out that it could be the simple process of shaping our own distinctive story about how we were involved. On the other hand, it could be the result of rehearsal because these are precisely the sorts of stories we tend to tell repeatedly. (Even Brown & Kulik, 1982, found a high positive correlation between subjects' ratings of an event's consequentiality and their reports of rehearsals—see Brewer, 1992.) Or it could be both.

The one thing that Neisser and his colleagues stressed is that emotional arousal does not seem to play any special role. They provided at least two reasons. First, most of their California subjects did not report great arousal at the moment they felt the quake. Earthquakes are common in California and most of the subjects did not perceive any imminent danger to themselves. Second, the California subjects' various reports of their emotional arousal (during and immediately after the quake and on learning about the Bay Bridge) did not correlate with the accuracy of their memories.

That the processes undergirding the consolidation of narratives rather than emotional arousal are the principal variables funding the California subjects' extraordinary performance makes sense.[7] As Neisser et al. (1996)

---

[7]Approximately one third of the California subjects were from Santa Cruz. Logistical difficulties prevented data collection with these subjects until the third week after the disaster. By Rubin's (1992) estimate, this would be enough time for them to have consolidated their stories. Of course, conformity to narrative conventions may have subtly distorting effects on those stories' accuracy.

emphasized, most of their subjects did not find the experience of the earthquake itself greatly arousing. Experiencing a nonarousing event would not seem to contribute to extraordinary recall. Moreover, the news of the earthquake's more serious effects accumulated bit-by-bit over a few hours (at least). Again, by the subjects' own reports, no single consequence (not even learning the news about the Bay Bridge) produced startling arousal levels. (The means of the two California groups' ratings of their level of affect on learning of the Bay Bridge collapse was 5.28 and 5.29 on a 7-point scale.) Presumably, it would be learning of the event's momentous consequences (concerning the Nimitz freeway, the Bay Bridge, the damage throughout the region, etc.) that would provide the incentive for subjects to remember where they were at the time and to share that information with others. Gradually coming to realize—probably over many hours for most subjects—that they were participating in a (literally) earth-shattering event surely does produce a benchmark in subjects' life stories—as Neisser (1982) maintained—even if it does not produce any specific moments of exceptional emotional arousal.

A hypothesis that looks to the processes behind narrative consolidation does make better sense of the earthquake findings than does any hypothesis that features emotional arousal. In light of other studies, however, it is not clear that a narrative consolidation hypothesis alone will suffice to explain all examples of accurate flashbulb memories. After all, in Christianson (1989), recall 1 year later for what were, presumably, well-consolidated, 6-week-old narratives did not yield the sorts of ceiling-level effects for accuracy that the Loma Prieta earthquake produced (whether the original 6-week-old narratives were accurate or not; see Neisser et al., 1996). Still, if the critical variable underlying narrative consolidation is rehearsal, perhaps destructive earthquakes in California simply provoke significantly more retellings (or rethinkings), at least among the public, than assassinations in Sweden (or even explosions of manned spacecraft) do. This, of course, is a matter about which these various studies provide little useful evidence (see Neisser et al., 1996).

Neisser and his colleagues (1996) were clear that their findings did not defeat an emotional arousal theory of flashbulb memory. On the assumption that they have interpreted those findings correctly, however, they certainly raise problems for theorists who hold that extraordinary emotional arousal is either a necessary condition or, *a fortiori*, a necessary and sufficient condition either for accurate flashbulb memories or for flashbulb experiences generally. The possibility remains, of course, that substantial levels of emotional arousal may still be a sufficient condition (or at least one of some number of jointly sufficient conditions) for flashbulb experiences—at least when those experiences are connected with personally or socially significant events.

In the next section, I briefly sketch how various prominent variables considered in these psychological studies play out in the transmission of one nonliterate culture's secret, infrequently performed, nonrepeated religious rituals. While discussing the Baktaman system of male initiation, I will make a case for the following three claims:

1. that all of the psychological variables pertaining to flashbulb memory that researchers have noted are manipulated regularly (save, perhaps, one) in the Baktaman system;
2. that emotional arousal has an important role to play in memory for these rituals, whether it contributes to the recollection of the rituals' details or not; and
3. that the rehearsal associated with narrative consolidation does not appear sufficient to explain memory for these rituals.

MEMORY FOR RITUAL AMONG THE BAKTAMAN

The seven stages of male initiation among the Baktaman of New Guinea are useful for examining how memory mechanisms are enlisted in the transmission of religious rituals. The Baktaman numbered 183 (with six deaths and three births) at the time of Barth's fieldwork in 1968. All of the evidence indicates that prior to 1968 the Baktaman had only two fleeting contacts (in 1927 and 1964) with anyone outside related groups occupying the lands within 30 miles or so of their own territory. Barth described the Baktaman as "persons entirely unacquainted with Man in any other form than themselves" (1975, p. 6).

Prior to colonial pacification in 1964, the Baktaman's relations with their neighbors were rocky. Although these groups are close enough to intermarry, to recognize clan relations across groups, and to invite one another to observe religious rituals, suspicions of sorcery and comparable offenses were sufficient to instigate frequent wars. Barth's research indicates that one third of Baktaman deaths over the previous couple of decades had resulted from war.

The system of male initiation among the Baktaman fulfills all of the conditions outlined previously in this chapter. In addition, this system introduces a few additional barriers to ready transmission that I have not discussed. The Baktaman are a small, nonliterate, isolated group of hunters and subsistence farmers in central New Guinea. They move within their region every few years as nearby land for gardens is exhausted. Males go through seven degrees of (nonrepeated) initiation in their lives. (A cohort of men—most of whom were in their thirties—had yet to undergo the seventh degree initiation in 1968.) Because entire age cohorts undergo these rituals together, they occur quite infrequently—roughly once every 10 years (although occasional opportunities arise to observe comparable initiations among neighboring groups). The rituals are long, ranging from a few days to a few weeks. Posing another barrier to easy recollection, earlier initiation rituals are also deceptive. Later rituals often reveal how earlier rituals were misleading on one point or another. On at least one count, the deception is double layered (across three initiations).

All of the rituals include parts kept secret from noninitiates; that is, from females and junior males.[8] Baktaman expectations about secrecy are extraordinary. Senior males threaten initiates with death, if they violate ritual secrecy. Not only are initiates prohibited from discussing these secrets with noninitiates; most of the time they are also prohibited from discussing them among themselves. Incredibly, they even seem to exhibit "a wariness and vagueness in *thinking* about them" (Barth, 1975, p. 221). As far as Barth could tell, initiates respected the prohibitions on overt behaviors, at least. (One cult leader was so concerned with secrecy that he hid his clan's sacred relics in the forest, and when he died unexpectedly, these articles were lost.)

Barth maintained that Baktaman secrecy is inimical to ready transmission of the religious system's symbols in another way. The impact of these demands for secrecy is so substantial that it undermines any hope of forging widespread logical coherence among Baktaman beliefs. Barth argued at length that analogic coding grounds whatever order inheres in the cultural knowledge of the Baktaman (1975).

Mostly, he characterized analogic coding negatively. It is not like a digital code. Although the Baktaman analogic code exhibits some compositional relations, its productivity is not based on any systematicity[9] in the code nor on any "logical closure" nor on some "limited set of alternatives" (Barth, 1975, p. 208). Instead, each symbol turns on "a very simple non-verbal metaphor sketchily exploited" yielding "complex harmonies." (This and all further citations in this paragraph are from 1975, p. 229.) Apparently, the underlying "metaphors" are "non-verbal" because the symbols are (non-linguistic) concrete objects and because the Baktaman either are generally

---

[8] . . . however, not with someone, Barth, who was so clearly an outsider. The principal cult leader bent rules to make Barth "a participant in his religion" (1975, p. 5). Sharing knowledge with Barth was, apparently, regarded as relatively harmless after Barth had gained the seniors' trust and made it clear that he would only reveal their knowledge to "others who had passed through all *our* initiations" in Barth's "distant homeland" (1975, p. 7). Finally, the only world the secrets of Baktaman initiations need stratify is their own (and, perhaps, those of the only neighbors they knew of). The crucial point was to keep these secrets from uninitiated Baktaman.

[9] For a discussion of the role of compositionality, productivity, and systematicity in symbolic systems, see Fodor and Pylyshyn, 1988.

unwilling to articulate these symbolic relations or are incapable of doing so or both.[10] Barth insisted that "an analogic code must . . . be understood in the context of its praxis," noting that secrecy and the complete absence of both exegesis and texts are the pivotal aspects of Baktaman praxis that give this code its form and that shape the processes of transmission. He underscored that the Baktaman not only have no writing; they are not even aware of its possibility. The tools the Baktaman have invented for retaining knowledge are meager.

> The total corpus of Baktaman knowledge is stored in 183 Baktaman minds, aided only by a modest assemblage of cryptic concrete symbols (the meanings of which depend on the associations built up around them in the consciousness of a few seniors) and by limited, suspicious communication with the members of a few surrounding communities. . . . such a corpus will only persist to the extent that its parts are frequently re-created as messages and thereby transmitted. (1975, p. 255)

The inevitable vagueness surrounding the use of symbols in such an analogic code requires that an analysis of transmission highlight neither the sayable nor the said but only what is received, reactivated, and "frequently re-created" (1975, p. 255); that is, those themes that "catch on and are re-used" (1975, p. 229).

Barth explicated these themes in terms of general resonances among the concrete symbols that figure in Baktaman myth and ritual from one symbolic context to the next. He identified broad themes (relations with the ancestors, fertility, security and welfare, etc.) with which various concrete symbols are associated in particular Baktaman rites. Barth headlined these thematic connections underlying the analogic code as the knowledge Baktaman initiations present. It is "the repetition of the knowledge they [i.e., the initiations] contain in numerous other temple performances" that is pivotal for their perpetuation (1975, p. 258). To explain the retention and transmission of Baktaman ritual knowledge, then, Barth looked primarily to the frequency with which initiates engage, in the repeated rituals of the Baktaman, the themes underlying the analogic code at the heart of the (nonrepeated) initiations. Barth seems to hold that the clusterings around these prominent themes—by way of associations among concrete objects in various symbolic contexts—impose enough constraints to explain as much transmission of Baktaman ritual knowledge as occurs. Thus, he listed the characteristic features of Baktaman ritual knowledge

---

[10]Barth did not consider the possibility that such symbolic relations simply do not exist (see Sperber, 1975).

as "constantly communicated about [in the repeated rituals of the Bak-taman] yet poorly shared and precariously transmitted . . ." (1975, p. 222).

Note that Barth did not look to the frequency with which initiates confront the concrete symbols themselves because their connections to these themes are relatively loose (hence, the coding is analogical) and many of those symbols are multivalent from one context to the next. Thus, although Whitehouse's (1992) gloss on Barth's notion of analogic coding in terms of the mental imagery associated with the concrete symbols makes perfect sense cognitively, it is not obvious that this is what Barth intended.

Whitehouse stressed that the Baktaman manipulate concrete, nonlin-guistic symbols in their rites rather than memorize linguistic formulae. (The very rare formulaic utterances that occur in Baktaman initiations are extremely simple statements that never involve more than a few words and are usually sung.) Baktaman rituals, however, do stimulate all of an initiate's senses (more on this later this chapter). Barth remarked often on the wide range of sensory cues associated with Baktaman rituals and symbols, which provide the materials for subsequent mental imagery. Experimental re-search has revealed the ability of mental images to organize memories, to distinguish specific episodes, and to serve as cues—especially for spatially and dynamically related materials (Paivio, 1986; Rubin, 1995).

In the absence of a fuller cognitive (or, for that matter, cultural) story about how familiarity with the broad themes underlying analogical coding in Baktaman initiations will suffice to explain the retention and transmis-sion of such an extensive, secret, and elaborate set of rituals, it does not seem inappropriate to suggest that other cognitive dynamics may be in-volved. Frequently confronting these analogically represented themes need not signal the marginality of other variables influencing memory. Consid-ering the character of these rituals, I think it reasonable to propose that the psychological research on flashbulb memory points to additional vari-ables that may influence the retrieval, reconstruction, and transmission of Baktaman rituals. The question is how these other factors affecting memory help in the retention of what is received so that it can be constantly recreated. Presumably, such variables would be responsible, in part, for a symbolic idiom's catchiness.[11]

All religious systems enlist various cultural mechanisms—the most popular of which is literacy—to aid in their transmission. We have good

---

[11]Barth provided two sorts of indirect evidence that pertain to the stability of these rites. He cited the coincidences among various informants' reports, which were collected independently of one another, and opportunities to observe corresponding rites among neighboring groups. By reviewing the place of these other mnemonically significant variables in Baktaman rituals and by examining the place of accuracy in forging a sense of community and continuity, I aim, in effect, to supply two additional forms of indirect evidence.

reason to expect that—in cultural settings like that of the Baktaman, where many of these cultural mechanisms, and literacy in particular, have yet to be invented—persisting religious systems will evolve so as to (a) exploit naturally available mnemonic aids disproportionately (compared, for example, to religions in literate cultures) and (b) develop alternative cultural mechanisms that capitalize on just the variables experimental research is finding are relevant to enhanced memory. What follows is a quick inventory of how the system of Baktaman initiations fulfills those expectations.

Although these rituals are of interest precisely because the Baktaman are nonliterate and they perform their rituals so infrequently, considerations of frequency still arise on two additional fronts. First, as noted, the Baktaman occasionally have the opportunity to observe the rituals of neighboring groups, which are similar to Baktaman rites. However, because the number of neighboring groups is small, because unhappy relations sometimes preclude invitations, because the invitations involve only parts of the performances, because these other groups perform these rites no more frequently than the Baktaman do, and because other groups' rites differ from those of the Baktaman on various fronts, these opportunities are less important aids to memory than they might initially appear. In addition, Barth reported that at least once in memory, the resulting visit from such an invitation provided the hosts with an opportunity to ambush and slaughter their guests! With such possibilities in mind, observers might be somewhat distracted.

What might be called the partial compositionality of Baktaman initiations constitutes a second sort of frequency effect. Familiar repeated rituals, such as sacrifices, occur as parts of these nonrepeated initiations (not unlike the role of the repeated communion ritual in the nonrepeated First Communion or confirmation rituals in Christianity). In both the fourth- and fifth-degree initiations, frequently performed, repeated rituals that are well known to the seniors serve as central components. They surely anchor memories for each initiation as a whole.

The structures of the other five initiations, however, depend less on such familiar rites. Moreover, even when familiar repeated rituals surface in these other initiations, they often amount to but a few among scores of separate actions that collectively constitute the initiation. So, because it seems unlikely that either opportunities to observe others' rituals or the partial compositionality of Baktaman initiations will prove to be toweringly effective aids to memory, it should come as no surprise that other variables also play a role.

Neisser and his colleagues (1996) suspected that experiencing the Loma Prieta earthquake firsthand and, thereby, having a sense of having participated in an important event for the entire community were critical variables in their subjects' astonishing performance. Their California subjects were not remembering when they heard the news; they were remembering when they experienced the news (even when they didn't!—see Neisser et al., 1996). Baktaman initiations almost certainly instill in initiates as much a sense of having participated in a significant event in the history of their community as experiencing an earthquake that eventually proves to be moderately destructive does in our own.

Defending the first side of this claim is less complicated than defending the second. Individual involvement is inherent in initiations. Typically, initiates do not sit idly by observing what goes on. At least in Baktaman initiations, the initiates are constantly forced to do one thing or another and they have plenty of things done to them. Here too initiates do not remember when they heard about an important event. Instead, they remember participating in it.

Two further Baktaman practices promote among initiates a sense of participation in these events. By initiating entire age cohorts at once, the Baktaman insure that although participation is individual, it is not isolated. Throughout their lives, initiates interact daily with age-mates with whom they have participated in their most culturally significant moments and who share their most culturally significant secrets. Baktaman practice also requires that the most recently initiated cohort help the cult leader conduct the next performance of the initiation (for the next age cohort). This clarifies an expectation that initiates strive to remember what they have learned and what they have undergone. It also insures that the knowledge remains distributed throughout the various cohorts of initiates. Like the practice of using altar boys, the Baktaman opt for the most recently acquainted individuals (though, recall that the gap between two performances averages 10 years) instead of the most experienced to serve as ritual assistants.

Turning to the second side of my claim, the Baktaman ritual system employs many means for impressing initiates with the social and cultural significance of these initiations. Besides both secrecy and its enforcement, the duration and scope of the initiations also mark their importance. For example, according to three independent informants, seventh-degree initiation takes a couple of weeks, including a period of 8 days when the entire population abandons the village. Barth (1975) noted that such measures suggest to the initiates that their whole community's fate is directly connected with their own ritual accomplishments. Undoubtedly, the most important means for impressing participants with the importance of their initiations, however, is through emotional arousal.

Whether emotional arousal contributes to enhanced recall for the details of an event is not my concern here.[12] The critical point is that it can serve to flag an event as one worth remembering. Doing so need not initiate some special now-print mechanism or contribute in any further way to the recollection of particulars. I am not endorsing Brown and Kulik's (1982) proposal but sketching an alternative; that sudden, substantial emotional arousal is a kind of general alarm for the cognitive system. It is an especially efficient means for signaling events and materials meriting our attention. Emotional arousal may have nothing to do with filling in the details in memory but only with occasioning a heightened sense of an event's significance. The assumption is that will increase the attention and cognitive resources we devote to it, which, in turn, will increase the probability of its subsequent recollection.

Neither possessing nor rehearsing flashbulb memories for reception events makes any sense if subjects have not also remembered that those events are connected with some initially provocative event deemed personally or socially significant.[13] The detail, vividness, confidence, and, perhaps, even accuracy associated with flashbulb memories may completely depend on perfectly ordinary processes. Emotional arousal may do nothing more than alert us that the events in question are ones worth remembering (even if they are not!).

Humans often react emotionally when they perceive present events to be important for their lives. Taking advantage of that association, Baktaman initiations manipulate initiates so that they feel considerable emotion during these rituals. This stimulation of initiates' emotions shapes their perceptions of the relative importance of these rites, marking them as culturally significant events that merit their complete attention currently and their faithful recollection in the future. Barth (1975) stated, for example, that "major discomforts characteristically follow immediately after the revelation of major secrets, and are consistent with their forbidden and esoteric character" (p. 54).

The Baktaman use two standard techniques for stimulating initiates' emotions. The first is surprise. Baktaman initiations begin unexpectedly. Many commence with senior men awakening initiates in the middle of the night and driving them into the forest. Once the initiations begin, seniors subject the initiates to a wide array of sensory stimulation. This is the second technique for arousing initiates' emotions—to subject them to all sorts of positive and negative sensory excitement. Some initiations end

---

[12]At least one Baktaman senior seemed to think not (Barth, 1975): "You know how it is during your initiation: your *finik* (spirit, consciousness) does not hear, you are afraid, you do not understand. Who can remember the acts and the words?" (p. 101).

[13]Presumably, they will also remember why it was significant as well. See Brewer (1992).

with communal meals and celebrations, but usually before initiates reach those stages of these rituals, they will have often undergone extreme deprivation and excruciating torture.[14] Substantial hardships and torture (and associated deceptions and surprises) invariably accompany the communication of each piece of previously forbidden knowledge.

The measures for stimulating initiates' emotions that the Baktaman have built into their rituals may enhance memory in another way. Rubin (1995) emphasized that a genre's formal constraints can substantially reduce the range of possibilities at any particular point in a text. Analogously, the temporal coincidence of distinctive stimuli in multiple sensory modalities may also restrict the set of possible events that could have occurred. Simultaneously experiencing a specific constellation of stimuli across our various sensory modalities may serve to triangulate (at least) on some very small set of possible events and corresponding actions (to be remembered). In short, the sensory experiences in question may jointly define a distinctive action profile.[15]

Whether the extreme emotions such treatment is likely to induce enhance participants' memories for these rituals directly is unclear. Far tamer laboratory studies suggest that subjects' recollections for both central and peripheral information about emotionally arousing stimuli can exceed that for neutral stimuli (Heuer & Reisberg, 1990). At least one study of flashbulb memory (Bohannon & Symons, 1992) found that subjects' reports of their initial emotional arousal on hearing about the Challenger predicted both the amount of information they generated and the consistency of their stories over time. As noted earlier, the earthquake findings notwithstanding, extreme emotion may be one of some

---

[14]Consider some of the details from the third degree initiation:

> Each novice is held and has his elbows pounded with sacred black stones. ... The novices are also assured that this is the only hardship they will suffer.
>
> As soon as this is completed, however, the seniors grab bunches of nettles and whip the novices over the face and chest ... They are then presented with the leaf package of the dog's black gut contents and cooked penis. They are forced to eat the black mixture and at least lick and suck the penis ... they are encouraged by the assurance that this is the very last trial they must endure. ... The novices are made to crawl on their hands and knees between the legs of the line of men; each man they pass under whips them with the burning nettles over back, legs, and particularly the genitalia. ... The novices are then assured that this completes their tortures ...
>
> They are ... made to sit around the two fires ... crowding them closer as the flames grow hotter. ... This starts a four-day ordeal: blistered and burned by the fires they are now kept continuously awake ... they are allowed no water. ... At irregular intervals they are again forced into the fires and burned. (Barth, 1975, pp. 64–65)

[15]I am grateful to David Rubin for this proposal.

number of conditions that are jointly sufficient to produce such effects (see Brewer, 1992).

I will not be resolving that one here, but I do want to emphasize that it is not clear that the processes of narrative consolidation and rehearsal in particular can do enough of the work with memory for Baktaman initiations (no matter whether those memories are accurate or not). The reason is that many features of Baktaman culture, including taboos, hyper-secretiveness, a fear of sorcery, and "a more diffuse wariness and reluctance to speak about . . . occult forces" (Barth, 1975, pp. 258–259), militate against initiates rehearsing narratives about their initiation experiences (even in their own minds!). Initiates make up a "*mute* fellowship of privileged participation" (Barth, 1975, p. 221, italics added). Barth (1975) asserted that ". . . in their initiations and temple organizations the Baktaman have constructed a communicative apparatus which they themselves approach with such reluctance and trepidation as to endanger the very knowledge it contains" (p. 260).

Presumably, during the short time between the seniors' decision to perform an initiation and the performance itself, some conversation about ritual details occurs. Although such review may not invite full-blown rehearsals of initiates' narratives, it encourages them to run through these events again in their minds.

Barth did report on one sort of circumstance where less inhibited discussion of the initiation rituals among the seniors is, apparently, acceptable; for example, when the decision to perform an initiation occurs during a power struggle over cult leadership. Such struggles can result from dissatisfaction with either the conscientiousness or the effectiveness of the current leadership or from sheer individual assertiveness by the pretender(s). On completion of the seventh-degree initiation, men are eligible to take over cult leadership. Not only is succession to these posts open, but rivals can unseat current cult leaders. In the face of rivals' criticisms, cult leaders may decide to consult with other seniors about their memories for ritual details and in the process try to garner their support as well.

Either the triumph of dissidents or a cult leader's flexibility in response to such dissent can result in innovations. For example, in the single instance of such conflict that Barth observed, the cult leader compromised. He agreed to changes in the performance of the sixth-degree initiation that the dissidents had advocated on the basis of their knowledge of how neighboring groups to the west performed a similar ritual.

Two points deserve attention. First, this episode notwithstanding, Barth repeatedly underscored how formidable the cultural barriers are to discussions of myth, ritual, and cosmology. Most of the time Baktaman hyper-secrecy and associated taboos seem to preclude the rehearsal that makes for the consolidation of stable narratives. Note that I am not claiming that these cultural mechanisms preclude the formation of narratives, but only that whatever stability initiates' narratives possess does not look as though it results from their rehearsal. These are precisely the considerations that led Barth to place so much emphasis on analogic coding in his account of the transmission of Baktaman ritual knowledge. Whether frequent exposure to abstract themes underlying the analogic coding will suffice to explain the retention and transmission of Baktaman initiation rituals, I cannot say. However, that religious systems in such settings will evolve to take advantage of other aids to memory seems a reasonable proposal and that the Baktaman system of male initiation manipulates most of the variables on which researchers on flashbulb memory have focused seems clear.

Second, all of those participating in the particular episode that Barth observed regarded these changes as innovations; that is, everyone agreed that these adjustments were new and that they did not accord with what they remembered about previous performances. The resulting compromise, of course, shows that perfect fidelity to past practice is not an unwavering ideal for the Baktaman, but, more important, it also suggests that a collective view about accuracy in memory sustains such conversations.

Collectively, participants must retain enough knowledge of these rituals to preserve a sense of both continuity and community. The functionally relevant measure of continuity is participants' sense that what they are doing presently is the same type of ritual action that they or their forbears did before and (although not necessarily with the Baktaman) that their compatriots might be doing contemporaneously somewhere else. From such temporal factors as timing and sequence to such structural factors as the identities and properties of agents, various features of actions condition participants' judgments about the similarities and differences of religious ritual performances (Lawson & McCauley, 1990).

Concurrence both about the criteria for ritual types and about the facts concerning particular ritual performances is diagnostic in identifying religious communities. Rituals, after all, are not incidental to religious systems. Their performance is integral both to situating individuals in the larger religious community and to sustaining that community.

The rivalry for cult leadership on which Barth reported shows unequivocally that innovations may be introduced into Baktaman initiations. But (a) the two factions participating in the discussion (and the resistance of the more conservative seniors especially), (b) the universal recognition that the proposed changes constituted innovations, and (c) the general acceptance of the eventual compromise each suggests that a common conception of what would count as a sixth-degree initiation informed this dispute throughout.

Whatever participants' criteria for identifying types of ritual acts, however, usually the issue is not so much whether the current ritual undertaking, in fact, matches its predecessors on all relevant counts but simply whether enough of the current participants are satisfied that it does. Most of the time this seems to turn on the accuracy of participants' memories, but accurate memory is not the only means for accomplishing such an end. Reaching consensus about such matters may rely, in part, on any number of devices from coercion to codification. The history of the great world religions alone provides countless instances when religious authorities have readily resorted to ruthless methods for imposing consensus about matters of ritual and belief. Moreover, plenty of forms of social negotiation less extreme than those that prevailed during, say, the Counter Reformation, are available for resolving these problems, and these are forms of negotiation in which the question of the accuracy of memory is only somewhat more likely to arise in the explanation of their operations (Barth, 1987). Arguably, these more subtle forms of social coercion are all the more effective precisely because they so often go undetected.

Without fierce coercion, however, and often even with it, memory is vital to these determinations and accuracy a prominent, if not preeminent, value. (Great dangers regularly accompany inattentiveness to the gods' decrees.) My claim here is not merely about desires for and perceptions of accurate memory at the object level but about genuine accuracy as an explanatory mechanism at the theoretical level. Collective recollection is not, after all, utterly unconstrained. Absent irresistibly powerful forms of coercion about such matters in a culture, some standards must restrict these negotiations or, otherwise, the problem of explaining the community's collective sense of continuity in these proceedings looms ominously. On the other hand, that said, recall Rubin's (1995) cautioning about what counts as accuracy in processes of cultural transmission where literacy plays no role. My emphasis in this discussion is not on the achievement of perfect accuracy in these settings but on the contributions of mechanisms that make for more faithful recall to this communal sense of continuity.

ACKNOWLEDGMENTS

I wish to express my gratitude to Marshall Gregory, E. Thomas Lawson, David Rubin, Harvey Whitehouse, and Eugene Winograd for their helpful comments on an earlier version of this chapter. I also wish to thank William Hirst, Robyn Fivush, and Eugene Winograd for their kindness and patience as editors.

Finally, I have so many things (stimulation, encouragement, support, criticism, good food, great coffee, puns, laughs, . . .) to thank Dick and Arden Neisser for that I hardly know where to begin. Space limitations require that I sum it all up by simply thanking them for their friendship.

REFERENCES

Barth, F. (1975). *Ritual and knowledge among the Baktaman of New Guinea.* New Haven, CT: Yale University Press.

Barth, F. (1987). *Cosmologies in the making: A generative approach to cultural variation in inner New Guinea.* Cambridge, England: Cambridge University Press.

Bohannon, J. N., & Symons, V. L. (1992). Flashbulb memories: Confidence, consistency, and quantity. In E. Winograd & U. Neisser (Eds.), *Affect and accuracy in recall* (pp. 65–91). New York: Cambridge University Press.

Brewer, W. F. (1992). The theoretical and empirical status of the flashbulb memory hypothesis. In E. Winograd & U. Neisser (Eds.), *Affect and accuracy in recall* (pp. 274–305). New York: Cambridge University Press.

Brown, R., & Kulik, J. (1982). Flashbulb memories. In U. Neisser (Ed.), *Memory observed* (pp. 23–40). San Francisco: Freeman.

Christianson, S. A. (1989). Flashbulb memories: Special, but not so special. *Memory & Cognition, 17,* 435–443.

Colegrove, F. W. (1982). The day they heard about Lincoln. In U. Neisser (Ed.), *Memory observed* (pp. 41–42). San Francisco: Freeman. (Original work published 1899)

Fodor, J. A., & Pylyshyn, Z. W. (1988). Connectionism and cognitive architecture: A critical analysis. *Cognition, 28,* 3–71.

Goody, J. (1987). *The interface between the written and the oral.* Cambridge, England: Cambridge University Press.

Heuer, F., & Reisberg, D. (1990). Vivid memories of emotional events: The accuracy of remembered minutiae. *Memory and Cognition, 18,* 496–506.

Hunter, I. M. L. (1985). Lengthy verbatim recall: The role of text. In A. Ellis (Ed.), *Progress in the psychology of language* (pp. 207–235). Hillsdale, NJ: Lawrence Erlbaum Associates.

Larsen, S. F. (1988). Remembering without experiencing: Memory for reported events. In U. Neisser & E. Winograd (Eds.), *Remembering reconsidered: Ecological and traditional approaches to the study of memory* (pp. 326–355). New York: Cambridge University Press.

Lawson, E. T., & McCauley, R. N. (1990). *Rethinking religion: Connecting cognition and culture.* Cambridge, England: Cambridge University Press.

Lawson, E. T., & McCauley, R. N. (1993). Crisis of conscience, riddle of identity: Making space for a cognitive approach to religious phenomena. *Journal of the American Academy of Religion, 61,* 201–223.

McCauley, R. N. (in press). "Overcoming barriers to a cognitive psychology of religion." In A. Geertz & R. McCutcheon (Eds.), *Proceedings of the XIII Congress of the International Association of the History of Religions.* New York: deGruyter.

McCauley, R. N., & Lawson, E. T. (1993). Connecting the cognitive and the cultural: Artificial minds as methodological devices in the study of the sociocultural. In R. Burton (Ed.), *Minds: Natural and artificial* (pp. 121–145). Albany: State University of New York Press.

McCauley, R. N., & Lawson, E. T. (1996). Who owns 'culture'? *Method and Theory in the Study of Religion, 8,* 171–190.

McCauley, R. N., & Lawson, E. T. (1998a). Interactionism and the non-obviousness of scientific theories. *Method and Theory in the Study of Religion, 10,* 61–77.

McCauley, R. N., & Lawson, E. T. (in preparation). *Ritual, agency, and memory: Elementary forms of religious performance.* (manuscript in preparation).

Neisser, U. (1982). Snapshots or benchmarks? In U. Neisser (Ed.), *Memory observed* (pp. 43–48). San Francisco: Freeman.

Neisser, U. (1986). Remembering Pearl Harbor: Reply to Thomson and Cowan. *Cognition, 23,* 285–286.

Neisser, U., & Harsch, N. (1992). Phantom flashbulbs: False recollections of hearing the news about *Challenger*. In E. Winograd & U. Neisser (Eds.), *Affect and accuracy in recall* (pp. 9–31). New York: Cambridge University Press.

Neisser, U., Winograd, E., Bergman, E., Schreiber, C., Palmer, S., & Weldon, M. S. (1996). Remembering the earthquake: Direct experience vs. hearing the news. *Memory, 4*, 337–357.

Paivio, A. (1986). *Mental representations: A dual coding approach*. New York: Oxford University Press.

Reber, A. S. (1993). *Implicit learning and tacit knowledge: An essay on the cognitive unconscious*. New York: Oxford University Press.

Roediger, H. L. (1990). Implicit memory: Retention without remembering. *American Psychologist, 45*, 1043–1056.

Rubin, D. (1992). Constraints on memory. In E. Winograd & U. Neisser (Eds.), *Affect and accuracy in recall* (pp. 265–273). New York: Cambridge University Press.

Rubin, D. (1995). *Memory in oral tradition: The cognitive psychology of epic, ballads, and counting-out rhymes*. New York: Oxford University Press.

Schank, R. C., & Abelson, R. P. (1977). *Scripts, plans, goals, and understanding: An inquiry into human knowledge structures*. Hillsdale, NJ: Lawrence Erlbaum Associates.

Scribner, S., & Cole, M. (1981). *The psychology of literacy*. Cambridge, MA: Harvard University Press.

Somayajipad, C. V., Nambudiri, M. I. R., & Nambudiri, E. R. (1983). Recent Nambudiri performances of Agnistoma and Agnicayana. In F. Staal (Ed.), *Agni (Volume II)* (pp. 252–255). Berkeley, CA: Asian Humanities Press.

Sperber, D. (1975). *Rethinking symbolism* (A. Morton, Trans.). Cambridge, England: Cambridge University Press.

Sperber, D. (1996). *Explaining culture: A naturalistic approach*. Oxford, England: Blackwell.

Staal, F. (1979). The meaningless of ritual. *Numen, 26*, 2–22.

Wells, G. L., & Murray, D. (1984). Eyewitness confidence. In G. L. Wells & E. F. Loftus (Eds.), *Eyewitness testimony* (pp. 155–170). New York: Cambridge University Press.

Whitehouse, H. (1992). Memorable religions: Transmission, codification and change in divergent Melanesian contexts. *Man (N.S.), 27*, 777–797.

Whitehouse, H. (1995). *Inside the cult: Religious innovation and transmission in Papua New Guinea*. Oxford, England: Clarendon.

Winograd, E., & Killinger, W. A. (1983). Relating age at encoding in early childhood to adult recall: Development of flashbulb memories. *Journal of Experimental Psychology: General, 117*, 413–422.

Chapter 13

Five Kinds of Self-Ignorance

David A. Jopling
York University

> *Ale, man, ale's the stuff to drink*
> *For fellows whom it hurts to think:*
> *Look into the pewter pot*
> *To see the world as the world's not.*
>
> —A. E. Housman (1946, p. 88)

Is ignorance preferable to knowledge? Would it be preferable if the payoff were increased contentment? The Biblical philosopher Ecclesiastes (1962, 1:18) seemed to think so: "For in much wisdom," he wrote, "is much vexation, and he who increases knowledge increases sorrow." Responding to Ecclesiastes centuries later, Spinoza (1677/1992) denied that "ignorance is preferable to knowledge, or that there is no difference between a fool and a wise man. . . . [It] is necessary," he wrote, "to know both the power of our nature and its lack of power, so that we can determine what reason can and cannot do . . ." (Part IV, Prop. 17, Sch.).

Generally, people tend to side with Spinoza rather than Ecclesiastes. We value seeing things as they are, rather than through a veil of illusion, fantasy, or ignorance, and we are loathe to exchange a clear-headed awareness and knowledge of reality for deluded contentment.

But on what grounds do we value seeing things as they are? Is there any rational justification for it?

Take the evil demon of *Meditation One*, the most extreme form of skepticism Descartes (1641/1993) could imagine. The all-powerful demon produces in us a convincing and internally consistent replica of our normal experiential contact with the world. So seamlessly woven is the replica that we are unaware of the demon's handiwork, naively believing that our experiences have their usual cause in a physical world impinging directly on our sensory apparatus. But the demon has pulled the plug on this world; all that remains is the demon's mind and mine, tangoing in a tortured *folie à deux*, the demon leading at every step.

The point of the thought experiment is to show that subjective experience could be just the way that it is, without its being the case that it is causally connected to physical, mind-independent reality.

Whatever the plausibility of his escape from this nightmarish system, Descartes assumed that genuine contact with reality is preferable to even the most pleasant demon-generated experience, which delivers merely the illusion of contact. Descartes is right, but why?

Consider how this question looks from another angle, one that is pertinent to Neisser's (1988) theory of the self: Is self-ignorance preferable to self-knowledge? Would it be preferable if the payoff were increased contentment and well-being?

Consider the following truisms. Normally, it is a matter of fundamental concern to us that we are aware of who we are, where we are in the social and physical environments, what we are currently doing and acting on, and what is occurring around us. Normally, we assume that as as more and more of the relevant features of actions and situations come into our purview, the more responsive we can be to the demands and affordances of the world; and the more accurately calibrated and better targeted our actions and reactions. Without this level of self-awareness, we would find it difficult to accept responsibility for what we do. We therefore tend to feel that any attempt to reduce our awareness of self, world, and others is generally bad. All these claims are true, but why? What is wrong with apprehending the self through a veil of illusion, fantasy, or false consciousness?

Enter again the evil demon. Imagine that it produces in us a convincing replica of our normal experience of ourselves. Because of its elaborate deception, we are radically mistaken about the various dimensions of the self: what Neisser (1988) called the ecological self, the interpersonal self, the extended self, the private self, and the conceptual self. Nothing that we perceive or think about ourselves corresponds to what we really are— even though subjectively it seems that we are in touch with ourselves.

This is a bad situation to be in. Would it be any less bad if we were to suppose that the demon-generated experience of self also happens to be pleasant, adaptive, and highly functional? Is there anything intrinsically wrong with exchanging contact with the reality of ourselves for a comfortable, user-friendly, and internally coherent bubble of self-deception or self-illusion?

Questions like these are not merely epistemological fantasies. They help shed light on a recent post-modern trend in clinical and social psychology that supports the cultivation of bubbles of illusion, subjective fantasy, and ignorance, on the grounds that: (a) these states are essential for well-being; and (b) that the goal of seeing things as they are is a philosophical fiction.

The concept of well-being is undergoing a profound revision in contemporary clinical and social psychology. Behind the revision is a turn toward subjectivism. Instead of accurate perception and realistic acceptance of self and world, well-being is now thought to involve the positively enhanced perception of self and world; that is, perception that is selective, self-serving, esteem-preserving, productivity-oriented, and comfort-inducing. The perception of self and world through a positively tinted user-friendly veil of illusions, wishful thinking, creative self-deception, fictionalization, or confabulation is considered to be more important for well-being than clear-headed, sober awareness. Well-being, in other words, involves diminished contact with reality. From a therapeutic point of view, contact with the real may even be inimical to well-being.

The subjectivist redefinition of well-being is a curious development. With the exception of Janet's (1925) deliberate cultivation of deceptive memories through hypnosis and suggestion, most forms of clinical psychology and psychotherapy have been committed to the traditional goal of helping people develop more accurate and more rational ways to think about themselves and the world. Traditionally, mental health has been viewed as involving the maintainance of an accurate contact with reality. Jahoda summed this up by saying, "The perception of reality is called mentally healthy when what the individual sees corresponds to what is actually there" (1958, p. 6); and "Mentally healthy perception means a process of viewing the world so that one is able to take in matters one wishes were different without distorting them to fit these wishes" (1953, p. 349).

To see how the ideal of contact with reality is undergoing a revision in contemporary clinical and social psychology, in favor of the ideal of subjective contentment, I look at five kinds of self-ignorance, each of which appear at the clinical level as normative ideals and each of which masquerades as mentally healthy self-insight. This serves a double purpose, for it will also show how Neisser's theory of self, and his commitment to realism and ecological validity, is relevant to the pursuit of self-knowledge at the clinical level. The five kinds of self-ignorance are:

1. creatively self-deceived insight;
2. placebo insight;
3. narrative insight;
4. cosmetic psycho-pharmacological insight (or Prozac insight); and
5. experientialist insight.

However disparate the theories and clinical practices supporting these forms of insight may appear to be, there are a number of common underlying threads. Each practice secures a form of well-being at the cost of diminished contact with reality; each one requires a shrinkage of the range of human experience in order to make experience more manageable and comfortable; each one tends to subjectivize truth; each one defends a culturally parochial model of well-being that reflects the implicit values of the technologically advanced and performance-driven culture of the Western world; and each one regards the ideal of accurate contact with reality as therapeutically dispensable.

CREATIVELY SELF-DECEIVED INSIGHT

> *Take away the life-lie from the average person, and you take his happiness along with it.*
>
> —Ibsen, *The Wild Duck* (1968, p. 64)

Nietzsche argued that untruth—a will to ignorance—is a fundamental condition of human life. Illusion, ignorance, deception, blind stupidity, oversimplification, and falsification are adaptive and life-enhancing. The unqualified commitment to truth, on the other hand, can be destructive of the blind momentum of life.

> It is not enough that you understand in what ignorance humans as well as animals live; you must also have and acquire the *will* to ignorance. You need to grasp that without this kind of ignorance life itself would be impossible, that it is a condition under which alone the living thing can preserve itself and prosper: a great, firm dome of ignorance must encompass you. (Nietzsche, 1968, p. 609)

Human beings cannot survive without limited perceptual, affective, and cognitive horizons: a "*narrowing of our perspective*, and thus in a certain sense stupidity, [is] a condition of life and growth" (Nietzsche, 1886/1966, p. 188; Nietzsche, 1968). Falsity and illusion are not therefore to be eradicated as part of the methodical purging of the web of belief (as Descartes advised). "The falseness of a judgment is not for us necessarily an objection to a judgment. ... The question is to what extent it is life-promoting, life-preserving, species-preserving, perhaps even species-cultivating" (Nietzsche, 1886/1966, p. 4). Nietzsche added that the will to ignorance is disguised: Part of what it means to be wholeheartedly committed to a view or a belief is to feel that it is the only correct view to be held and that it is untainted by illusion.

The plays of Henrik Ibsen and Eugene O'Neill illustrate these Nietzschean themes at the intrapersonal and interpersonal levels and call into question our normal assumptions about the goal of seeing things—including self and other—as they are. They show how life for the average person can be tolerable only with a veil of comforting and self-serving illusions filtering out life's harsher elements: pipe dreams and life-lies (Jopling, 1996a).

Without psychological crutches and other encompassing domes of ignorance, most people would not be able to function normally and maintain adaptive self-regarding attitudes such as self-esteem and self-contentment (Martin, 1985; Rorty, 1975, 1994). The plays of Ibsen and O'Neill thus focus on a recurrent theme: When pipe dreams and life-lies are burst, in the name of an honest confrontation with reality, tragedy and despair inevitably follow. Too much self-knowledge is psychologically de-stabilizing. "To hell with the truth!" says the barfly Larry Slade, a besotten regular at Harry Hope's bar, in O'Neill's (1957) play *The Iceman Cometh.* "The lie of a pipe dream is what gives life to the whole misbegotten mad lot of us, drunk or sober" (pp. 9–10).

There is some truth in this sage barroom advice: Pipe dreaming may be as adaptive as it is pleasant, just as liquid courage may be as effective as real courage. The problem is that the advice also serves as a defense for remaining permanently cocooned in an alcoholic daze; or as a lame rationalization for wantonness; or as a convenient strategy for avoiding facing up to the vicissitudes of life, and therefore of learning and growing from the experience of suffering.

A psychologically sophisticated version of Larry Slade's advice is defended in certain branches of social and clinical psychology. Taylor and Brown (1988; Taylor, 1989) adduced a wealth of convincing experimental evidence to show that positively biased creative illusions about the self play a more significant role in the maintenance of mental health, as well as in the maintenance of caring interpersonal relations and a sense of well-being, than do accurate self-perception and self-knowledge. These illusions include unrealistically positive self-evaluations, exaggerated perceptions of personal control, and unrealistic optimism about the future.

> The individual who responds to negative, ambiguous, or unsupportive feedback with a positive sense of self, a belief in personal efficacy, and an optimistic sense of the future will, we maintain, be happier, more caring, and more productive than the individual who perceives this same information accurately and integrates it into his or her view of the self, the world, and the future. (Taylor & Brown, 1988, p. 205)

According to Taylor and Brown, accurate self-knowledge is neither an indispensable ingredient of well-being (see also Rorty, 1975, 1994), nor an essential component of functioning in a complex social environment. They also make a strong prescriptive claim: the cultivation of illusions about the self—not their eradication and replacement, as the Jahoda model suggests—has positive therapeutic benefits:

> [The] capacity to develop and maintain positive illusions may be thought of as a valuable human resource to be nurtured and promoted, rather than an error-prone processing system to be corrected. In any case, these illusions help make each individual's world a warmer and more active and beneficent place in which to live. (Taylor & Brown, 1988, p. 205)

From a strictly self-regarding first-person point of view, the cultivation of positive illusions and creative self-deceptions may be desirable: They seem to guarantee temporary feelings of well-being; they cushion the often-painful impact of reality; they sweeten memories; they are an antidote to sorrow; and they are an addictive anodyne for dealing with the criticisms, negative judgments, and hurt feelings of others. But there is a price for cultivating illusions to make the world "a warmer and . . . more beneficent place," and it is paid by the people who must live with creative self-deceivers.

Taylor and Brown likened positive illusions to cognitive filters that select and organize self-relevant information in a self-serving direction: filters that distort negative information, prevent contradictory information from being acknowledged, enhance positive information, and disambiguate ambiguous information. But what is this other than a description of the cognitive mechanisms by means of which negative feedback from other people—criticisms, advice, disapprovals, hurt feelings—is edited, filtered out, or self-servingly candy-coated, thereby allowing self-deceivers to remain systematically unaware of the effects their actions and words are having on others? The creatively self-deceived, in other words, suffer from a level of other-blindness that the undeceived do not (Jopling, 1996a). But because they are less responsive to negative feedback, they are also less capable of experiencing the kinds of moral and personal growth that are only possible in contexts of interpersonal relations.

The creative self-deception hypothesis is marked by two culturally parochial assumptions. First, it assumes that there is no more to well-being than purely intrasubjective feelings, as if the self is a socially discrete atom uninfluenced by genuine interpersonal and dialogic connectedness. There is no interpersonal self here. Second, it assumes that all forms of negative feedback are equally bad and to be avoided. But the painful experiences of life that would otherwise be tranquilized with positive illusions are also opportunities for learning to face up to the trials of life, of learning from suffering, and of learning to accept human foibles in all their forms in the same objective way that one accepts the processes of nature.

The most curious aspects of Taylor and Brown's prescriptive claims are their political and social consequences. Were positive illusions to be systematically nurtured and promoted, as they advocate, duplicity, moral evasiveness and selfishness may come to replace the specifically social virtues of honesty, trust, and personal responsibility. For the lost souls of *The Iceman Cometh*, ensconced in the protective bubble of their alcohol-fueled pipe dreams, nothing is more tempting than to put off owning up to their deeds and misdeeds and taking responsibility for themselves.

PLACEBO INSIGHT

> *What pledge can be afforded that the boasted remedies of the present day will not be like their predecessors, fall into disrepute, and in their turn serve only as a humiliating memorial of the credulity and infatuation of the physicians who recommended and prescribed them?*
>
> *The Paris Pharmacologia* (Haggard, 1934, p. 395)

Insight-oriented psychotherapy is another form of contemporary psychology that tends to subjectivize truth, and to secure well-being at the cost of diminished contact with reality. The curious fact here is that it unwittingly exchanges contact with reality for psychic contentment. Most psychotherapists simply assume uncritically that insight-oriented psychotherapy is a valid and truth-tracking method of personal discovery. Working together with the therapist, the patient comes to see him or herself from a more accurate and rational perspective. This, it is assumed, is an authentic experience. With persistence and courage, the patient achieves what therapists consider to be genuine self-knowledge. The fundamental assumption here is that the acquisition of self-knowledge is an essential step for personal change in therapeutic improvement; and that the therapist's specific treatment method and theoretical orientation is directly instrumental in helping the patient gain self-knowledge.

Psychotherapeutic healing sometimes works this way—but not always. Neither the acquisition of insight, nor the occurrence of therapeutic change following insight, nor the patient's feeling of being more insightful, nor the patient's command of a more psychologically sophisticated vocabulary of the self, is sufficient to guarantee that the insight is true or authentic (Farrell, 1981). Something else may be occasioning these therapeutic changes that has little to do with the acquisition of an authentic, truth-tracking self-knowledge.

However carefully controlled and practiced, all forms of insight-oriented psychotherapy have the capacity to bring about therapeutic changes through nonrational means; by suggestion, for instance, or persuasion, or placebo effect. All forms of insight-oriented psychotherapy have the capacity to induce in suggestible patients pseudo-insight, or self-deception that masquerades convincingly as insight.

Naturally, this is vigorously denied by therapists, who are heavily invested in their methods. But it has long been known that healing is not always governed by reason and guided by truth. Observing the soul doctors of ancient Greece and their use of rhetoric, word-sorcery, and nonrational persuasion, Socrates remarked that, "the cure of the soul has to be effected by the use of certain charms, and these charms are fair words" (Plato, 1961). Socrates might have added that talking cures work as much by dazzling and bewitching as they do by enlightening: The soul-doctor's word is like a *pharmakon*, at once curative and poisonous (Lain Etralgo, 1970).

Socrates anticipated by 2,500 years the view that today is known as the common factors approach. According to this, psychotherapeutic improvement is often a function of factors that are not unique to a particular theoretical orientation or to a particular method of treatment. Improvement occurs largely because of factors that are shared by all forms of psychotherapy and perhaps by all forms of healing (including shamanism; Eysenck, 1965; Frank & Frank, 1991; Haley, 1963; Luborsky, Singer, & Luborsky, 1975; Strupp, 1972; Strupp & Luborsky, 1962). These factors include: suggestibility, seduction by a technical discourse, self-validating interpretations, placebo effects (Shapiro & Morris, 1978), the desire to reduce the cognitive dissonance generated by the therapeutic encounter, social consensus about the authority of the therapist, and therapist charisma and supportiveness.

These common factors explain not only therapeutic improvement, they also account for unwanted therapeutic changes such as deterioration effects and negative outcomes. One of the less acknowledged forms of unwanted change involves suggestion-driven insight. With the pressure of common factors, patients may be more disposed to accept from the therapist as true what are in fact psychologically and historically incorrect interpretations and to formulate for themselves psychologically and historically incorrect insights, based on evidentiary and interpretive criteria that have been reshaped by continued exposure to the therapist's theoretical orientation. This kind of negative change should not be surprising.[1] In the volatized setting of the therapeutic encounter there is a constant risk that the patient may be misled by incorrect, inexact, or illusory insights—which nonetheless appear to the patient to be true. We might call this phenomenon placebo insight: That is, insights that, unbeknownst to patients, have no more explanatory power and descriptive validity than psychological sugar pills but which are placebologically effective, and subjectively pleasing.

---

[1]See Sundberg (1966). Sundberg's experiment indicates that there is a tendency to accept bogus personality assessment statements as containing true descriptions about the self.

Vulnerability to placebo insight is complicated by a number of factors. With continued exposure to the therapist's theoretical orientation, for instance, the patient's self-understanding may be reformulated in terms of a theory-laden explanatory terminology that conflicts with the pre-therapeutic self-conception. Moreover, the patient's insights may be subtly reinforced by the therapist, who naturally desires confirmation for his or her theoretical orientation. Given these factors, the treatment methods used in insight-oriented psychotherapies may be self-confirming (Farrell, 1981): That is, they may be potent enough to create the very conditions under which the therapist can obtain empirical support for his or her theoretical orientation. As patients learn to think of themselves in terms of a psychologically sophisticated theory and to restructure their self-concepts and self-reports accordingly, the therapist receives back from them information that supports that theory, and that in turn encourages the therapist to continue to apply the treatment and to further develop the ongoing interpretation. Such a dynamic guides the patient's acquisition of insight along a path that would not otherwise have been followed.

Even Freud admitted that the agent of therapeutic change is not always the truth of the psychoanalyst's interpretation, nor the truth of the analysand's insight, but the analysand's belief in their truth-value—a state that is compatible with therapeutic suggestion, persuasion, and the reduction of cognitive dissonance.

> Quite often we do not succeed in bringing the patient to recollect what has been repressed. Instead of that, if the analysis is carried out correctly, we produce in him an assured conviction of the truth of the construction which achieves the same therapeutic result as a recaptured memory. (Freud, 1964, p. 260)

Incorrect interpretations, then, can be as therapeutically effective as correct ones, as long as other nontruth-valuable factors obtain: They can supply a coherent and persuasive—although false or inexact—explanation for otherwise incoherent and alien sufferings.[2]

---

[2]Lévi-Strauss (1963) described the case of Quesalid, a shaman who successfully cured his patients but who did not believe in the validity of his treatment methods nor in his own aetiologic explanations. Quesalid's cure involved extracting from his mouth a concealed tuft of bloodied down and then offering to his patients the explanation that he had sucked out the offending pathology in the form of a bloody worm. He knew that there was no aetiological connection between the tuft, the presenting illness, and the eventual cure, yet he was widely successful in the application of the procedure and the mythological explanation. The case illustrates the importance of social consensus in effecting a cure, and the importance of the patient's acceptance of the shaman's authority. It is a clear example of how mythological explanations can be effective not because they are true but because they supply patients with a coherent and socially endorsable explanation for otherwise incoherent and alien sufferings. Lévi-Strauss argued that psychoanalytical explanations work in much the same way.

If psychotherapeutic change can be explained in terms of placebo insights, then the demarcation line is blurred between psychotherapy as an authentic method of personal discovery and as a healing method that trades in convenient fictions, creative illusions, rationalizations, complicating insight-mimicking overlays, and nonrational persusasion. Obviously not all forms of insight-oriented psychotherapy do this but many unwittingly sustain placebo insight, thereby gaining psychic contentment at the cost of diminished contact with the reality of the self.

NARRATIVE INSIGHT

Narrativist psychotherapy is another form of contemporary psychology that tends to subjectivize truth and to secure well-being at the cost of diminished contact with reality. Unlike traditional insight-oriented psychotherapy, however, it advocates exchanging contact with reality for psychic contentment by appealing to the antirealist idea that historical and psychological truth is irrelevant with respect to the patient's creation of a coherent and subjectively satisfying narrative. Spence (1982) argued that:

> it was once accepted that psychotherapy worked by digging into the unconscious ... and curing symptoms by exposing truth. Conflicting therapies disagreed about the meanings or factors behind symptoms, but all believed that only dealing with these "real things" in their "real places" could really cure. These metaphors are no longer valid. (p. 203)

The critical distinction in narrativist psychotherapy is between historical and narrative truth (Spence, 1982). Historical truth is established by ascertaining a statement's correspondence to extralinguistic matters of fact. Narrative truth pertains to the narrative framework in terms of which extralinguistic facts are organized and given meaning and it is established by appealing to the internal coherence of the narrative, the goodness of fit between the narrative and the data, and the narrative's congruence with a consensually recognized knowledge base. Coherence is not merely a sign of truth, but is itself the condition of truth.

The kind of truth relevant to narrativist psychotherapy, and its specific form of insight, is narrative truth. In this view, a true narrative insight does not consist in getting an objectively correct representation of the facts of the self and personal life-history; truth emerges with the creation of an adaptive, personally acceptable, internally coherent system of meaningful connections amongst the facts. This is a creative process that involves imaginative selection and abstraction, very much as artists select materials with a view to constructing a unique synthetic whole. A narratively true insight is therefore flexible enough to accommodate factual errors, false memories, and psychologically incorrect descriptions. These inconveniences are relatively insignificant with respect to "the effort of a creator to give the meaning of his own mythic tale. . . . [T]he truth of facts is subordinate to the truth of the man" (Gusdorf, 1980, p. 48; McNamee & Gergen, 1992).

How could the acquisition of an internally coherent narrative insight that floats free of the facts be therapeutically effective? It is principally because patients are suffering from a surfeit of unintelligibility in their lives—not because they lack objectively true representations of the self. Their life-stories are broken and discrepant; events do not add up for them. The idea that psychic suffering is occasioned by unintelligibility presupposes the validity of a counterfactual principle of contrast: Without narrative structuring, experience would disintegrate into a degraded incoherent state. Narrative coherence is "the standard which determines even that which deviates from it. When plans go awry, when things fall apart, it is by reference to or by contrast with story-like projections, scenarios, that they do so" (Carr, 1986, p. 88).

What narrative therapy supplies to the patient is an adaptive and personally scaled framework of meaning. The narrative therapist's interpretation, wrote Spence (1982):

> may bring about a positive effect not because it corresponds to a specific piece of the past but because it appears to relate the known to the unknown, to provide explanation in place of uncertainty. . . . We have come to see that certain kinds of pragmatic statements can produce changes in behaviour simply by virtue of being stated. (p. 290)

In narratives as in artworks, there is a certain degree of interpretive and criteriological slack to allow playing with the evidentiary materials at hand. The construction of a self-narrative involves giving free rein to imaginative editing, re-writing, historical neglect, and the narrative smoothing over of factual discrepancies. The exact mirroring of psychological and historical reality is less important for the acquisition of insight and psychological healing than the patient's creation of a coherent narrative account of previously unidentified experiences—that is, relating the unknown to the known, and naming that which was hitherto lived as unnamed:

> Meanings are not objectively *there* to be found, but are *constructions* of therapists' and clients' minds. The story of clients' lives, which develops in therapy, is not the real history, archaeologically reconstructed, but is one possible *narrative*: perhaps more orderly, detailed and coherent than the pretherapeutic one, but not necessarily more true. (Spence, 1982, p. 100)

This leaves a number of questions unanswered. First, can the narrativist approach to psychotherapy supply clear grounds for upholding the distinction between mere storytelling and truth-tracking storytelling? The mere acquisition of therapeutically effective narrative insight is not sufficient to establish the insight as truth-tracking: It may simply be a case of exercising a knack for formulating narratives that have a semblance of plausibility. The reverse is also possible: Robust truth-tracking insight is compatible with narrative ineptitude. Moreover, a narrative insight that merely happens to be historically and psychologically true is not *ipso facto* equivalent to genuine insight. A patient in narrative psychotherapy may know enough about herself to produce a historically and psychologically plausible narrative, but she may not be genuinely insightful because her actions are jarringly mismatched to her narratives. There must be something more to insight (and healing) than merely the production of a coherent narrative life story.

Second, how much narrative arti-factuality is enough? At what point does narratively constructed insight slide down the slope into arbitrary subjectivism? When does the imaginative narrating of a life story become so empirically underdetermined that implausible personal fantasy takes over?

With enough interpretive slack and evidentiary malleability, and enough coherence-preserving revisions in their narrative life stories, the patients of narrative psychotherapy would be free to develop insights that express simply the most morally convenient and self-serving life stories, without fear of external correction and intersubjective corroboration. The failure to ground narrative in an extranarrative reality places into jeopardy the distinction between a coherent and factually accurate life story, and a coherent but systematically self-deceived life story that is driven by personal preference or fantasy (Jopling, 1996b). Narrative relativism thus has undesirable moral consequences because it blurs the distinction between truth-telling and outright lying (Held, 1995).

Without a sufficiently objective grounding, narrative psychotherapy legitimates retreating into the protective bubble of an aesthetically pleasing narrative that softens the impact of reality; it exchanges contact with historical and psychological reality for one of a number of dubiously subjectivist ideals: contentment, aesthetic self-expressiveness, or subjective meaningfulness.

PROZAC INSIGHT

> *Since you only live once, why not do it as a blonde? Why not as a peppy blonde?*
>
> —Peter Kramer, *Listening to Prozac* (1993, p. 15)

Psycho-pharmacology is only in its adolescence, but like all adolescents it is experimenting with cosmetics for the first time. Just as there are now medications powerful enough to induce global personality and mood changes without serious side effects, so there are now psychiatrists willing to give these drugs to people who have no diagnosable psychological disorders but simply require a touch of pharmacologically boosted mood brightening or personality enhancement for such varied reasons as lifestyle management and career performance.

Extravagant claims have been made about the cosmetic benefits of drugs like Prozac to remake the self (Kramer, 1993; see also Cebuliak, 1995): It gives confidence to the habitually timid, brashness to the sensitive, and the social skills of a salesman to the introvert. People who have lived for many years with inhibiting but nonpathological character traits (e.g., shyness, melancholy, hesitancy, feelings of vulnerability) not only report feeling better than well on the drug; they also identify wholeheartedly with the new medicated self, and disavow the old premedicated self, which they view as alien. The drug, it is claimed, has enabled them to finally be themselves and to finally know who they really are.

From a clinical point of view, Prozac and other SSRIs have been relatively successful in the treatment of depression and other psychological ailments. They have helped many people live meaningful and productive lives, where only years before these same people would have struggled with debilitating depression.[3] But the goals of clinical psycho-pharmacology are quite distinct from those of cosmetic psycho-pharmacology; success in the former does not entail success in the latter. And just as there is a distinction between clinically necessary surgery and cosmetic surgery, so there is still a clear line of demarcation between clinically necessary pharmacologic treatment and mere lifestyle management or mood brightening, despite the intensifying nonmedical pressures from the pharmaceutical industry and the performance-oriented marketplace to see this distinction blurred.

What then is to be made of the puzzling claim that Prozac has restored people with no clearly discernable diagnosable psychological disorders to some original state—that it is a neuro-chemical short-cut to the real self, a "self that feels true, normal and whole" (Kramer, 1993, p. 20)? Does it make sense to say that the real self is the self on the drug, and that insight is drug-induced? Does Prozac yield accurate and truth-tracking insight, or merely tranquillized self-contentment that, with the help of undetectably lowered epistemic standards, masquerades as insight?

---

[3]The critique of Prozac that I am defending here is not a critique of the effectiveness of Prozac as an antidepressant or as an aid to people who suffer from diagnosable psychological disorders; it is a critique of Prozac only insofar as it is used as a cosmetic personality enhancer in those cases where there is no diagnosable psychological disorder.

In *Listening to Prozac,* Kramer (1993) argued that Prozac functions both as a chemical prosthetic that enhances self-perception and as a chemical agent that transforms the self that is perceived. Patients on cosmetic Prozac experience "a sense of a leap forward, of communication with aspects of the self that had been closed off" for many years (p. 106). Emotions and memories, he claimed, are more accessible than they have ever been. The drug "seems to aid rather than inhibit the struggle to locate the self" (p. 278). "Many patients, including some who may never have had a diagnosable mental illness, are better able to explore both their past and their current circumstances while they are taking Prozac" (p. 278). Finally, Prozac helps to redefine patients' understanding of what is essential to their identity, and what is intrusive and pathological (Kramer, 1993). While on the drug, they accept that it is "an occasionally necessary adjunct to the maintenance" of their identity (p. 20).

At the same time, however, Prozac is claimed to transform the newly located self. Patients are bolder, less troubled by habitual worries, more at one with themselves, keener of thought, and more open to ordinary pleasures (Kramer, 1993); they "relate differently to their anxiety, guilt, shame, timidity, depression and low self-worth, experiencing them no longer as uniquely human or preferentially responsive to insight and self-understanding" (Kramer, 1993, p. 282). Self-reports of patients on cosmetically prescribed Prozac include: "I feel like myself without the lead boots," "I am myself without swimming through Jell-O," "I am myself on a good day, although I've never had days this good," and "I am myself without fears."

What Kramer fails to mention is that if there is such a state as pharmacologically boosted insight, then there must also be such states as pharmacologically induced self-deception and self-ignorance. There is no pharmacological cure for epistemological ailments such as falsity, illusion, bad reasoning, self-deception, or ignorance; a pill may enhance the desire for insight, and may surreptitiously alter the threshold for the acceptability of certain kinds of insight, but it cannot guarantee that any newly acquired insight is true. All the epistemic possibilities for self-relating that are open to people in the drugless state are also there in the drugged state: Insights are still to be assessed on independent grounds as true or false, plausible or implausible, complete or incomplete, well-supported or under-evidenced. Thus with pharmacologically boosted personality enhancement comes the possibility of pharmacologically boosted self-alienation; with pharmacologically boosted autobiographical memory comes the possibility of pharmacologically boosted false memory. Epistemically, nothing has changed from the drugless to the drugged condition. There is no such thing as insight on the cheap, with none of the hard work that characterizes drugless routes to insight.

Perhaps here it is helpful to remember Spinoza's logical maxim *omnis determinatio est negatio* (all determination is a negation). For every avenue of self-perception opened up by cosmetic uses of Prozac, other avenues—those involving anxiety, guilt, melancholy, or shame—are closed down. The drug distances patients from a disclosive dimension of their experience: It is experience shrinking, rendering experience more manageable and pleasant, but also less variegated, and less accessible to extremes of emotion, mood, and thought. As patients are relieved of the need to struggle head-on with the hardships of life, they come to reconceptualize as illness, and as pharmacologically malleable, aspects of the self that may be normal.

Like positive illusions and narrative fabrications, Prozac can serve as a protective psychic crutch that softens the impact of negative, unsupportive, or ambiguous feedback. But there is a price for securing drug-induced self-contentment at the expense of diminished contact with reality. Walker Percy's (1987) novel *The Thanatos Syndrome* drives home this point, depicting the bizarre social consequences that arise when the public water supply is laced with a powerful personality-altering drug called Heavy Sodium. People who are normally shy, anxious, and neurotic suddenly become bold, competitive, and thick-skinned: There occurs "a sloughing away of the old terrors, worries, rages, a shedding of guilt like last year's snakeskin, and in its place is a mild fond vacancy, a species of animal good spirits" (Percy, 1987, p. 21).

Perhaps this seems like a trade worth making: medicated contentment and mood brightening in exchange for anxious moods, uncertainties, and vulnerabilities. But Percy regarded Heavy Sodium as a soul-deadening distraction. The person who is anxious, confused, or suffering is in touch with a dimension of human experience for which there is no adequate chemical substitute: He or she may be less ill than the person who is tranquillized, artificially content, and superficially insightful. On the drug, Percy wrote, people are not "hurting, they are not worrying the same old bone, but there is something missing, not merely the old terrors but a sense in each of her—her what? her self?" (pp. 21–22).

Heavy Sodium shrinks the range of human experience. The emotions it tranquillizes—shame, guilt, anxiety, sorrow—are not the symptoms of pathologies, like cold sweats are to fevers or dizziness is to vertigo; they are meaningful and potentially edifying ontological moods,[4] disclosive of

---

[4]This is a term used by Heidegger (1927/1962), Sartre (1943/1969), Ricoeur (1986), and other existential phenomenologists to characterize moods such as anxiety, boredom, nausea, and joy—moods that have the power to awaken human beings from illusions and false securities and to disclose important truths about the human condition. Like Heidegger and Sartre, Percy characterized anxiety as "a summons to authentic existence" (1991, p. 259).

self and world. Percy (1991) described them as signposts of the quest each person is pursuing in his or her life: signposts in a strange land.

Heidegger (1977) once remarked that technology is the destiny of Western reason. The advent of normalizing and cosmetic psychotechnologies is clearly a culturally parochial phenomenon. The perception of one's nose as too big or one's wrinkles as too ugly can only be made in a culture that treats these features as flaws; similarly, the perception of grief, despondency, or anxiety as undesirable can only be made in a productivity-driven culture that treats these states as abnormal and in which the threshold for suffering has been systematically lowered over time. In a culture that takes shiny happy people as the psychological norm, more and more dimensions of human experience will be threatened with cosmetic-pharmacological extinction.

EXPERIENTIALIST INSIGHT

Truth is usually considered to be a forensic matter; it is public, accessible, intersubjectively endorsable, and objective. We are as skeptical of truth-claims based exclusively on private experiences as we are of religious truth-claims requiring us for their verification as a one-way religious conversion.

Experientialist epistemology, and its offshoot in experientialist psychotherapy, challenge this objectivist bias and in so doing call into question the ideal of accurate contact with reality. In its weak version, experientialism defends the claim that nothing can adequately substitute for the access to the real that is supplied by personal experience; no one can understand better than I can what I have experienced. The most authentic kind of truth is therefore first-person; it serves as the ground and touchstone for subsequent reasoning. In its strong version, experientialism is committed to the claim that no one, logically, can refute or correct truth-claims based on firsthand lived experience. From the evidentiary point of view, all first-person experiential reports are intrinsically valid and truth-bearing.

Variations of weak and strong experientialism are defended in postcolonialist theory, feminist theory, Foucauldian genealogical analysis, anti-psychiatry, as well as in psychotherapy devoted to the recovery of repressed memories. Common to all of these disciplines is the concern to rectify the injustices of those practices where paternalistic power-mongering masquerades as epistemic authority. These are practices where disinterested masters of truth, sitting in judgment on a person's testimony—and thereby validating it, correcting it, or dismissing it—can cause that person to doubt the veracity of his or her own experiences and his or her own voice. Experientialists argue that one's experience as a member of an oppressed minority, for example, yields access to a fund of evidence that no nonmember's evidence (or evidentiary criteria) can rationally supplant. It also insures a certain epistemic autonomy: Insights based on personal experience are one's own and cannot be authorized or prescribed by anyone else. The proprietary character of the self-relationship guarantees the authority of one's knowledge-claims.

Experientialism has some degree of plausibility: What could be truer than a person's own account of what he or she has lived through firsthand? For certain kinds of claims, especially claims about the private self, personal experience is often taken as incontestable evidence. My self-concept, for instance, is intrinsically valid not because it is objectively true or false, but precisely because it is my own and concerns me in a way that no one else can possibly replicate; no third-person observer, however well-informed, can challenge the validity of my firsthand experience and concept of who I am. As Collingwood (1956) argued, to respect the claim of firsthand experience is to respect the autonomy of the person experiencing.[5]

One of the drawbacks of strong experientialism, however, is that it is committed to holding that first-person truth-claims are logically unassailable. There is no way to rationally decide between competing claims about facts if these are expressions of personal experience. My claim that "A is the case" is as legitimate as your claim that "A is not the case" because each is based on irrefutable personal experience. This has the undesirable consequence that contradictory claims are simultaneously true (Grant, 1987).

There is another drawback of strong experientialism as an approach to psychotherapy, and as a supporting theoretical orientation for the development of therapeutic insight. By underestimating the role of extraexperiential reality and third-personal evidentiary criteria in the assessment of truth-claims and insights reported during therapy, experientialism opens the way for personal fantasy and mnemnic distortion, in much the same way as does narrative psychotherapy. False memory syndrome is the most notorious example of this. Therapists convinced—without independent evidence—that they are on the trail of repressed memories of childhood sexual abuse may unwittingly participate in the patient's confabulation, construing every feeling and glimmer of memory as evidence for the reality of abuse—as if the reality of the abuse is established by the memories themselves.

For therapist and patient, as Neisser (1994) pointed out, the vividness of the memories that first come to the surface during the therapy, and "the coherence of the narrative that they support, seem to be self-validating" (p. 4). Despite the lack of independent evidence, "the presumptive expe-

---

[5]From this can be derived a principle of respect for persons. Treating a person as a person involves taking that person's sense of herself or himself into account in a respectful manner, without adopting toward it a mastering or hermeneutically suspicious stance.

rience of childhood sexual abuse becomes the turning point of the patient's life narrative" (Neisser, 1994, p. 3).

This disregard of historical fact, complicated by the various common factors cited earlier, can wreak havoc with the development of therapeutic insight. Patients who are uncertain whether they have in fact been abused may be suggestible enough in the volatized therapeutic setting to endorse psychologically and historically incorrect interpretations. With the support of the therapist, they may formulate for themselves subjectively plausible but psychologically and historically incorrect insights based on evidentiary criteria that have been adopted uncritically as a result of exposure to the therapist's experientialist orientation and evidence-fishing.

In the now-famous treatise on repressed memory and child abuse, *The Courage to Heal*, Bass and Davis (1994) offered experientialist advice to possible survivors of childhood abuse who are uncertain about the status of their memories as confabulated or real: Honor your own truth. The issue of whether a memory of abuse is objectively true or mere fantasy, they claimed, is not relevant at the beginning of memory retrieval work: What matters is validating the victim's experience, without any master of truth intervening to deny it, redefine it, or pass judgment on it as objectively true or false (see Herman, 1992).

If other people demand factual evidence to back up the allegations of abuse, Bass and Davis (1994) advised that "you are not responsible for proving that you were abused" (p. 137). Moreover, the patient's own desire for objective confirmation of childhood abuse (e.g., by consulting pediatric records) must be tempered because it may be yet another way of continuing the denial and thereby playing into the hands of the abusive family's denial system. More harm may be occasioned by becoming caught up in the search for external proof rather than internal relief. Thus Bass and Davis's advice to therapists is the following:

> You must believe that your client was sexually abused, even if she sometimes doubts it herself. . . . If a client is unsure that she was abused but thinks she might have been, work as though she was. . . . [N]o one fantasizes abuse. . . . Be willing to believe the unbelievable. (pp. 345–349)

Although honoring your own truth may be good therapeutic advice for victims of childhood sexual abuse, it is disastrous for those who have not in fact suffered abuse but are in the hands of therapists convinced they have. It matters whether or not something happened and it matters that the truth is independently accessible and intersubjectively endorsable. Without preserving these distinctions, there would be no difference between unchecked fabrication and sober report and no difference between a false accusation and a true one (Neisser, 1994, pp. 2–3). Experientialist psychotherapy erects a kind of epistemic Maginot Line around the self to protect the validity of claims based on first-person experience, but it acheives this subjectivist ideal only at the cost of diminished contact with the reality of the past and the perspectives and knowledge-claims of others.

CONCLUSION

Hume remarked that errors in religion are dangerous, but that errors in philosophy are merely ridiculous. But the philosophical views underpinning clinical and social psychology's emphasis on the importance of personal fantasy, wishful thinking, positive illusion, subjective contentment—and their corresponding suspicion about the value of contact with reality—surely puts the lie to Hume's remark.

There is something unsettling about clinical and social psychology's willingness to exchange self-knowledge for contented self-ignorance or creative self-deception and its willingness to embrace positive illusions, narrative fabrications, or pharmacological quick-fixes for what may well be normal reactions to life's hardships and challenges. As the threshold for hardship tolerance creeps lower and lower, normalizing psychotechnologies offer more and more tempting forms of rapid solace, tapping an already well-tapped propensity for denial and self-deception. Well-being, however, is not enhanced by making people less aware and less self-aware; that is, less responsive to the real, and more immune to suffering. This only diminishes their humanity and shrinks the range of experience.

The more people can get used to looking reality in the face without becoming dependent on the crutch of comforting illusions, chemical prosthetics, or placebo insights, the greater the range of human responses—and human responsibility—open to them (Jopling, 1996a).

Perhaps the most concrete argument against comforting user-friendly illusions was made by the poet Housman, in addressing the relative merits of a life of poetic sensitivity and a life of alcohol-fueled pipe dreaming.[6] Housman's suggestion is that it is simply too difficult to sustain a consistent and robust level of alcoholic illusion for very long. Reality catches up eventually: The mischief is, but it will not last.

> Ale, man, ale's the stuff to drink
> For fellows whom it hurts to think:
> Look into the pewterpot
> To see the world as the world's not.
> And faith, 'tis pleasant till 'tis past:

---

[6]I would like to thank Dick Neisser for informing me of this apt poetic example.

The mischief is that 'twill not last.
Oh I have been to Ludlow fair
And left my necktie God knows where,
And carried half-way home, or near,
Pints and quarts of Ludlow beer:
Then the world seemed none so bad,
And I myself a sterling lad;
And down in lovely muck I've lain,
Happy till I woke again.
Then I saw the morning sky:
Heigho, the tale was all a lie;
The world, it was the old world yet,
And I was I; my things were wet,
And nothing now remained to do,
But begin the game anew.
(Housman, 1946, pp. 88–89)

REFERENCES

Bass, E., & Davis, L. (1994). *The courage to heal: A guide for women survivors of child sexual abuse* (3rd ed.). New York: HarperPerennial.

Carr, D. (1986). *Time, narrative and history.* Bloomington: Indiana University Press.

Cebuliak, C. (1995). Life as a blonde: The use of Prozac in the 90's. *Alberta Law Review, 33*(3), 612–625.

Collingwood, R. G. (1956). *The idea of history.* New York: Oxford University Press.

Descartes, R. (1641/1993). *Meditations on first philosophy.* (Trans., D. Cress.) Indianapolis, IN: Hackett.

Ecclesiastes. (1962). Ecclesiastes, 1:18. In H. May & B. Metzger (Eds.), *The Oxford annotated Bible* (Revised Standard Ed., pp. 805–814). New York: Oxford University Press.

Eysenck, H. (1965). The effects of psychotherapy. *International Journal of Psychiatry, 1,* 97–168.

Farrell, B. A. (1981). *The standing of psychoanalysis.* Oxford, England: Oxford University Press.

Frank, J. D., & Frank, J. B. (1991). *Persuasion and healing* (3rd ed.). Baltimore: Johns Hopkins University Press.

Freud, S. (1964). Constructions in analysis. In J. Strachey (Ed. and Trans.), *The Standard Edition of the Complete Psychological Works of Sigmund Freud* (Vol. 23, pp. 255–269). London: Hogarth.

Grant, J. (1987). I feel therefore I am: A critique of female experience as the basis for a feminist epistemology. *Women and Politics, 7*(3), 99–114.

Gusdorf, G. (1980). Conditions and limits of autobiography. In J. Olney (Ed.), *Autobiography: Essays theoretical and critical* (pp. 101–123). Princeton, NJ: Princeton University Press.

Haggard, H. (1934). *The doctor in history.* New Haven, CT: Yale University Press.

Haley, J. (1963). *Strategies of psychotherapy.* New York: Grune & Stratton.

Heidegger, M. (1927/1962). *Being and time.* (Trans., J. Macquarrie & E. Robinson). New York: HarperCollins.

Heidegger, M. (1977). *The question concerning technology and other essays.* (Trans., W. Lovitt.) New York: Harper & Row.

Held, B. (1995). *Back to reality: A critique of post-modern theory in therapy.* New York: Norton.

Herman, J. L. (1992). *Trauma and recovery.* New York: Basic Books.

Housman, A. E. (1946). "A Shropshire Lad." *The collected poems of A. E. Housman* (pp. 88–89). London: Jonathon Cape.

Ibsen, H. (1968). *The wild duck.* (Trans., D. B. Christiani). New York: Norton.

Jahoda, M. (1953). The meaning of psychological health. *Social Casework, 34*, 349.

Jahoda, M. (1958). *Current concepts of positive mental health.* New York: Basic Books.

Janet, P. (1925). *Psychological healing: A historical and clinical study.* (Trans., E. Paul & C. Paul). New York: Macmillan.

Jopling, D. A. (1996a). 'Take away the life-lie': Positive illusions and creative self-deception. *Philosophical Psychology, 9*(4), 525–544.

Jopling, D. A. (1996b). Philosophical counselling, truth, and self-interpretation. *Journal of Applied Philosophy, 13*(3), 297–310.

Kramer, P. (1993). *Listening to Prozac.* New York: Penguin.

Lain Entralgo, P. (1970). *The therapy of the word in classical antiquity.* (Trans., L. J. Rather & J. M. Sharp). New Haven, CT: Yale University Press.

Lévi-Strauss, C. (1963). *Structural anthropology.* New York: Basic Books.

Luborsky, L., Singer, B., & Luborsky, L. (1975). Comparative studies of psychotherapies. *Archives of General Psychiatry, 32*, 995–1008.

Martin, M. (Ed.). (1985). *Self-deception and self-understanding.* Lawrence: University of Kansas Press.

McNamee, S., & Gergen, K. (Eds.). (1992). *Therapy as social construction.* Newbury Park, CA: Sage.

Neisser, U. (1988). Five kinds of self-knowledge. *Philosophical Psychology, 1*, 35–59.

Neisser, U. (1994). Self-narratives: True and false. In U. Neisser & R. Fivush (Eds.), *The remembering self* (pp. 1–18). New York: Cambridge University Press.

Nietzsche, F. (1886/1966). *Beyond good and evil.* (Trans., W. Kaufmann). New York: Vintage Press.

Nietzsche, F. (1968). *The will to power.* (Trans., W. Kaufmann & R. J. Hollingdale). New York: Vintage Press.

O'Neill, E. (1957). *The iceman cometh.* New York: Vintage Books.

Percy, W. (1987). *The Thanatos syndrome.* New York: Ivy/Ballantine.

Percy, W. (1991). The coming crisis in psychiatry. In W. Percy, *Signposts in a strange land.* New York: Farrar, Straus & Giroux.

Plato. (1961). *Charmides.* (Trans., B. Jowett). In E. Hamilton & H. Cairns (Eds.), *The complete dialogues of Plato* (pp. 100–122). Princeton, NJ: Princeton University Press.

Ricoeur, P. (1986). *Fallible man.* (Trans., C. A. Kelby). New York: Fordham University Press.

Rorty, A. O. (1975). Adaptivity and self-knowledge. *Inquiry, 18,* 1–22.

Rorty, A. O. (1994). User-friendly self-deception. *Philosophy, 69,* 211–228.

Sartre, J. P. (1943/1969). *Being and nothingness.* (Trans. H. Barnes). London: Methuen.

Shapiro, A. K., & Morris, L. (1978). The placebo effect in medical and psychological therapies. In S. Garfield & A. Bergin (Eds.), *Handbook of psychotherapy and behavior change: An empirical analysis* (2nd ed., pp. 369–410). New York: Wiley.

Spence, D. (1982). *Narrative truth and historical truth: Meaning and interpretation in psychoanalysis.* New York: Norton.

Spinoza, B. (1677/1992). *The ethics.* (Trans., S. Shirley). Indianapolis, IN: Hackett.

Strupp, H. (1972). Needed: A reformulation of the psychotherapeutic influence. *International Journal of Psychiatry, 10,* 114–120.

Strupp, H., & Luborsky, L. (Eds.). (1962). *Research in psychotherapy.* Washington, DC: American Psychological Association.

Sundberg, N. D. (1966). The acceptability of 'fake' versus *bona fide* personality test interpretations. *Journal of Abnormal Social Psychology, 50,* 145–147.

Taylor, S. (1989). *Positive illusions: Creative self-deception and the healthy mind.* New York: Basic Books.

Taylor, S., & Brown, J. (1988). Illusion and well-being: A social-psychological perspective on mental health. *Psychological Bulletin, 103,* 193–210.

Chapter 14

How Does an Advisor Influence a Student?: A Case Study

Yohtaro Takano
University of Tokyo

How do academic advisors exert influence on their graduate students? Do they simply transmit knowledge? Or do they impose their theoretical preference on their students? Not always. In this chapter, I present my own case as an instance. More specifically, I review my past studies while showing how they were influenced by my own advisor, Professor Ulric Neisser.

I was a foreign graduate student from Japan at Cornell University from 1981 to 1985. As soon as my first year started, I asked Professor Neisser to become my academic advisor. After a couple of weeks, he agreed, fortunately. Although he moved to Emory University after the end of my second year, he continued to be my advisor and awarded me a Ph.D. after 2 years of supervision by mail.

When I was enrolled in Cornell University, I was already over 30 years old and had completed the course work in a Ph.D. program at the University of Tokyo. At that time, a doctoral degree was not awarded to a graduate student who had just completed a Ph.D. program in the fields of humanities and social sciences at Japanese universities. (Incidentally, the system is now rapidly changing.) However, I decided to repeat graduate work at Cornell not simply to get a degree. I wanted to find the know-how of conducting original studies in cognitive psychology.

It was as late as 1976 that I learned the very existence of cognitive psychology. In psychology, the time lag between the United States and Japan was so large. (Incidentally, it has shrunk considerably since then owing to the recent speedup of information flow.) At that time, Japanese experimental psychology was still dominated by behaviorism. I chose psychology as my undergraduate major because I wanted to study epistemology not only philosophically but also scientifically. I was deeply disappointed by the psychology that I found. How can one study epistemology with rats? No cognitive psychologist will have difficulty in imagining how much I was excited by my first contact with cognitive psychology. It had already actualized scientific epistemology! Furthermore, I faced all at once the whole accomplishments accumulated over 10 years after the "cognitive revolution." They were dazzling and overwhelming.

Japanese was one of the many languages into which Professor Neisser's (1967) *Cognitive Psychology* was translated. It was this book that sent me to Cornell. However, he had already changed (Neisser, 1976). It took me a long time to realize that his change was quite radical. I needed more than 5 years after leaving Cornell to understand the real significance of his ecological approach.

A THEORY OF INFORMATION TYPES

Before going to Cornell, I had written a paper (Takano, 1981) on the mental imagery debate: whether the mental representation of imagery is like a picture or propositions (Kosslyn, 1980; Pylyshyn, 1973, 1984; see Tye, 1991, for review). I analyzed the debate from a philosophical point of view and concluded that it could not be settled decisively by any empirical data. I had two reasons for this conclusion: First, the concepts, picture and proposition, were not defined strictly enough so that they could be conceived of as mutually exclusive. Second, the core assumption about the nature of a picture or that of a proposition could be defended in the face of apparently contradictory evidence by adding appropriate peripheral assumptions, as the Duhem–Quine thesis (Duhem, 1954; Quine, 1953) maintains. The presence of this paper led Professor Neisser to believe that I should choose mental imagery as the subject of my dissertation study.

I focused on the presence and absence of "mental rotation" (Shepard & Cooper, 1982; Shepard & Metzler, 1971). I attempted to construct an account that would explain all the related empirical findings without any inconsistency. I soon realized that this issue was closely related to form recognition, especially to its success or failure due to the change in orientation (Marr, 1982; Rock, 1973). When I succeeded in explaining all the related empirical findings, I ended up with 11 different types of information that were supposed to be used for constructing the mental representation of a form. Some of them appeared to be redundant, however. Then I changed my goal of theory construction from comprehensiveness to simplicity. When I managed to reduce the number of information types from 11 to 4, it became difficult to proceed further. After struggling for further simplification, I found that the four information types are given as results of combining two dichotomies: the information that is affected by orientational change (*orientation-bound information*) and the one that is not (*orientation-free information*), on the one hand; and the information specifying basic figural elements (*elementary information*) and the one specifying how to combine them (*conjunctive information*), on the other. This finding enhanced confidence in the validity of the assumed four information types.

In a typical mental rotation experiment, subjects are required to discriminate between a rotated form and its mirror image (e.g., Shepard & Metzler, 1971). They differ solely in the information that specifies orientational relations among the figural elements: that is, the information that is conjunctive and orientation-bound (*relative orientation information*). Compare, for example, an upper-case letter *L* and its mirror image. The shorter line is to the right of the longer one in the original, whereas it is to the left in the mirror image. They do not differ in any other respects. This relative orientation information is modified by rotation. When *L* is rotated through 180° in the picture plane, for example, the shorter line is not to the right of the longer one but to its left. Therefore, the relative orientation information has to be made comparable in some way to judge whether a rotated form is identical to the original or to its mirror image. Mental rotation is one of the possible strategies. It is also the one most frequently used. Thus, subjects typically conduct mental rotation to align the orientations of forms when mirror-image discrimination is required. They do not have to conduct mental rotation when mirror-image discrimination is not required and thus they can utilize orientation-free information to discriminate among a given set of forms (e.g., Corballis & Nagourney, 1978; Eley, 1982).

I found ample evidence to support the orientation-bound/free distinction. However, I had little empirical basis to support the elementary/conjunctive distinction, though it was indirectly suggested by studies of perception. When I told Professor Neisser the outline of this information type theory for the first time, he informed me of the feature integration theory (Treisman & Gelade, 1980), which had not become a "modal model" as it is today. It had exactly proposed the elementary/conjunctive distinction along with persuasive empirical evidence, though the issue of orientation was not included in its scope. It convinced me of the validity of my own theory.

I conducted seven experiments to confirm the basic assumptions of my theory and reported them in my dissertation, which was published later (Takano, 1989a). In one of the subsequent studies (Takano, 1993), I confirmed that the information type theory is valid in the case of depth rotation as well as picture plane rotation, though the classification of information into orientation-bound/free has to be made somewhat differently.

Quite a few researchers seem to consider the presence or absence of mental rotation as a direct indicator of whether mental representation of form is orientation-bound or orientation-free. However, they have no one-to-one correspondence. Mental rotation is not an automatic process but a controlled strategy that can be invoked when unnecessary (Takano, 1989a, Experiment 2) or replaced by other strategies even when necessary (Takano, Takenaka, Nagai, & Handa, 1998). We have to be careful in inferring the properties of a form's mental representation from the presence or absence of mental rotation.

MIRROR REVERSAL

While examining mental rotation experiments, the task of which was mirror image discrimination, I encountered the mirror reversal problem: Why does a mirror reverse left and right without reversing up and down? Optically, a plane mirror reverses neither left and right nor up and down; it reverses only front and back when we face it (see Gardner, 1964). Nevertheless, a clock's hands rotate counterclockwise and its figures look left–right reversed in a mirror; a watch around your left wrist is seen around the right wrist of your own mirror image. Everybody knows this mirror reversal as a phenomenon; however, its reason has been a mystery for centuries. Although a number of attempts have been made to elucidate the reason of the mirror reversal by philosophers, physicists, mathematicians, as well as psychologists, no satisfactory solution has ever been obtained (Ittelson, Mowafy, & Magid, 1991; Morris, 1993).

In 1988, I focused my effort on this problem because my chronic fatigue syndrome did not allow me to conduct experimental studies. Fortunately, I succeeded in finding a consistent account of all the phenomena related to the mirror reversal (Takano, 1997, 1998). The key to the solution was to realize that the so-called mirror reversal is actually composed of three different types of reversal that are produced by different underlying principles. The typical instance of the Type I reversal is the reversal of our own mirror image; that of the Type II is the reversal of an alphanumeric character. Both of them cannot be explained by optics alone. By contrast, the Type III reversal can be explained in purely optical terms and is not related to particular kinds of objects. The mirror reversal problem was unexpectedly difficult because every past attempt implicitly presupposed a single principle underlying all the mirror reversal phenomena.

The difference between the Types I and II will be intuitively realized by attending to the following fact. Suppose that a viewer with a watch around the left wrist faces a mirror. The viewer's mirror image has a watch around the right wrist; hence a left–right mirror reversal. However, this right is the direction that is judged from the mirror image's viewpoint. By contrast, the position of the real watch, left, is judged from the real viewer's viewpoint. If the direction of the mirror image is likewise judged from the real viewer's viewpoint, the mirror image watch is also on the left; hence no reversal in direction. In short, the left–right mirror reversal is recognized only when the left and right of the mirror image are judged from the mirror image's viewpoint, whereas those of the real viewer are judged from the real viewer's viewpoint. In the case of a character, however, the left–right mirror reversal is recognized when the left and right of the real character and those of its mirror image are both judged from the real viewer's viewpoint. The viewer does not have to assume the mirror image character's viewpoint. Thus, it is evident from the mirror reversal of a viewer and that of a character are produced by different underlying principles, respectively.

With past studies on object recognition in mind, the above "viewpoints" can be identified with the following two coordinate systems: A *viewer-centered coordinate system* (Marr, 1982) is used to recognize the orientational relations (i.e., relative orientation information; see earlier this chapter) among figural elements of a real object. In general, this orientational framework is a basis to encode perceptual input and is always aligned with a viewer's body. A *subject-centered coordinate system* (Takano, 1989a) is used to recognize the orientational relations among figural elements of a viewer's own mirror image. In general, this orientational framework is a basis to construct and process an object's mental representation. Although it may be also aligned with a viewer's body, it can be rotated away from the body to recognize the object's representation from a different hypothetical viewpoint.

How can we explain the Type I reversal? Suppose that you have a watch around the left wrist while facing a mirror. You judge that the real watch is around the left wrist of your real body in reference to the viewer-centered coordinate system. To judge the position of the watch in your own mirror image, you will automatically rotate your subject-centered coordinate system through 180° about a vertical axis to assume your own mirror image's viewpoint. This rotation reverses both left–right and front–back axes of the subject-centered coordinate system, which can be easily understood with basic geometry. The front–back direction of the mirror image, which has already been reversed optically by the mirror, looks unchanged when judged by this reversed front–back axis. However, the left–right direction, which has not been reversed by the mirror, looks reversed when judged by this reversed left–right axis. Accordingly, you judge that the watch in your own mirror image is around its right wrist. When you compare the position of the real watch to that of the mirror image watch, you will thus recognize a left–right reversal.

Why do we rotate the subject-centered coordinate system through 180° about a vertical axis? It is because this rotation is appropriate to assume our own mirror image's viewpoint. But why do we try to assume our own mirror image's viewpoint?

Our body is approximately bilaterally symmetrical. Accordingly, we have to use the words, left and right, to specify a symmetric body part (e.g., "Raise your right hand"). It is our convention to judge such left and right in reference to the orientational framework of the person who possesses that body instead of the orientational framework of our own. Suppose, for example, that a surgeon faces a patient to conduct an operation on the left lung. The surgeon has to open the chest that is on the left in reference to the patient's orientational framework. Otherwise, the consequence will be disastrous for both of them. Usually, we are even unaware of the fact that we use different orientational frameworks when we specify body parts, depending on whether they belong to ourselves or to others. The employment of an orientational framework aligned with another person has become so automatic that we apply it to our own mirror image as well in judging its left and right. This is why we assume our own mirror image's viewpoint.

The Type II reversal is recognized between a mirror image of an object and its mental representation. The orientational relations in the mirror image are judged in reference to a viewer-centered coordinate system, which is aligned with the viewer's body; those in the mental representation are judged in reference to a subject-centered coordinate system, which is also aligned with the viewer's body. Suppose, for example, that you are looking at an alphanumeric character in a mirror while facing it. On the one hand, your mental representation of that character is in the position from which it has to be rotated through 180° about a vertical axis, if it has to be aligned with the real character. This means that both left–right and front–back directions are reversed between them. On the other hand, only the front–back direction is reversed optically between the real character and its mirror image. When you compare the mirror image with your mental representation, you will find no front–back reversal because this direction is reversed in both. However, you will recognize a left–right reversal because this direction is reversed only in your mental representation. This is why the mirror image of a character looks left–right reversed. In this Type II reversal, no rotation of a subject-centered coordinate system is involved; and a comparison is made between a mirror image and a mental representation, not between a mirror image and a real object.

The Type III reversal is observed when the left–right direction of an object is perpendicular to a mirror. Suppose that you are standing in front of a mirror while showing your left shoulder to the mirror and holding a sheet of paper carrying a character so that it is perpendicular to the mirror. Then you will see that your own mirror image has a watch around the right wrist though the real watch is around your left wrist, and that the mirror image of the character is left-right reversed. These reversals are produced purely by the mirror, which optically reverses the direction that is perpendicular to its surface. When the up–down direction is perpendicular to a mirror, therefore, an up–down reversal is observed instead of a left–right one. When a tree or a person is reflected on the surface of a lake, for example, it looks upside down with the left and right unchanged.

Professor Neisser was the first person who appreciated the validity of this account of mine. Without his backup, it would have been difficult for me to publish this study in English (Takano, 1998).

FOREIGN LANGUAGE EFFECT

The most difficult problem for a foreign student is language. Psycholinguistic studies have shown that the later one begins to learn a second language, the lower the level of proficiency that can be attained (e.g., Johnson & Newport, 1989). I began to learn oral English when I was nearly 30 years old. It is not surprising that I had extreme difficulty in aural–oral English. The difficulty was much more far-reaching than I had expected before going to the United States. It was not confined to communication. While using English, I felt that I was childish and stupid, and moreover, that my personality was distorted. I even felt that I had lost human dignity. This experience naturally led me to become interested in language. In addition, Professor Neisser's seminar on language and thought provided me with an opportunity to think deeply about their relation.

When I took part in discussions at seminars in Japan, I had no difficulty in finding out, for example, what was wrong in another member's statement and what would be the most effective way to refute it. When I was attending seminars at Cornell, I had much difficulty in understanding what others were arguing in English. What was more important, even when I realized what they said, no ideas came to mind as to how I should cope with those statements. I felt that I had become an idiot.

Initially, I attributed all the difficulty to my poor ability with English, as most foreign language users do. After more than a year of such experience, however, I began to suspect that my difficulty might actually consist of two components: the difficulty in using English and that in thinking. In other words, I suspected that my thinking ability might be actually lowered while I was using English. At that time, I was attending Professor Neisser's seminar on attention. While learning about empirical and theoretical studies of attention, I found the idea that using an unskilled foreign language causes a real decline of thinking ability not absurd theoretically.

When we try to perform two demanding cognitive tasks in parallel, they interfere with each other and the performance of one or both declines (e.g.,

Broadbent, 1958; Treisman, 1969). However, extensive practice reduces or even extinguishes the interference (e.g., Hirst, Spelke, Reaves, Caharack, & Neisser, 1980; Spelke, Hirst, & Neisser, 1976). Meanwhile, ordinary verbal activities (e.g., conversation and negotiation) consist of two cognitive tasks: linguistic processing and thinking. Usually, we have to perform both in parallel: We have to think while listening or speaking. As a result, the performance of one or both should decline. We typically sacrifice thinking because we have to complete linguistic processing if we want to make meaningful communication: We cannot focus on thinking while ignoring what is being said or emitting incomprehensible sounds. When we are using our own native language, the decline of thinking ability is not serious because we have been practicing the dual task of native language processing and thinking extensively for our lifetime. However, when we have to use a foreign language in which we are not so proficient as in our own native language, the decline of thinking ability should be serious because of much less practice. Thus, our thinking ability should be lower when we are using a foreign language than when we are using our own native language. I named this phenomenon the *foreign language effect.*

I have to stress that the foreign language effect is not equal to the well-known difficulty in using a foreign language. Although the former can be considered as a side effect of the latter, they are separate phenomena in principle. The latter is a difficulty with linguistic processing (e.g., parsing), whereas the former is a difficulty with nonlinguistic information processing. However, they are not incompatible: We may well suffer from both at the same time. The foreign language effect is not a permanent damage to intelligence: Our thinking ability declines temporarily only while we are actually using a foreign language. Therefore, this effect has to be distinguished from the debated retardation in intellectual development of bilinguals (see Macnamara, 1966; Peal & Lambert, 1962).

I employed the dual-task paradigm to verify the predicted foreign language effect while separating it from the well-known linguistic difficulty in using a foreign language: I asked my subjects to perform a linguistic task and a thinking task concurrently. In the linguistic task, they had to orally answer easy questions (e.g., "Is a lion an animal that lives in water?") that were read at a constant rate. The questions were asked in Japanese in one condition; in English in the other. The thinking task was either calculation or intelligence test problems designed to assess spatial reasoning ability (e.g., maze and pattern matching). These problems were printed on paper and the subjects answered with a pencil. It is important to note that no language was used at all in the thinking task. The subjects had to perform both tasks in parallel: several minutes of torture. When I was at Cornell, I tested foreign students from Japan. When I was later teaching at Waseda University in Japan, my student tested native speakers of English.

In these experiments (Takano & Noda, 1993), the performance in the thinking task was significantly and evidently lower when the foreign language was used in the concurrent linguistic task than when the native language was used. These results were common to both groups of subjects. The observed decline in the thinking task performance cannot be attributed directly to the well-known linguistic difficulty in using a foreign language because no foreign language was used in the thinking task. Thus, the foreign language effect was experimentally verified while separated from the linguistic difficulty per se.

When I was at Cornell, I told my prediction of this effect to a foreign graduate student from Germany. He insisted that he was not suffering from lowered thinking ability while using English. His English was obviously better than mine. Then I suspected a relation between the magnitude of foreign language effect and linguistic similarity. Suppose that he and I had learned English for a comparable period of time. Nevertheless, he should have been more proficient in English than I because German is much more similar to English than Japanese. Both German and English belong to the Germanic branch of the Indo-European family, whereas Japanese is close to the Altaic family. The more proficient in a foreign language, the smaller the foreign language effect. This may be the reason why the foreign language effect did not appear real for the German student.

Later, my student and I tested this hypothesis (Takano & Noda, 1995). In the same dual-task paradigm, we compared Japanese students with foreign students from Germany, employing English as a common foreign language. Although the length of learning English was a little longer for the Japanese-speakers, the performance was better for the German-speakers in the linguistic task when it was given in English. More important, the magnitude of foreign language effect in the thinking task was much smaller for the German-speakers as predicted, though it was still significant statistically. We replicated these results with students from Korea and those from English-speaking countries, employing Japanese as a common foreign language. Both Korean and Japanese are close to the Altaic family and similar to each other; English is very different from these languages. Although the length of learning Japanese was comparable, the Korean-speakers outperformed the English-speakers in the linguistic task when it was given in Japanese. More important, the magnitude of foreign language effect in the thinking task was much smaller for the Korean speakers, as predicted. Thus, we concluded that a foreign language more similar to a native language causes a smaller decline of thinking ability.

I also found that an observer responds to the decline in the thinking ability of a foreign language user by underestimating the user's intelligence (Takano, Saito, & Nagai, 1998). This means that the foreign language effect has an important social implication. We routinely make intuitive assessments about the intelligence of a person we meet (Sternberg, Conway, Ketron, & Bernstein, 1981). When a foreigner uses our language, we usually try to ignore erroneous or childish expressions because most of us have some idea about the difficulty in using a foreign language. Our effort may not be 100% successful due to our underestimation of that difficulty as well as insufficient discount (Ross, Amabile, & Steinmetz, 1977). At any rate, we try to base our intuitive assessment of intelligence on the contents of the foreigner's speech. However, this strategy may be grossly misleading: We may confidently underestimate the foreigner's intelligence due to the foreign language effect. If the presence of the foreign language effect is known to the public, however, many educated people will make an attempt to avoid this underestimation, and thus international misunderstanding may be reduced to some extent.

LINGUISTIC RELATIVITY

When I was at Cornell, Professor Neisser held a seminar on cross-cultural psychology together with other professors in psychology and anthropology. In this seminar, we discussed a book titled *The linguistic shaping of thought: A study in the impact of language on thinking in China and the West*, which had been just published (Bloom, 1981). It claimed that the ability of Chinese people in theoretical thinking is lower than that of Americans because the Chinese language lacks specialized grammatical devices that are present in English and alleged to play critical roles in theoretical thinking: Bloom called them *counterfactual* (i.e., subjunctive as in "If John had gone to the library, he would have seen Mary") and *entification* (i.e., nominalization as in "the approval of that measure by Congress" from "Congress approved that measure"). Bloom also reported a series of experiments that showed that Chinese college students were consistently inferior to American counterparts in forced-choice tests that were alleged to assess the ability of theoretical thinking.

It seemed to me that most people in the seminar were persuaded by Bloom's (1981) arguments and evidence. A young professor exclaimed, "That's why the Chinese could not develop science!" though Professor Neisser reproved him for this premature conclusion. I could not ignore this study because the Japanese language is similar to the Chinese language in lacking counterfactual and entification. In fact, Bloom (1984) later reported that Japanese college students were also inferior to American counterparts in essentially the same forced-choice tests. It is an undeniable fact that modern science has been developed primarily by Europeans and Americans whose languages are all equipped with counterfactual and entification. Are we Asians destined to be inferior in scientific ability? I could not help starting the third series of experiments while at the same time conducting experiments on form perception for my dissertation and those on the foreign language effect.

With one exception, Bloom's experiments had no control conditions designed to confirm that his American subjects were comparable to his Chinese or Japanese subjects. Therefore, their results were uninterpretable; for example, his American subjects may have happened to have higher general intelligence, which may have been confounded with the alleged higher ability of reasoning through counterfactual or entification. Au (1983) and Liu (1985) failed to replicate Bloom's (1981) results concerning counterfactual. Due to the lack of the appropriate control conditions, however, the debate (Au, 1984; Bloom, 1984) did not attain a clear-cut conclusion (McNeill, 1987).

The only experiment with a control condition concerned entification. American and Chinese college students read one of two paragraphs in their respective native language and answered a forced-choice question. Both paragraphs described functional relationships among four variables, and their contents were supposed to be identical except that the degree of entification was higher in Paragraph 2 than in Paragraph 1. Thus, Paragraph 1 served as a control condition, in which both groups of subjects showed comparable performance. In contrast, the American subjects out-performed the Chinese subjects in Paragraph 2. Although Bloom (1981) interpreted these results as support for his hypothesis, I found that the contents of the two paragraphs were not actually the same and that Bloom's "correct" alternative was not actually correct for Paragraph 2. However, I could not figure out why only the Chinese subjects responded to this unintended procedural flaw.

I asked my academic advisor at the University of Tokyo, Professor Hiroto Katori, and two friends of mine in Japan to test Japanese college students with Bloom's (1981) paragraphs that I translated into Japanese. They kindly conducted the experiment in two classes of introductory psychology: one consisting exclusively of students majoring in natural sciences and the other consisting exclusively of those majoring in humanities and social sciences. While processing the answer sheets that they sent to me at Cornell, I happened to notice that the two classes of students showed very different patterns of results: Although the students in natural sciences replicated Bloom's Chinese subjects, those in humanities and social sciences replicated Bloom's American subjects. Seeing this difference, I reasoned as follows: The former students had richer experience with mathematical functions and thus a larger portion of them succeeded in avoiding Bloom's "correct" alternative for Paragraph 2, whereas the latter students had poorer experience with mathematical functions and thus a smaller portion of them succeeded in avoiding it. If this reasoning was correct, American college students should also show both patterns of results. This prediction was confirmed: Although Cornell students in humanities and social sciences replicated Bloom's American students, Cornell students in physics replicated Bloom's Chinese students. The difference in the pattern of results cannot be attributed to any difference in language because both patterns of results were observed in both linguistic groups. Thus, no reliable evidence is left for Bloom's hypothesis.

Incidentally, I should not have succeeded in identifying the true cause of Bloom's (1981) findings in the entification experiment if my cooperators had not kindly tested two classes, instead of one. In my course of cognitive psychology, I refer to this study (Takano, 1989b) as my own experience of serendipity.

INDIVIDUALISM AND COLLECTIVISM

My initial undergraduate major was anthropology, though I soon moved to psychology. Professor Neisser's seminar in cross-cultural psychology together with my own experience in a different (i.e., American) culture revived my interests in culture, not only the relationship between language and thought but also other aspects of culture. Specifically, my interests have been centered on cognitive biases in understanding other cultures as well as one's own culture. While studying the past literature, I found that a commonly held view that the Japanese are more collectivistic than the Americans was not supported by recent empirical studies (Takano & Osaka, 1997).

On the one hand, it has been widely believed that the Americans are extremely individualistic (e.g., Bellah, Madsen, Sullivan, Swindler, & Tipton, 1985; Riesman, 1954) since Tocqueville (1840/1946) referred to individualism as a marked characteristic of the Americans. On the other hand, it has also been widely believed that the Japanese are extremely collectivistic. For instance, Reischauer (1988), who was professor of history at Harvard University and a former ambassador to Japan, wrote, ". . . Japan is made up of a uniform race of pliant, obedient robots, meekly conforming to rigid social rules and endlessly repeating the established patterns of their society. This is a concept widely held in the West . . ." (p. 159), though he did not endorse this view himself. The most influential book that established this view was *The Chrysanthemum and the Sword* written by anthropologist Benedict (1946). It strongly suggested that the past totalitarian political system of Japan is rooted in its collective culture, though she never used the term *collectivism*.

Collectivism carries a negative connotation (Kâgitçibasi, 1994) mainly because it has been related to totalitarianism such as fascism and communism, though both individualism and collectivism actually have both positive and negative consequences, respectively (see Triandis, 1990). Accordingly, the alleged collectivism of the Japanese has been often invoked to explain its negative social phenomena. As for bullying in Japanese schools, for example, Rohlen, who is professor at Stanford University, commented, "This is embarrassing for Japan because the country is trying so hard to evolve away from the group-action stereotype, and this is evidence the old ways of Japan are at work" (see Sanger, 1993), though in actuality bullying is a serious problem in Western countries such as Norway and Britain as well.

A dictionary of social sciences (Gould & Kolb, 1964) defines individualism as "a belief that the individual is an end in himself, and as such ought to realize his 'self' and cultivate his own judgment, notwithstanding the weight of pervasive social pressure in the direction of conformity" (p. 325). This core meaning is common to most ordinary uses of the term *individualism*, though other peripheral meanings have been attached to it by some researchers. The term *collectivism* is usually used as its antonym.

We found 10 empirical studies that provided direct tests for the common view that the Japanese are more collectivistic than the Americans: six questionnaire studies and four behavioral studies. The common view was supported by only one of them, a questionnaire study by Hofstede (1980). He delivered questionnaires concerning "work-related values" to IBM employees all over the world. He factor-analyzed the answers to 14 "work goals" questions obtained in 50 countries and three regions, and extracted four factors; one of them was an "individualism factor." On the basis of its factor scores, he ordered those countries and regions. The United States ranked first (i.e., the most individualistic); Japan ranked 22nd. These results are consistent with the common view as far as the relation between the two nations is concerned.

However, a close examination of the exact wordings of the questions that had high loadings on this factor discloses that it does not exactly correspond to individualism. The questions with high positive loadings (in the parentheses) were as follows (all the questions took the form of "How important is it to you to . . ."): "Have a job which leaves you sufficient time for your personal or family life?" (.86), "Have considerable freedom to adopt your own approach to the job?" (.49), and "Have challenging work to do—work from which you can get a personal sense of accomplishment?" (.46). The questions with high negative loadings were as follows: "Have training opportunities (to improve your skills or to learn new skills)?" (−.82), "Have good physical working conditions (good ventilation and lighting, adequate work space, etc.)?" (−.69), and "Fully use your skills and abilities on the job?" (−.63). Obviously, these questions have little to do with the above ordinary meaning of individualism. Hofstede's (1980) "individualism factor" seems to be related actually to something like "personal satisfaction versus workplace satisfaction in occupation." Triandis (1990; see also Triandis, Bontempo, Villareal, Asai, & Lucca, 1988) reported that this factor had a significant rank correlation only with "Family Integrity (good and lasting relationships between parents and children)," which was one of the four factors extracted by Triandis et al. (1986) in their questionnaire study on collectivism in nine countries. Thus, it is hard to assume that Hofstede's ranking accurately reflects the degree of individualism in the listed countries and regions.

The other five questionnaire studies have not found the alleged difference between the United States and Japan. Leung and Iwawaki (1988) compared college students of the two countries with Hui's (1984) collectivism scale and found no significant difference. Triandis et al. (1988) used their own collectivism scale to compare American college students with Japanese college students and adults. According to Asai (1987), who reported the same data in more detail, the Japanese subjects were significantly more collectivistic in 25 questions, whereas the American subjects in 23, with the remaining 91 questions nonsignificant (cf., Triandis et al., 1988, erroneously reported that the total number of questions was 138 instead of 139). Triandis et al. (1993) delivered the individualism/collectivism questionnaire developed by Triandis et al. (1986) in 10 countries including the United States and Japan. They extracted six factors related to individualism and collectivism. When the factor scores of the countries are simply summed up after aligning their signs so that positive values indicate individualism, Japan was the most individualistic with 254, whereas the United States was fifth with −10. Yamaguchi, Kuhlman, and Sugimori (1995) compared college students of the two countries employing Yamaguchi's (1994) collectivism scale concerning goal conflict (e.g., "I do things in my way regardless of what my group members expect me to do"). They found no significant difference. Kashima et al. (1995) compared college students in five countries, using the extended version of Yamaguchi's (1994) collectivism scale, Kakimoto's (1989) relatedness scale, an allocentrism scale, and a friendship questionnaire. Among the extracted seven factors, the Japanese sample was more individualistic than the U.S. sample on four factors, whereas the converse was true on the other three factors.

In sum, none of these studies supported the common view. The questionnaires used by these five groups of researchers are closely related to the ordinary meaning of individualism and collectivism because they were developed specifically to assess this dimension and thus avoid the validity problem that Hofstede's (1980) questionnaire had. Incidentally, Schwartz (1994) found no consistent differences between the United States and Japan on three factors (i.e., Conservatism, Affective Autonomy, and Intellectual Autonomy) that appear to be related to individualism/collectivism, though he refused to endorse this construct (Schwartz, 1990).

It may be argued that the answers to the questionnaires may not accurately reflect actual behavior. We found four behavioral studies that are directly related to the ordinary meaning of individualism/collectivism. Two of them are related to conformity, whereas the remaining two to cooperation.

Conformity is mentioned in the above definition of individualism and usually considered to be an essential part of collectivism. Frager (1970) hypothesized that the Japanese should show stronger conformity in the Asch-type conformity experiment where confederates make obviously erroneous answers unanimously in some trials. However, he found that the rate of conformity was 25% for Japanese college students, whereas it was 32% when Asch (1956) tested American college students in a comparable condition. In addition, Frager observed "anticonformity" (i.e., erroneous answers when the confederates unanimously made correct answers), which Asch had not reported. Williams and Sogon (1984) reported that the conformity rate was 27% for Japanese college students when the confederates were unfamiliar to the real subjects as in Asch's original study. Incidentally, these findings were replicated in two graduation theses: Sako (1975) reported a conformity rate of 18%, and Shindo (1993) reported 20%. She observed anticonformity as well (Shindo, personal communication, 1996).

Bond and Smith (1996) found that the conformity rate has declined over time in the United States; the average of the conformity rates observed in eight studies conducted between 1955 and 1990 after Asch's original work is 25% (Smith & Bond, 1993). Therefore, the conformity rates observed in Japan are best conceived as roughly comparable to those in the United States.

Ross and Nisbett (1991) and Triandis (1990) conjectured that Frager's (1970) conformity rate was not higher than Asch's (1956) because his Japanese confederates were not in-group members. However, the available evidence concerning the in-group/out-group difference is mixed. Matsuda (1985) compared friends and strangers among female college students. Although his results cannot be directly compared to the previous conformity rates because his procedure differed from Asch's standard procedure in critical respects, it is justifiable to compare the results of friends and strangers in the study. He observed no systematic difference. By contrast, Williams and Sogon (1984) reported that the conformity rate was 51% when their confederates and real subjects were from the same formal sports clubs (taiikukai). This discrepancy may have resulted from the difference in the nature of the in-groups: Formal sports clubs at Japanese universities are infamous among the Japanese for their unusually rigid discipline. At any rate, a cross-cultural comparison is impossible until a comparable in-group is tested in the United States because it is known that the conformity rate tends to be higher for in-group members (Bond & Smith, 1996).

Collectivists are generally considered to subordinate their own goals to group goals (e.g., Triandis, 1990). If the Japanese are collectivists, they will maintain cooperation even at the sacrifice of their individual profits. Yamagishi (1988a) compared American and Japanese college students in a setting like the prisoner's dilemma. In his experiment, cooperation increased a money reward, though the reward decreased when individual members tried to increase their own reward further by acting selfishly. When the selfish behavior was sanctioned, no difference in cooperation was observed between the American and Japanese subjects. When it was not sanctioned, however, the American subjects showed a significantly higher level of cooperation.

Yamagishi (1988b) compared American and Japanese college students with regard to secession from cooperation as well. In every trial, each subject in a small group was free to choose between his or her own individual record and the group record of performance as a basis for getting a money reward. When the amount of reward was identical for the two kinds of record, both samples chose the individual record in 7 to 8 trials out of 20. When the amount of reward for the individual record was reduced to the half of that for the group record, however, the American subjects chose the individual record only in about one trial, whereas the Japanese subjects still chose it in about eight trials. All the subjects obtained smaller amounts of reward in individual-record trials than in group-record ones in this half-reward condition. These results suggest that the Japanese subjects preferred to perform individually even at the cost of a reduced reward.

All these empirical studies, except for the questionable study by Hofstede (1980), are unanimously in contradiction to the common view that the Japanese are more collectivistic than the Americans. It is thus highly probable that this view is a product of misinterpreting reality. But how was it produced?

The common view was formed principally on the basis of intuitive interpretations of casual observations (Mouer & Sugimoto, 1986), which are susceptible to many cognitive biases. It seems to me that the most critical bias responsible for this misinterpretation is the *fundamental attribution error* (Nisbett & Ross, 1980; Ross, 1977), a prevailing bias to attribute the causes of others' behaviors to their dispositions while underestimating the power of situations. More specifically, universal reactions of the Japanese to their situations may have been erroneously attributed to their stable "national character."

The most critical situational determinant of individualism in modern societies seems to be military and economic power. When a society is threatened by outside military force, it typically seeks to unite its members to protect itself, and thus cannot afford to allow their individualistic behavior. As symbolized by McCarthyism, even the United States attempted to tighten the control over its nation when it faced the threat of communism. Japan faced the overwhelming military power of Western colonialism when it was forced to open its country by Commodore M. C. Perry's gunboat diplomacy in 1854. Japan demolished the decentralization of power in its feudal system to construct a centralized political and military system. The newly established government utilized education, civil law, and police power to unite the nation. This attempt culminated before World War II when Japan had to confront the United States, whose GNP (gross national product) is estimated to have been 13 to 20 times as much as that of Japan. It is not surprising that the behavior of the Japanese at that time appeared to be collectivistic. Most observations about them were made during this period by Western observers including Benedict (1946).

After Japan was defeated in the War, the situation changed drastically. Under the umbrella of American military power, Japan had no need (or no ability) to defend itself against the communist nations, and thus tight control was unnecessary. Japan had no conscription, for example, while American youngsters were sent to Korea or Vietnam. In this respect, therefore, the situation for the Japanese was more favorable for individualism than that for the Americans. From an economic point of view, however, Japan still had to compete with the stronger economic powers of the Western countries. Accordingly, collectivism was needed especially by enterprises at least until the end of the high growth of Japanese economy in 1973. Thereafter, a serious threat virtually disappeared in the economic sector as well. Now Japan has little necessity for tight unity.

Triandis (1990) listed subsistence (hunting/gathering and industrial contrasted with agricultural), affluence, social and geographic mobility, social complexity, and exposure to mass media as situational preconditions of individualism. In every respect, Japan has become similar to the United States in recent years. For example, the percentage of city population is 77.4% for Japan and 75.2% for the United States in 1990, which are both much higher than 25.2% for China. If the magnitude of individualism is largely determined by situational factors, therefore, it is not surprising at all if the Japanese are presently as individualistic as the Americans. The past totalitarian political system of Japan may be better conceived as a universal reaction to the particular international situation at that time rather than an unavoidable consequence of the Japanese culture.

The long debate on cross-situational consistency of human behavior (see Kenrick & Funder, 1988; Mischel, 1968; Ross & Nisbett, 1991) has revealed that human behavior is more dependent on situations than is commonly assumed. As Ross and Nisbett (1991) suggested, the common overestimation of the cross-situational stability of personality traits may well be due to the fundamental attribution error. Although no systematic investigation has been conducted, it seems highly probable that the same holds true for "national character." Its cross-situational stability may be grossly overestimated: A "national character," if any, may be a dominant pattern of response by a nation to a dominant situation for that nation at a particular time and may readily change when the situation changes.

I was led to think of this possibility partly by the ecological approach which Professor Neisser introduced to me. When I was at Cornell, however, I had difficulty in understanding Gibson's (1966) theory and the significance of his ecological approach. It did not appeal to me mainly because it appeared to contradict the obvious effects of learning in perception. In 1990, Professor Neisser was invited by the Japanese Psychological Association to give the principal address at its annual convention, where I had the honor of introducing him to the audience. In this address, he offered a distinction between direct perception and recognition. It made me realize for the first time that the notion of direct perception is not unreasonable. Once direct perception was separated from recognition, its "contradiction" with learning disappeared. If I understand Professor Neisser's theory correctly, what direct perception is tuned to are stable properties of the terrestrial environment, which have been essentially identical for several hundred millions of years. Humans may well have evolved to detect these stable properties directly with built-in mechanisms. Thus, it is not surprising that a part of the human perceptual system "resonates" to the stable properties of the environment without referring to learned information. However, the environment has changing aspects as well as stable ones. To adapt to the numerous minor changes of the environment, learning is obviously superior to evolving built-in mechanisms. In fact, it is commonly believed that humans have acquired the highest learning ability on the whole in the course of their evolution. If learned information is used almost exclusively in the recognition process, there is no reason to question the notion of direct perception. Thus, Professor Neisser's address made me to think of the ecological approach more seriously.

The ecological approach leads us to attend to the properties of the environment. This is especially pertinent in the study of culture because it is formed primarily as a means of better adaptation to the environment. The ecological approach was one of the factors that drove me to examine the issue of individualism/collectivism in the context of natural and social environments. Although the consideration of environments may appear to be a matter of course, not a few cultural studies are still conducted only with cultural and spiritual terms.

CONCLUSION

This review of my past research has revealed that the influence of Professor Neisser is imprinted on its various aspects, though I have been simply investigating what I was interested in without following his research or theoretical framework intentionally. This review has also revealed that advisors' influence could take various forms. To list a few, they may be sources of valuable information, their interests in particular domains may stimulate those of their students, and their theoretical frameworks may lead their students to apply them to new problems. Fifteen years ago when Professor Neisser became my advisor, I could not predict in what ways my research would be affected by him. Perhaps, he could not either.

REFERENCES

Asai, M. (1987). *Nichi-bei-kan niokeru kojinshugi to shudanshugi nikansuru kousa-bunka-shinrigaku-teki kenkyu* [Cross-cultural study of collectivism and individualism: U.S. and Japan]. (Tech. Rep. No. 34). Tokyo: Nihon University, Institute of Humanities and Social Sciences.

Asch, S. E. (1956). Studies of independence and conformity: I. A minority of one against a unanimous majority. *Psychological Monographs, 70*(9, Whole No. 416).

Au, T. K.-F. (1983). Chinese and English counterfactuals: The Sapir-Whorf hypothesis revisited. *Cognition, 15*, 155–187.

Au, T. K.-F. (1984). Counterfactuals: In reply to Alfred Bloom. *Cognition, 17*, 289–302.

Bellah, R. N., Madsen, R., Sullivan, W. M., Swindler, A., & Tipton, S. M. (1985). *Habits of the heart: Individualism and commitment in American life*. Berkeley: University of California Press.

Benedict, R. (1946). *The chrysanthemum and the sword: Patterns of Japanese culture*. Boston: Houghton Mifflin.

Bloom, A. H. (1981). *The linguistic shaping of thought: A study in the impact of language on thinking in China and the West*. Hillsdale, NJ: Lawrence Erlbaum Associates.

Bloom, A. H. (1984). Caution—the words you use may affect what you say: A response to Au. *Cognition, 17*, 275–287.

Bond R., & Smith, P. B. (1996). Culture and conformity: A meta-analysis of studies using Asch's (1952b, 1956) line judgment task. *Psychological Bulletin, 119*, 111–137.

Broadbent, D. (1958). *Perception and communication*. Oxford, England: Pergamon.

Corballis, M. C., & Nagourney, B. A. (1978). Latency to categorize disoriented alphanumeric characters as letters or digits. *Canadian Journal of Psychology, 32*, 186–188.

Duhem, P. (1954). *The aim and structure of physical theory*. (P. P. Wiener, Trans.). Princeton, NJ: Princeton University Press. (Original work published 1914)

Eley, M. G. (1982). Identifying rotated letter-like symbols. *Memory & Cognition, 10*, 25–32.

Frager, R. (1970). Conformity and anticonformity in Japan. *Journal of Personality and Social Psychology, 15*, 203–210.

Gardner, M. (1964). *The ambidextrous universe*. New York: Basic Books.

Gibson, J. J. (1966). *The senses considered as perceptual systems*. Boston: Houghton Mifflin.

Gould, J., & Kolb, W. L. (1964). *A dictionary of the social sciences*. Glencoe, IL: The Free Press.

Hirst, W., Spelke, E. S., Reaves, C. C., Caharack, G., & Neisser, U. (1980). Dividing attention without alternation or automaticity. *Journal of Experimental Psychology: General, 109*, 98–117.

Hofstede, G. (1980). *Culture's consequences*. Beverly Hills, CA: Sage.

Hui, C. H. (1984). *Individualism-collectivism: Theory, measurement, and its relation to reward allocation*. Unpublished doctoral dissertation, University of Illinois at Urbana-Champaign.

Ittelson, W. H., Mowafy, L., & Magid, D. (1991). The perception of mirror-reflected objects. *Perception, 20*, 567–584.

Johnson, J. S., & Newport, E. L. (1989). Critical period effects in second language learning: The influence of maturational state on the acquisition of English as a second language. *Cognitive Psychology, 21*, 60–99.

Kâgitçibasi, Ç. (1994). A critical appraisal of individualism and collectivism: Toward a new formulation. In U. Kim, H. C. Triandis, Ç. Kâgitçibasi, S.-C. Choi, & G. Yoon (Eds.), *Individualism and collectivism: Theory, method, and applications* (pp. 52–65). Thousand Oaks, CA: Sage.

Kakimoto, T. (1989). *Shakaiteki kategorii-ka no kouka no kojinsa ni kansuru kenkyu (1): Kojin-kanjin shakudo no kentou* [An examination of individual differences in the effect of social categorization (1): Validation of individual-kanjin scale]. *Proceedings of the Japanese Society of Social Psychology, Japan, 30*, 21–22.

Kashima, Y., Yamaguchi, S., Kim, U., Choi, S.-C., Gelfand, M. J., & Yuki, M. (1995). Culture, gender, and self: A perspective from individualism-collectivism research. *Journal of Personality and Social Psychology, 69*, 925–937.

Kenrick, D. T., & Funder, D. C. (1988). Profiting from controversy: Lessons from the person-situation debate. *American Psychologist, 43*, 23–34.

Kosslyn, S. M. (1980). *Image and mind.* Cambridge, MA: Harvard University Press.

Leung, K., & Iwawaki, S. (1988). Cultural collectivism and distributive behavior. *Journal of Cross-Cultural Psychology, 19*, 35–49.

Liu, L. G. (1985). Reasoning counterfactually in Chinese: Are there any obstacles? *Cognition, 21*, 239–270.

Macnamara, J. T. (1966). *Bilingualism and primary education: A study of Irish experience.* Edinburgh: Edinburgh University Press.

Marr, D. (1982). *Vision.* San Francisco: Freeman.

Matsuda, N. (1985). Strong, quasi-, and weak conformity among Japanese in the modified Asch procedure. *Journal of Cross-Cultural Psychology, 16*, 83–97.

McNeill, D. (1987). *Psycholinguistics: A new approach.* New York: Harper & Row.

Mischel, W. (1968). *Personality and assessment.* New York: Wiley.

Morris, R. C. (1993). Mirror image reversal: Is what we see what we present? *Perception, 22*, 869–876.

Mouer, R., & Sugimoto, Y. (1986). *Images of Japanese society: A study in the social construction of reality.* London: Routledge & Kegan Paul.

Neisser, U. (1967). *Cognitive psychology.* New York: Appleton.

Neisser, U. (1976). *Cognition and reality: Principles and implications of cognitive psychology.* San Francisco: Freeman.

Nisbett, R., & Ross, L. (1980). *Human inference: Strategies and shortcomings of social judgment.* Englewood Cliffs, NJ: Prentice-Hall.

Peal, E., & Lambert, W. E. (1962). The relation of bilingualism to intelligence. *Psychological Monographs, 76*(27, Whole No. 546).

Pylyshyn, Z. W. (1973). What the mind's eye tells the mind's brain: A critique of mental imagery. *Psychological Bulletin, 80*, 1–24.

Pylyshyn, Z. W. (1984). *Computation and cognition: Toward a foundation for cognitive science.* Cambridge, MA: MIT Press.

Quine, W. V. O. (1953). *From a logical point of view: A logico-philosophical essays.* Cambridge, MA: Harvard University Press.

Reischauer, E. O. (1988). *The Japanese today: Change and continuity.* Cambridge, MA: Harvard University Press.

Riesman, D. (1954). *Individualism reconsidered and other essays.* New York: The Free Press.

Rock, I. (1973). *Orientation and form.* New York: Academic Press.

Ross, L. (1977). The intuitive psychologist and his shortcomings. In L. Berkowitz (Ed.), *Advances in experimental social psychology* (Vol. 10, pp. 173–220). New York: Academic Press.

Ross, L. D., Amabile, T. M., & Steinmetz, J. L. (1977). Social roles, social control, and biases in social-perception processes. *Journal of Personality and Social Psychology, 35*, 485–494.

Ross, L., & Nisbett, R. E. (1991). *The person and the situation: Perspectives of social psychology.* Philadelphia: Temple University Press.

Sako, S. (1975). *Douchou-koudou no jikken-bunka-shinrigaku-teki kenkyu* [An experimental approach to the cross-cultural study of conformity behavior]. Unpublished graduation thesis, University of Osaka, Osaka, Japan.

Sanger, D. (1993, April 3). Student's killing displays dark side of Japanese schools. *The New York Times*, pp. 1–3.

Schwartz, S. H. (1990). Individualism-collectivism: Critique and proposed refinements. *Journal of Cross-Cultural Psychology, 21,* 139–157.

Schwartz, S. H. (1994). Beyond individualism/collectivism: New cultural dimensions of values. In U. Kim, H. C. Triandis, Ç. Kâgitçibasi, S.-C. Choi, & G. Yoon (Eds.), *Individualism and collectivism: Theory, method, and applications* (pp. 85–119). Thousand Oaks, CA: Sage.

Shepard, R. N., & Cooper, L. A. (1982). *Mental images and their transformations.* Cambridge, MA: MIT Press.

Shepard, R. N., & Metzler, J. (1971). Mental rotation of three-dimensional objects. *Science, 171,* 701–703.

Shindo, M. (1993). *Douchou-koudou ni kansuru jikken-shakai-shinrigaku-teki kenkyu: Shudan-shugi, kojin-shugi tono kankei* [A social psychological study on conformity behavior: Its relation to collectivism and individualism]. Unpublished graduation thesis, Nihon University, Tokyo, Japan.

Smith, P. B., & Bond, M. H. (1993). *Social psychology across cultures: Analysis and perspectives.* London: Harvester Wheatsheaf.

Spelke, E. S., Hirst, W. C., & Neisser, U. (1976). Skills of divided attention. *Cognition, 4,* 215–230.

Sternberg, R. J., Conway, B. E., Ketron, J. L., & Bernstein, M. (1981). People's conceptions of intelligence. *Journal of Personality and Social Psychology, 41,* 37–55.

Takano, Y. (1981). Shinzou no gainenteki kousatsu [A conceptual analysis of mental imagery]. *Japanese Psychological Review, 24,* 66–84.

Takano, Y. (1989a). Perception of rotated forms: A theory of information types. *Cognitive Psychology, 21,* 1–59.

Takano, Y. (1989b). Methodological problems in cross-cultural studies of linguistic relativity. *Cognition, 31,* 141–162.

Takano, Y. (1993). Recognition of forms rotated in depth: A test of the information type theory. *Japanese Psychological Research, 35,* 204–214.

Takano, Y. (1997). *Kagami nonakano misuterii: Sayu gyakuten no nazo ni idomu* [The mystery in the mirror: Challenging the puzzle of left-right reversal]. Tokyo: Iwanami Shoten.

Takano, Y. (1998). Why does a mirror image look left–right reversed?: A hypothesis of multiple processes. *Psychonomic Bulletin & Review, 5,* 37–55.

Takano, Y., & Noda, A. (1993). A temporary decline of thinking ability during foreign language processing. *Journal of Cross-Cultural Psychology, 24,* 445–462.

Takano, Y., & Noda, A. (1995). Interlanguage dissimilarity enhances the decline of thinking ability during foreign language processing. *Language Learning, 45,* 657–681.

Takano, Y., & Osaka, E. (1997). "Shudanshugi-tekina nihonjin" to "kojinshugi-tekina amerikajin": Tsusetsu no saikentou ["Collectivistic Japanese" and "individualistic Americans": Reexamining the dominant view]. *Japanese Journal of Psychology, 68,* 312–327.

Takano, Y., Saito, A., & Nagai, J. (1998). *Underestimation in perceived intelligence of foreign language users due to foreign language effect.* Manuscript submitted for publication.

Takano, Y., Takenaka, H., Nagai, J., & Handa, M. (1998). *Humans could perform as pigeons in discrimination of rotated mirror images.* Manuscript in preparation.

Tocqueville, A. C. H. M. C. de. (1946). *Democracy in America.* (H. Reeve, Trans.). New York: Knopf. (Original work published 1840)

Treisman, A. M. (1969). Strategies and models of selective attention. *Psychological Review, 76,* 282–299.

Treisman, A. M., & Gelade, G. (1980). A feature-integration theory of attention. *Cognitive Psychology, 12,* 97–136.

Triandis, H. C. (1990). Cross-cultural studies of individualism and collectivism. In J. J. Berman (Ed.), *Nebraska Symposium on Motivation 1989* (pp. 41–133). Lincoln: University of Nebraska Press.

Triandis, H. C., Bontempo, R., Betancourt, H., Bond, M., Leung, K., Brenes, A., Georgas, J., Hui, C. H., Marin, G., Setiadi, B., Sinha, J. B. P., Verma, J., Spangenberg, J., Touzard, H., & de Montmollin, G. (1986). The measurement of the etic aspects of individualism and collectivism across cultures. *Australian Journal of Psychology, 38,* 257–267.

Triandis, H. C., Bontempo, R., Villareal, M., Asai, M., & Lucca, N. (1988). Individualism-collectivism: Cross-cultural perspectives on self-in-group relationships. *Journal of Personality and Social Psychology, 54,* 323–338.

Triandis, H., McCusker, C., Betancourt, H., Iwao, S., Leung, K., Salazar, J. M., Setiadi, B., Sinha, J. B. P., Touzard, H., & Zaleski, Z. (1993). An etic-emic analysis of individualism and collectivism. *Journal of Cross-Cultural Psychology, 24,* 366–383.

Tye, M. (1991). *The imagery debate.* Cambridge, MA: MIT Press.

Williams, T. P., & Sogon, S. (1984). Group composition and conforming behavior in Japanese students. *Japanese Psychological Research, 26,* 231–234.

Yamagishi, T. (1988a). The provision of a sanctioning system in the United States and Japan. *Social Psychology Quarterly, 51,* 265–271.

Yamagishi, T. (1988b). Exit from the group as an individualistic solution to the free rider problem in the United States and Japan. *Journal of Experimental Social Psychology, 24,* 530–542.

Yamaguchi, S. (1994). Collectivism among the Japanese: A perspective from the self. In U. Kim, H. C. Triandis, Ç. Kâgitçibasi, S.-C. Choi, & G. Yoon (Eds.), *Individualism and collectivism: Theory, method, and applications* (pp. 175–188). Thousand Oaks, CA: Sage.

Yamaguchi, S., Kuhlman, D. M., & Sugimori, S. (1995). Personality correlations of allocentric tendencies in individualistic and collective cultures. *Journal of Cross-Cultural Psychology, 26,* 658–672.

AUTHOR INDEX

SUBJECT INDEX

A

Action development, *see* Perception-action process; Affordances
Action, recall for, 293-294
Adaptation, 4, 5, 18, 140, 322, 352, *see also* Infant problem solving
Advisor influence, 335-336, 341, 352-353
Affordances, 5, 13, *see also* Causal understanding; Cultural/social ecology
action development/representation and, 6, 21-24, 28
Agency, 21, 135, 136, 137
American Psychological Society, 135
Analogic code, *see* Memory for ritual
Analytic ability, 219, 222
Anxiety, 326, 327, 328
Artifacts, 175-176, 182, *see also* Object perception/manipulation
Associative pairing, 52-53
Attention, 33, 135, 139, 161, 171, 172, *see also* Visual research
Auditory exploration, 16-18
Auditory feedback, objectification and, 15-16
Auditory memory, *see* Williams syndrome cognitive profile
Auditory research, 130
Autism, 159, 199
Autobiographical memory errors
constructivist viewpoint, 230
flashbulb memories and, 229, 230, 235, 237, 246-247
self-definition and, 245
social pressures and, 242-246
source monitoring errors and, 241-242
Avoidance responses, 45-47, 52, 54
Awareness, 134, 314

cognition and, 177-178
metacognitive, 187

B

Baktaman people, *see* Memory for ritual
Balance control, *see* Infant problem solving
Base-rate fallacy, 256
Bayesian decision theory, 185
Behavior, 8, 56, 145, *see also* Exploratory behaviors; Means/ends behavior
cognition and, 135, 137
cross-situatinal stability, 351-352
hallmarks, 135-136
psychology and, 176-177
Behavioral studies, individualism v. collectivism, 348-350
Behaviorism, 336
Bell curve, 223
Biological determinism, 286
Biological processes, 181
Biomechanical issues, *see* Infant problem solving

C

Caregivers, 32, 55, 155
Cartesian system, 69, 71
Categorization, *see* Causal understanding
Causal understanding, *see also* Self-understanding
affordances and, 175, 180, 182, 188
categorization and, 174-176, 181-182
causal intuition and, 180-183
causal patterns and, 181
cognition and, 177-182